The African City

The African City

Anthony O'Connor

Lecturer in Geography, University College London

Africana Publishing Company
a division of Holmes & Meier Publishers, Inc.
New York

First published in the United States of America 1983 by

Africana Publishing Company
a division of Holmes & Meier Publishers, Inc.
30 Irving Place
New York, N.Y. 10003

First published 1983
© Anthony O'Connor 1983

Set in VIP Times Roman by
D. P. Media Limited, Hitchin, Hertfordshire

Printed in Great Britain by The Anchor Press Ltd
and bound by Wm Brendon & Son Ltd
both of Tiptree, Essex

Library of Congress Cataloging in Publication Data

O'Connor, Anthony M. (Anthony Michael)
  The African city.
  Bibliography: p.
  Includes index.
  1. Cities and towns – Africa, sub-Saharan.
2. Rural–urban migration – Africa, sub-Saharan.
3. Housing – Africa, sub-Saharan. 4. Ethnic groups.
5. Urban economics. I. Title.
HT148.A357025   1983
307.7'64'096   83-10648
ISBN 0–8419–0881–8
ISBN 0–8419–0882–6 (pbk.)

Printed in Great Britain

Contents

Figures

Tables

Preface

This book aims to explore some of the characteristics of tropical African cities, with special reference to change in the post-independence period. In particular, as a geographical study, it investigates the diversity of urban forms and urban experience to be found within the region, and distinguishes the more widespread features from those peculiar to individual cities or groups of cities. Such reviews form a necessary foundation both for theoretical formulations on the process of urbanization and for practical planning decisions, yet very few exist at present for tropical Africa. Much has been written on African cities, but most of the existing literature is concerned with an individual city, and often with a highly specific aspect of it. This attempt at a synthesis, discussing briefly many aspects of many cities, should provide a context for such more narrowly-focused studies.

No grand theory is formulated here, but hopefully the book will be of value to students and teachers, both in Africa and elsewhere, seeking an understanding of the empirical reality of this aspect of contemporary Africa. It is not intended as a planning manual, but it may perhaps also be of value to some of those directly involved in the affairs of African cities.

Tropical Africa is here taken as the area extending south from the Sahara as far as Zimbabwe, but no attempt is made to cover this area comprehensively. The emphasis is placed on the Commonwealth countries of both western and eastern Africa, which together illustrate a wide range of urban forms, though some comparisons with the francophone countries are made. The cities of Angola, Mozambique, Ethiopia and Somalia receive only brief mention. Furthermore, no volume such as this could cover all aspects of the cities. Here they are seen basically as settlements and as foci of economic activity: themes such as urban politics, labour relations and emerging class structures are left to other writers.

The book could not have been written if I had not had the good fortune to work in universities in four African cities. The writing has been done in London, however, where I have benefited from both the ideal working environment of University College Department of Geography and access to the superb library resources of the School of Oriental and African Studies. I owe much to many colleagues both in Africa and in London, but particularly to Alan Gilbert, Peggie Hobson, Peter Jackson and Peter Ward, who read and commented on various chapters, and to Paul Richards, who reviewed the whole manuscript and – together with Mark Cohen at Hutchinson – offered encouragement whenever it was most needed.

I am also most grateful to Annabel Swindells, who undertook much of the typing, to Anne Mason and Sarah Skinner who drew the maps, and to my family for their tolerance of a husband and father preoccupied quite excessively with this project. To them I promise: no more book-writing for quite some time!

London, December 1982

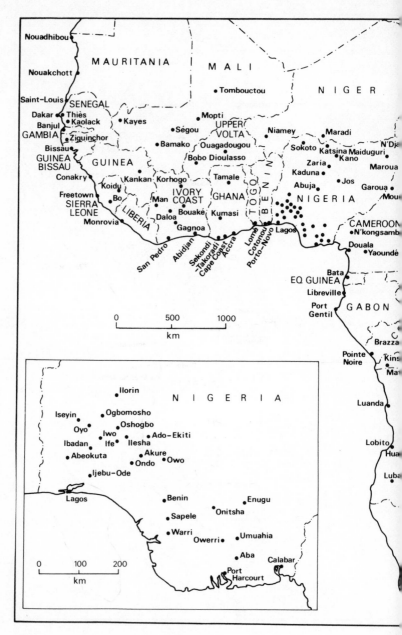

Figure 1   *Tropical Africa: reference map*

1 Introduction

Why write – or indeed read – a book on the city in tropical Africa? For the author the interest and importance of the subject is totally compelling, but some who glance at these pages may not share that view. For those elsewhere in the world with an interest in urban studies, tropical Africa might seem of little importance. It is one of the least urbanized world regions, and in most of its component countries less than a quarter of the population live in cities or towns. Although it is quite wrong to regard its cities as entirely products of the recent colonial era, it does not have continuous urban traditions extending back several millennia as in the Middle East. It has no cities yet comparable in size to the largest in Europe or North America, or to Bombay, Calcutta, Pekin and Shanghai; and it has not experienced twentieth century urban growth on the scale of Sao Paulo or Mexico City. Each of the two giants in tropical African terms, namely Lagos and Kinshasa, reached a population of two million only in the 1970s.

For people within Africa, and for others interested in the African scene, the question may not be 'why study Africa?' but 'why study the cities?', since the vast majority of people live in a rural environment. In terms of development, for instance, it is declared government policy almost everywhere that priority attention should be given to the rural areas, even if such policies are often less evident in practice. Most academic observers share this view, as increasingly do outside advisers such as those in the aid agencies.

So why should the cities of tropical Africa command our attention? The very fact that the level of urbanization is so low is surely itself of interest, and raises challenging questions. Coupled with that is the fact that while *levels* of urbanization are low, the present *rates* of urbanization, in the sense of progressive increase in the proportion of the total population who live in cities and towns, are among the world's highest. Until recently rates were higher in Latin America, but now that a clear majority of people in many Latin

American countries are urban dwellers, Africa has taken the lead in respect of current change. Despite data limitations there is no doubt that the present urbanization rate in most African countries is much higher than in most parts of Asia, including both India and China (Table 1).

The combination of low levels, but high rates, of urbanization means that tropical Africa provides almost unparalleled opportunities for the outside observer to see 'cities in the making'. It also provides enormous challenges for all who are directly involved in the process – whether as a government minister in an air-conditioned office or as a squatter living in a disused quarry.

It can certainly be argued that no other contemporary change in tropical Africa is either as dramatic or as significant as the growth of its cities, especially now that the transfer of nominal political power from London, Paris, Brussels and Lisbon is complete. That change was largely concentrated into the early 1960s, and many would say that the actual change, both in terms of real power and in terms of most people's lives, was by no means as far-reaching as had been hoped.

The direct impact of rapid urbanization is of course greatest for those who actually move, permanently or temporarily, from a rural to an urban home; but profound effects are also felt by the existing urban dwellers, and by the rural residents whose sons and daughters or even second cousins move to town. The importance of the extended family throughout tropical Africa contributes greatly to the social and economic impact of city growth.

The significance of the urbanization process in tropical Africa is enhanced by the fact that the cities exert all kinds of influence out of all proportion to their modest size. This is emphasized in much of the writing of Gutkind (1974 etc), while Hanna and Hanna (1981: 3) assert that 'the towns of Africa are the epicenters of their societies . . . the centers of polity, society, economy and culture.'* Many other observers share this view, whether they see the influence as largely benevolent, with the cities providing services for the rural population and acting as agents for the spread of whatever is meant by 'modernization', or as largely malevolent, with the cities exploiting the rural population, extracting a surplus from them and becoming parasitic upon them. Undoubtedly, the cities form the critical links in every country between the population as a whole and the outside world. Nearly all transactions are channelled through

* Full references quoted in the text appear in the Bibliography section at the end of this book.

Table 1   *Urban population in four world regions*

	Estimate				Forecast	Annual growth
	1960	*1970*	*1975*	*1980*	*1990*	*1975–80*
	millions					%
Latin America	107	162	198	241	343	3.9
East Asia	195	265	309	359	476	3.0
South Asia	147	217	266	330	516	4.3
TROPICAL AFRICA	23	40	53	71	126	5.9
World total	1012	1354	1561	1807	2422	2.9

Source: Patterns of Urban and Rural Population Growth, United Nations, New York, 1980, p. 11.

Note: 'Urban' is here based on national definitions, and generally includes all centres over 5000 or 10,000.

them; and they have largely determined the evolving structure of the space economy, as a glance at any road map would demonstrate.

The speed and significance of contemporary urbanization mean that many difficult decisions are faced as a matter of urgency. Collectively, the decisions of all the inhabitants are vitally important, but much responsibility lies with a limited number of decision-makers in national and municipal administrations and in private concerns which include multinational corporations. Their decisions, made today while the cities are still small and situations fluid, will largely determine the structure – spatial as well as economic, social and political – of the much larger African cities of the future. This book does not aim at offering recommendations to the policy-makers, but it does aim to spread an awareness of some of the issues involved.

Terms and concepts

Having already made frequent references to 'urbanization' perhaps we should note that there are at least two senses in which that word is commonly used. Hauser (1965: 8–9), for instance, distinguishes between urbanization as a change in the pattern of settlement and urbanization as a social process. Little (1974: 4–5) does likewise with special reference to Africa, and then concentrates especially on the latter aspect. Friedmann (1973: chapter 4) has spelled out the distinction more fully than anyone else, and has written essentially about the former aspect. Throughout this book also the emphasis is firmly placed upon urbanization in the first sense, essentially from a geographical standpoint, leaving social change to the sociologists. In both senses 'urbanization' is, of course, a mental construct rather than a material phenomenon, and since this book is concerned more with diverse and changing reality than with theoretical formulations 'the city' has been preferred for its title.

We shall not even delve into the meaning of 'the city', since this has already been done with special reference to Africa by several writers (e.g. Mabogunje 1968: chapter 2; Peil 1977: 259–72), generally by referring back to scholars such as Wirth (1938). An outstanding recent discussion, conducted at a global scale but with much reference to Africa, is that of Hannerz (1980). Our concern is simply with the growth, distribution, character and relationships of those large and concentrated settlements that are cities in every sense of the word. There is of course no clear-cut division between cities and towns, though the latter word is used whenever centres with fewer than about 100,000 people are being discussed. These smaller towns merit more attention than they receive here, or from most writers on urban Africa, but they have at least been the subject of a recent symposium volume (Southall 1979) and bibliography (Schatzberg 1979).

While we refer constantly to the urban population, this is really a much less clearly defined group in tropical Africa than in many parts of the world. This is not because of problems in defining cities as settlements, which are no greater than elsewhere, but because so many people are involved with, and move frequently between, city and countryside. 'They participate in the urban economy while remaining loyal to a rural community; they operate in geographically separate but culturally and economically integrated systems' (Gugler and Flanagan 1978: 64). In speaking of the urban population, therefore, we refer not to a highly discrete set of people, but rather to those living within the cities and towns at a particular point in time.

In contrast to some studies, no specific chapter is devoted to women, for the discussion throughout concerns women as much as men. As in nearly all writings, however, there is a heavy emphasis on the adults despite the fact that almost half the inhabitants of most African cities are children. Indeed, education is one of many important topics not covered here. Even more glaring omissions in the eyes of some readers will be the matters of urban politics and social stratification or class. Fortunately, these are the central issues in an Africa-wide study by Sandbrook (1982), which is thus largely complementary to the present volume.

Problems of data availability

On questions such as the emergence of classes and the concentration of political power precise data can hardly be gathered anywhere in the world. Other phenomena lend themselves more readily to measurement, but in many cases lack of data is a major problem in tropical Africa. Population censuses have been conducted in most countries, but the figures which they provide are sometimes unreliable and often very out of date. The range of questions asked in these censuses varies greatly over time and space, and often it is very limited. It is particularly unfortunate that all recent Nigerian censuses have yielded grossly distorted results (officially declared invalid in some cases), since that country probably accounts for over 30 per cent of tropical Africa's urban dwellers. Other statistics, such as those for employment, may be both reliable and up to date, but may provide only a partial coverage of the situation. In addition to many subjects on which the facts are simply not known for many cities, there are of course others on which data do exist but are kept secret – justifiably or otherwise.

As a result it is very rarely possible to provide a series of comparative statistics for a wide range of cities, especially in tabular or map form. Sophisticated data analysis can be applied to specific aspects of individual cities (Ayeni 1979), but on a pan-African scale this is normally out of the question. Generally, it is far more realistic to aim for an appreciation of broad orders of magnitude, with such recent and reliable figures as are available provided merely as illustrations of specific situations. On most of the topics discussed here, such broad orders of magnitude *can* be indicated, and they often differ from what is widely believed.

Africa and elsewhere

A further purpose in writing on this subject is indeed to challenge some of the views that are held in various quarters at present. One is that urbanization involves largely the same processes throughout the world (Rayfield 1974: 183; McNulty and Horton 1976: 179), and that Africa is simply following a path trodden at an earlier date by Europe, North America and the Soviet Union. This view has, of course, been challenged by many others, one notable recent discussion of the subject being that by Berry (1973), who stresses the co-existence of divergent paths of urbanization. However, he and others do suggest that while the less developed countries are not following the same path as the more developed, they are all following a single distinct path.

In their valuable review of the literature on urbanization in these countries, Friedmann and Wulff (1975: 40) observe that 'constructing broad generalizations about Third World cities is always a hazardous business'. Yet academics have frequently met to discuss 'The Third World City', and several books have appeared with this theme, if not this title (e.g. Breese 1966, 1969, McGee 1971, Dwyer 1974, 1975, Bromley and Gerry 1979, Nelson 1979a, Gilbert and Gugler 1982). Abu-Lughod (1977: 2) introduces another volume as 'an introduction to urbanization in the Third World within a unified theoretical framework which we believe is powerful in illuminating many of the phenomena consistently found in the cities of Asia, Africa and Latin America'. But how much do they really have in common? She rightly stresses that students of urbanization must not 'dismiss as "deviant" more than half the world's largest cities', but is it likely that we can make many valid generalizations about so many? Or even about the cities of the whole continent of Africa? Does a knowledge of either Mexico City or Calcutta, or even of Cairo or Johannesburg, give much indication of what is happening in Lagos or Kinshasa? Perhaps there are some common features, but in many ways the tropical African situation differs sharply from those of North Africa and South Africa, as well as those of Asia and Latin America. Indeed, it is often hard to generalize even for the whole of tropical Africa, and a major theme of this book is the diversity to be found within this region. So is there really even such a thing as 'The African City'?

Themes in the study of the African city

A few features are common to nearly all tropical African cities. One is the dire poverty in material terms. Many studies of Latin American cities single out 'the urban poor' for special attention, but across Africa from Dakar to Maputo this would mean the vast majority of the inhabitants. Perhaps fewer are totally destitute than, say, in

Calcutta; but no more than 5 per cent could be considered affluent, with a further 10 to 15 per cent in a middle-income range (though even these would be distinctly poor by European standards).

Another widespread feature is ethnic diversity, with sharper divisions between racial groups than in some other parts of the world, and sharp ethnic divisions within the indigenous population. These are important enough in African urban life to warrant a chapter to themselves, and are, perhaps, especially significant in so far as they cut across class divisions. A third feature shared by most tropical African cities is the maintenance of intense urban–rural relationships arising out of the fact that most men and women living in them were born and brought up in the countryside. Specific attention is given to these relationships in chapter 9, but the way in which the cities are bound up with indigenous peasant society, as well as the international capitalist economy, is relevant to every topic discussed.

One of the most important common characteristics of tropical African countries is their common experience of colonial rule and the recent attainment of political independence. Most have existed as entities for less than a hundred years, and as independent states for less than twenty-five, and so they are engaged in a critical process of nation-building in which the cities play a vital role. The colonial episode provided a major impetus for urban growth everywhere, but a distinction must be made between those areas where it brought this for the first time and those where it impinged upon well-established indigenous urban traditions.

This provides a recurring theme throughout the book, qualifying almost every attempted generalization. Thus, while throughout tropical Africa people feel a powerful attachment to 'home', the significance of this sentiment is very different in those cities which are regarded as 'home' by many of their inhabitants from that in the larger number of cities where almost everyone thinks of some rural locality as 'home'.

A geographical study in the 1980s can hardly reject all efforts at generalization, but it can be much concerned with the issue of how widely any generalizations apply. It can also raise queries about excessively crude dichotomies which are so widely used in the social science literature. If developed *v*. less-developed countries is one such dichotomy of which we must beware, indigenous *v*. colonial cities may be another. Other examples are generative *v*. parasitic cities, and formal *v*. informal sectors within cities. Perhaps we even need to challenge the urban *v.* rural dichotomy itself. Every one of these certainly has some value, but all can distort reality if overused. Brookfield (1975: 53) has noted that dichotomies, or polarized constructs, are necessary for social science theory, but warns that 'inevitably they grow into stereotypes'. In respect of most phenomena a spectrum or continuum is far closer to reality.

One specific aim of this book is to provide a context for the numerous individual city studies that now exist (O'Connor 1981), both on the topics discussed here, and also on others such as urban administration and politics (e.g. Werlin 1974, Wolpe 1974) or labour relations (e.g. Grillo 1973, Jeffries 1978, Peace 1979). These topics should obviously be included in any comprehensive study of African urbanization, but they are beyond the competence of this author. The observation that many individual city studies exist does not, of course, imply that there is no scope for more. More are urgently needed, for there are many aspects of many cities on which virtually nothing has yet been published.

It has lately become fashionable to criticize both case studies and broad reviews such as this for a lack of firm theoretical foundations. Indeed, the leading African writer on urbanization, Akin Mabogunje (1980: 339–43), in a much wider-ranging volume in this series, felt obliged to explain why he had not adopted a single consistent theoretical framework such as that provided by Marx. His arguments apply to the present work also.

It would be *possible* to present a single theory of African urbanization, even perhaps 'Third World' urbanization, and to provide evidence to support it. Unfortunately, it would be bound to fly in the face of all the contradictory evidence. One could build an argument around the undoubted fact that African urbanization is diverging from the path trodden by Europe, North America and Japan over the past 200 years, if only because the world context for contemporary Africa is utterly different. One could equally well build an argument around the fact that many processes now at work in African cities are similar to those now operating in post-industrial Europe and North America, so producing convergence. One could argue that the relationships between overseas metropolises and African capitals, between these capitals and provincial towns, between these towns and the countryside, are all basically exploitative, analysing each issue from migration to trade in these terms: but this would be no more complete a picture than an analysis based on the premise that all such relationships are mutually beneficial. Fortunately there are at last a few voices saying 'the old Left–Right axis is not much use to us in handling such questions' (Seers 1979: 13), and even presenting general pleas for pragmatism (Streeten 1979).

It would be quite *impossible* to write a book within a clear-cut theoretical framework that incorporated within it such diverse approaches as those of Berry (1973), Friedmann (1973), the later Friedmann (1979), Harvey (1973), Lipton (1977), McGee (1971) and Santos (1979), yet there is clear evidence to support *all* of their propositions. Most urban–rural relationships, for example, involve some benefits to certain rural dwellers, and some harm done to others – or even to the same people.

Others are now preparing books which consider a wide range of models and theories of urban geography and urban sociology, largely derived from 'Western' experience, and examine their relevance to Africa. This is not the approach adopted here, for our starting point is the African experience itself. This book attempts to arrive at conclusions, and to make partial generalizations, on the basis of the evidence available, rather than to see how far the empirical findings fit any preconceived theory.

The next chapter starts with the proposition that there are several quite distinct urban traditions in tropical Africa, and that African cities can only be understood in terms of these. However, while that undoubtedly applies to the legacy inherited at the time of independence around 1960, later chapters will suggest that even this basic framework is now of steadily decreasing validity, as a result of a great variety of contemporary processes. It remains helpful, but really only as a starting point. We begin by considering the urban pattern on a broad scale, then narrow down to spatial structures within the cities, and finally widen out again to a discussion of the cities' relationships with each other and with their rural hinterlands.

2 Urban traditions, distribution and growth

Urban origins and urban traditions in tropical Africa

One source of the diversity of tropical Africa's cities lies in their origins. While this book is sharply focused on the contemporary scene, a proper understanding of this demands some historical depth – ideally far more than can be provided here. As Peel (1980) has argued, there is a need for more historical study of African urbanization, as exemplified by Cole (1975) and Gouellain (1975) for individual cities, and on a wider scale by Howard (1975). A full chronological account of the emergence of cities in Africa will not be given, partly because the story is still shrouded in mystery and partly because summaries of what is known have been provided elsewhere (e.g. Hance 1970: 211–16, Vennetier 1976: 12–22). For the pre-colonial period an account at greater length is provided by Hull (1976). We shall simply identify certain urban traditions, and the initiatives for urban growth lying behind these.

With respect to chronology we should at least note that although really ancient cities on the African continent are confined to those such as Cairo and Alexandria in the far north, continuous urban settlement within parts of tropical Africa certainly extends back for over a thousand years; and also that in sharp contrast to Latin America, where nearly all the capital cities were founded in the sixteenth century, African cities are very diverse in their dates of origin. While Kano, Zaria, Ife, Benin, Mogadishu and Mombasa were all established long before the sixteenth century, Luanda, Accra, Kumasi and Ouagadougou date from about that period. Other cities, including Banjul, Freetown, Monrovia, Ibadan, Sokoto and Khartoum, first developed in the early nineteenth century; while Bamako, Abidjan, Lomé, Cotonou, Yaoundé, Brazzaville, Kinshasa, Addis Ababa, Kampala, Nairobi and Harare all had late-nineteenth-century or early-twentieth-century origins. This was undoubtedly the main period of city foundation in tropical Africa, when the greater part of the present spatial framework for urban development was laid down. However, a number of cities such as Lusaka and those of the Zambian Copperbelt are even more recent, while the Mauritanian capital, Nouakchott, is a creation of the 1950s, and the new Nigerian capital is still largely on the drawing board.

Clearly, the difference in age between, say, Kano and Lusaka, is significant in many ways; but the importance of dates of origin could certainly be exaggerated, especially in the many cases where old-established settlements declined almost to nothing before experiencing a twentieth-century burst of growth. (There are, of course, ancient urban settlements that were totally abandoned or destroyed, as the Zimbabwe ruins indicate, and others such as Axum in Ethiopia, Kilwa in Tanzania, and Gao and Tombouctou in Mali that are now only very minor settlements.) It is suggested here that 'urban traditions' are of greater significance for the present characteristics of African cities than mere chronology, and that Sokoto and Ibadan, for instance, have much more in common with Zaria and Ife respectively – in each case 800 years older – than with other cities of nineteenth-century origin such as Monrovia or Dar es Salaam. In any case, most of the cities which originated hundreds of years ago remained extremely small until recent times, so that the growth of Accra or Luanda as colonial cities is a twentieth-century phenomenon almost to the same extent as the growth of Brazzaville or Kinshasa.

The crudest form of differentiation of African urban traditions would have to be based on a dichotomy either between 'traditional' and 'modern', or between 'indigenous' and 'alien', or else on some compromise incorporating all of these. These terms are extremely vague, and have been used by different writers with substantially different meanings, while there are some scholars who reject all such dualistic thinking. However, as purely descriptive devices, such dichotomies do have some validity in many aspects of African life – far more so than in, say, Latin America.

Within every tropical African country elements that are wholly indigenous dominate society in general, and still loom large in both economic and political life despite around seventy years of colonial rule; and many of these can appropriately be regarded as 'traditional'. Yet every country has been profoundly influenced by the colonial impact (or comparable intrusions in the case of Ethiopia and Liberia). In most areas this came so abruptly that it super-imposed rather than infused the alien elements ranging from local government to physical infrastructure that tend to be included in the notion of 'modern'. This applies to the urban as well as the rural scene; and while every city combines indigenous and alien elements to a certain extent, there are some where the former remain dominant as well as many where the latter have always predominated.

Without doubt most of the urban centres in south-western Nigeria are indigenous in origin and are a traditional feature of Yoruba culture (Mabogunje 1968: chapter 4; Ojo 1966a: chapter 5). Local initiatives have been responsible for most of their growth and their present character, while the colonial intrusion brought only modifications, albeit major ones in the case of cities like Ibadan. Conversely, most urban centres in Kenya and Zambia are entirely of colonial origin (Morgan 1969, Kay 1967b), and until recently Europeans were responsible for most of the major decisions affecting their growth and character. There were earlier urban traditions in various parts of eastern Africa (Southall 1971), but there is no continuity between those and the present Nairobi, Lusaka and Harare. The site of Nairobi, for example, was a no-man's land between Kikuyu and Masai territory when the British arrived in 1899.

To some extent this form of differentiation fits in with the classic distinction between orthogenetic and heterogenetic cities made by Redfield and Singer (1954), and is comparable with forms of differentiation adopted for south-east Asia by Ginsburg (1955) and McGee (1967) even though it coincides with the age of the cities much less closely than in south-east Asia.

However, a simple dichotomy between traditional/indigenous cities and modern/colonial cities is far too crude to be of much use in the study of African urbanization. The frequency with which Southall's (1961: 6–13) differentiation of Type A and Type B cities has been quoted is a reflection of how superficial has been the discussion of spatial differentiation in most of the literature on the subject. One study after another has referred to, and made use of, this dichotomy without elaborating on it, and some writers have even implied that all West African cities are of one type while all East and Central African cities are of the other type.

If the whole range of tropical African cities is to be forced into a simple typology, so that reasonably valid generalizations can be made, then at least six categories must be recognized. Even then many individual cities will occupy only marginal positions between these categories. Here we shall distinguish the truly indigenous city and the Islamic city, the colonial city and the 'European' city, the dual city and the hybrid city.

Six types of African city

The indigenous city

A variety of indigenous urban traditions exists within tropical Africa, but much the strongest is that found among the Yoruba people of south-western Nigeria (Figure 2). This has been the subject of one substantial book (Krapf–Askari 1969) and numerous briefer writings (Bascom 1962, 1968, Mabogunje 1962, Ojo 1966a, Wheatley 1970, Lloyd 1973). Little is known of the origins of the earliest Yoruba cities, or of any links that they may have had with cities elsewhere, but Ife is thought to date back at least to the tenth century. Urbanism there was associated with the institution of divine kingship, and probably spread northwards to Old Oyo and eastwards to Benin as they also became centres of authority. Many other Yoruba towns, such as Ilesha, Ondo and Oshogbo, were probably well established by the seventeenth century.

The nineteenth century brought massive changes in the urban pattern of this region, with warfare causing the abandonment of some settlements and defence requiring the foundation of others. Thus in the 1830s Oyo shifted southwards over 150 kilometres, Ibadan and Abeokuta were newly established, Ilorin was growing further to the north, and many refugees swelled the populations of Iwo, Ogbomosho and Oshogbo. By the end of the century and the coming of colonial rule there were at least ten settlements with populations exceeding 50,000, and by now many more have grown to this size. Precise figures cannot be given, partly because reliable census data are lacking, and partly because – in contrast to all other parts of Africa – there are many who stay in town only at weekends, going out to their farms for the week, and others who normally live outside the town yet who claim to belong to it.

The lack of any sharp cultural distinction between the urban and rural population, the cohesion of large kinship units, and the dependence of many town dwellers on farming for their livelihood, have caused some observers to question whether these are truly 'urban' settlements at all (Schwab 1965, Lloyd 1973). However, provided the term is not defined in a narrow ethnocentric way, they surely did represent one form of urbanism even in the past. Today,

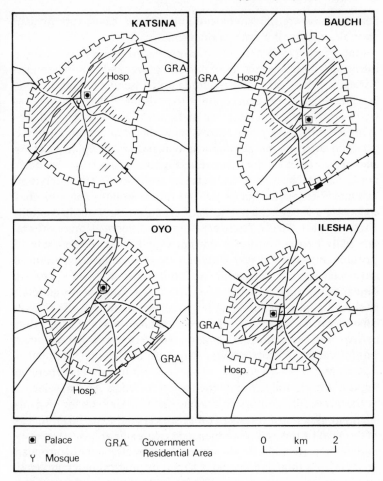

Figure 2   *Four indigenous Nigerian cities*

no one making their way across Ibadan could doubt that it is a truly urban centre. Certainly these indigenous towns lack the ethnic diversity characteristic of most urban settlements elsewhere, some having populations that are 99 per cent Yoruba and 90 per cent local-born. They do not fit Wirth's concept of urbanism as a way of life marked by largely impersonal relationships and so on, and in their origins they did not meet Sjoberg's criterion of literacy; but perhaps these are reflections more upon these classic authors than upon the reality of Yoruba urbanism.

Mabogunje (1968: 78–82) stresses that in origin most of these towns were basically centres of political power and thus of administration, but that both crafts and trade were essential to their survival and growth. Most of them continue to perform all these functions as well as providing a home for many farmers. Wheatley (1970) sees them essentially as cult centres, with the *Oba*, or king, as the personification of the city, and he concludes that far from being anomalous oddities they provide a good example of an early developmental phase of worldwide city evolution. In historical terms this may well be so, but as will be shown in later chapters they constitute a very distinctive form of urbanism even within contemporary tropical Africa. There are of course differences among them, especially between those of the north and those of the south of Yoruba country, and now between those that have experienced most and least external impact, but they still show enough similarities in most respects to be treated as a group. Many generalizations can be made for them: few observations for African cities in general can be applied to them. In cultural terms at least, they perhaps still have more in common with Yoruba rural areas than with other urban centres, even elsewhere in Nigeria.

Perhaps the best example of an indigenous city elsewhere in tropical Africa, and certainly the largest, is Addis Ababa, selected by the nineteenth-century Ethiopian emperor Menelik for his capital in succession to a variety of other sites (Pankhurst 1961). Just as all the Yoruba towns were influenced to a greater or lesser extent by colonial rule, so Addis Ababa was profoundly affected by European contacts even though Ethiopia retained its political independence. One consequence may indeed have been the ending of the tradition of moving the capital at frequent intervals (Horvath 1969), while many others are apparent in the physical fabric of the present city. None the less, the growth and the evolving character of Addis Ababa has depended on indigenous initiatives to a far greater extent than that of the great majority of African cities (Palen 1976).

In various other regions there is clear evidence of the spontaneous emergence of urbanism in past centuries, but no real representatives of these urban traditions today. In southern Nigeria the city of Benin arose well outside the Yoruba area, but externally-induced twentieth-century growth has made it into more of a hybrid today (Onokerhoraye 1975, 1976). Indigenous urban traditions have also been largely swamped in Kumasi, Ghana, and in Kampala, Uganda (Gutkind 1963); while those of the Kongo and Loango kingdoms of eighteenth-century equatorial Africa had disappeared entirely even before the colonial development of cities such as Kinshasa and Brazzaville began.

The Islamic city

A second set of urban traditions is represented by many cities and towns in the savanna belt or Sahel of West Africa, and by some in eastern Africa also. The term 'the Islamic city' has been used for these forms of urbanism, for they owe much to Islam and have much in common with the 'traditional' cities of the Middle East (Costello 1977, Blake and Lawless 1980). There is much debate on how far these cities can be regarded as indigenous to tropical Africa and how far they represent an urban tradition brought across the Sahara. To some extent they vary among themselves in this regard. In many cases the idea of urban life was imported, and some of these cities were founded by invaders from far outside the local area. Most were built by Africans, with African initiatives dominant at each stage of their early growth, but this growth usually depended on external contacts to a much greater extent than in the case of Yoruba urbanism.

The historical basis of this urban tradition in northern Nigeria has been outlined by Mabogunje (1968: chapter 3), and accounts of individual cities there are provided in Usman (1977). A detailed study of some in Mali has been undertaken by Brasseur (1968: 403–34), and this urban tradition is well exemplified by Miner's (1953) account of the rise and decline of Tombouctou, also in Mali. Gugler and Flanagan (1978: 5–13) show how some cities flourished as capitals of empires, others partly as religious centres and partly as terminals in trans-Saharan trade. Some such as Kano, Zaria, Djenné and Ségou are ancient, while others such as Bauchi and Sokoto date only from the *Jihad* of 1809 and Maiduguri only from 1907. Some have been so much altered during this century that only parts of them now exemplify this urban tradition, Kano and Zaria being among these; others largely retain their character, an outstanding example being Katsina (Figure 2) in the extreme north of Nigeria (Dihoff 1970).

These Islamic cities occupied mainly by Hausa people in northern Nigeria, like those of the Yoruba, show much cultural continuity with the surrounding rural areas, although they have always housed a distinct elite. Much change has occurred during this century, but it has been largely incorporated within the traditional social system rather than producing a very different system as in cities in many other parts of Africa.

In Niger and Chad the capital cities, Niamey and N'Djamena, are colonial creations but the Muslim urban tradition is well represented in the smaller towns of Agadez and Abéché (Works 1976). In eastern Africa both Mogadishu and Zanzibar have experienced other strong influences, but both Hargeisa and Merca in Somalia retain much of their traditional character, as does the small Kenya coastal town of Lamu.

The colonial city

Contrasting sharply with the urban traditions just considered are those arising out of the colonial experience. The great majority of tropical Africa's urban centres, large and small, are of colonial origin, most dating from the late nineteenth century and some from the early years of this century. Even those first established much earlier along the coasts remained extremely small until that time. These numerous towns were created by Europeans for their own purposes of administration and trade, playing a critical role in the process of colonial political domination and in the extraction of profit by colonial business enterprise. Many of those that have prospered are ports (Figure 3), developed at the main points of contact between the colonial powers and the local population.

In some cases the new town absorbed one or more traditional African settlements, but it was generally in-migration that ensured an African majority among the population from the earliest years. Much of this migration was of a relatively long-term nature, although very few people permanently broke their ties with their rural homelands; and the character of these towns came to depend to a considerable extent on African decisions and initiatives, although within a framework set up by the European minority. In these respects what we are terming 'colonial' towns differed from the 'European' towns considered in the next section.

Political independence has naturally brought many changes to these towns, but perhaps fewer than might have been expected. The new national administrations in the capital cities often wish to retain many of the inherited structures, while it is through these cities that strong economic ties with Europe continue to be maintained. In contrast to the situation in cities representing indigenous urban traditions, European languages are most often used for both administration and large-scale commerce, although the majority of the inhabitants use indigenous languages at home. While many decisions affecting the cities' character are now made locally, they are still constrained both by the inherited colonial framework and by continuing ties with the international urban system.

In physical terms the inherited structures generally include sharper contrasts between functional and residential zones than in the cities of indigenous origin, while the residential zones are themselves sharply differentiated, with income now replacing race as the basis for this. Even today in some of the francophone capitals a distinction is often made between 'la ville blanche' and 'la ville

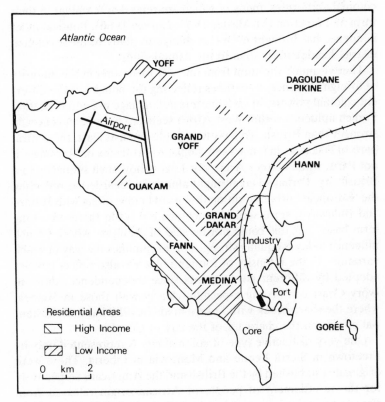

Figure 3 *A colonial city: Dakar*

noire'; the first including both the central administrative and commercial areas and the formerly European residential zones, though it is 'Westernized' Africans who increasingly dominate this section whether in Cotonou, in Bangui or in Libreville. To a greater extent than in the 'dual' cities discussed below as a distinct type, there is much striving after European cultural norms, in dress, in diet and so on, especially among the younger generation, even in 'la ville noire'.

This group of urban centres is so large that inevitably it is in many respects highly diverse. It includes not only most capital cities, but also the majority of the provincial towns such as Thiès (Senegal), Bouaké (Ivory Coast), Tamale (Ghana), Kaduna and Enugu (Nigeria), Kananga and Lubumbashi (Zaire), Mwanza (Tanzania), and many very much smaller centres. Even in countries where the capital cities are rather distinctive, such as Uganda and Sierra Leone, there is a series of small district headquarters set up by the colonial authorities, many of which are remarkably similar in their form and function (McMaster 1968, Harvey 1966). Political independence has brought even less change to many of these colonial district headquarters than to the capital cities.

There is much variation from one city to another in the intensity of foreign influence, sometimes reflecting the policies of the different colonial powers. In such matters as language use and education French influence within West Africa seems to have been generally stronger than British. To a visiting Englishman at least, the central parts of Dakar seem remarkably similar to Bordeaux or Marseilles, if not Paris, while neither Accra nor Lagos show such similarity to a British city. Perhaps Dakar might almost be regarded as reflecting the 'European' urban tradition discussed below, along with Harare and Bulawayo, since some Frenchmen did settle there on a long term basis: but this could not be said of Abidjan, where French influence today is equally strong. This exemplifies the way in which variations in the intensity of foreign influence also reflect policies adopted by different governments since independence, those in Ivory Coast contrasting especially clearly with those in Guinea, where the sharp break with France made in 1958 has had substantial effects on the character of the city of Conakry.

One very distinctive type of colonial city is represented only by Freetown in Sierra Leone and Monrovia in Liberia. These were originally established by the British and the Americans respectively for the resettlement of people of African origin released from slavery. Liberia was never administered as a colonial territory, but it long provided the clearest example within tropical Africa of internal colonialism, the Americo-Liberians being culturally very distinct from the indigenous population, and dominating them politically and economically from their base in Monrovia. Freetown did become a British colonial capital (Fyfe and Jones 1968), but with the Creole community greatly influencing its character, which in certain ways resembles Kingston, Jamaica, more than most African capitals.

The 'European' city

The fourth group of cities might be regarded as a special case of the colonial city, but from the point of view of urban traditions they are quite distinct. They might even be regarded as the true 'colonial' cities in the original sense of colony as a place of permanent new settlement, but the word is not normally used in this sense in writing on tropical Africa – nor in the most notable recent study of 'The Colonial City' (King 1976) which is based largely on Indian experience. Such cities as Harare (formerly Salisbury), Bulawayo, Lusaka and Nairobi were set up by Europeans with little regard for any pre-existing settlement, primarily as places for Europeans to live in, and to a large extent to provide urban services for permanent European settlers in the surrounding rural areas (Hake 1977, Kay and Smout 1977). In terms of origins, therefore, they differ little from Cape Town, or even Melbourne and Montreal. As in the more numerous colonial cities, administration and trade have been the chief functions, but here more manufacturing was permitted, and even encouraged, again largely to meet the needs of European settlers.

Inevitably there was some interaction with the local population from the start, since they also came under the new territorial administration, and since they offered a source of cheap labour. Large numbers of Africans quickly converged upon these new towns, but generally only for a temporary stay: and while they soon constituted a majority of the population, the residential areas set aside for them occupied only a very small part of the total. In contrast to Lagos or Kinshasa these towns were designed to be replicas of towns in Europe. Some reflected European town planning ideas more clearly than many towns in Europe, partly because they were twentieth-century creations, and partly because they were established under highly authoritarian governments.

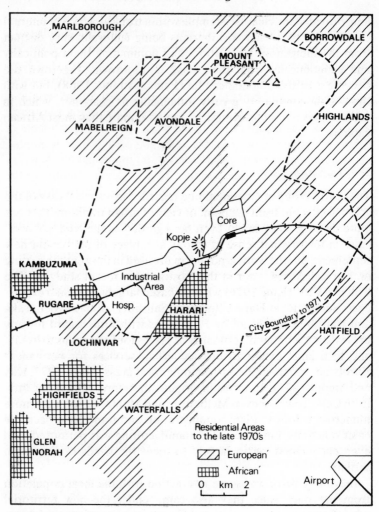

Figure 4   *A 'European' city: Salisbury/Harare*

By the 1950s some of these places had become substantial cities (Figure 4), but the citizens were still by definition only the people who had come from overseas, with Africans resident there only on the Europeans' terms. On the Zambian Copperbelt 'Africans were by definition temporary sojourners. This thinking was incorporated into the legal and administrative structure from the earliest days of settlement' (Mitchell 1969b: 161). Government reports in the late 1940s had asserted that 'the African' was essentially a member of a rural society with his urban activities regarded as a temporary deviation from the norm. This was an entirely different view from any which prevailed in Nigeria, even in relation to colonial cities such as Kaduna and Port Harcourt. There were of course variations within this small group of European cities: in Nairobi, for instance, the picture was complicated by the presence of large numbers of people of Asian origin, who had to be accepted as long-term residents and who won representation on the municipal council.

The attainment of independence by Kenya and Zambia in the early 1960s naturally brought dramatic changes to these cities, and similar changes are now occurring in Zimbabwe. These changes are far more substantial than any taking place in such cities as Abidjan or Accra, or even Dar es Salaam, and much attention is given to them in subsequent chapters. Yet there is little doubt that even in twenty years' time there will be many aspects of these cities that cannot be understood without reference to the circumstances in which they developed.

Meanwhile, Harare and Bulawayo were in 1980 still cities in which a European viewpoint continued to dominate most aspects of urban life. Each consisted of two largely separate communities, with social interaction between them near the minimum. For most of the Europeans they were spacious cities designed for people like themselves into which an uncomfortably large number of Africans had intruded. For most Africans they were places where the great majority were like themselves, living in crowded conditions and commuting to some part of the foreigners' city for employment. The changes there in the 1980s should be fascinating to observe.

The dual city

Among the most interesting of African cities are those which combine elements of two or more of the types already considered in sectors which can be clearly distinguished on the ground. Kano, for instance (Figure 17), incorporates both an ancient Muslim city similar in its population structure and its physical character to Katsina, and beyond the old city walls a newly built-up area whose population and physical character have more in common with a city of colonial origin such as Kaduna. The two very distinct parts are broadly comparable in their number of residents, although the newer part is now considerably larger in extent, and is itself sub-divided into what was essentially the European quarter and the zones that were set aside for migrants from within Nigeria (Becker 1969).

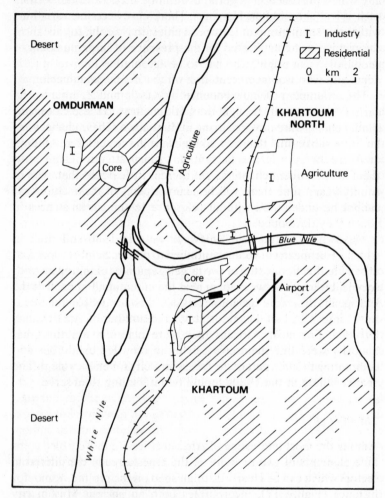

Figure 5   *A dual city: Khartoum–Omdurman*

Another example is Greater Khartoum (Figure 5), where the essentially indigenous city of Omdurman developed on the west bank of the Nile roughly simultaneously with the colonial city of

Khartoum on the opposite bank (El Bushra 1976). Again the two are of comparable size, although the latter has an extension in the form of Khartoum North, from which it is separated by the Blue Nile. While commonly known as 'the Three Towns', this is in most respects one urban agglomeration, with one major and one minor division within it. Kampala might also once have been included, but the colonial element became dominant there, while the city took on a more hybrid character after the establishment of a single municipal authority for the whole agglomeration in 1966.

Some observers would argue that when indigenous and colonial elements are juxtaposed the latter will always dominate, but this can be challenged. For the rest of the world Omdurman is perhaps an appendage of Khartoum, but many Sudanese look to Omdurman as their chief city and regard Khartoum as the appendage. Many Hausa would regard old and new Kano in the same way. These dual cities are distinguished by physically separate components, each with a full range of urban functions, each with a certain degree of independence and self-respect, and each developing in its own way. The relationships between the component parts are those of interdependence rather than those of dominance and subservience.

The whole notion of dualism is rejected in some quarters, but it is often only the more extreme forms of dualistic thinking, or invalid theories based upon the notion, that are successfully demolished. As long as dualism is not taken to mean absence of any relationships, and as long as it is not seen as differentiating between rich and poor but rather as the juxtaposition of two cultural traditions, its existence can hardly be doubted (Brookfield 1975: 69). The two halves of Kano are not totally different worlds, but they do differ greatly. There are banks and motor vehicles in the old city, but far fewer than in the new. Some English is spoken there, but the dominance of Hausa is far greater than in the new city. For major crimes the same legal system applies throughout, but for minor offences there are two quite separate systems.

The extent and nature of the interaction between the different parts of these cities would make a fascinating area for research. Little is known about how many residents of one sector work in the other, about the extent of movements for education and medical care, or about their trading relationships. There are many such links, even though the hallmark of dual cities is that they are weaker than might be expected for such large groups of people in such close proximity (on the principle of the gravity model). Indeed, many residents of new Kano have much stronger links with people else-where in Nigeria, and beyond, than with any residents of old Kano.

A second major subject for inquiry is whether the distinction between sectors in these cities has generally become less sharp since independence. There is no doubt that the presence of an adjacent colonial urban settlement, along with colonial rule in general, brought great changes within the pre-existing cities, undermining some elements of the economy, for instance, while perhaps stimulating others. To what extent has independence reversed or accelerated these processes? The alien character of the colonial sector of these cities has clearly been modified, but has a great increase in interaction necessarily resulted?

The same questions are relevant, but would be even harder to answer, in other cities where both indigenous and colonial elements are present, but where there is no such clear physical separation. In some of these one element is so clearly dominant that the city can be regarded as falling into one of the previous categories, but in many the balance is such that they constitute yet another category.

The hybrid city

This final category is reserved for those cities which combine in-digenous and alien elements in roughly equal proportions, but in which they are to a large extent integrated, rather than merely juxtaposed as in the dual city. As subsequent chapters will indicate, more and more cities might be regarded as moving into this category, including originally indigenous cities such as Addis Ababa and Ibadan, cities that were clearly colonial in origin such as Dar es Salaam and Freetown, and cities of dual origin such as Kampala. An example of a city which has had this hybrid character throughout this century is Kumasi in Ghana which was the capital of the Ashanti empire in the seventeenth and eighteenth centuries with a popula-tion once reaching over 50,000, which shrank to a mere 3000 in 1901 after the British occupation, which was adopted as a major provincial headquarters by them, and which then flourished again as a centre of trade quite largely through local initiative.

There are good reasons for regarding Lagos also as a hybrid city, for it comprises an indigenous Yoruba settlement, vastly enlarged as a colonial capital but with strong local influence throughout its growth, and has its Yoruba core and its colonial city centre sharing the heart of the city rather than as nuclei of two separate halves. A similar case might even be made out for Accra. The best example of a hybrid city from francophone Africa is probably Ouagadougou, which has long been the focal centre for the Mossi people but which was adopted by the French as the capital of Upper Volta. This city has been the subject of a detailed study (in English) by Skinner (1974).

While various other examples of hybrid cities could have been found at any time during this century it is probable that up to the time of independence most of the cities of tropical Africa could appropriately have been fitted into one of the other categories. It is possible that this is no longer the case, and that the urbanization processes occurring in each type of city over the past twenty years have been making it more of a hybrid. This would imply a substantial degree of convergence taking place with respect to these contrasting types of city. This is a theme to which further reference will be made in later chapters, and to which we shall return in the Conclusion.

The geographical distribution of urban development

What total geographical pattern has resulted from these various urban traditions? In the mid nineteenth century large towns were almost entirely confined to south-western Nigeria, but a series of medium-sized towns extended across the savanna zone of West Africa, and many small settlements were strung along the coasts from Saint-Louis to Lobito and from Mogadishu to Maputo. By the mid twentieth century a great dispersal had taken place, although Ibadan was still the largest city in tropical Africa in 1950, with almost half a million inhabitants, and Ogbomosho, Oshogbo, Ife, Abeokuta, Kano, Katsina, Sokoto and Zaria were all among the fifty or so cities which then had over 50,000 inhabitants. Along the Atlantic coast the population of both Dakar and Lagos had then reached 250,000, and both Accra and Luanda around 150,000, while a short way inland Kinshasa had reached 200,000. Meanwhile, in eastern Africa, Addis Ababa almost rivalled Ibadan in size, while Khartoum, Nairobi, Harare and Maputo all exceeded 100,000.

The pattern in 1980, shown in Figure 6, is not greatly different from that in 1950, for urban growth since independence in most African countries has taken place largely on the basis of the framework established during the pre-colonial and colonial periods. A notable feature in comparison with Latin America and

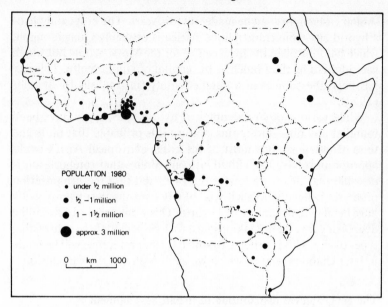

Figure 6   *Tropical Africa: distribution of cities*

Asia is the absence of real giants, for even Lagos and Kinshasa only reached a population of 2 million in the 1970s. From Table 2 it is evident that African capitals occupy a wide spectrum of sizes, many still having populations of under 300,000.

The greatest concentration of towns is still in south-western Nigeria, where there are not only the major cities of Lagos and Ibadan only 150 kilometres apart, but also about twenty other towns with a population of 50,000 or more, many within fifty kilometres of each other (Krapf-Askari 1969). A second cluster is now provided by the Copperbelt of Zambia and Zaire, where a zone only 100 kilometres in length and fifteen kilometres in width includes five out of the seven Zambian towns with over 100,000 inhabitants (Figure 24) and where three further towns of this size are found, somewhat more spread out, in the Shaba Province of Zaire.

Elsewhere there is a remarkably even spread of cities across tropical Africa, but one other notable feature is still a concentration along the coasts. In 1980 about sixty cities outside Nigeria had populations exceeding 100,000, and of these twenty-five have a

Table 2 *Population estimates for the major cities of tropical Africa, 1980*

(Population in thousands)			
Lagos, Nigeria	3000	Bamako, Mali	450
Kinshasa, Zaire	2700	Mogadishu, Somalia	450
Addis Ababa, Ethiopia	1300	Ogbomosho, Nigeria	450
Abidjan, Ivory Coast	1200	Asmara, Ethiopia	400
Accra, Ghana	1100	Brazzaville, Congo	400
Ibadan, Nigeria	1100	Bulawayo, Zimbabwe	400
Khartoum, Sudan	1100	Kananga, Zaire	400
Dakar, Senegal	950	Freetown, Sierra Leone	350
Nairobi, Kenya	900	Ilorin, Nigeria	350
Dar es Salaam, Tanzania	800	Kisangani, Zaire	350
Harare, Zimbabwe	800	Kitwe, Zambia	350
Kano, Nigeria	750	Mbuji-Mayi, Zaire	350
Luanda, Angola	750	Mombasa, Kenya	350
Lubumbashi, Zaire	600	Oshogbo, Nigeria	350
Douala, Cameroon	550	Yaoundé, Cameroon	350
Kumasi, Ghana	550		
Lusaka, Zambia	550	Bangui, CAR	350?
Maputo, Mozambique	550	Conakry, Guinea	500?
Kampala, Uganda	500		

Cities with around 300,000 include Abeokuta, Port Harcourt, Zaria (Nigeria); N'Djamena (Chad); Ndola (Zambia). Cities with around 250,000 include Ado-Ekiti, Aba, Enugu, Ife, Ilesha, Kaduna, Onitsha (Nigeria); Blantyre (Malawi); Bouaké (Ivory Coast); Lomé (Togo); Monrovia (Liberia); Niamey (Niger); Takoradi (Ghana).

Source: Author's estimates based on diverse national sources.

coastal location (even though the coastline of Africa, and especially tropical Africa, is very short in relation to its area). Of the coastal states all but five have their largest city located on the coast – including every one in West Africa. This clearly reflects the role of contact between indigenous and alien peoples as a primary stimulus to urban growth.

Table 3 and Figure 7 indicate the urban population and level of urbanization in each country. Nigeria accounts for over a quarter of the urban population of tropical Africa, and around 20 per cent of Nigerians now live in cities or towns (Mabogunje 1977). Countries with a higher level of urbanization include Congo, Ghana, Ivory Coast, Senegal and Zambia, while at the other end of the scale are

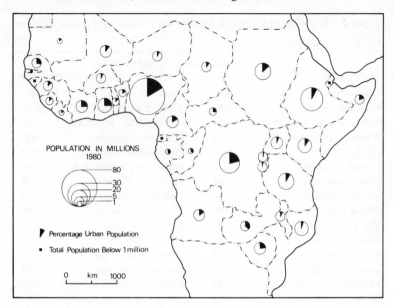

POPULATION IN MILLIONS
1980

80
30
20
5
1

▶ Percentage Urban Population

• Total Population Below 1 million

0   km   1000

Figure 7   *Tropical Africa: urban population by country*

countries such as Burundi and Rwanda where less than 5 per cent live in towns. A fuller country by country analysis has been made elsewhere (O'Connor 1978: 171–80), and this will not be repeated here.

Distribution within countries

While the 'Balkanization' of Africa, and the need for an adminis-trative apparatus in each country, may have encouraged a relatively even spread of urban development on a macro scale, the same is not true of the distribution patterns within countries. While most have a wide scatter of provincial towns, these are often extremely small. At the national scale, spatial concentration of urban development, rather than dispersal, is the keynote.

One of the few generalizations that can be made about urbaniz-ation throughout the world is that all countries have some form of urban hierarchy in which small centres are more numerous than large centres. Some observers have carried generalization further, and have suggested that patterns of urban size-distribution tend to conform to a rank-size 'rule' by which the largest city is roughly

Table 3 *Total urban population and level of urbanization in tropical African countries*

	Urban population in thousands 1975	Urban % of total population 1975	1955		Urban population in thousands 1975	Urban % of total population 1975	1955
Angola	900	15	6	Mali	600	10	3
Benin	400	14	5	Mauritania	140	11	0
Burundi	120	3	2	Mozambique	700	7	3
Cameroon	1200	18	5	Niger	300	7	2
CAR	550	26	7	Nigeria	12000	17	8
Chad	370	10	2	Rwanda	80	2	0
Congo	450	34	17	Senegal	1350	28	16
Ethiopia	2100	8	4	Sierra Leone	480	15	5
Gabon	300	25	4	Somalia	700	20	8
Gambia	60	12	7	Sudan	1900	12	5
Ghana	2500	25	10	Tanzania	1200	8	3
Guinea	600	14	4	Togo	260	12	4
Guinea-Bissau	100	20	5	Uganda	650	6	2
Ivory Coast	1630	25	6	Upper Volta	350	6	2
Kenya	1350	10	5	Zaire	5500	22	8
Liberia	260	15	4	Zambia	1500	34	14
Malawi	300	6	2	Zimbabwe	1200	19	15
				TROPICAL AFRICA	42300	15	6

Note: Urban population is taken as that in towns over 20,000.
The tropical Africa total includes estimates of 100,000 for Djibouti, and 70,000 for Equatorial Guinea in 1975.

Sources: Diverse.

twice the size of the second city, three times the size of the third, and so on (Zipf 1941). On the other hand, as early as 1939 Jefferson noted that many countries have a 'primate' city which is substantially larger than its nearest rival, and many writers have examined the phenomenon of urban primacy in more recent years (Berry 1961, Mehta 1964, Linsky 1965, El Shakhs 1972, Gilbert and Gugler 1982).

These studies have tended to confirm the widely-held belief that urban primacy is particularly prevalent in the less developed countries, although no close correlation has been found with measures such as per capita income since there are other relevant factors such as size of country. Writers who have looked specifically at the African situation (Hance 1970, Clarke 1972, 1975) have demonstrated a generally high level of primacy (Table 4). It will be shown in chapter 8 that this is in fact now intensifying in many countries, and that it is even more marked if we use criteria other than mere population numbers.

Table 4   *Urban size distribution patterns in selected African countries*

	City population in thousands				
	Largest	Second	Third	Fourth	Fifth
Angola 1970	475	62	60	41	32
Cameroon 1976	396	286	79	69	67
Ethiopia 1980	1277	425	82	77	70
Ghana 1970	849	343	161	84	52
Ivory Coast 1975	921	175	61	50	45
Kenya 1979	828	341	120	93	50
Malawi 1977	226	103	21	16	12
Mali 1976	404	65	54	47	45
Niger 1977	225	58	46	31	20
Senegal 1976	800	117	107	88	73
Sierra Leone 1974	274	76	39	31	27
Sudan 1973	784	133	107	90	66
Tanzania 1978	757	111	111	103	77
Togo 1970	148	30	20	17	16
Uganda 1969	331	53	24	21	18
Zaire 1975	1680	481	317	292	283
Zambia 1980	538	315	282	150	146
Zimbabwe 1980	800*	373	72	64	52

* This figure, like most others, is for the urban agglomeration. The official mid 1980 estimate for Harare municipal area was 654,000.

Sources: Census Reports and National Statistical Yearbooks.

However, since this is a phenomenon shared with most countries in Latin America, many in south-east Asia and the Middle East, and several in Europe, it should not be regarded as an aberration requiring special explanation. Probably the rank-size 'rule' is now best forgotten.

Factors influencing the distribution

Explanations of all aspects of African development (and under-development) are increasingly sought in forces operating inter-nationally. The effects of both colonial rule and today's neo-colonialism have profoundly affected the distribution of cities, but factors internal to the continent have also been significant. These include the distribution of rural population, the resource base, and cultural preferences for nucleated or dispersed settlement. Other factors, such as suitable port sites and the pattern of cash crop production have become important through the interaction of internal and external forces (Steel 1961). Arising more specifically out of the colonial experience, the political fragmentation of Africa has contributed to a relatively wide dispersal of city development, while specific colonial structures explain features such as the large size of Dakar and Brazzaville in relation to present-day Senegal and Congo. The high levels of urban primacy within most countries owe much to the fact that most urban growth has depended largely on alien initiatives.

In so far as the distribution of urban centres reflects colonial interests rather than local needs, major modifications may now be required. McNulty (1976) argues this for West African countries in general, despite the existence of powerful pre-colonial urban traditions there. Soja and Weaver (1976) are even more emphatic in the case of East Africa. They observe that 'the location, size and distribution of urban centers in contemporary East Africa is almost entirely the product of British and German decision-making' (p. 236). It 'can thus be best understood as an expression of the more comprehensive and pervasive process of underdevelopment', constituting a 'pattern of urbanization which is inherently antithetical to an autonomously controlled and socially just process of development' (p. 240). The first observation is clearly true, but not all would agree that the others necessarily follow.

Urban growth and rising levels of urbanization

One outstanding feature of most African cities is their current rate of growth. Tropical Africa's total urban population is rising by over 5 per cent per year, and that of many individual cities by over 7 per cent to produce a doubling within ten years. In part this reflects high rates of natural increase, which prevail in the rural areas also, and therefore the rate of *urbanization* is substantially lower. Nevertheless rural–urban migration is so extensive that levels of urbanization are rising everywhere. The relative contributions of these and other components of the urban growth are discussed later.

The growth of urban population continues unabated in absolute terms, and indeed the annual increment is larger every year: but after an acceleration in the 1950s and 1960s it is now slowing somewhat in relative terms. While many cities with around 100,000 inhabitants in 1960 had doubled to 200,000 by 1970, the increase by 1980 was most often to around 350,000 rather than 400,000. Further slight deceleration seems likely through the 1980s, but the rate of growth will probably remain the world's highest, and far higher than that of the rural population.

Variations in recent growth rates

Most cities of indigenous origin continue to grow more slowly than those of colonial origin, but there are marked variations among the latter while a few of the former have been rejuvenated. Sharp national contrasts are revealed by Table 3 and estimates for individual cities are given in Table 5. The highest rates of growth have occurred in those countries which attained independence almost without urban centres, notably Mauritania and Rwanda. The French governed Mauritania from Saint-Louis in Senegal, and its new capital of Nouakchott grew from almost nothing in 1960 to a town of 135,000 people by 1977, the growth accelerated by the Sahel drought (Pitte 1977). The Belgians administered Rwanda from Bujumbura in Burundi, and even its largest town, Kigali, chosen as capital in 1962, then had less than 10,000 inhabitants (Nwafor 1981). By 1977 the figure had reached 90,000.

Table 5   *Population growth in tropical African cities, 1950–80*

| | Estimated population in thousands | | | |
	1950	1960	1970	1980
Ibadan	430	550	750	1100
Addis Ababa	350	500	850	1300
Lagos	250	600	1600	3000
Kinshasa	220	500	1400	2700
Khartoum	210	380	650	1100
Dakar	180	380	600	950
Accra	160	390	740	1100
Luanda	150	250	470	750
Harare	140	280	400	800
Nairobi	130	270	510	900
Abidjan	80	220	600	1200
Dar es Salaam	80	170	380	800

Note: Figures are for the whole urban agglomeration.

Sources: Diverse.

Other countries experiencing particularly rapid urban growth include Gabon, Ivory Coast, Malawi and Somalia, i.e. two of the most affluent and two of the poorest. In the first two, booming primary product exports are supporting some industrial growth and rapid expansion in the tertiary sector. In Ivory Coast the population of Abidjan rose from 130,000 in 1955 to 920,000 in 1975, and the urban share of the total population rose from 6 per cent to 25 per cent. Malawi is vastly poorer, but has recently experienced faster economic growth than most African countries, while urban expansion there has been boosted by reductions in labour migration to South Africa and Zimbabwe and by the construction of a new capital city at Lilongwe. Somalia's economic growth has been minimal, and the influx to Mogadishu and other urban areas reflects both extreme drought and a resulting desperate plight for many rural dwellers, and also a refugee stream from Ethiopia.

Political factors are well illustrated by both Zaire and Tanzania. In Zaire the urban population rose from 1.2 million in 1955 to almost 6 million in 1975, while numbers in Kinshasa rose from 350,000 to 1.7 million. Political problems throughout the post-independence period brought disastrous breakdown to the rural economy in many areas, while many people fled to the cities hoping for greater physical security there.

Tanzania has been spared such civil strife: but during the 1970s government policies dedicated to improving rural life and intended to curb rural–urban migration may have had the reverse effect in the short run. The 1978 census reveals that urban growth has been at least as rapid as in most African countries. Many rural dwellers have been dissatisfied with policies requiring them to move into new *ujamaa* villages, most of which have had inevitable teething troubles and some of which have been either badly sited or badly managed.

Slower rates of urban growth in Congo and Senegal represent the reverse of the Rwanda and Mauritania situation, for each came to independence with an oversize capital, Brazzaville and Dakar having been the foci for the whole of French Equatorial Africa and French West Africa respectively; and it is hard to see how either country has sustained increased urbanization. In Zimbabwe too urban growth was slowed in the 1960s by the break-up of the Central African Federation, and then in the 1970s by UDI: but now the removal of constraints placed upon rural–urban migration under previous regimes and the upheavals of the late 1970s in many rural areas are contributing to rapid expansion of the cities. For a while growth may be exceptionally rapid, as wives come to join husbands already there and as the resulting boost to natural increase is felt.

Patterns of growth within countries

Few meaningful generalizations can be made about urban growth in Nigeria in view of the size and complexity of its urban system; despite data problems sharp contrast among its cities are quite evident. Lagos has been among the fastest growing throughout the past thirty years. Its population was around 270,000 in 1952, while by 1963 there were about 650,000 people within the municipality and a further 400,000 in the outer suburbs. The agglomeration reached its second million in the mid 1970s, and most 1980 estimates are between 2.5 and 3 million. This contrasts sharply with the picture for Ibadan, still tropical Africa's largest city in 1952 when the census recorded 460,000 inhabitants, but soon to fall way behind Lagos. The official 1963 census figure of 635,000 was more accurate than that for many Nigerian cities, and the total reached 1 million only in the late 1970s.

The growth rate for Kano lies between those for Lagos and Ibadan, as does that for other northern cities such as Kaduna and Zaria. Elsewhere, changing circumstances have greatly affected growth rates. The oil boom brought a burst of growth first to Port Harcourt and then to Warri; and the civil war brought a sudden influx of refugees to cities such as Aba and Enugu. Other changes were provided by the creation of twelve States in 1967 and their further subdivision in 1976, elevation to the position of State capital bringing accelerated growth first to towns such as Calabar, Jos, Maiduguri and Sokoto, and then to others such as Abeokuta, Akure, Bauchi, Makurdi, Minna and Owerri. Before gaining their new status, Calabar and Sokoto, Abeokuta and Bauchi were among the slowest growing urban centres in Africa.

The number and diversity of Nigeria's cities presents a great planning challenge, since to a far greater extent than elsewhere decisions involve not only how far urban growth should be aided but also where it should be concentrated. One major decision already taken concerns the new capital city at Abuja (see chapter 8), which will surely be the fastest growing of all African cities in the mid 1980s.

Zambia is of interest here because of the contrast between

mining-based urbanization on the Copperbelt and more orthodox urban growth in Lusaka. Census figures for 1963, 1969 and 1980 show some notably constant trends. Over this whole post-independence period the Zambian urban population has risen by 220 per cent, but that of the five main Copperbelt towns has risen by only 140 per cent, while there has been a 330 per cent increase in the capital city.

In Zaire too growth has been more modest in the copper mining towns of Kolwezi and Likasi, and even in the main commercial centre of that region, Lubumbashi, than in various other urban centres (De Saint Moulin 1977). The capital city, Kinshasa, has grown faster than most, but the greatest growth in the 1960s was experienced by the Kasai cities of Kananga and Mbuji-Mayi in the most strife-torn area.

The most interesting question in relation to the growth rates of different urban centres within most countries, and the only one of a general nature that can be asked for tropical Africa as a whole, concerns the evidence for increasing or decreasing levels of urban primacy; but this will be taken up in chapter 8.

The components of urban growth

The main components of the rapid growth of urban population are natural increase, discussed below, and rural–urban migration, the subject of chapter 3. Two smaller components to be noted first are the engulfing of rural communities as cities expand, and the transformation of villages into small towns. Both of these may involve real changes in the way of life of formerly rural groups, who have become more urbanized without moving: but related to each there is the possibility of misleading statistics which exaggerate urban growth.

One source of error arises from the problem of defining the limits of the urban area. As any city's population rises the area that it occupies naturally expands, and census figures ten years apart which relate to the same tract of land will understate the urban growth. However, in most African countries city boundaries have been greatly extended since independence, and this may inflate the population growth figures if either the old boundary excluded part of the effective urban area at that time or the new boundary enclosed a substantial rural population. The 1959 Uganda census recorded

47,000 inhabitants in Kampala, but this referred to the municipality only and the real urban population exceeded 100,000. The boundaries were later greatly extended, so that the 1969 census indicated a meteoric rise to 332,000, a figure which was technically fairly accurate but which included many people still living in a rural environment.

The other source of error results from the need for some minimum 'urban' threshold. If a lower population limit such as 20,000 is used, a country's level of urbanization would appear to rise sharply if, say, it had one large city and five other settlements all increasing over an intercensal period from 18,000 to 22,000. Adams (1972b) has argued that this has led to false statements about rates of urban growth and urbanization in West Africa. However, it should be recognized that in most countries the whole urbanization process does include the addition of urban functions to settlements that were once wholly rural in nature, and indeed some would argue that this should become a much larger component in preference to the massive rural–urban migration that currently takes place. Thus, while the *ujamaa vijijini* programme in Tanzania has been undertaken as a programme of rural resettlement, it is perhaps desirable as well as probable that the largest or best located of the new nucleated villages will take on sufficient central place functions to become small towns.

The engulfing of rural communities is perhaps much less desirable, but it is quite inevitable as cities expand in physical terms. Numerous examples could be quoted, from the absorption of villages like Yoff into Dakar to the spreading of Nairobi's tentacles over areas of dense rural settlements in Kiambu District. Not only the largest cities such as Kinshasa, but even smaller centres such as Blantyre and most of the towns in the densely-populated south-east of Nigeria have absorbed several small rural communities. There is clearly much scope for study of the responses of the former rural communities in such cases, and it is surprising that more has not been undertaken. Two substantial studies which indicate less impact than might be expected are that of Buurri al Lamaab on the eastern edge of Khartoum, by Barclay (1964), and that of a village just outside Kano, by Hill (1977).

Natural increase

An excess of births over deaths is contributing much to the growth of every African city, and the share of such natural increase in the overall growth is generally rising. However, the precise share is known nowhere, and estimates often vary widely. During the 1950s and even the 1960s migration accounted for a larger share in most cities, but as demographic structures have changed natural increase has become the dominant element in more and more cities. In some cases in-migration has shown only arithmetical progression while growth from natural increase has shown geometrical progression.

In assessing the role of natural increase it is important to note that it is occurring not only among the long-settled population, but among the recent migrants too. Some writers have suggested that rates of net in-migration can be obtained by noting total population growth over a fixed period and subtracting the growth that normal natural increase would have produced: but if a city of 100,000 in 1970 has gained an extra 35,000 through normal natural increase of around 3 per cent a year, and an extra 35,000 through net in-migration at a similar rate, it is likely to have gained a further 5000 to 6000 through the natural increase produced by these migrants within their one to ten years in the city. As a result the share of migration in urban population growth has commonly been exaggerated, and the share of natural increase understated.

Even so, natural increase will be given less attention here than migration, because it is in no way a peculiarly urban phenomenon. In every African country the cities are involved in a national process of rapid population growth that has been documented in volumes edited by Brass (1968), Caldwell (1975) and Udo (1979). Death rates in every country are still shockingly high, but they are falling steadily while birth rates remain as high as ever. The result has been a rate of natural increase for tropical Africa as a whole which has been rising from 2 per cent a year towards 3 per cent, and which differs relatively little from one country to another.

The question of greatest interest in the present context is whether the rate of natural increase in the cities is higher or lower than in the rural areas. Unfortunately, with little or no registration of births and deaths, not much is known about this. Several specific surveys have yielded very inconclusive results, partly because some factors producing rural–urban differences cancel each other out, but it seems likely that most cities now have a slightly higher rate of natural increase than most rural areas.

Relevant factors include both the demographic structure of the urban population, which in turn reflects migration patterns and is therefore discussed more fully later, and various aspects of the urban and rural environment. Death rates are generally lower than in the rural areas, partly because there are fewer elderly people among the urban dwellers and partly because, in contrast to Europe in past centuries, health conditions tend to be better in the cities and health care is much more readily available there. Crude birth rates are also lower in some cities, especially those which have a highly unbalanced sex ratio, but they are particularly high in those cities which have a disproportionately large number of young adults of both sexes.

The main focus of attention in some demographic surveys is the question of whether urban life has encouraged a decline in fertility, as much conventional theory would suggest. If African countries are to experience a demographic transition with falling mortality followed by falling fertility, as has occurred elsewhere, it might be expected that the cities will lead the way. However, as yet there is very little evidence that this is happening, except among a small part of the elite. Several surveys indicate that among the great majority of urban African families the preferred number of children is still at least five or six. Even wives with advanced education and careers have less incentive to reduce the number than in, say, Europe since they invariably have domestic help. For most parents of more lowly status, children are still seen as providing the security in old age which the state cannot offer.

Morgan (1975) found that the average level of fertility in Ibadan was actually higher than in the surrounding rural areas, and that it was higher still in Lagos. Similarly, Thompson (1978) found higher urban than rural fertility rates in Uganda. The lowest rates of fertility in urban areas are reported from Ethiopia, where crude birth rates also seem to be much lower than in the countryside.

Caldwell (1975: 11) has pointed specifically to apparent variations from country to country. 'Urban fertility is definitely lower than rural fertility in Ghana and may have been so for at least half a century' but 'On the other hand, there is equally strong evidence of higher urban fertility in Zaire and Gabon'. No one has yet provided a full explanation of these national contrasts, although various contributory factors have been noted. The urban fertility rate is raised in certain countries primarily by the relaxing of customs by which pregnancy would be avoided while another infant was still being nursed, so that some women give birth every two years or so rather than every three or four years. It is raised elsewhere by changes in diet and by medical care which reduces the number of stillbirths as well as the level of infant mortality.

Conversely, fertility rates are lowered to varying degrees by later marriage, especially with the spread of secondary education, by awareness of falling infant mortality rates so that there is less need to produce ten children in order to ensure the survival of five, and by use of new methods of contraception. In some cities the fertility rate may also be lowered by the presence of many women who are there to escape from the norms of village life, and some who have been rejected by village society because they have been unable to bear children. The particularly low rate in Addis Ababa and other Ethiopian towns is certainly related to the large number of divorced women present there.

Despite the variations among cities, we can suggest a general picture of mortality, including infant mortality, much lower than in most rural areas, of fertility only slightly lower, and therefore of natural increase rather higher. Natural increase is therefore contributing slightly to rising levels of urbanization, as well as massively to urban growth. Migration plays a far larger part in increasing urbanization, however, and so merits a chapter to itself.

3 Rural–urban migration

Until very recently migration was the chief contributor to total urban population growth in most parts of Africa: it remains everywhere the chief cause of a rising level of urbanization. Even today in most African cities there are far more migrant than local-born adults, and in relation to the size of the existing urban population the scale of such migration is greater than in any other part of the world. Net migration out of certain rural areas has actually reduced their population, as in parts of Zambia, although rural natural increase is too high, and the urban share of the total population too low, for this yet to be widespread.

Population movements are constantly occurring throughout Africa, as they have always done (Prothero 1968, Gould and Prothero 1975, Clarke and Kosiński 1982). Prior to this century few were focused on cities, for even where these existed they grew mainly by natural increase. Today rural–to–urban movement is the dominant element in long-distance migration in most countries, though rural–rural local movements (for example, for marriage) may involve even more people.

In examining rural–urban migration we are concerned with its extent, nature, causes and consequences, but all too little is known about each of these. Even the simple rate of net in-migration, either at present or in the recent past, is not known for any city. Subtracting a presumed rate of natural increase from total population growth provides only a crude indicator, even after allowing for births to recent migrants. Census data on birthplace are relevant for past movements, though influenced by such factors as women returning to the rural home area for childbirth. One might compare the size of each age group at the latest census with the size of the group ten years younger at a census ten years earlier, allowing for deaths: but truly comparable data are rarely available, age is often mis-reported, and even school terms and holidays may distort the figures.

Other indicators include sex ratios and ethnic structures, but they provide only very rough guides. While a high sex ratio suggests (selective) migration, an even balance does not indicate little migration; and while the presence of Ibo in Lagos or Luo in Nairobi was once evidence of migration, increasing numbers from such groups are now born outside their home areas.

The distinction between *gross* and *net* rates of in-migration is highly significant in a continent where return migration is widespread. In terms of urban growth it is net movements that matter, whereas for urban impact gross flows may be of greater concern. Return migration to rural homes is rarely revealed by census data, so the size of gross flows can often only be guessed.

A small contribution to urban growth has been made by people coming from overseas rather than from rural Africa. In some cities short-contract expatriates have increased the annual *gross* inflow from overseas since independence, but the *net* inflow is now small, and often there has been a net outflow. The largest outflow was of Portuguese from Luanda in 1975–7, but many Cubans then provided another type of in-migrant there.

Scores of questions might be asked about African rural–urban migration. What are its spatial patterns? To what extent is it age- and sex-selective? Do people move mainly as individuals or as families? Are the moves short-term, long-term or permanent? Do people move primarily for economic or for other motives? How well-informed are they about conditions in the cities? A few writers have considered these questions in depth for individual countries (Deniel 1968, Caldwell 1969, Heisler 1974, Sabot 1979), but they have been considered for tropical Africa as a whole only briefly (e.g. Gugler 1969, Hance 1970, Byerlee 1974, Prothero 1976). Before tackling such questions, however, we should try to establish the extent of rural–urban migration.

The extent of migration

Eastern Africa   Of the 828,000 people recorded in Nairobi by the 1979 census only 26 per cent were born within the city, and most of these were small children. For residents over 15 years of age the proportion fell to under 5 per cent, so there were then about 500,000 adults who must have moved in, mostly from Kenya's rural areas. The situation in Mombasa is rather different, for 39 per cent of the inhabitants were born in the city, though even there the vast majority of adults were in-migrants. This difference reflects the longer history of Mombasa, which already had a small nucleus of long-settled urban families by 1900, when Nairobi was still only a railway base camp. The population within Nairobi's 1979 boundaries had been about 350,000 in 1962, so even with the highest plausible estimates for natural increase there must have been net in-migration of at least 200,000 people over that seventeen-year period.

In Dar es Salaam only 32 per cent of the 1967 population was local-born, and the figure dropped to 15 per cent for the adult population. The proportion local-born was very similar in most Tanzanian provincial towns, ranging only between 28 per cent and 36 per cent. In every town most local-born were small children, so nearly all the adults were migrants. No birthplace figures are yet available from the 1978 census, but the totals indicate that migration into Dar es Salaam and various provincial towns probably accelerated in the 1970s. Net in-migration during this period into the capital city must have exceeded 25,000 a year, which is considerably more than the annual rate for Nairobi.

The 1969 Uganda census also recorded birthplace, but did not distinguish between towns and their surrounding districts. Even so, it is evident that the great majority of the urban dwellers were migrants. Less than 30 per cent of Kampala's population was born anywhere within West Mengo District, so the proportion born within the city must have been much lower than for Dar es Salaam. The extent of migration is also indicated by the sample of 200 unemployed men in Kampala and Jinja studied by Hutton (1973), for only one was city born and bred.

The rate of rural–urban migration during the 1960s and 1970s was even greater in Zambia than in Kenya, Tanzania and Uganda. Nearly all the adult urban residents are migrants who have arrived within the past thirty years. Among the earliest migrants few stayed more than two or three years, and indeed Zambia now has not only a large proportion of urban dwellers but also a large proportion in the adult rural population who have had some experience of urban life. The 1969 census indicated that only 26 per cent of Lusaka's population was born there, and that nearly all of these were children. Of those aged between 25 and 29, only 7 per cent were born within the city. The situation was very similar in the Copperbelt towns, and also in Kabwe and Livingstone. Thus of Zambia's total 1969 adult population of 2.2 million, over 700,000 had moved from rural homes to their present urban locations. The population growth in all towns between 1962 and 1969, allowing for both natural increase and boundary changes, indicates a net inflow of at least 250,000 people. There is no evidence that this inflow decreased in the 1970s, though it probably levelled off at about 50,000 a year, giving rise to a 7 per cent annual growth in the urban population compared with about 1.2 per cent for the rural population.

Malawi is one of the few countries where the scale of internal rural–urban migration has actually accelerated in recent years. The proportion of local-born is rather higher in Blantyre than in Lusaka mainly because urban growth there has absorbed a dense previously rural population, but it is of course particularly low in the new capital city of Lilongwe. Much of this inflow to Malawi's cities represents a deflection from 'traditional' labour migration to the gold mines of South Africa. It is therefore producing an increased outflow from the rural areas only in so far as it now involves the movement of whole families rather than just young men.

Western Africa   In many West African countries migration to cities is only slightly less extensive in relation to their size than in eastern Africa (Zachariah and Condé 1981: chapter 5). In Ghana the 1970 census showed that of Accra's total population of 636,000 just half were born within the city. Perhaps surprisingly, the proportion dropped to 43 per cent in the older city of Kumasi, while it was only 37 per cent in Sekondi-Takoradi. In these three centres alone there were 700,000 people who had moved in from elsewhere. Rather more than in eastern Africa had moved from smaller towns, but most had come from rural areas.

Comparison with 1960 figures suggests that there must have been a net movement into Accra proper of at least 100,000 people during the decade, along with 70,000 moving into the new town of Tema. In a survey of Accra factory workers, Peil (1972: 128) found that only 19 per cent had grown up locally, while 7 per cent had come from other large towns, 28 per cent from small towns, and 46 per cent from rural areas. Among workers in Kumasi just 27 per cent had been brought up there.

Caldwell's (1969) survey provided complementary information, especially since he directed much attention to the rural areas. In those which he surveyed 11 per cent of the adult population whose 'homes' were said to be there were away in town, 14 per cent had formerly lived for a while in town, and a further 9 per cent planned to go to town. For males aged 25 to 29 the proportions were 18 per cent, 23 per cent and 9 per cent. Caldwell concludes that rural–urban migration is extensive enough to have a direct impact on the majority of the population.

In Ivory Coast the proportion of urban dwellers who were born and brought up in the cities and towns is even lower than in Ghana, and the extent of rural–urban migration there has been much greater. Over the decade of the 1960s there must have been a net movement into Abidjan alone of at least 250,000; and there was an acceleration in the early 1970s, when net migration into Abidjan reached almost 50,000 a year.

In Senegal the rate of rural–urban migration has for many years been much lower. As early as 1955 more than half the African population of Dakar, and almost one-third of the adults, had been born within the city, and the proportions have probably increased since then. The Sahel drought of the 1970s brought a renewed influx of rural migrants, but the generally rather slow growth of Senegal's urban centres now depends much more on natural increase than on in-migration.

Nigeria presents some notable exceptions to the general pattern of massive cityward migration. A great diversity among Nigerian towns in demographic structure reflects sharp contrasts in respect of past and present migration patterns (Green 1974). There has for many years been a flow of migrants into Lagos broadly comparable in character to the flows into other West African capital cities, though larger in scale. The increase in the recorded population of the municipal area from 272,000 in 1952 to 665,000 in 1963 included a net inflow of at least 200,000 people, while there was a further net inflow of over 200,000 into areas such as Shomolu, Mushin and Ajeromi just outside the city boundaries. It is likely that the rate of net inflow then rose, with increasing centralization of many aspects of national life and with the boost given to the urban economy by oil revenues, levelling off at around 50,000 a year in the 1970s.

The experience of some other cities such as Kaduna and Jos has been similar to that of cities of colonial origin elsewhere. Lock (1967) showed that only 31 per cent of the 1965 population of Kaduna, and only 7 per cent of the adults, were born locally, and that most adults had arrived since 1960. The predominance of migrants in the population of Jos is clear from the work of Plotnicov

(1967). There was also much migration into the eastern towns such as Enugu, Onitsha, Aba and Port Harcourt during the colonial period, and the first three of these received a further massive influx in the late 1960s due to Ibo withdrawal from northern Nigeria and the dislocations of the civil war.

In contrast, there is little evidence of any net migration in recent years into various old towns of northern and south-western Nigeria. Some people have moved into Katsina and into Oyo and Ogbomosho, but they are probably outnumbered by those who have moved out. Even cities such as Kano and Ibadan have experienced only modest in-migration during the past thirty years. The rise in population recorded for Ibadan City between the 1952 (probably undercounted) and 1963 (probably exaggerated) censuses was no more than would be expected from natural increase, and was slower than that recorded for the rural areas of Ibadan Division (which do not include a large peri-urban population).

There is certainly ample evidence of people moving out of the pre-colonial urban centres and into either Lagos or the newer cities such as Kaduna. Berry (1975) has suggested that in western Nigeria there has also been a substantial movement of farmers from homes in the old Yoruba towns to new homes on their farmlands. So while urban–rural movement in Africa is common enough in respect of return migration, here is an exceptional case where it is the primary movement. The explanation of this phenomenon is in one sense simple, since people are moving nearer to their source of livelihood, and in one sense very difficult since the real question is why these farmers were living in town previously.

General assessment   The general picture that emerges is one of continuing net in-migration to almost every city, but certainly not one of a rapidly accelerating flow everywhere as some of the literature would suggest. In absolute terms the annual net flow is still increasing in some countries, but in many it seems now more or less constant, in which case it represents a slowly falling proportion of the rural population – which continues to rise almost everywhere. Certainly over most of tropical Africa there is no prospect of rural depopulation in any foreseeable future. Meanwhile the share of in-migration in the total population growth of almost every city is falling steadily, as natural increase takes a progressively larger share.

There is, none the less, considerable variation in these respects from one city to another, as there is also in the degree to which an urban–rural outflow of return migrants is part of the total picture. There are also increasing numbers of children in some rural areas who were born in the cities, notably in Kenya, so that crude data on the birthplace of the urban population may tend to exaggerate the extent of net rural–urban migration. Furthermore, in countries with relatively elaborate urban systems, especially Nigeria, some of those born outside a particular city will have come in from another urban centre rather than from the countryside. Although such interurban migrants are far less numerous than, say, in Latin America, they are an increasingly significant element throughout tropical Africa.

Spatial and temporal patterns

Spatial patterns

To understand the nature of migration into the cities of, say, Ghana or Kenya, we must distinguish between movements from certain regions and those from others. The spatial pattern is important not only in itself but also with respect to both the causes and the consequences of the movements. Thus Caldwell notes that propensity to migrate depends on where the individual lives (1969: 212), and that migrants from some areas adjust to city life more easily than those from other areas (1969: 219).

Western Africa   As regards the actual patterns of movement in Ghana, the 1960 and 1970 censuses are even more informative than Caldwell's survey, both providing a wealth of birthplace information. Migrants in Greater Accra in 1970 included 129,000 from the surrounding Eastern Region, 86,000 from Central and Western Regions, 77,000 from Volta Region, 38,000 from Ashanti, a mere 6000 from Brong-Ahafo, and 24,000 from Northern and Upper Regions. This clearly indicates both the wide area from which migrants are drawn and the general inverse relationship to distance. It also suggests that local opportunities both in cocoa farming and in Kumasi have reduced the medium-distance flow from Ashanti and Brong-Ahafo.

A further 58,000 people in Greater Accra were born outside Ghana. Some were children of Ghanaians who had been temporarily resident abroad, but most were labour migrants. Togo provided the largest contingent (19,000), followed by Upper Volta. The numbers had been much higher two years earlier, for the 1970 census came just after massive expulsions of non-Ghanaians (Peil 1979), and probably increased again in the 1970s despite Ghana's economic stagnation.

Ivory Coast provides a useful comparison. Migrants come to Abidjan from all over the country, and also from other countries, especially Upper Volta. The rate of migration to the capital city seems particularly high among the Baoulé in the centre of the country, even though the second city, Bouaké, lies within their area: and it has been suggested that urban influences emanating from Bouaké have encouraged this flow to Abidjan, perhaps involving some step movement through the provincial capital. The disparity in the relative attraction of the two urban centres is clearly far greater than in the case of Accra and Kumasi.

Cultural, as well as physical, distance deters some Upper Volta migrants from travelling to Abidjan, and they constitute a higher proportion of the population in the small towns of the north than in Bouaké or Abidjan. Many also find work in the rural areas of Ivory Coast, so that the total spatial pattern includes many Upper Volta migrants taking the place of Ivory Coast rural dwellers who are moving to the cities.

In Nigeria the patterns of migration are far more complex. The abortive 1973 census could have been extremely valuable as a guide to these patterns, since it included questions both on birthplace and on what people regarded as 'home place'. On the basis of 1952–3 census data, Mabogunje (1970a) pointed out that in contrast to Ghana and Ivory Coast the main orientation of rural–urban movements was not from north to south but rather the reverse, as southerners moved into cities such as Kaduna, Zaria and Kano. However, southward movement to Lagos greatly increased in the 1960s (Green 1974) as did the westward flow to Lagos from the Ibo homeland. Political conflict in the 1960s added complications, and more is known about the exodus of Ibo from various cities than about the origins of those who moved in to fill the resulting vacuum.

Migration fields often expand and increasingly overlap, especially as communications improve, and this applies to Lagos; but the migration fields of other cities in Nigeria may now be smaller than in the past, and overlap less. As education spreads, while the rural economy stagnates, the urge to move into town becomes more widespread: and since urban centres are more scattered than in most African countries, this could mean a reduction in the average distance of movement. A circular process may be at work in which rural dwellers around a town such as Kaduna or Jos both increasingly regard it as 'their' town, and increasingly dominate the flow of in-migrants. However, an important countervailing trend in Nigeria is increasing movement from one city to another. A survey of the sources of recent migrants to Nigerian cities could be most revealing, while priority should be given to monitoring the pattern of migration into the new capital city of Abuja.

Eastern Africa   Several studies of spatial patterns of migration in East Africa are based on census data for tribal affiliation (e.g. Hirst 1970), and do not distinguish movements to towns from movements between rural areas. However, unpublished birthplace data from the 1962 Kenya census have been used by Ominde (1968) to analyse movements to Nairobi and Mombasa, while a very full analysis of unpublished 1967 Tanzania census data has been undertaken by Claeson and Egero (1971).

In Tanzania the nationwide dominance of Dar es Salaam is very evident. The local region is the chief source of migrants for most towns, and the local town is a major destination for the migrants from each region; but while it is the chief destination in eight of the regions, it is second to Dar es Salaam in all the remaining ten.

The patterns in Kenya are more complex than those in Tanzania, partly because the urban system does not consist of a national capital and a set of roughly comparable regional capitals, and partly because of the greater regional contrasts in rural population densities. Movement to Nairobi is predominantly from the adjacent overcrowded areas of Central Province, but there is also a large flow from the equally overcrowded areas 500 kilometres to the west. Of the migrant population of Mombasa one-third have come from elsewhere in Coast Province, and a quarter from adjacent Kitui and Machakos Districts. The flow from Central Province has been small, but larger numbers have undertaken the much longer journey from Nyanza and Western Provinces. So whereas most migrants from Central Province have been absorbed within Nairobi, many from Nyanza and Western Provinces have bypassed it and moved on to Mombasa (Figure 8).

In Zambia, too, the spatial pattern of migration is complex, especially since Lusaka and the Copperbelt provide twin foci for such movement. To some extent they draw on different source

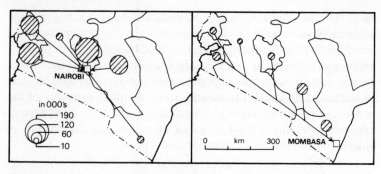

Figure 8   *Provincial origin of migrants to Nairobi and Mombasa*

areas, migrants from Northern, North-Western and Luapula Provinces going mainly to the Copperbelt, and those from Central, Eastern and Southern Provinces going mainly to Lusaka, but there is much overlap. Eastern Province progressively surpassed the local Central Province as a source of migrants to Lusaka during the 1950s and 1960s. A survey undertaken in Lusaka in 1968–9 by Ohadike (1975) showed that the average distance of migration to Lusaka had risen steadily from 425 kilometres for those who moved before 1945 to 515 kilometres for those moving between 1965 and 1969.

General features   Neither these brief outlines for individual countries, nor even the fuller studies on which they are based, provide clear answers to most general questions about the spatial pattern of rural–urban movements. In some countries these are predominantly short-distance, while in others much longer distances are normally involved. Much depends on the distribution of population around each city, and on factors such as local income opportunities in each rural community. There is no conclusive evidence on whether the distances involved are now tending to increase or to decrease. People all over Africa have been willing to move remarkably long distances, especially in view of poor transport facilities, their very limited funds for meeting transport costs, and their general wish to remain in close touch with their home areas; and this willingness seems to continue. One clear trend, however, is for fewer movements to be across national boundaries as national sentiment has become stronger, and as increasing unemployment has led various governments to discriminate against foreign workers. This change has tended to reduce the average distance of migration, perhaps offsetting the contrary effects of transport improvements.

It is also not possible to offer any generalization on the extent to which cities have discrete or overlapping migration hinterlands. In Cameroon, the two main cities of Douala and Yaoundé draw largely on different rural areas (Marguerat 1975, Dongmo 1982), whereas in Kenya the two cities of Nairobi and Mombasa have largely overlapping hinterlands even though they are considerably further apart.

Rural–urban migration sometimes takes place in a series of steps, up the urban hierarchy, so that provincial towns serve as staging posts with a transient population on their way from the rural areas to the capital city. On this matter, too, there is no clear evidence for tropical Africa as a whole, partly because the various countries differ greatly in the nature and extent of their urban hierarchies. An ILO survey suggested that many migrants in Lagos had previously lived in other towns, whereas Peil (1972: 149) found that among Ghanaian factory workers step migration culminating in a move to the city was rare. A study by Riddell and Harvey (1972) specifically concerned with this matter in Sierra Leone found some evidence of step-wise migration, and an ILO survey in Khartoum (1976: 353) found that about 12 per cent of recent in-migrants had moved via other towns. So provincial towns sometimes assist the process of cityward migration while at other times diverting it.

Temporal patterns

There is much debate about the prevalence of short-term and long-term movements to African cities, sometimes expressed in terms of whether or not a proletariat is emerging (Elkan 1967, 1976, Lloyd 1981, Sandbrook 1982: 125–8). In every city some migrants have come for only a few months to acquire cash for a particular purpose, some have come for a year or two as part of a labour circulation process – and may do so for a second and third time, some have come intending to stay for most or all of their working lives but then to return to their rural homeland, and some regard the move as permanent. The uncertainties relate to the relative size of each group, and also to how far reality matches intentions.

Some debate takes place at cross-purposes, with one observer saying that most migrants come to the city for only a short period while another says that most of the migrant population has been in the city a long time. Both statements might be true, for if each year 2000 people came in for a long stay of ten years or more, while 5000 came in for short stays of around one year, the migrant population would soon consist mainly of long-stay individuals. Indeed, for many cities something like this is the case today, although of course the length of stay occupies a wide spectrum rather than two discrete categories.

Truly conflicting views often reflect experience in different areas, but disagreements even extend to particular regions. Thus Ross and Weisner (1977: 363) suggest that 'unlike migrants in West African cities, Kenyans for the most part have not committed themselves economically to permanent urban life'. Yet Peil (1976: 156–8) quotes surveys which imply the opposite, and so asks 'why should West Africans be less permanent urbanites than other Africans?' This lack of consensus partly reflects lack of data. Urban censuses and surveys reveal nothing about those who left after a short stay in the city, and longitudinal studies are needed, both in the cities and in the rural areas.

Most rural–urban migration certainly differs from rural mass movements which involve the setting of new lands with no intention of return: but most is also now quite different from the recruitment of labour for short fixed periods which was widespread earlier in this century (Heisler 1974). Most migrants in the cities intend to return eventually to their rural homelands, in sharp contrast to the situation in many other world regions, but throughout tropical Africa the length of stay is certainly tending to increase, partly in line with a shift from individual to family migration.

Evidence for individual cities, discussed later, supports these general statements, but it also points to great variations from place to place. The movements within southern Ghana examined by Caldwell (1969) are frequently of a long-term nature, although they are rarely permanent; and the same applies to movements to Dakar (Vernière 1977). Gugler and Flanagan (1978: 63) claim for West Africa in general that 'short-term and intermittent labour migration has become the exception'. Yet within the West African Sahel seasonal movements into towns remain widespread (Swindell 1979). Far away in Zimbabwe most migration in the 1970s was still of the type described by Mitchell (1969b) as labour circulation, young men going to town without families for periods ranging from a few months to two or three years.

Within eastern Africa change has been particularly evident in Zambia. Heisler (1974) has shown that short-term circulation is now far less common there than is often supposed, suggesting that even before independence more permanent movements had become the norm. In a survey of Lusaka, Ohadike (1975) found that 18 per cent of the population had moved to the city within the previous twelve months, while 51 per cent had moved in earlier than that. The figure for recent arrivals is high compared with most of the world's cities, but it reflects acceleration of in-migration as well as the presence of short-term migrants; and such migrants evidently now make up only a small minority of the population.

The situation clearly differs from country to country, and not just between western and eastern Africa; yet perhaps we can make a broad distinction which might resolve some apparent contradictions. West African cities such as Lagos and Accra seem to have a larger proportion of long-term migrants than many in eastern Africa, but few who have moved permanently: in some eastern African cities there are now more who have moved in permanently, but also more who continue to migrate for only short periods.

The migrants: sex and age

Male and female migration

Closely related to the short-term or long-term nature of migration is the male/female balance. Much writing about 'migrants' seems to imply that this word applies only to men, and several surveys have been directed exclusively to males. This cannot be excused on the grounds that men are the main decision-makers, for women's role in major household decisions varies greatly across Africa and is often substantial. In any case, many women have moved independently into African cities (Little 1973, Obbo 1980). No doubt over tropical Africa as a whole more men than women have moved, and while the balance has been changing lately, there are still slightly more males leaving most rural areas. However, both in past patterns and in recent trends there are great differences from place to place.

Past labour circulation in eastern Africa certainly involved mainly men, who were either single or accustomed to leaving their wives in the rural areas, and in Zimbabwe this pattern continued through the 1960s and 1970s. In Kenya and Tanzania more changes took place, but male migrants still outnumbered females. In Nairobi males increased by 290,000 between 1962 and 1979, while females increased by only 225,000. The trend was similar in Dar es Salaam in the 1960s, and although Sabot (1979: 89) suggests that women provided the majority of new arrivals there in the early 1970s, the 1978 census indicates that a greater absolute increase of males has continued – 256,000 between 1967 and 1978, compared with 231,000 females.

As in the shift to long-term migration, Zambia provides the clearest example of post-independence change. Heisler (1974) documents very fully the change there from male to family migration, and Ohadike's (1975) study in Lusaka indicated that among those who had arrived there within the 12 months up to his survey, women formed a majority. As with Sabot's Tanzania findings, however, we do not know how many of these women stayed in the city on a long-term basis after the survey: if large numbers left after a few months, the net inflow could still include more men.

In eastern Africa women have tended to move to the cities either for shorter periods than men, if going only during the slack agricultural seasons to join husbands, or else for a longer time than men, if they were outcasts from, or rebels against, rural society. Where the former is still common, as in Nairobi, the gross inflow or the total number of arrivals certainly includes more women than men, but they are even more preponderant in the gross outflow. The general trend, however, is for more and more women to move on just the same time-scale as the men.

There is conflicting evidence from eastern Africa about the distances over which men and women migrate. In Dar es Salaam males outnumber females among the migrants from every Region, but far more so among those from distant Ruvuma and Mara than among those from the rural areas of Coast Region. In some Tanzanian provincial towns there are more women than men among migrants from the local Region, but rarely among those from elsewhere. The 1969 Uganda census showed five males for every two females among migrants to Kampala from Rwanda, compared with a very even balance among the local Ganda. In Kenya, however, there is much long-distance female migration, especially among the Luo of Nyanza Province, and much short-distance movement of men on their own.

In Lusaka, Ohadike (1975) showed that men outnumbered women to a greater extent in the migration streams from distant provinces than in those from closer by. Among migrants from origins within 320 kilometres he found a sex ratio of 103:100, while among those from over 640 kilometres it was 132:100. This contrasts with the situation in Harare, where Garbett (1975: 123) suggests that men who migrate from long distances have wives with them more often than those who come from closer areas.

In Zaire there is a long tradition of family migration, partly resulting from Belgian colonial policies which differed from those of the British in the present Zambia and Zimbabwe. The accelerated migration of the 1960s also involved women just as much as men, perhaps not surprisingly since political insecurity in the countryside was one of its causes. Within Zaire, however, there are substantial regional variations.

In many West African countries too, different strands produce a complex total picture, though in general there was more family migration during the colonial period than in eastern Africa. The long-term migration prevailing in southern Ghana involves as many women as men, but men predominate in the flows to Accra and Kumasi from the far north and from Upper Volta. There is even greater diversity within Nigeria, but the total situation there shows more imbalance than in Ghana, and possibly more than now prevails in Zambia.

The chief exception to the general African pattern of male majorities in the migration streams is provided by Ethiopia. Not only do more women than men move to the city there, but they more often stay permanently, and this applies particularly to the large number who are divorced.

Unfortunately, little evidence is available on how far female migration consists of wives coming with their husbands, wives joining husbands, or women moving independently of men, although these distinctions are highly relevant to any analysis of motives for migration. The studies by Little (1973) on African women in towns shed little light on this question, and it was not covered in the Caldwell and Ohadike surveys.

Probably the majority of women moving into most West African cities are wives moving with their husbands, and such movement is increasing in eastern Africa also. In both areas, however, a single man will often migrate to town, become established there, and then marry a woman from his home area who joins him in town. It has also been common in eastern Africa for married men to move to town on their own, and to be followed by their wives, temporarily or permanently, only after a job and a room have been secured.

Women moving on this basis account for much of the apparent excess of female migrants in Tanzania and Zambia in the 1970s.

In most countries only a minority of women are moving quite independently of men, but their numbers are steadily increasing, especially as female education is extended and as traditional social attitudes in rural communities are weakened. Studies in Kampala by Halpenny (1975) and Obbo (1975, 1980) revealed many women who had moved into the city without husbands. Some were unmarried, and came seeking work on the same basis as men, while others were married women who had become dissatisfied with rural life or with their husbands, and had left them to come into town.

The shift to more females arriving unmarried has been documented for Tanzania by Sabot (1979: 92). The figure was only 13 per cent for women who had arrived in the towns as adults more than 20 years before the 1971 survey, but was 33 per cent for those who had arrived as adults within 1970 and 1971. To some extent this reflects a general increase in the age of marriage, but that itself is related to increasing independence on the part of many young women. The change makes the issue of job opportunities for women (chapter 5) ever more important.

Adults and children among the migrants

Most studies of rural–urban migration fail to distinguish between movements of adults and of children. Clearly the movements both of small children with their parents, and of older children moving in search of education, are each quite different in nature from adult labour migration. We might also distinguish teenage school leavers seeking work, since these are accounting for an increasing share of the annual inflow into many cities.

During the colonial period there were very few children among the migrants to the cities of eastern Africa, but there was rather more family migration in Zaire, and considerably more in many parts of West Africa. Even among the migrants to Lagos, Accra and Dakar, however, adults then greatly outnumbered children. The proportion of children in the migrant streams has probably now increased everywhere, although little firm evidence is available on this point. Ohadike (1975) found that in Lusaka the average age at migration had fallen during the 1960s, which could mean that adults were moving at a younger age, as he implies, or that the migrants included more children, or both. In fact, of 21,000 people who had arrived within the previous 12 months, 44 per cent were under 15 years of age. Surprisingly, Caldwell's (1969) very thorough survey of migration in Ghana offers little on this subject; and while Ominde's (1968) work in Kenya examines both migration streams and urban age-structures, it also has little to say about the numbers of children among the migrants.

The Tanzania survey reported by Sabot (1979) related specifically to migrants who were at least 14 on arrival in town, but this revealed that 36 per cent of the men and 44 per cent of the women had arrived between the ages of 14 and 19. However, we do not know how many were school leavers, how many were seeking further education, how many were young wives, and how many came at that age with parents.

There is conflicting evidence on how the availability of primary education affects the movement of children. Some adult migrants are keen to bring their small children to town because more and better schools are available than in the rural areas, while others send infants back to the rural areas when they reach school age because of pressure on places in urban primary schools. Much depends on the adequacy of educational provision in each city, or even each part of the city, and in various home areas even within the same country. For individual families it is also affected by such factors as the presence of kinsmen with whom the children could stay at home, the respective level of fees in urban and rural schools, and the language of instruction in each.

There is more consistency with regard to secondary education, which is much more readily available in the cities than in most rural areas. In some francophone countries, such as Ivory Coast, nearly all schools are concentrated in the towns; and even in Kenya and Uganda, where early mission boarding schools were set up outside the towns, the emphasis has shifted to urban day schools. As a result, many older children move into the urban areas either to take up school places or just to seek them. These children, unlike those mentioned above, have themselves made the decision to move, often with parental support but not invariably so. They are not normally moving either with or to their parents, although they often intend to live with a relative who is already in town. Few studies of such migration have yet been made, apart from those in Ivory Coast by Saint-Vil (1981) and in Uganda by Gould (1975).

Causes of migration to the cities

Several valuable discussions of the causes of rural–urban migration in tropical Africa already exist (e.g. Mitchell 1959, Gugler 1969, Byerlee 1974, Riddell 1978, Swindell 1979). Increasingly, debate has come to focus on how far explanations should be sought in the reasons given by migrants themselves and how far true explanations must lie in the broad structures of socio-economic change in Africa brought about by its involvement in the global capitalist economy. The latter view has been forcefully presented by Amin (1974), and is to a large degree adopted in the latest statement by Riddell (1981).

The broad context of the colonial experience and the continuing dependent situation of African countries is clearly highly relevant, and certainly constrains the individual's choice. However, migration was taking place in Africa long before the colonial impact, and is a worldwide phenomenon. Furthermore, the fact that most rural dwellers still do not move to the cities suggests that some freedom to choose remains; and here we shall confine attention to some of the factors that influence the choices that are made.

In his much-quoted paper on causes of labour migration, Mitchell (1959) distinguished between factors affecting the rate of migration from or to each area, which he considered to be primarily economic, and those affecting the incidence among individuals within source areas, which were often social or cultural. One might also distinguish between factors leading to migration, and those which cause many such moves to be temporary and encourage people to return to their rural homes at some stage. Again perhaps the first are primarily economic and the second primarily social. A further distinction might be made between the actual motives for migration, such as the search for higher income, and characteristics of either areas or individuals, such as levels of education, which may favour or hinder it, rather than really forming motives.

A distinction not made here is between so-called 'push' and 'pull' factors. It seems pointless to argue whether people are pushed from the countryside by poor conditions there, or pulled to the town by its greater opportunities: it is surely the differential between the two areas, or the perceived differential, which matters. Some people are in a sense forced into the cities either by land shortage or by the collapse of the rural economy in times of drought, but most surveys indicate that migrants come from a wide range of rural circumstances, each individual perceiving that prospects are better in the city.

There is certainly a clear consensus that throughout tropical Africa the primary motive for rural–urban migration is a search for higher income. Mitchell, Gugler, Caldwell and many others all agree on that. Todaro (1969, 1971) goes further in formulating a model in which rural–urban migration is a direct response to differences between rural and urban areas in anticipated earnings, which reflect both wage levels and the perceived chances of obtaining employment, and in which social factors have no part. Even from a strictly economic viewpoint other sources of income must surely be taken into account along with wages; but in fact other motives for migration are also of great importance, even for potential wage-earners.

A wish for freedom from the social constraints of life in closely-knit rural communities is probably the primary motive for some young men, and women, and a subsidiary motive for many more. The 'bright lights' hypothesis need not be rejected entirely, for the belief that life is more exciting in town is often one reason for moving (Nabila 1979). Further motives are curiosity, especially about places of which so many stories are told by returning migrants, and the prospect of enhanced social status after a spell in town, when one can tell the stories oneself.

One large group of migrants for whom the economic motive is at most indirect are the wives moving to join their husbands either temporarily or permanently. Another distinct group are the children whose primary motive is to obtain secondary education, even if this is partly seen as the key to higher income in the future. At the same time better schools, like better medical facilities, water supplies and so on, are often a subsidiary motive for the migration of whole families. These factors are themselves interlinked: for instance, when all the children are sent to school the fetching of water becomes an intensified problem in many rural areas.

Education is clearly relevant to migration in many ways, for while better prospects for obtaining it sometimes provide a motive for moving, the existing educational level of the rural population seems to be an important influence on the propensity to move. Most surveys and census analyses, such as those of Caldwell (1969) and Riddell (1970) show a positive correlation between prevailing levels of education and the rate of out-migration from each rural area. Even a basic primary education makes many young people dissatisfied with life in the countryside, and opens their eyes to the alternative provided by the towns. Even more significant perhaps than education itself, is the socialization process by which those who have been sent to school by rural parents are now expected to seek work in the city. They may go more because it has been assumed that they will than because of any deliberate economic calculation.

Other factors affecting the propensity to migrate are of a socio-political nature, such as the degree to which the town appears to most rural dwellers as an alien place. This is clearly something which in the past discouraged migration, especially long-term migration, in countries such as Kenya and Zambia, and which has changed drastically since independence. On the other hand, even since independence it influences the people of some rural areas, especially where those who now dominate city life, although African, are of a different ethnic group. A more specifically political factor that has been important in countries such as Zaire has been the way in which the cities have been seen to offer greater personal safety.

One feature of all parts of tropical Africa which assists the migration process is the strength of kinship ties. These generally ensure that the decision to migrate is not irrevocable, and that the migrant can return home if things do not work out as planned. Even if the move proves successful, these family ties provide a sense of security and make the upheaval less severe. Furthermore, kinship ties generally provide the migrant with an initial base in town; and it is very doubtful if so many people would migrate to African towns if they could not rely on kinsmen to provide them with board and lodging until they find a job and a house.

While there are major regional variations in the factors affecting the nature of migration, the general reluctance to move *permanently* to the cities reflects the fact that so many are largely colonial creations and so perceived as somewhat alien, and the fact that people feel a very close attachment to their homeland. The rural areas can offer greater social security when employment ceases, while age-graded social roles provide an incentive for the young to leave the rural areas but for the old to return to a position of influence and esteem. The possibility of such return is often ensured by prevailing systems of communal, rather than individual, land tenure.

The generally greater amount of male than female migration largely reflects the respective positions of men and women in both rural and urban society, and also in the rural and urban economy. Throughout tropical Africa there are far more urban employment opportunities for men than for women, and as the cash economy has spread in the rural areas it has involved men more directly than women. On the other hand the women are often largely responsible for food production. Where this is so, and where they have few earning opportunities in town, there is a strong economic incentive for wives to remain in the countryside when their husbands move to town, perhaps visiting them during the agricultural slack season but maintaining the family farm.

Tightly structured rural societies make it more possible for wives to remain behind than in many other parts of the world, while there is widespread social disapproval of young women moving to the cities before they are married. Since education is a powerful influence on migration, the generally better provision for boys than for girls is also clearly relevant, as is the recent trend to greater equality in this respect.

Other factors that affect the decision to migrate, but especially the decision to move as a family, include the housing situation in each city, and the costs of living at a given standard compared with the costs in the rural home, as well as the extent to which the city seems to offer a real alternative to the social security of the rural community. Yet another vital consideration in the change from labour circulation to long-term migration is the increasing difficulty in finding employment again once a job is given up.

There is no doubt that some attempts to explain patterns of rural–urban migration in Africa have been too mechanistic and too narrow. A contrast is provided by Mabogunje's (1970b) systems approach in which he emphasizes the general aspiration and expectations of particular groups of people. It is often possible to show that particular urban centres could be expected to draw migrants from some rural areas because such migration would give them a much better income without incurring too many social costs, but to offer much less attraction to the people of other rural areas. Probably for some overcrowded rural communities substantial out-migration is essential for sheer survival, although this still need not be to towns. Generally, however, the migrants have had a choice between staying and moving, as well as choices with regard to the nature and direction of the move. That choice will be affected not only by differences in actual conditions in particular rural and urban areas, but also by their knowledge of those differences, in some cases by false impressions, and in all cases by the intensity of their desire for a better life. Even among the migrants from one village to the nearest town, motives are likely to differ from one individual to another as well as being mixed for each of them. Any explanation of aggregate patterns over broad areas should be considered with this in mind.

Consequences of migration

Demographic structures

Changing migration patterns greatly affect the demographic structure of each city. Many discussions of African urbanization emphasize unbalanced sex ratios, and some also show how city age-profiles differ from national averages. Not all, however, indicate the variation among cities, nor the extent of current change. Thus, the excess of males and the preponderance of young adults so often described for Africa in general were always more characteristic of colonial than indigenous cities, and more marked in eastern than western Africa. Today these features are becoming less extreme even in Nairobi and Harare.

Sex ratios   Table 6 indicates much diversity in sex ratios, but contrasts among and within countries were even sharper thirty years ago. The Nigeria 1952 census recorded 170 males for every 100 females in the five main Eastern Region towns, and 140 in the mining town of Jos. By contrast, Ibadan and Kano had ratios of only 107 and 103 respectively, while females outnumbered males in many smaller indigenous towns. Lagos then occupied an intermediate position, with 116 males per 100 females, and the ratios were similar in both Accra and Kumasi. In eastern Africa, however, they then exceeded 150 in most cities, while for the adult African

Table 6   *Sex ratios in selected African cities (males per 100 females)*

Harare 1969	151	Douala 1976	113
Nairobi 1979	138	Kinshasa 1975	110
Khartoum 1973	131	Accra 1970	106
Kampala 1969	124	Lusaka 1980	106
Blantyre 1977	123	Kumasi 1970	102
Abidjan 1975	123	Brazzaville 1974	101
Dar es Salaam 1978	115	Addis Ababa 1978	95

Sources: Census Reports and Demographic Surveys.

population alone males often outnumbered females by three to one. Among adult Africans in Nairobi, men were actually four times more numerous than women in 1948.

The extreme imbalances were reduced through the 1950s and 1960s. A process of convergence within Nigeria indicated by the 1963 census has been confirmed by later surveys. Likewise, while the ratios in several major West African cities fell over twenty years from around 115 to around 105, that in Kinshasa fell from 135 in 1955 to 110 in 1975, and those in Lusaka and on the Copperbelt fell equally sharply. The latest figures to appear are those for Dar es Salaam, where the 1978 census indicated a fall since 1967 from 123 to 115. In Harare the ratio was still about 150:100 in 1969, but even there it has now fallen sharply.

An exception to the general picture of falling sex ratios is provided by Sudan, where census figures indicate an increase for adults in Khartoum agglomeration from 128:100 in 1956 to 131 in 1973. It dropped in both Khartoum proper and Khartoum North, but rose substantially in the more indigenous sector, Omdurman, producing a case of convergence within one city. Neighbouring Ethiopia is also exceptional, for as noted earlier there has always been an excess of females among migrants to its cities. In Addis Ababa there were only 95 males for every 100 females in 1978. A survey of 91 smaller towns around 1970 indicated an average ratio of 85:100, and there was little difference between, for example, the old town of Harer and the newer, more industrial Dire Dawa.

The discussion of sex ratios could be carried further, since it is a topic on which data are widely available. Clearly it is an important issue wherever ratios are gravely distorted, and shifts in cities such as Lusaka have brought profound social change. However, now that ratios are generally within the range 95 to 115 (or 90 to 130 for adults), the differences are perhaps not highly significant, especially in societies where polygyny is widespread. The ratios have economic implications, but false assumptions can easily be made about these since male/female economic roles vary greatly from place to place (chapter 5). Sex ratios do still matter in various ways, but possibly age structures are more important.

Age structures   As a result of consistently high birth rates and still appallingly high death rates, tropical African countries have very young populations. Indeed, few discussions of 'the people' of tropical Africa take full account of the fact that half are children.

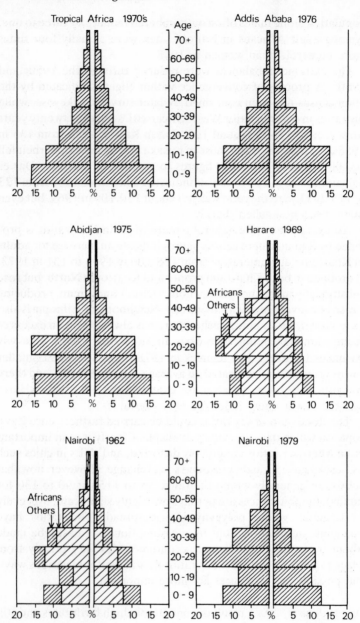

Figure 9 *Demographic structures in selected cities*

The situation differs little from country to country, but there is more variation between rural and urban areas, largely because so much migration has been both recent and age-selective.

Analysis of age structures is potentially more complex than that of sex ratios, since any number of categories can be distinguished. Census data are often published for ten-year or five-year age groups, and sometimes for each individual year. A simple distinction between children and adults often provides the basis for calculation of 'dependency ratios', using 15 as the cut-off age since this is thought of as school-leaving age. However, this concept is of limited value in Africa, where most leave school far sooner while some 15 to 19s are still in fairly early stages of education. Similarly, although the elderly should be distinguished, there is no standard age of retirement.

In general, the proportion of children is slightly lower in the cities than in the countries as a whole (Table 7). In Tanzania those under 10 accounted for 34 per cent of the national population in 1978, but for only 30 per cent in Dar es Salaam. Equivalent figures for Ghana and Accra in 1970 were 35 per cent and 31 per cent. In Kenya and Zimbabwe the contrasts are even more marked (Figure 9), whereas in some indigenous cities of Nigeria small children are as numerous as in most rural areas. However, the correlation between urban origins and the proportion of children is less close now than twenty

Table 7 *Age structures in selected African cities*

| | Percentage of total population | | |
	under 10	20 to 29	over 50
Nairobi 1979	25.4	29.2	5.0
Kampala 1969	27.0	24.2	5.3
Blantyre 1977	30.8	23.2	5.1
Kinshasa 1975	36.7	17.5	3.9
Brazzaville 1974	32.0	17.2	5.5
Douala 1976	29.1	23.1	5.2
Abidjan 1975	30.4	26.4	2.7
Accra 1970	30.7	21.9	5.5
	33.5	15.0	8.8
National averages	to	to	to
	34.8	16.1	11.3

Sources: Census Reports and Demographic Surveys.

years ago. In Harare migration still brings in many adults without children, but even there the proportion of children is rising rapidly, while in Kinshasa most households have many small children and the proportion of under 10s is actually above the national average. It is thus the cities of countries such as Zaire, Congo and Ivory Coast that have the largest number of young children, especially now that a balanced sex ratio among the recent migrants has raised rates of natural increase. These cities are surely set for further rapid growth over the next thirty years whatever the trends in respect of migration.

Contrasts among cities are equally great with respect to the proportion in the 20 to 29 age group. As we should expect, this is higher in cities than in most rural areas, was exceptionally high in the 'European' cities in the past, and has always been lowest in the cities of indigenous origin. In Kenya adults of 20 to 29 accounted for only 15 per cent of the national population in 1979, but for 26 per cent in all urban centres and for 29 per cent in Nairobi. In several of the Yoruba towns, however, the 1963 census indicated a proportion in their 20s little different from that in Nigeria as a whole, while estimates for Addis Ababa in 1978 indicate only 18 per cent aged 20 to 29 (Figure 9). These contrasts clearly reflect both the scale and the nature of in-migration to each city. This in turn may reflect the availability of jobs, as in the case of the contrast between Abidjan and Brazzaville (Table 7).

Not only are children as numerous as adults in most African countries, but there is also a sharp falling off in numbers among the adults with each successive age group. Generally, fewer than 10 per cent of all people are over 50, and fewer than 5 per cent are over 65. Yet the lack of old people is far more extreme in most cities, where in addition to the nationally low levels of life expectancy and the effects of age-selective migration, return to the rural areas later in life and simply the recency of the main surge of urban growth both have to be taken into account. People over 65 constitute 3 to 4 per cent of the population of some of the Yoruba cities and almost 3 per cent in Addis Ababa, but only 1.5 per cent in Dar es Salaam (1978), 1.1 per cent in Nairobi (1979), and 0.6 per cent in Kinshasa (1975).

Since age structures have a profound effect on both present and future rates of population increase they are of indirect importance for every aspect of urban planning; but they are very directly significant in respects such as educational provision. There is much criticism of an undue favouring of urban areas in this regard, but in evaluating capital expenditure for education it must be noted that the numbers of children are rising far faster in most cities than in most rural areas.

Even if we cannot precisely measure the dependency ratio, it is clearly often lower than in the rural areas. There is a large potential labour force, with relatively few dependants within the city, although many are supporting dependants who remain in the countryside. Some argue that the age structure makes the cities places of high productivity, others that urbanization causes economically disastrous age structures in the rural areas, but if urban–rural links remain strong enough both claims lose some of their force. A clearer consequence of a disproportionate number of young adults in the cities is the heightened need for employment opportunities. Where there is a great employment problem certain age structures may intensify it, but on the other hand the failure of employment to expand in line with the total population in cities such as Lusaka may not seem quite so catastrophic if it is realized that the proportion of adults in that population has been declining.

As far as the social life of African city dwellers is concerned household structures may be even more significant than age structures, and some information on this is provided in various recent surveys and censuses. It is clear that single-person households are much more common in some cities than in others, while the extent to which larger households include non-relatives also varies. This topic is taken up below in case studies which bring together various aspects of migration and population structure for particular cities.

Other consequences of migration

While some consequences of massive rural–urban migration are perfectly obvious, others are matters of intense dispute, producing diverse attitudes towards it among academics and within African governments. The academic literature has increasingly stressed its negative consequences (e.g. Amin 1974, Gregory 1974, Gugler and Flanagan 1977, 1978, Van Binsbergen 1978, Riddell 1978, 1981).

The impact on the cities in terms of accelerated population growth and resulting desperate need for extra housing, schools, water and so on, is not too hard to assess. The effects of the extra labour on the urban economy are more complex. The influx is

significant through increased consumption as well as a very uncertain amount of increased production, while it affects the
balance between larger- and smaller-scale activities and the level of
earnings within each.

Since such migration shows every sign of continuing, we must
surely assume that it is proving beneficial to many of those who
move – from their own viewpoint: and fortunately most of those for
whom it does not work out well can return to their home areas
having gained experience and lost very little. Few assumptions can
be made, however, about the consequences for the existing urban
population. Most city dwellers are glad to welcome their own kinsfolk, as long as they do not expect free hospitality for too many
months, but many reckon that the total flow is too great in view of
the competition it creates for jobs, housing and school places. One
possibility is that additional in-migration tends to benefit the rich
businessmen by increasing markets, lowering wages and raising
rents, while harming the poor.

The consequences for the cities are not only economic. The
migrants bring with them ideas and attitudes that may differ from
those of many existing urban dwellers. They may alter the balance
among ethnic groups, and influence patterns of language use.
Where overt political activity is permitted they are bound to
influence that also. In view of all this, it is surprising how few studies
have been explicitly directed to the (real and imagined) impact of
continuing in-migration on the people already in the cities,
especially as this must greatly influence urban-based policy
makers.

More academic attention has been given to the effects of out-
migration on the rural areas of origin. The negative stance of the
literature mentioned above contrasts with the emphasis on
beneficial effects in Van Velsen (1960), Skinner (1965), Smock
(1971), Hart (1974) and Bates (1976). In part the differences result
from certain discussions concentrating on the impact on agricultural
systems while others are concerned with the general welfare of rural
communities. In part they result from variations in how far the
assessment is of the migration alone or of the migration together
with subsequent urban–rural relationships – including the remittances so often sent to rural kinsfolk. Also relevant are marked
regional contrasts in terms of both prevailing rural conditions and
the character of the migration.

In areas such as south-eastern Nigeria and western Kenya, where population pressure upon the land is severe, out-migration helps to relieve that pressure, ensuring greater availability of land for some of those who remain, and reducing the number of mouths to be fed. It is true that many urban dwellers retain rights to a patch of land, but this is generally occupied and cultivated by other members of their family. Indeed, in many ways we must differentiate between consequences for migrants' families and those for other members of the rural society.

In some other areas, from Sierra Leone to Zambia, where there is no land shortage and where customary agricultural practice involves frequent land clearance, out-migration has had a more disruptive effect, and posed labour problems for those remaining behind. It has often reduced the incentive for, and the practicability of, the local development of cash crops. In respects such as this it is often the selectivity of the migration that is of most significance, not only in terms of a preponderance of males but also in terms of the loss of the best educated and most ambitious members of the rural society.

The social consequences perhaps depend even more upon the nature of the migration. There is no doubt that the absence of large numbers of men for long periods of time, even after they were married, was severely disruptive in many parts of Africa in the past; and the widespread shift towards family migration is changing the nature of the social repercussions. Even family migration has major consequences, however, for societies in which relationships throughout the extended family are of major importance. It is perhaps the elderly, whose children and grandchildren are away in the city, who are most affected by out-migration, and who have most cause to be thankful that throughout tropical Africa it rarely means a total severing of ties with the rural homeland.

In many societies the traditional authority of the elders is also undermined, especially when the rest of the community begins to give greater respect to younger people who are making a success of life in town. The younger generation have less reason to respect that authority when they have the alternative of escape to the city. Yet there are also ways in which out-migration provides a safety-valve which helps to preserve traditional social structures. There is no consensus on which of these effects are good or bad, but all are relevant for policy decisions.

Five countries compared

Zimbabwe

Zimbabwe lies at one extreme among tropical African countries with regard to the prevailing type of rural–urban migration and the demographic structure of its cities. At least up to the late 1970s its situation had changed little over many years, and it is these patterns, characteristic of the 'European' city in Africa, that are discussed here. No information is yet available on changes resulting from the struggle for, and attainment of, majority rule: some of these, notably an influx of refugees into the cities, may have been temporary, while others may prove to have been permanent.

In 1962 the ratio of males to females among the total population in Harare was about 160:100, and even in 1969 it was still 150:100; but the aggregate included an evenly balanced European community, and the ratios for Africans alone were 190:100 and 180:100 respectively. The situation was similar in the second city, Bulawayo, and in smaller towns such as Gweru and Mutare. Among the Africans over 15 in all the urban centres taken together there were 208,000 men and only 82,000 women at the 1962 census. By 1969 these figures had risen to 295,000 men and 142,000 women, representing only modest equalization in relative terms and reflecting a net in-migration of men far greater than that of women. The age structure shows less distortion: the 20 to 34 age group accounted for only 31 per cent of the inhabitants of all towns in 1969, a much lower proportion than in many African cities.

The age structure reflects both the presence of a large European group, and also health conditions much superior to those in many African cities, which contribute to a low infant mortality rate and to relatively high life expectancy. The level of fertility remains very high, and the numbers of children are now growing particularly fast. However, the age structure, as well as the sex ratio, also reflects specific patterns of in-migration, with male labour circulation continuing well into middle age, and with a new influx of younger migrants strongly discouraged in the late 1960s.

A pattern of 'labour circulation' was encouraged in the colonial period over much of eastern and southern Africa, and what was then Southern Rhodesia was no exception (Barber 1967, Mitchell 1969b). The cities were regarded as 'White Man's Country' in which Africans had no right to permanent settlement, yet their economic growth depended greatly upon African labour. In the case of Harare much of this labour came from outside the country, notably from Malawi (then Nyasaland). Housing was provided for the migrant workers, but often in dormitories rather than in family homes, while wages were hardly adequate to support whole families in the city. There were few (formal or informal) employment opportunities for women, whereas the agricultural economy in the rural areas depended primarily upon their efforts. There was thus little economic incentive for women to join the migration stream, and much for them to stay on the land.

Furthermore, the cities were seen by the vast majority of the African population as totally alien culturally, and when the migrants had accumulated enough cash to meet the needs that had led them to move they were only too glad to return, both to their families and to a familiar environment. In the early stages at least, few men and even fewer women had any wish to change their whole life-style indefinitely by moving to such 'European' cities. There were, of course, disadvantages for employers in a rapid turnover of labour, but it ensured that Africans remained largely in unskilled work rather than challenging the Europeans who were present in such relatively large numbers, and was therefore politically advantageous to those in power. All these factors led most migrants to be male and temporary – but there was no more reason than elsewhere for them to be young. In fact most first-time migrants were men in their twenties, needing cash both as they became liable for tax and for marriage, but a notable characteristic of the labour circulation system was that a large proportion returned to the city after each extended visit home. This reflected, and indeed still reflects, not only the continuing need for cash, but also the narrower range of opportunities for obtaining it in the home areas of Zimbabwe than in many other African countries. Whereas many men in Uganda or Nigeria would take up cash crop cultivation or start a small rural business after their early stay in the city, there has never been the chance to do this for most migrants to Harare and Bulawayo. Indeed, pressure on the land in many of the 'African' rural areas of Zimbabwe has now become so intense that many families are dependent for survival on a periodically-renewed urban wage.

In many respects the basic pattern remained little changed into the 1970s (Garbett 1975), substantial numbers of men continuing to come to the city periodically through their 30s and 40s. Indeed, for some it was more a matter of periodic visits home than temporary migration to the city. This is the picture presented by Moller (1978) as a result of extensive surveys in Harare in the mid 1970s. While less than 10 per cent of the adults were born in the city, and most even had their education in the rural areas, the great majority were committed to urban residence for the duration of their working lives. However, there were still many men living in hostels, without their wives, and even among those settled as families in the city it was common for the wife to return to the rural home area for the main farming season. Furthermore, over 80 per cent of those interviewed planned to return to a rural area on retirement.

In the independent Zimbabwe of the 1980s several of the factors mentioned above have begun to change, and so substantial changes in migration patterns can now be expected. The small group identified by Moller as developing a total commitment to the city may soon be greatly augmented. The nature, magnitude and pace of change will of course depend to a large extent on the policies adopted in the new state.

Ghana

We have referred several times to Ghana in the discussion of migration patterns, as exemplifying a very different case from Zimbabwe. Its second city, Kumasi, is a hybrid owing much to both local initiative and European influence, while the capital, Accra, lies somewhere between a hybrid and a typical colonial city. Either city could in various respects be regarded as approximating to a 'norm' for West Africa. These are also cities for which an exceptionally large amount of information is available, as a result of two very detailed and relatively reliable censuses, taken in 1960 and 1970, as well as the studies by Caldwell (1969) and Peil (1972) quoted earlier.

In an area such as southern Ghana both government policy and the popular image of the city were quite different throughout the colonial period from those in what is now Zimbabwe. Kumasi and even Accra have always been places where Africans have lived by right, and where they have played a large part in many of the decision-making processes that have determined the character of the cities. In that area, also, various forms of modernization diffused widely through the rural communities early in this century, so not only did a long-term move to town involve less of a cultural upheaval, but there was a greater desire for some of the changes in life-style that might result, rather than just a desire for limited amounts of cash – which cocoa growing could in any case provide.

For those moving from northern Ghana and from Upper Volta to Kumasi and Accra the situation was, and still is, different (as it is for the larger numbers from Upper Volta who now migrate to Abidjan). These cities are alien to them, so there is more pressure on them to return home after a while rather than settle permanently (Nabila 1979). Since most are Muslims, religion as well as ethnic identity is important here. More of these people have moved essentially to acquire some cash, the opportunities for which are very limited within their homelands; while sheer distance makes it impossible for them to maintain links with home while they are in town in the way that those from rural areas in the south can do. Yet even among these groups there has been more long-term and more female movement than in Zimbabwe (Schildkrout 1978).

Even in 1960, therefore, males outnumbered females in Accra by only 114 to 100 (207,000 and 181,000 at the census), while in Kumasi the ratio was 112 to 100 (115,000 and 103,000). Between 1960 and 1970 there were apparently more female net in-migrants than males, for the absolute figures had risen to 287,000 males and 277,000 females for Accra (104:100) and to 174,000 males and 171,000 females for Kumasi (102:100). A key factor here was probably the massive expulsion of aliens in 1969–70, since males clearly predominated in this group. The age structure in Accra and Kumasi is also very different from that in Harare and Bulawayo. By 1970 children under 10 accounted for 31 per cent of the total Accra population, and far outnumbered young adults of 20 to 29.

A convenient summary indicator of the age–sex structure is provided by the proportion of adult males in the total urban population – 31 per cent for Accra and 29 per cent for Kumasi in 1970 compared with 43 per cent for Harare in 1969. These figures tie in well with the general impression of Ghanaian migration flows in which men play the dominant role, but in which they are accompanied by wives and children, given in both Caldwell's migration study and Peil's work on factory employees. Both writers suggest that very few of the migrants intend to stay permanently in town, but both indicate that many stay as families until retirement.

Nigeria

If Harare and Bulawayo lie at one extreme of the diverse migration and demographic patterns among tropical African cities, the other extreme is occupied not by Accra and Kumasi but by many of the traditional Yoruba towns such as Oshogbo and Iwo, and by old Islamic and predominantly Hausa towns such as Katsina. No recent census data are available for Nigeria, but in many of these towns patterns and structures have changed little over the past thirty years. In certain cases, of course, there have been great changes, as where one of these towns has been elevated to the position of a State capital. Ilorin, in the north of Yoruba territory, and the largely Hausa town of Bauchi, are examples.

According to the 1952 census the sex ratio at that time was only 92:100 in Sokoto and 96:100 in Katsina, while it was only 87:100 in the oldest of all the Yoruba towns, Ife, and 88:100 in the larger but more recent Yoruba town of Abeokuta. By the 1963 census there were apparently almost exactly equal numbers of males and females in all these towns, although there was still a slight surplus of females in some others, such as Owo. In most of these towns the age structures are also similar to those in the country as a whole.

In such towns there is no evidence, either from demographic structures or otherwise, for any net in-migration at all. Indeed towns such as Owo and Ilesha are growing no faster than the population as a whole. There is a vast amount of movement into and out of the Yoruba towns, but most is movement on a daily or weekly basis between town house and country house (Goddard 1965, Bender 1971). The longer-term movement from the rural areas of south-western Nigeria, especially among school-leavers, is concentrated upon the larger cities of Ibadan and especially Lagos. There are of course some migrants in every one of the Yoruba towns, and the results of a survey of such migrants in two of them have been recorded by Adepoju (1974), but they are generally outnumbered by school-leavers from the town moving off to Lagos.

The reasons for the slow growth of some of these traditional towns in both the south-west and the north of Nigeria are discussed very fully by Mabogunje (1968). In one sense they are cultural and historical, reflecting their early origins, and in another sense they are economic, reflecting the lack of new income-earning opportunities in the twentieth century. Northern cities such as Katsina, Gombe and Sokoto attracted many migrants in the eighteenth or nineteenth century, but later those leaving the land found economically more attractive alternatives in the form of new cities such as Kaduna or concentrated upon the rejuvenated ones such as Kano and Zaria. There are now signs, however, that a booming economy is bringing a belated influx of migrants and consequent change in demographic structures to at least some of the previously rather moribund towns.

Within Nigeria some very different situations are also found, both in Lagos (Morgan 1979) and elsewhere. Port Harcourt and Warri have experienced rapid in-migration, much in the form of short-term male labour circulation. In much of the south-east, intense population pressure on the land encourages male out-migration, but induces families to maintain their stake and security by wives remaining on the farm. In the north the Islamic requirement for female seclusion has discouraged family migration to those cities where this cannot easily be maintained. Powerful ethnic rivalries have also led minority groups in various Nigerian cities to regard them as suitable for only a temporary stay. Generalization about migration is thus almost as difficult for Nigeria as for tropical Africa in general.

Zambia

Lusaka formerly had a pattern of in-migration characteristic of the centres founded by Europeans largely for their own settlement, but the patterns there have changed dramatically. Similar changes have also occurred in Kitwe and Ndola on the Zambian Copperbelt, and Heisler (1974) has drawn evidence for his study of such changes both from these and from Lusaka. Other evidence is provided by a 1968–9 survey conducted in Lusaka by Ohadike (1975), and by census material.

Heisler has shown that the change has been a gradual process of transition from what he terms 'Labour Camps' to 'Towns for Africans' and then ultimately to 'African Towns'. The system of labour circulation set up before World War II was little different from that in Zimbabwe; but by the 1950s change had begun, with increasing amounts of family housing being provided, with urban wages rising much faster than the number of jobs and thus more incentive to hold on to those jobs, and with substantial numbers of women joining the men in the towns. Change was even more rapid in the 1960s, as these trends continued while political independence brought other developments such as the transfer of the municipal authorities from European control.

Between 1963 and 1969 the sex ratio for Lusaka's adult population fell from 160:100 to 120:100. In 1963 there was still a heavy concentration of people in the 20 to 29 age group, but by 1969 this group accounted for only 21 per cent, comparable to the 1970 figure for Accra and lower than that for many African cities. Children under 10 made up 34 per cent of the population, compared with 31 per cent in Accra. Within the 20 to 24 age group there were more women than men, and over 80 per cent of them were married. This, together with the large number of small children, clearly indicates family migration rather than male labour circulation, as well as the beginnings of population born and brought up in the city.

More direct information on migration into Lusaka comes from Ohadike's survey. Among migrants who had arrived during the previous twelve months he found more females than males, but of course this could just reflect a more rapid turnover for women, with some intending to make only a short stay. More significant was the finding that 44 per cent of these recent arrivals were children under 15. One observation directly bearing upon change does relate to the sex ratio, for the figure of 114:100 for migrants who had arrived during the 1960s compared with 131:100 for those arriving in the 1950s, and 196:100 for those arriving even earlier.

Yet another indicator of the changing pattern of migration into Lusaka is provided by the rapidly increasing demand for family housing, and the proliferation of squatter settlements (see chapter 6). This shows the emergence of a large group who are identifying with the city and intending to settle in it for a long period, if not permanently, as well as highlighting a major consequence of the change. Another consequence, discussed in chapter 9, is the implication for national integration, and especially for urban–rural relationships, as a constant flow of people between town and country is replaced by a long-term rural exodus, often over long distances. In many ways the nature of rural–urban migration in Zambia is approaching that which has long prevailed in countries such as Ghana, but it is not yet clear whether the type of continuing links so prevalent there will be maintained in Zambia.

It is hardly necessary to explain why this change has been occurring in Zambia, for the labour circulation system was clearly highly unsatisfactory in social terms and depended entirely on colonial policy. The speed and extent of the change is, however, surprising in economic terms, in view of the very slight impact of independence on the structure of the Zambian economy, the role of women in agriculture throughout the country, the limited income opportunities for them in the cities, and the high cost of bringing up a family in the city. Some explanation is therefore required, but this might best be provided by a comparison with Kenya, and especially with Nairobi, where less change has occurred.

Kenya

Nairobi still has a severely distorted demographic structure, which reflects continuing streams of age-selective and sex-selective in-migration. The total sex ratio fell between 1962 and 1979 only from 154:100 to 138:100, and among adults there were still 170 males per 100 females in 1979, reflecting mainly the number of men who leave their wives in the rural areas. Children under 15 accounted for only 34 per cent of the Nairobi population, compared with 48 per cent in the country as a whole. It is notable that infants up to four years of age accounted for 17 per cent of the Nairobi total in both 1962 and 1979, suggesting no increase in the proportion of people setting up a family home in the city, while the proportion of the population aged fifty or above actually fell from 8 per cent to 5 per cent. Numbers in the 20 to 29 age range (241,000) remained far higher than numbers in the 10 to 19 range (156,000) or the 30 to 39 range (118,000).

Nairobi differs from Lusaka in the presence of a very large Asian population in 1962 – whose share of the total had fallen greatly by 1979. Since this group had a high proportion of women and children, its shrinkage has influenced the overall trend; but exclusion of this group reveals an even greater contrast between the African population of Nairobi and that of Zambian cities.

It is clear that males still greatly outnumbered females in net in-migration to Nairobi during the 1970s, their total rising by 176,000 between 1969 and 1979 while the number of females rose by only 142,000. More women than men may arrive in the city on the long-distance buses and trains, but many are wives joining their husbands for only part of the year. In some polygynous households they may be changing places with a second wife, but more often the movements depend on the farming calendar. There is no clear evidence of a shift to longer-term migration. A few families are firmly settled in the city, and surveys by Parkin (1975) and Ross

(1975) indicated average lengths of residence in Nairobi of between nine and eighteen years among specific groups: but some of these people have both a base in the city and a base in the rural homeland, while many others still come only for a year or two to meet a specific cash need, not to mention those who fail to find work and return home after two or three months.

The total pattern of movements is extremely complex, and does not lend itself to ready generalization even for this one city. For instance, pregnant wives often return to the rural home to give birth, yet some come to the city just at this time because of superior maternity facilities there. This must account for some of those recorded in the census as born in Nairobi but resident elsewhere. Similarly, there are many movements in both directions for education. Many parents, even those well settled in Nairobi, prefer to send their young children to rural primary schools away from harmful city influences, while others, including some of the truly rural population, send their children to what they hope are better quality city schools if they have relatives with whom they can lodge. One notable recent trend has been an increased inflow of both boys and girls to private secondary schools in the city, and to a host of commercial and secretarial colleges. Many of these young people stay on in the city to seek work, but some return to the rural areas or at least to small towns in their home regions. However, in spite of these complexities it is clear that in respect of migration and demography Nairobi now differs considerably from Lusaka.

The large Asian community in Kenya's cities is one factor discouraging some African migrants from making a long-term commitment to them in the way that so many are now doing in Zambia. Ethnic divisions within the African population are also important, especially in Nairobi. The Kikuyu are increasingly identifying with Nairobi as 'their' city (see chapter 4), but this means that other groups such as the Luo and Luhya still regard themselves as strangers there almost as much as in colonial days. So while men from these groups may work in the city for many years, many leave their wives in the rural homeland, while few intend to end their days in the city (Ferraro 1979: 5). Both in Lusaka and on the Copperbelt there is much less alienation of particular ethnic groups.

Another important consideration is the proximity to Nairobi of the rural homes of those who do now feel most 'at home' there. Whereas nearly all migrants to Lusaka and the Copperbelt cities come from far away, most Kikuyu or Kamba in Nairobi can make frequent visits to the family farm, while men who have wives and children still living there can receive visits from them. As a result, family migration is no more widespread among these groups than among the Luo and Luhya from the far west.

Two other factors of critical importance relate to conditions in the rural areas rather than within the cities. One is the existence of high quality land in the central highlands of Kenya from which farmers can obtain a much higher income than in most African rural areas. Many young men who move to Nairobi leave when they inherit this land on the death of their fathers, the stay in the city having helped them to build up a little capital which can be invested in the farm. The widespread establishment of freehold title to land, the success-ful establishment of coffee and tea as cash crops in the small-scale farming areas, and the resettlement programmes on former European farms all contribute to this process. Even for Kenya as a whole it could be argued that rural–urban income differentials are not as great as in Zambia, where only the urban areas seem to offer long-term economic prospects and where the incentive to abandon rural life altogether is greater, at least at times when copper prices are high.

A second factor is the density of rural settlement and consequent pressure on the land in both the fertile central highlands of Kenya and the poorer Luo and Luhya areas of the west. This means that as long as urban livelihoods are insecure people cannot risk losing their stake in the traditional rural homeland, and so there is great incentive for wives to remain on the farm. If the whole family were settled in the city for a long period, it might prove difficult to regain a foothold in such overcrowded rural areas. In few parts of Zambia is land shortage such a problem, so that any migrants returning home even after a long absence would be allocated land on which to establish a farm.

Clearly a host of interlocking factors combine to maintain movement into and out of Nairobi, and to make the establishment of a stable urban population a slower process than in Lusaka. This shows how each of the inherited urban traditions may be represen-ted by cities which actually differ greatly, and suggests that policy recommendations can often be made only in the light of each city's unique circumstances.

Summary and conclusions

Rising levels of urbanization in tropical Africa result largely from rural–urban migration, which continues at a high, though no longer accelerating, rate. Such migration is generally beneficial to the individuals concerned, and some contributes to the national welfare, but the rate of migration into many cities is probably excessive. However, there are important variations from place to place.

The indigenous urban centres that were largely bypassed by colonially-induced economic change have few migrants, and have often experienced net out-migration to cities offering better job opportunities: but far more towns and cities have experienced net in-migration throughout this century.

A preponderance of short-term male migration is associated with what were earlier termed 'European' cities, where a pattern of labour circulation was established to suit the interests of the European settlers. Wages were too low to support whole families in town, housing was provided for employees but not for wives and children, and few economic opportunities existed for women. Most rural dwellers saw the city as a totally alien environment, and governments encouraged that view. Most of these considerations have now changed, but in Nairobi as well as Harare their effects are still evident.

Most of the colonial cities of equatorial and western Africa, such as Kinshasa, Lagos and Dakar, also have a continuous record of net in-migration, but involving whole families to a much larger extent than in Nairobi or Harare, and on a much more long-term basis. The result has been sex ratios and age structures intermediate between the two types of city just discussed. There have been sufficient short-term male migrants to produce some deviation from the national figures, but not a gross distortion. Even in these cities there have been far more wage employment opportunities for men than for women, and the migration has been most often initiated by the men: but husbands have been accompanied or followed by their wives much more often in Zaire or Senegal than in Kenya or Zimbabwe. In some cases economic factors have made a critical difference, especially where women play no larger a role than men in farming and where there is a strong tradition of their engaging in trade, which can be continued in the cities. Contrasting housing policies, and the existence of a larger private housing market, have also been important. In addition, social differences between city and country are often less sharp in these countries. Men are therefore more willing to plan for a long stay, to bring their wives with them, and to have their children brought up in the city environment.

This crude threefold division does not cover all the variations. Dar es Salaam shares some features with the cities just considered but others with the 'European' cities. The sex ratio is lower than in Nairobi, but higher than in Kinshasa or Accra, perhaps primarily because of Tanzanian women's farming rather than trading role. A marked lack of children in the 5 to 14 age range there indicates a clear preference for having them brought up in the rural areas. Some Nigerian cities have more short-term male labour migrants than is normal in West Africa, both land shortage in the south-east and religious custom in the north having contributed to this.

Some contrasts among cities have persisted for decades, but others have emerged only recently, such as that between Nairobi and Lusaka. In Zambia a quite remarkable change has occurred, with many families now feeling quite 'at home' in the cities, and having little incentive to leave them until retirement. A similar change may be in store in Harare and Bulawayo, but the experience of Nairobi suggests that it is not inevitable.

Broadly speaking, independence has brought greater changes in eastern than in western Africa, and greater changes in cities of colonial origin than in those of indigenous origin. In various respects there has been convergence between contrasting patterns of migration, and this seems likely to continue. Within individual countries, however, government policy is an important variable.

Most African governments are very conscious of the harmful effects of excessive rural–urban migration, and wish to reduce it, but few have found effective ways of achieving this. Policies dealing only with the symptoms of the real problems include restrictions on entering the cities, such as the former Rhodesian authorities applied, and periodic efforts to round up unemployed migrants and to transport them back to rural areas, such as Tanzania and Mozambique have attempted. Policies which go closer to the root of the problems include efforts to provide jobs and to improve service provision within the rural areas – the more constructive aspect of Tanzania's approach.

Since migration depends largely on the rural dweller's perception of rural–urban differences in income prospects, job creation in the cities may well increase the flow. Clearly the same applies to provision of piped water, schools and health care in the cities. So although their inadequacy is a major urban problem, exacerbated by excessive migration, there is a strong case for giving priority to extending these services in rural rather than urban areas.

Even this may be too simplistic an approach, because of the complex linkages among the elements involved. While the immediate impact of better schools in the rural areas may be to reduce one incentive for migration, the long term effect of education there may be to increase awareness of what the city offers. A partial answer to the paradox may lie in the school syllabus, but if this is very different in urban and rural schools both parents and pupils may show a clear preference for the former.

Other national policies may have different repercussions for city and country dwellers. One concerns the sources of government revenue, for in some countries there is a heavy dependence on income tax and company taxes felt mainly in the cities, while in other taxes on agricultural exports are far greater. The reduction of such export taxes which oil revenues permitted in Nigeria should have made rural life slightly more attractive there. Also of importance in Nigeria, as elsewhere, is policy with regard to the fixing of food prices. Often these have been artificially low, assisting urban consumers at the expense of rural producers.

All these policy issues relate to the *volume* of rural–urban migration, but governments must also consider how far the present *nature* of migration is optimal. Thus the authorities in the former Rhodesia chose to maintain the labour circulation system rather than to foster a stabilized African urban population, whereas in Zambia policy moved towards the latter even before independence. Many countries might be well advised to encourage certain types of migration and to discourage others: undoubtedly, it should be encouraged more from certain rural districts than from others.

The strategies available for influencing the nature and the spatial patterns of migration are as diverse as those relevant to its volume. Indeed, migration policy can rarely be separated from other aspects of government policy when decisions of so many different kinds affect who moves where. Yet it is most important that each national and municipal government should consider how its actions may affect rural–urban migration, and policy must involve more than generalized encouragement or discouragement.

Migration policies will also, of course, influence future demographic structures, and may affect the nature of the urban population in terms of ethnic groups, the topic to which we next turn.

4 Ethnic groups

Migration has brought into African cities people of extremely diverse origins and cultures, most of whom are keenly aware of this diversity. Ethnicity is always a sensitive subject, and academic writers, as well as politicians and census-takers, are sometimes reluctant to give explicit attention to it: but a discussion of cities in tropical Africa cannot avoid it. For good or ill, ethnic identity matters greatly to most people.

Cultural heterogeneity is universally regarded as a hallmark of urbanism, but rarely is the rural–urban contrast as great as in this region. One of the most consistent, and exciting, features of African cities is that they form the meeting point of different cultures – generally including several indigenous and several alien elements. Pluralism in Africa is the subject of a major symposium volume (Kuper and Smith 1969), and it is surprising that this does not focus more sharply on the cities, for these surely provide 'plural societies' – however that term might be defined. In the past Harare and Nairobi were so ethnically divided that they perhaps did not form 'societies' at all: but that is less true today.

In some regions such plurality is based on an attribute such as religion, but this is generally not so in tropical Africa despite the great importance of religion to most people. In northern Nigeria this powerfully reinforces other divisions, but there are many cities from Dakar to Dar es Salaam where even a close juxtaposition of Christians and Muslims has created no great social barriers. In India the caste system provides a form of pluralism cutting across ethnic divisions, but there is nothing comparable in Africa.

Nationality is now of increasing significance, especially as this provides an acceptable basis for official policies of discrimination. In cities such as Accra and Abidjan the large number of non-nationals has become a matter of great concern, and the 'nation-building' process will increase the importance of this issue everywhere. However, the most widely recognized distinctions at present are still those among ethnic groups which rarely coincide with nationality.

People of Asian origin in Dar es Salaam are seen as Asians whether or not they are Tanzanian citizens, and immigrant fishermen in Monrovia are more often seen as Fanti than as Ghanaians. Ethnic categories may be imprecise, and in part even fictional, and they may be played down by governments, but they are very real to most people. Nairobi's inhabitants, for instance, almost invariably perceive their neighbours not only as old or young, rich or poor, but also as African, Asian or European, as Kikuyu, Kamba or Luo; and this greatly influences their attitudes towards them.

Ethnicity as a social phenomenon is sometimes defined in terms of strife (Cohen 1969: 4), but although ethnic strife is all too common this seems too restrictive. Peaceful, and even cordial, relationships may exist between groups that are ethnically quite distinct. The distinction is generally based on a combination of physical differences, notions of ancestry, area of origin, cultural heritage, and especially language; but perhaps the most important criterion for ethnic distinctiveness is self-identification. In this book people are assumed to belong to a particular ethnic group if they themselves consider that they do, and ethnicity refers simply to awareness of such identities – which may of course differ from one situation to another.

Whether such groups are major racial divisions of mankind, or entities within the African population, identification with them affects many aspects of people's behaviour. Race is not of course all-important as it is in South Africa, partly because Africans constitute a massive majority everywhere, and partly because there are now no official policies of racial segregation. It is also less significant today than during the colonial period, when racial groups were often treated as totally discrete entities, especially in eastern and central Africa. (A minor, but apposite, example was the conducting of African and non-African censuses as quite separate exercises.) Nevertheless, the present character of each city has been much influenced by both past and present racial composition, while in day-to-day life most people still tend to associate with others of the same race.

While race has become less important since independence, as power has shifted from the minority to the majority group, and as a small African elite has begun to share the privileged position formerly held exclusively by Europeans, the same is not true of ethnic distinctions within the African population. The term 'tribe' will at times be used for these, despite its undoubted imprecision, since it is widely used by the people in question and since no better alternative exists. However, it should be stressed that such groups vary in size from a few thousand people to several million, and that the categories are fluid and ever-changing, large groups such as the Yoruba having their own sub-divisions.

Colonial decision-makers often treated the African urban population as a single entity, and common opposition to alien rule was a powerful unifying force. But as control increasingly passed to Africans it was almost inevitable that ethnic differences among them came to assume more prominence, especially in situations of competition for political or economic power. At the level of personal relationships they have always been important. Urban life is sometimes seen as leading to 'detribalization' (Gluckman 1961), but when people of diverse origins have only recently come together, and most retain close ties with their home areas, 'tribal' feeling tends to be more intense than within the more homogeneous rural societies.

This is one respect in which tropical Africa differs markedly from most parts of Asia and Latin America. Even there 'tribes' are recognized, but only a very small portion of the urban population is regarded as 'tribal'. Tropical Africa is exceptional in that in each city virtually all who are not members of racial minorities can say without hesitation to which 'tribe' they belong. One of the many implications is that most people in most cities have a home language that is not shared by the majority of their fellow citizens.

Language is one way in which ethnic differences hinder national integration throughout tropical Africa (Smock and Bentsi-Enchill 1975, Paden 1980); and any evaluation of ethnic differentiation within the cities must be made in the context of its crucial political importance on this wider national scale. In countries such as Nigeria and Zaire ethnicity has contributed to large-scale conflict, and almost everywhere governments are trying to persuade people to identify more strongly with the whole country than with smaller ethnic groups. Most governments would actually express it as identity with the whole 'nation' even though many people share Van den Berghe's view (1975: xviii) that 'the real nations of Africa (are) not Nigeria, Uganda or Tanzania, but rather the Ibo, Kikuyu or Baganda'.

Except perhaps in Zimbabwe, broad racial divisions are of much less significance for national integration. They also influence urban life in very different ways from 'tribal' divisions, since they so largely coincide with income and class differences rather than cutting across them. So the two will now be considered separately.

The minority racial groups

The concept of race creates extreme confusion, partly because the extent and nature of physical and cultural differentiation among people varies so much from place to place. Mankind in general is not divided into clear-cut racial categories, and in areas such as the Middle East and Latin America there are gradations rather than sharp distinctions. In tropical Africa, however, it is widely accepted that all indigenous peoples, from Senegal to Zimbabwe, constitute one racial group, while most intruders have come so recently and from so far away that they are quite distinct physically and culturally. While physical anthropologists might prefer such terms as Negroid and Caucasoid, most people in tropical Africa think in terms of Africans and Europeans, with Asians as a third widely-recognized category. Where these categories are mutually agreed by all the people in question they really should not cause confusion.

While there are some Europeans and Asians in every city, there are very few in the indigenous Yoruba cities of south-western Nigeria and in the Islamic cities of the West African interior. Even in Ibadan, which became a colonial regional headquarters and where some Lebanese traders have long been established, Africans have always made up over 99 per cent of the population. In Abeokuta the 1963 census recorded only 158 non-Africans in a population of 220,000, and the ratio in towns such as Ilesha and Ogbomosho was, and still is, similar.

In the colonial cities of West and Equatorial Africa more Europeans were employed both in the administration and in trading companies. In both Lagos and Freetown 1.6 per cent of the inhabitants in 1963 were non-Africans. In those cities absolute numbers have stayed about constant since then, as administrators have been replaced by expatriates working in education, medicine, finance and industry, but in Abidjan the number of Europeans rose steeply after independence (Cohen 1974), reaching 23,000 by 1975. In colonial times Dakar had the largest concentration of Europeans in West Africa, but some decrease has occurred there, as the city has lost many supra-national functions. In many West African cities non-Africans also include a few Indian merchants and rather more traders from Lebanon and Syria (Little 1974: 69–73, Van der Laan 1975).

In most East African cities the proportion of non-Africans is far higher (Table 8), and Europeans are far outnumbered by Asians (Ghai 1965, Mangat 1969). This group, largely originating from India and Pakistan but now including adults born within East Africa, accounted for one-third of the population of Nairobi, Dar es Salaam and Kampala just before independence. This share fell sharply during the 1960s, as absolute numbers fell slightly, and then 1972 brought mass expulsion of Asians from Kampala and other Uganda towns (Twaddle 1975). A net outflow persisted elsewhere through the 1970s (Table 9), but even in 1982 much of the wholesale and larger-scale retail trade of Nairobi and Mombasa remained in Asian hands.

In Zambia there are far fewer Asians, but in the colonial period Europeans made up almost 10 per cent of the urban population. However, their numbers fell between 1961 and 1969 from 12,000

Table 8 *Inhabitants of European and Asian origin in selected African cities*

| | Population (thousands) | | | Percentage of total | |
	Total	Europeans	Asians	Europeans	Asians
Harare 1969	386	97	4	25	1
Bulawayo 1969	245	50	2	20	1
Lusaka 1969	262	9	3	4	1
Kitwe 1969	200	7	1	4	0
Nairobi 1979	828	19	39	2	5
Mombasa 1979	341	6	24	2	7
Dar es Salaam 1967	272	3	28	1	10
Kampala 1969	331	4	32	1	10
Blantyre 1977	219	3	3	1	1
Douala 1976	396	5	1	1	0
Abidjan 1975	951	23	2	2	0
Accra 1970	636	5	2	1	0
Kumasi 1970	345	1	1	0	0
Freetown 1963	128	1	1	1	1
Khartoum 1973	800	1	0	0	0

Source: Census Reports.

to 9000 in Lusaka, from 12,000 to 7000 in Kitwe, and from 9000 to 6000 in Ndola. They accounted for only about 4 per cent of these cities' inhabitants by 1969, and under 2 per cent by 1980.

A massive exodus of Portuguese from Angola and Mozambique in the 1970s has left Zimbabwe highly distinctive within tropical Africa. Even there the proportion of Europeans dropped between 1962 and 1969 – from 28 per cent to 25 per cent in Harare and from 25 per cent to 20 per cent in Bulawayo – but the absolute number increased throughout the 1960s and early 1970s. Official estimates for this group in 1975 were 135,000 in Harare and 60,000 in Bulawayo, but the advance to legal independence in 1980 has brought some fall.

The decline in the proportion of Europeans and Asians in cities such as Nairobi and Lusaka, and now even Harare, offers another case of convergence among African cities of contrasting origins. There could be no comparable fall in those of indigenous origin, and in a few of these, such as Maiduguri and Sokoto, there may even have been a slight rise during the 1970s.

Characteristics of non-African groups

There are qualitative as well as quantitative differences between the Europeans in Harare and those in Lagos or Accra. The former include many who were born in Zimbabwe and regard themselves as permanently settled there, whereas the latter consist almost entirely of short-term expatriates. In neither case has the situation changed greatly in recent years, although the average length of stay of the expatriates in Lagos and Accra has decreased, while their origins have diversified. Even less change has taken place in most francophone countries, so that most Europeans in Abidjan or Libreville are still from France.

The greatest changes have occurred in Zambia and Kenya, where many Europeans considered themselves to be permanently settled up to the 1960s. Now the pattern in their cities is similar to that elsewhere in tropical Africa. The same is true of Dakar, although a small community of Europeans intend to remain there most of their lives (Cruise O'Brien 1972). Changes in the nature of the Asian populations of the cities of Kenya and Tanzania are less evident.

One feature of the non-Africans varying little over space or time is their privileged social and economic status, and particularly their close association with a few high-income occupations. The role of

Asians in the more profitable forms of trade has already been mentioned: they also occupy many relatively well-paid posts in government service and in industrial concerns, especially those requiring technical skills. Most Europeans occupy very highly paid administrative, managerial or professional posts, and their concentration in these is now greater than ever, but cities differ considerably in the extent to which Africans share such positions. In this respect change over the past twenty years has been dramatic almost everywhere (Adedeji 1981), but Abidjan and Blantyre, for example, are still some way behind Accra and Lagos.

Africanization policies have broken the former close correspondence between race and income. No longer in Nairobi and Dar es Salaam do the Europeans form the high-income group, the Asians the middle-income group and the Africans the low-income group – but only because some Africans have entered the first two categories. The mean or median incomes of each racial group in these cities still show the same pattern now as during the colonial period, and the same is true in the smaller towns. In this respect a neo-colonial structure remains, one result of which is to slow down the development of income-based class divisions among the African population.

Even more important than the income levels of the non-African groups is the power and influence that they have exerted. This is not discussed at length here, since the position of the cities as meeting points of indigenous and alien cultures, and contrasts between those where external influence has dominated and those where it has been weaker, are themes running through the whole book. In some cities the Europeans long regarded all Africans as intruders who 'belonged' elsewhere – and many Africans reciprocated, perceiving the city as an utterly alien place. The ideas and plans of the European minority largely determined the broad spatial structure of most tropical African cities, though both the areas they reserved for themselves and the extent of their control of daily life elsewhere varied greatly. Innumerable aspects of their culture, such as language, were implanted everywhere, but to sharply differing degrees.

Asians played a major role in the development of all East African cities, and many have had a strong commitment to them. Until recently both Europeans and Africans were temporary sojourners to such an extent that people of Asian origin could claim to form a majority of the permanent residents. Yet, while some central parts of Nairobi, Dar es Salaam and Kampala even in the 1960s had a predominantly Indian character, there was little transfer of Indian culture.

Just as the non-African groups continue to enjoy high incomes, so also they generally retain a high social status (however defined), and a disproportionate share of power – even if not in direct political terms. In Nairobi and Lusaka non-Africans continued to dominate the city councils for a short period even after Africans had taken control at national level, and as technical officers they still wield much influence. Kimani (1972) has shown how far Asians still controlled land in Nairobi in 1970 and further studies of land ownership there and elsewhere are much needed.

The continuing influence of non-Africans in specifically urban affairs has been noted in a few city studies (e.g. Werlin 1974), but there is little on the subject in most writing on neo-colonialism in Africa. In so far as whole national economies are still controlled from outside Africa, this control is largely exercised through Europeans resident in the cities – now in partnership with a local elite. Their activities are therefore relevant to the whole question of the cities' role, positive and negative, in national development. The perceptions and priorities of most residents of European or Asian origin undoubtedly differ greatly from those of most African city dwellers: but since they are increasingly shared by a small African elite this is no longer so clearly an ethnic issue, and it is perhaps the power and influence of the entire elite, local and expatriate, that is most important today. In other ways, however, differences of race may remain highly significant.

Relationships among the races

In most rural areas relationships between the African majority and the few scattered Europeans have always been remarkably cordial, but there has been rather more hostility in the cities, where many Africans have not shared their rural cousins' view of Europeans as people of higher status whose lifestyle should obviously differ from their own. It was largely in the cities that the independence movement gathered force, and rapid adjustments had to be made there as Africanization proceeded. Even so, relationships remained generally amicable in many cities through the transition to independence (Little 1974: 61–4), and remain so today.

More problems have arisen where Europeans or Asians have been present in larger numbers and on a longer-term basis. Thus, although French policy in Dakar was far from segregation, and much effort was made to assimilate into French culture at least some 'évolués', attitudes hardened in the 1950s with the arrival of many 'petits blancs' with no special qualifications. Since independence, according to Cruise O'Brien (1972), the Europeans in Dakar have lived very separately from the new Senegalese elite, but largely by mutual consent and thus with little friction.

In East African cities, too, the racial groups tend to form distinct communities, living in separate even if overlapping worlds. The separation was far greater there in the past, and was indeed institutionalized, and this is still reflected in highly distinctive residential areas which were initially set up for specific racial groups (chapter 7). Today, Africans have become the majority not only in the former European residential areas of Nairobi and Dar es Salaam but also in the social clubs: yet a 'European community' still exists, even if not all Europeans identify with it. The Asian community, sub-divided largely along religious lines, remains even more distinct, and there are still parts of these cities where Asians predominate in the houses, in the schools, and on the sports fields. Both language and religion sometimes provide bonds between Africans and Europeans, but the Hindu faith and the use of languages such as Gujerati separate many Asians totally from other groups. Many have much closer social ties with Asians in other towns than with African or European fellow-citizens.

The hostility often felt towards the Asians was reflected in the popular support for Amin's purge in Uganda in 1972. Even the smaller numbers in West African cities tend to be unwelcome, and Cohen (1974: 128) describes the Lebanese as the 'most hated non-Africans' in Ivory Coast towns. In both East and West Africa various Asian groups may have not only attracted hostility by their 'middleman' role in the economy and their apparent cultural exclusiveness, but also have served as scapegoats for latent antagonism between Africans and Europeans.

African cities certainly constitute 'plural societies' in the sense that different sets of value systems coexist. During the colonial period wherever these conflicted the European view prevailed, and one result was a widening gulf between 'the alien town' and most rural areas. By the 1970s a European perspective was no longer dominant anywhere north of the Zambezi, but African perspectives are highly diverse, and those which prevail are often those most influenced by European contacts. This applies even to cities like

Lagos, Accra and Freetown, where much decision-making has always been in African hands; but it is most evident in post-colonial Lusaka or Nairobi, where it has rapidly passed to a highly 'Westernized' African elite. While friction along racial lines still arises, as in both Zimbabwe and Zambia in the late 1970s, it is giving way to class conflict – though how many classes exist and what are their distinctive characteristics is still far from clear.

Ethnic differences within the African population

Ethnic distinctions within the African population sometimes have a clearly evident physical basis, so that in Nairobi or Kampala, for example, most people of the Nilotic groups differ somewhat in appearance from the majority. The main distinctions, however, are cultural, and involve matters such as language and kinship structures. The most fundamental consideration of all, and the reason why the subject demands attention, is the way in which the people concerned identify themselves with a particular group or 'tribe'. Some of these ethnic entities such as the Hausa or Ganda are of long standing, while others such as the Luhya of Kenya date only from the colonial period, constituting an amalgamation of smaller entities (Southall 1976).

In the city context, a basic distinction can sometimes be made between 'indigene' and 'stranger' groups (Hanna and Hanna 1981: 124–7). Kuper (1965: 16) has even suggested that 'with the coming of independence under an urban-oriented African leadership, the dominant emerging cleavage in the towns appears to be along lines of the "indigenous" versus the "stranger" '. Parkin (1969a, 1969b, 1975a) makes a similar distinction between 'host' and 'migrant' groups – though even the former includes many who have moved in from the countryside.

Thus Yoruba in Lagos, Asante in Kumasi, Mossi in Ouagadougou, Amhara in Addis Ababa and Ganda in Kampala all regard themselves as 'indigenes' or 'hosts', and tend to regard all others as strangers or outsiders. In many cities, however, such as Lusaka, Kaduna or Abidjan, no 'host' group can be so readily identified, either because there are two or three rival claimants in cities set up in sparsely-populated regions, or because the local group has now been swamped by others. The site of the new Nigerian capital (Abuja) has been deliberately chosen so that there will be no dominant 'host' group there.

In a city such as Ibadan, where one group is totally dominant, the issue of ethnicity is most significant for small minorities, as it is in many other parts of the world. Cohen's (1969) study of the Hausa there has rightly attracted wide interest: but we should note that this situation is not typical of tropical Africa. Even where 'host' groups can be clearly distinguished these often account for less than half the city population, so that questions of ethnic identity involve not just specific minorities but everyone.

The different characteristics of each group can be important for our understanding of African cities. Analyses of Abidjan's demographic structure in terms of averages for the whole population reveal less than those which note the high proportion of adult males among Mossi migrants compared with the more balanced composition of other groups. There is, however, a danger here of reinforcing false ethnic stereotypes.

The importance of 'tribe' really lies in what people themselves feel about it, and its effects on attitudes. These topics are not easily documented, and it is not surprising that there is much debate on them. The bibliographies in Hanna and Hanna (1981) and Southall (1975) point to some of this debate, while Cohen's (1974) symposium volume on urban ethnicity is very largely concerned with Africa.

Ethnic identity

Few observers (and few African urban dwellers) suggest that ethnicity is of no importance, but sharply differing views have been expressed about how urbanization affects the intensity of ethnic awareness. Some people have referred to African cities as 'melting-pots' in which strongly felt tribal identities are gradually lost as diverse groups come together. Crowder (1962: 83) has said of Dakar 'maintenance of tribal cohesion is a difficult task in this city of French creation, where a new community of Dakarois is rapidly coming into existence'. Forde (1956: 39) suggested that tribal membership in African cities was a short-lived phenomenon, and Gluckman (1961: 69) once asserted 'the moment an African crosses his tribal boundary to go to the town, he is "detribalized" '.

Shack, writing on Addis Ababa (1973: 251), has firmly rejected this view, suggesting that entry into urban life greatly strengthens the bonds among members of the same tribe; and the Hannas (1981: 113) observe for Africa in general that the sense of ethnic identity is often increased in an urban setting. Plotnicov (1967: 61) has claimed that 'Nigerians in Jos cannot conceive that one may be both black and detribalized', and in discussing the strong self-identification of the Hausa minority in Ibadan, Cohen (1969) speaks of 're-tribalization'. Dike (1979: 26–8) insists that 'the basic normative superstructure of urban Ibadan or Kano is Yoruba or Hausa respectively, irrespective of metropolitan status', and suggests that 'ethnic consciousness and culture not only remain part of the urban socio-cultural order, but quite often strengthened under such conditions'.

There is some truth in both sets of views. This is partly because the situation differs from place to place; it is partly because it can change in one place quite quickly over time, as the post-independence experience of Nigeria has shown; and it is partly because short-term and long-term perspectives may differ even for a single individual. Ethnic identity is not something consciously and keenly felt by most people living in rural communities where all are members of the same ethnic group and there are few direct contacts with people of other groups. However attached one may be to various aspects of traditional life one just does not spend much time thinking about being an Ibo or a Luo. But moving into a city and into close contact with people of other groups, speaking other languages and so on, one becomes much more explicitly conscious of ethnic identity. This is especially true for all those who see themselves as in ethnic minorities, whether in a city dominated by one group or in one where a wide range of groups are all daily put into competitive situations. One aside on this point is that it rather undermines the notion that tribal identity is a 'rural' characteristic brought into town (e.g. Roberts 1978: 141).

Once people have been settled in the city for some while ethnic identity may diminish in importance, but this must depend on a host of factors, some external and some particular to the individual. In Dar es Salaam and Lusaka there are strong pressures on many people to think of themselves less and less as Chagga, Bemba or whatever, and more as Tanzanians or Zambians. In Nairobi and Kampala the equivalent pressures are often outweighed by pressures to retain powerful identification with one's tribe. Personal factors include level of education, the residential and work environment, and for some people such specific considerations as a marriage across an ethnic boundary.

Parkin (1969b) has shown the complexity of the situation in

Kampala. He found that 'tribal' affiliation was extremely important in many aspects of life there, but that in the 1960s independence was bringing some shift to a focus on nationality, especially Ugandan versus Kenyan, as well as to various trans-ethnic status groupings. The author's own experience in Kampala confirms this picture, but like Parkin's it pre-dates the Amin regime which greatly intensified the significance of ethnic identity, generally in the most unpleasant of ways.

Alternative groupings

Another complexity is the way in which the entity with which people identify themselves in the city may not be the same as that with which they would identify themselves in the rural homeland. Thus various people from western Kenya are brought together by life in Nairobi and Mombasa as the Luhya, and there is an important Abaluhya Union in those cities, but this is an entity which did not exist a hundred years ago, and the same people are much more aware of various sub-groups when they are in their home areas.

In some cases the question is merely one of scale, for many large groups have commonly-recognized subdivisions. The Egba and Ijebu, for instance, are distinct sub-groups of the Yoruba, Aronson (1978: 28) emphasizing Ijebu identity in Ibadan. In the towns of Aba and Enugu the Owerri Ibo are often regarded as strangers. In the reverse direction, Rouch discussed as early as 1954 the concept of 'supertribes', and this theme has been followed up by Cohen (1969: 204) and by Schildkrout (1979: 183), especially with reference to 'northerners' in the cities of the forest zone of West Africa. Schildkrout found that peoples such as the Dagomba and Frafra in Kumasi often regarded themselves collectively as northerners, and were even more often perceived as such by the local Asante; and she went so far as to suggest that 'in much of West Africa the most persistent category of inclusion and exclusion is neither tribe nor nation, but regional identity'. This is a rather extreme view, and in the same volume Peil (1979: 127) observes that the unity among northern peoples in Accra was reduced by the late 1960s: but in many countries besides Ghana regional, as well as tribal, identity is important. Thus in Lusaka and on the Zambian Copperbelt people are often placed in just three or four categories, such as Bemba for all from the north and Ngoni for all from the east. In Kampala the local Ganda are not greatly concerned to distinguish Acholi from

Lango, regarding both as northerners, while in Khartoum it is southerners who are distinguished by the majority rather than Dinka or Zande.

In all these cases there is a hierarchy of groupings, with a regional level of ethnicity exceeding the 'tribal' level in certain contexts. However, there are cases where a grouping commonly made by outsiders is firmly rejected by the people concerned. The Ibibio and Ijaw in south-eastern Nigeria are sometimes grouped with the Ibo, but they are intensely aware of their distinctiveness: a similar situation exists with regard to the Kanuri and Hausa in northern Nigeria. Elsewhere, other groups reject a regional label commonly applied to them because of a specific differentiating factor such as religion.

Ethnic groups in specific cities

Partly because of these complications, existing writing does not give a clear picture of the actual extent of ethnic mixture in most African cities. It gives still less indication of the rate, or even the direction, of current change. Marked contrasts exist, and there is evidence of increasing ethnic diversity in some cities and increasing homogeneity in others. Some contrasts simply reflect the ethnic setting, one city lying within a vast area occupied essentially by members of one group, while another lies close to the home areas of several small groups. Also relevant are the degree of mobility and the relative political power of different groups.

The data available do not permit compilation of an index of ethnic diversity in each city. Some censuses have classified people by tribe, but others have not done so. In Ghana and Uganda much attention was given to this in 1959–60, but the question was dropped for the next enumeration. A crude index might anyway be misleading wherever some groups form sub-sets of others. However, a general impression for various cities can be given, noting how far there is a dominant 'host' group.

Western Africa   Many Nigerian cities are notable for their ethnic homogeneity. Those of the south-west are described throughout this book, as elsewhere (Mabogunje 1962, Krapf-Askari (1969), as Yoruba cities. The 1963 census indicated that Yoruba people accounted for 94 per cent of the total urban population of the former Western Region. In Ibadan they form an overwhelming majority, although there is a small, socially-exclusive Hausa community (Cohen 1967, 1969). In Abeokuta the 1963 population was 96 per cent Yoruba, while the proportion reached 99 per cent in towns such as Iwo and Oyo.

Even in Lagos, not normally included among the 'Yoruba cities', this group constituted 70 per cent in 1963, as it had done in 1950. Many Ibo left during the 1967–70 civil war, and while some later returned, most recent in-migrants have been Yoruba. (The 1970s brought a great influx of non-Nigerians, especially Ghanaians, but most of these were summarily expelled early in 1983.)

Similarly, most northern Nigerian cities have a clear Hausa majority, together with a partly assimilated Fulani element. Katsina and parts of Kano and Zaria represent a manifestation of Hausa culture just as Ife and Oyo do of Yoruba culture. These cities received an influx of southerners, and especially Ibo, during the colonial period, but the 1966 massacres led to a mass exodus of Ibo (Paden 1971), and only a minority have returned. Both the role of these cities as a vehicle for a particular ethnic culture, and the distinctive but insecure position of a minority group, illustrate the significance of ethnicity in African urban life.

While eastern Nigerian cities differ in many ways from those of the west and north, most show equal ethnic homogeneity, for Ibo far outnumber all other groups in Aba, Enugu, Onitsha and Umuahia. The situation is less clear-cut in Port Harcourt. Ibo also formed a majority there in 1963, but the city lies within Ibibio/Ijaw territory (Wolpe 1974), and became in 1967 the capital of the essentially non-Ibo Rivers State.

The greatest ethnic mixture is found in 'middle belt' towns, Plotnicov (1972) indicating the interesting situation in a paper entitled 'Who owns Jos?'. People have come to Jos from all parts of Nigeria, but both the local Birom and the near-by Tiv have claimed it as 'their' city. The Birom had perhaps the greater claim until it became the capital of Tiv-dominated Benue–Plateau State in 1967. Tiv influence then increased, but subdivision of the state in 1976 may have deflected their attention to Makurdi, the new Benue State capital, allowing more Birom influence again in Jos. The new federal capital at Abuja also lies in the thinly populated 'middle belt', and is expected to draw people from every corner of Nigeria. It should become a fascinating laboratory for evolving ethnic relationships.

All Ghana's cities show great ethnic diversity, although this was reduced by the sudden expulsion of many non-Ghanaians in 1969

(Peil 1971). In Accra the Ga are the local group (Kilson 1974), but they are far outnumbered by a variety of others. Kumasi was the pre-colonial capital of the Asante Kingdom, and this large group still look to it as their focal point: but even so, Asante accounted for little over 40 per cent of its 1960 population, with 25 per cent from other southern Ghana groups and 35 per cent from the north or from outside the country. Between 1900 and 1930 these 'stranger' groups such as Dagomba and Hausa were heavily concentrated in the Zongo area (Schildkrout 1978), and each group was largely responsible for its own affairs with an officially recognized chief. Subsequently they dispersed more widely and were brought under the general municipal government: but ethnic identity or a broader regional identity remains strong.

The capital cities of two of Ghana's neighbours have sharply contrasting ethnic structures. In Ouagadougou the Mossi form a clear majority, though there are many minority groups, about most of whom Mossi tend to hold firm opinions (Skinner 1974: 195–9). In Abidjan numerous ethnic groups from within Ivory Coast and many more from outside are all well represented, and no single group is dominant. This perhaps makes ethnic affiliation a less critical issue than in some other cities, attention switching somewhat to the issue of nationality. The fullest discussion of ethnicity in a francophone West African capital is the study of Niamey by Bernus (1969), but the ethnic diversity of Bamako is also made clear by Meillassoux (1968).

In several West African cities a small local group was once dominant but has now been swamped by a larger group. Thus the Africans in Dakar were once mainly Lebou, but these now comprise only about 12 per cent of the population while Wolof account for over 40 per cent. The most notable feature of Dakar, however, is the limited significance of ethnicity there. Its component groups are similar enough, and have co-existed long enough, for many to become more Senegalese than Lebou, Wolof or Serer (Vernière 1977: 119).

Freetown and Monrovia are distinctive mainly because their populations include the descendants of the released slaves for whom the settlements were originally established (Fyfe and Jones 1968, Fraenkel 1964). In Freetown the Creoles have been far outnumbered by groups such as Temne and Mende, and their formerly dominant position has been undermined, but they still play a major role in the city and remain culturally very distinct (Cohen 1981).

The dominance of the equally distinct Americo-Liberians in Monrovia remained much greater until the 1980 coup. In both cities ethnicity among the indigenous majority was institutionalized in this century by an administrative system based upon Headmen, each responsible for all members of his 'tribe' living in the city (Banton 1957, Harrell-Bond *et al*. 1978). A countervailing influence, however, was common opposition to the dominant 'non-tribal' group, along with the decision by some people to break their traditional ties in order to join this elite.

With respect to ethnicity, Kinshasa is more typical than distinctive. The main pre-colonial settlements here were Teke fishing villages, but the surrounding area is the homeland of the far more numerous Kongo people, and these have provided the dominant element for the past eighty years (La Fontaine 1970). They probably account for half the total population. They certainly dominate the city both economically and politically, and since groups such as the Luba and Zombo include many political refugees, either from within Zaire or from Angola, these do not present a serious challenge to the Kongo. One factor assisting good relations at the personal level is the widespread use of Lingala rather than Kongo as a lingua franca.

Eastern Africa   Throughout eastern Africa the cities are places of 'tribal' as well as racial diversity. Rarely does one group account for half the population, and minorities often maintain a clear identity.

In 1979 Kikuyu made up 33 per cent of the total in Nairobi, compared with 21 per cent of the Kenya total; and Parkin (1975: 152) suggests that most inhabitants now regard it as an essentially Kikuyu city. However, Luhya, Luo and Kamba each added a further 12 per cent to 18 per cent of the Nairobi total (Table 9). In Mombasa the diversity is greater, for the local Mijikenda constituted only 26 per cent of the 1979 population, Kamba for 12 per cent, Luo for 13 per cent and Luhya for 8 per cent. A notable feature is that Kikuyu accounted for only a further 6 per cent, even though they are a larger group than the Luo and their home area lies far closer to Mombasa. Whereas Luo and Luhya have had to search widely for urban jobs, Kikuyu have had more opportunities available on their doorstep in Nairobi.

In Dar es Salaam the Zaramo are clearly the local resident group, and localities such as Kurasini and Mtoni were once Zaramo villages: but this group accounted for only 22 per cent of the population

Table 9   *Ethnic groups in Nairobi, 1969–79*

	1969 Thousands	Percentage of total	1979 Thousands	Percentage of total
Total population	509		828	
Kenyan African	408	80	740	89
Kikuyu	191	38	277	33
Luo	63	12	150	18
Luhya	65	13	134	16
Kamba	61	12	103	12
Other African	13	3	22	3
Kenyan Asian	25	5	20	2
Other Asian	42	8	18	2
Kenyan European	2	0	2	0
Other European	18	3	17	2

Source: Kenya 1969 and 1979 censuses.

in 1967, and certainly does not occupy a position matching the Kikuyu in Nairobi. The Tanzanian situation is notable for the small importance of ethnic differentiation there, due to a combination of cultural similarities among most groups, the existence of Swahili as a lingua franca, and government policy.

By contrast, ethnic differences have been a cause of much conflict in Uganda. The 1959 census suggested that the Ganda had a remarkably small stake in Kampala, for they were the country's largest ethnic group, dominated the whole surrounding area, yet constituted only 10 per cent of the city population. The main explanation for the anomaly lay in their preference for residence in the adjacent traditional capital of Mengo, brought within Kampala City only in 1966. Their share in the population of Greater Kampala was rather over 50 per cent. The 1969 census birthplace data indicated no great change over that decade, but the 1980 census should surely show some effects of the political traumas of the 1970s.

In Zambia, as in Tanzania, ethnic differences matter less than in most countries. Neither the Copperbelt nor the Lusaka area was heavily populated before this century, so that most people come from far away. Bemba are particularly numerous on the Copperbelt, while there are more Ngoni and Nsenga in Lusaka, but all cities are very mixed. People are well aware of ethnic differences, as

Mitchell (1956) has demonstrated, but these do not greatly affect where they live or what jobs they do.

In Addis Ababa ethnic diversity is much less than in Dar es Salaam or Lusaka, Amhara accounting for half the population and Galla and Gurage for almost 20 per cent each; but the differences matter more. 'Lower-status non-Amhara who seek upward mobility must do so within the Amhara cultural framework' (Shack 1973: 276). Yet most Gurage decline to do so, retaining very clear identity.

We should ideally consider variations over time as well as space. In what direction has the 'tribal' composition of most cities been changing in recent years? Are urban populations in tropical Africa generally becoming more heterogeneous, as has been suggested (e.g. Hanna and Hanna 1981: 122)? The evidence is most inconclusive. Kikuyu are often said to be increasingly dominant in Nairobi, but their share of the city's population fell during the 1970s from 38 per cent to 33 per cent (Table 9). With increasing migration from distant areas the population of Dar es Salaam and of Khartoum has tended to become more diverse, whereas Yoruba predominance has increased in Lagos as has that of the Amhara in Addis Ababa. Political factors have often been highly relevant but other factors range from changing education levels in different regions to variations in rainfall and hence farming conditions. Many Nigerian cities have experienced much change since independence, but the general picture over tropical Africa shows much stability of 'tribal' balance despite the huge changes in total numbers.

Consequences of ethnic differences

How does ethnic diversity influence African urban life? Firstly it affects the scale, direction and character of rural–urban migration. Most people prefer to move to a city where their own group is well represented rather than to one where they would be in a very small minority, and for some only the presence of co-ethnics permits a move. The nature of ethnic relationships also often influences the degree of permanence of such migration and how far it involves whole families. This in turn is related to the issue of identification with the city – which affects both social relationships and political processes.

Associations

A proliferation of ethnically-based voluntary associations or 'tribal unions' in many cities is both a consequence of ethnic diversity and a factor reinforcing ethnic identity. Little (1974: 91) observes that 'the immediate effect of the ethnic association is to increase tribal consciousness'. These associations have been examined in detail in Africa by Banton (1965), Little (1965) and Meillassoux (1968), while good examples from East Africa are the Luo Union branches discussed by Parkin (1969a: 151–4) and Southall (1975). Most of these writers show how associations assist migrants to cope with urban life, providing contacts with others already in the city and aiding the maintenance of rural homeland ties.

Peil (1977: 301), however, suggests that most newly arrived migrants depend on informal contacts, few joining associations until they have been in the city for some years. She considers that their main roles today are as pressure groups to protect minority interests in city politics, as an outlet for political activity where other forms are proscribed, and as organizations for assisting the home areas. The younger generation may not join if they find proceedings dominated by the older men, and if their own return home seems very distant. Certain more specific roles are still performed by many of these associations, such as the handling of deaths within the city and perhaps transporting the body back to the homeland for burial. This has led Gugler (1975: 300) to suggest that in some cases they are hardly 'voluntary'.

These formal associations tend to be more important for minority groups than for 'host' communities, e.g. for Ibo rather than Yoruba in Lagos, for Luo rather than Kikuyu in Nairobi and for Gurage rather than for Amhara in Addis Ababa (Shack 1973: 270). There are, however, many minority groups among whom they are not found, such as the Frafra in Accra (Hart 1971: 29). They may also relate to entities much smaller than the generally recognized ethnic groups, such as many 'village unions' in Nigeria, and these may be found even where the broader group forms a clear majority of the urban population. Thus Smock (1971) notes the importance of hometown associations among the Ibo in places such as Aba and Enugu.

Various associations which cut across ethnic groups are now of increasing importance. Trade unions provide obvious examples, while Little (1978) points to various women's associations which are not ethnically defined. Churches sometimes function in the same way, although in some cities religious differences largely coincide with ethnic differences. This may be true even within Christianity or Islam: in Nairobi past patterns of mission activity have brought widespread adherence to the Presbyterians among the Kikuyu, the Society of Friends among the Luhya, and so on (Ross 1975: 57). Sports clubs may also cut across ethnic lines, though in Nairobi football clubs tend to follow them (Parkin 1978: 42–3).

Both Cohen (1969: 195) and Peil (1977: 302) conclude that the role of ethnically-based voluntary associations in African cities has often been exaggerated. Even where they are important probably only a minority actually belong to them and just a few are really active – as with most associations elsewhere. However, this does not mean that the significance of ethnicity has been over-rated: its importance may not depend on formalized structures.

Personal links: ethnicity and kinship

Ethnic ties are certainly of profound importance in most cities as a source of social security, in providing for the few elderly who remain there, for the sick, and for the many un- and under-employed. However, in these respects, people rely more on their extended family or on a kinship group than on an ethnic group as a whole, so that ethnicity provides just the context for more intimate ties. The same applies to the provision of accommodation for new migrants.

Writers who have stressed the importance of kinship ties rather than wider ethnic affiliation for urban social life include Ferraro (1973) for Nairobi and Schildkrout (1978) for Kumasi. However, no sharp distinction can be drawn. The new migrant may depend on kinsmen for shelter, but may turn to an ever-wider group of co-ethnics in seeking a job. Those who do not have many kinsmen in the city must rely on others of their own tribe as a substitute. Ibo 'improvement unions' may centre on a particular home locality, but they extend far beyond immediate kin, as do numerous 'associations d'originaires' in the cities of francophone West Africa.

'Social distance' is such that friendship patterns are strongly influenced by ethnic affiliation. Even in the most ethnically diverse cities nine people out of ten specify a co-ethnic as their best friend. Both Ross (1975: 67–9) and Parkin (1974a) have shown this for Nairobi, as have Parkin (1969a) for Kampala and Peil (1975b) for several Nigerian cities.

There is much scope for research on how both length of urban residence and level of education affect the importance of ethnicity in people's day to day lives. Level of education is of course closely related to social status, and it is often suggested that ethnic origin matters less to the elite than to the majority (Baeck 1961, Parkin 1969b, Kileff 1975). Lloyd (1974) found evidence of this in Lagos and Ibadan, and Chilivumbo (1975) demonstrates it for Blantyre. In Nairobi, however, Ross (1975: 70) found that 'social networks within the city are based to a great extent on kinship and ethnicity at all socioeconomic levels', with social separation of Kikuyu and Luo as great among university lecturers as on a low-income housing estate. Differences between men and women in this respect also merit study. Past surveys have concentrated on men, and women may be more willing to make contacts across ethnic barriers.

Marriage patterns provide a key indicator of the significance of ethnic identity and are of particular importance since the children of mixed marriages may identify less strongly than others with the tribe of either parent. In Nairobi and Kampala the vast majority marry members of the same ethnic group (Parkin 1966; Grillo 1973). In Grillo's Kampala survey only 8 per cent of marriages were inter-ethnic, and in the case of the Luo and Luhya he found strong pressures even on the city-born to marry someone from within a very restricted 'home' area. Among the very heterogeneous population of Kisangani, Pons (1969: 96) found that 77 per cent of marriages taking place within the city were between co-ethnics.

Peil's (1972) study of Ghanaian factory workers indicated that 85 per cent of the married men had wives from their own tribe, and her surveys in eight West African urban areas indicated that 'interethnic marriage remains relatively rare' (1981: 149). Schildkrout's work in Kumasi (1978: 168–90) indicates more mixed marriages, rising from about 20 per cent of the total among the northern migrants to about 40 per cent among their urban-born children. The marriages are, however, almost entirely to fellow-northerners, such as between Mossi and Hausa, so that ethnicity at a broader level of aggregation remains highly significant.

Residence

Tribal, as well as racial, differences have some effect on residential patterns almost everywhere, but again there are great variations. Certain groups in some cities are almost entirely segregated into specific quarters, while elsewhere multi-ethnic occupation of dwellings is common. This topic will be discussed later, in the chapter on spatial structures.

Economy

There is also often some correlation between ethnic group and occupation. Thus, most Hausa in Ibadan are dependent directly or indirectly on the cattle and kola trades. Indeed, the Hausa have moved as merchants to many West African cities. In other regions too particular groups are associated with market trade, as in the case of the Gurage in Addis Ababa. In many towns on the West African coast fishing communities consist mainly of minority groups, such as the Fante from Ghana in Monrovia and Freetown. In some cities particular groups are heavily represented in domestic service, such as Ibo in Lagos, Batoro in Kampala, Luhya in Nairobi and Chewa and Ngoni from Malawi in Harare. Other groups are concentrated in jobs that the majority prefer to avoid: thus refuse disposal in Accra and Kumasi is largely the preserve of the Frafra.

It is not always clear why this occupational specialization occurs. Is the heavy concentration of Luo among the port workers of Mombasa simply a matter of personal choice? Or is it essentially a matter of tradition, the origins of which were largely accidental?

Grillo (1973) has discussed with reference to railway workers in Kampala the question of ethnic enclaves within sections of one industry. He shows that this often arises as people seek jobs where they have kin in influential positions, rather than because one occupation is reserved for one tribe: but the result of the chain reactions that follow may be such that job allocation is *seen* by many as a 'tribal' issue.

While kinship and ethnic ties together perform many positive roles in African cities, 'tribalism' is generally viewed by governments as harmful, causing divisions instead of unity for the common good. Negative effects may be seen when one group dominates elements of the urban economy so that others feel excluded, and especially when one predominates in activities which bring high status and high income. Thus it was largely the economic success of the Ibo within northern Nigerian cities which made them so unpopular there, while the justifications offered for the expulsion of many aliens from Ghana in 1969 were largely economic. Eades (1979) notes that while Yoruba constituted only 5 per cent of

Tamale's population at that time they occupied one-third of the stalls in the central market and dominated market trade in manufactured goods. In Nairobi today the situation is rather different, for it is the 'host' group, the Kikuyu, who are seen as excessively dominating the economy as they take over jobs and businesses from departing Europeans and Asians.

Politics

The main negative effects of ethnic identity are political, especially in this post-independence era when 'nation building' is a priority concern yet rivalries exist between groups seeking to fill the power vacuum left by the departing 'colonial masters'. In this respect ethnicity is far from just a sentimental relic, but is a critical contemporary issue, often seized upon as the basis for political action. Peil (1975b: 121) has observed that 'it is this political manipulation of ethnicity which is most dangerous'.

There have been many analyses of the appalling 1966 massacres of Ibo people in the cities of northern Nigeria, showing that numerous issues were involved, but the fact that the Ibo were a highly distinctive group was critical to most of these. There was much genuine resentment against them, there were fears of their possibly assuming a dominant position in national politics, and they formed a convenient scapegoat for various frustrations felt by the Hausa majority.

Anti-Ibo feelings in other Nigerian cities have been noted in several studies of urban politics. Baker (1974: 87) considers that in Lagos in the 1960s 'the myth of Ibo domination in local affairs had little basis in reality', noting that they owned little property, played only a very small role in trade, and were under-represented on the city council. Local Yoruba had taken increasing control in city politics, despite continued in-migration, perhaps partly because the political energies of others were then concentrated on competition for power at the national level. Wolpe (1974) shows that Ibo did occupy a much more dominant position in Port Harcourt, and tended to regard it as one of 'their' cities, even though it lies just south of their traditional homeland. He also shows that relationships between local Ijaw people and Ibo played a major part in most aspects of the political life of that city in the 1960s.

Two other studies by political scientists demonstrate in different ways the importance of ethnicity in urban politics in Nairobi. Werlin

(1974) is concerned with rivalries between Kikuyu and other groups as Africans took over control of the city council after independence, while Ross (1975) shows how ethnicity has influenced political behaviour at the grass roots level. With higher levels of both education and income than other groups, as well as numerical superiority, the Kikuyu became increasingly dominant through the 1970s in Nairobi as in Kenya generally, sometimes without needing to resort to chicanery. They now have to decide whether actually to discriminate in favour of other groups, in order to lessen political hostility and promote national integration.

Just as African cities could in theory be ranked in terms of degrees of ethnic mixtures, so also they could be ranked at any one point of time in intensity of ethnic awareness. Thus Dakar would now rank low, Kampala and Nairobi higher, on both counts; Ibadan and Kano low on diversity but high on intensity of feeling; Dar es Salaam and Lusaka high on diversity but particularly low on intensity. These variations in intensity often result largely from political circumstances, and Cohen (1969: 193) has even suggested that ethnicity is 'basically a political and not a cultural phenomenon'. However, it nearly always reflects one cultural attribute, and that is language.

Ethnicity and language use

Ethnic diversity produces great linguistic diversity in most African cities, and language plays a crucial part in determining the groups with which people identify. It is language more than anything else which causes Ibo in Lagos or Luo in Nairobi to be labelled, and to label themselves, as such. In these cities language is not only the vehicle of communication but also a frequent subject of discussion. Decisions regarding language policy (for example, in schools) face the leaders of all African states, and they may be even harder to make in the cosmopolitan cities than elsewhere.

The situation is quite different from that in most Latin American cities, where the vast majority speak only Spanish or Portuguese, or many cities in the Middle East, where Arabic is used by most people. In many African cities ten or even twenty languages are in constant use, and rarely can any one of these be understood by everyone. There are sharp contrasts among cities, however, and these do not coincide with the contrasts in urban traditions. Thus there is a single dominant African language, used together with a varying amount of English, not only in the pre-colonial Yoruba cities, but also in Enugu and even in Harare; whereas in Freetown, Monrovia, Kaduna, Kampala and Nairobi a much greater diversity of languages may be found.

Remarkably little has been written on this subject, either for Africa in general or for individual cities, Parkin's (1974) work on Nairobi providing a rare exception. Furthermore, censuses provide few data. The total picture would in any case be very difficult to quantify when people know several languages to varying degrees, and regularly use two or three. However, some general observations can be made.

Use of European languages

Most tropical African countries differ from those elsewhere in having an official language that is the home language of very few citizens. Generally this is English, French or Portuguese, inherited from the colonial power and still used in administration, high-level education, large-scale commerce and so on. This situation is not quite so disturbing as in many rural areas, where very few people have any knowledge of the language in which their government is conducted. One distinctive characteristic of the cities within the national scene is the relatively large number of people who have some familiarity with the ex-colonial language, and as education expands the proportion is rising. In some cities more than half the adult population make some use of it, though few speak fluently and many problems result. On the other hand, some observers would regard this knowledge of English, French or Portuguese in the cities as a liability, both in terms of cultural dependency and as a force encouraging the urban elite to ignore the needs of their rural compatriots.

The extent to which a European language is known and is used varies greatly among cities. In general the French legacy was stronger than the British, especially since the French nearly always made their language the medium of instruction in schools, even at primary level. However, British policy differed greatly from place to place, so that English is now far more widely spoken in Lusaka and Nairobi than in Ibadan and Kano. The extent of ethnic mixture has been a significant factor, so that French is more widely used in ethnically diverse Abidjan than among the more homogeneous population of Dakar.

Use of English or French tends to break down barriers among ethnic groups; but the use of either as the preferred home language is confined to a very small elite, and it tends to cut them off from the rest of society. Furthermore, ethnic conflict may be exacerbated if one group has a better command of the introduced language than another group, as in the case of Ibo and Hausa people in Nigeria. Before 1966 in the northern cities the immigrant Ibos' greater knowledge of English often helped them to obtain better jobs than the Hausa in both government and commerce.

In most – though not all – cities the use of a European language has become more widespread since independence, but local languages are still far more extensively used, and in the context of ethnicity must concern us more.

African languages in selected cities

In very few tropical African countries is one indigenous language sufficiently widely known to be acceptable as the national language, but at the scale of an individual city one may be accepted as a lingua franca. In Dakar a 1965 survey (Wioland 1968) found that among a large sample of schoolchildren Wolof was the home language of 72 per cent. Most others spoke it as a second language, and its use was steadily increasing. Some people who are not of Wolof origin have evidently adopted it as their first language, while it is normally used in families where just one parent is Wolof.

The situation is similar in various other cities from Accra to Addis Ababa. The language of an ethnic group who make up around half the population is now the home language of nearly two-thirds, as closely related groups have thought it expedient to adopt it. This is Twi in Accra, and Amharic in Addis Ababa (Cooper and Horvath 1976). The dominance of Susu in Conakry, Bambara in Bamako and More in Ouagadougou is greater still, though even in these cities many other languages are also spoken.

A rather different situation prevails in Kinshasa, for the language of the Kongo people has not been adopted by others there. Instead, a language known as Lingala, increasingly used as a lingua franca throughout the river basin, has been widely adopted in the city. However, it is the preferred home language of few people, so that an even higher proportion than in most cities are bi-lingual – or tri-lingual if they know some French.

Dar es Salaam also has a lingua franca, but Swahili differs from

Lingala in that it is becoming a truly national language. English was never as widely spoken as in most Commonwealth countries, partly because Britain ruled only after 1918, and official encouragement of Swahili meets with general approval. As yet, however, most people in Dar es Salaam, as elsewhere, use one of a host of local languages in the home.

Swahili is the home language of rather more people in Mombasa, and is widely spoken there, while even in Nairobi it is used increasingly as lingua franca – discouraging the adoption of Kikuyu by people of other groups. It is very appropriate that Nairobi should have been a focus for the socio-linguistic work mentioned earlier (Parkin 1974b), as it provides a microcosm of the African urban language situation. There are differences of home language both between racial groups and within the African population (and within the Asian population also), variations in knowledge and use of English largely related to education and social status, and a very fluid situation with regard to the role of Swahili as a language cutting across both ethnic and class divisions.

As in respect of ethnicity in general there is less linguistic diversity in most provincial towns than in the capital cities. Many lie within the heart of a single language area and have drawn few migrants from elsewhere. The fewer the speakers of each other language the greater is their incentive to learn either the local vernacular or a lingua franca. However, even in the smallest towns some use will be made of at least two languages, while in places such as Tamale, Jos, Kisangani or Jinja the patterns are just as complex as in the capital cities, and future trends just as uncertain. Another highly complex language situation must surely now be developing in the new Nigerian capital at Abuja.

Other aspects of the language situation

If few studies have been made of the dominant and subsidiary languages in African cities, even less is known about how far people are multi-lingual, and of the ways in which different languages are used for different purposes. Some people regularly use at least four languages. Many Kamba in Nairobi, for example, will know some Kikuyu, Swahili and English, as well as the Kamba language. Even in their home city of Maiduguri, some Kanuri will use Hausa, Arabic and English as well as Kanuri. Arabic is widely used within Muslim religious practice, while Hausa is the language of trade over a wide area of interior West Africa. There are many urban dwellers, especially those far from their area of origin, who commonly use one language in the home, another for neighbourhood socializing, and a third in their employment: but of course there are others whose knowledge of any language other than their own is very slight.

Another neglected dimension concerns the languages of communication from one city to another. Undoubtedly Yoruba is used for most interaction between Ibadan and Ife, and Hausa for most between Kano and Zaria, but what of that between Ibadan and Kano? Language patterns must influence patterns of interaction within national urban systems, sometimes hindering the establishment of truly integrated systems. On the other hand, languages such as Amharic in Ethiopia and Lingala in Zaire, which are spoken far more extensively in the towns than in rural areas, provide integrative bonds that are not available to most rural dwellers. The same is true of English and French, which are used for a much higher proportion of inter-city than of intra-city interactions; and it might even be argued that the use of Gujerati among many Asian traders contributed to the development of a relatively integrated urban system in Uganda in the colonial period.

It is, of course, at the international level that non-African languages have the largest role to play in communication patterns. The need for some citizens of Addis Ababa and Mogadishu, as well as Blantyre and Lusaka, to know English is heightened by the cities' role as link points between their rural hinterlands and the rest of the world. The links in this case are not only with London and New York, but also with neighbouring African countries. There is no alternative to English or French for most interaction among African capitals. Yet as in so many other ways language both unites and divides, for the English/French distinction greatly reduces interaction between cities such as Accra and Abidjan.

This is moving rather far from ethnicity, but it does indicate the range of ways in which language is affecting the process of urbanization. Some of these are intimately bound up with the whole issue of ethnicity, and research is needed to discover how far various patterns are the result of ethnic differentiation in general or of language in particular. Only then can we say for each city how far language influences the direction and character of migration, the operation of the labour market, patterns of social interaction and the conduct of urban politics, as well as the functioning of national and international urban systems. Meanwhile, we can affirm that it is a far more important consideration than in Britain, France, Brazil or Japan.

Conclusions

This chapter has indicated how tropical African cities vary both in their degree of ethnic diversity and in the apparent importance of ethnicity. We have examined some ways in which ethnic identity affects life in these cities. Partly because of the sharp variations that exist, and partly because of the many facets of ethnicity, few simple generalizations can be made for the whole region beyond the assertion that everywhere people's origins have much influence on where they live and what work they do, as well as on social relationships. This applies both to those cities which have a great mixture of ethnic groups and to those where one group is clearly dominant.

Some possible generalizations concern the relationships between ethnicity and class. Even today there is a very close connection between race and class in most cities, since Europeans almost invariably enjoy high incomes and social status, while most people of Asian origin occupy a position between the Europeans and the majority of Africans. Yet race and class no longer coincide exactly anywhere, for even in Nairobi and Harare independence has brought some Africans into the upper and middle income groups, producing a convergence towards those West African cities where this was true long ago.

Within the African population the relationships between ethnic origin and class are very much weaker, for those who have risen in income and social status are generally from a variety of ethnic groups. Distinctions of 'tribe' cut across those of class (Banton 1965: 144–6), and wherever they have become more important it could be argued that class barriers have weakened and that social mobility in this sense has increased. As Peil (1981: 265) observes, ethnic identities certainly tend to inhibit the emergence of a new clear-cut class structure, and to bind together people who in other societies would be sharply separated. Exploration of the many profound implications of this is left to other writers (e.g. Mitchell 1969a, Nelson 1979a: chapter 6).

At the same time certain African ethnic groups enjoy advantages over others, whether in respect of sheer numbers or of wealth, education or political power. The location and resources of their home areas may also be significant. In some cities, such as Dakar or Dar es Salaam, no major problems have arisen, but in others, such as Kano and Nairobi, perceived disparities have led to intergroup tension and conflict. The effects of ethnicity can thus be both integrative and divisive, and the resulting patterns of positive and negative interaction within the cities are highly complex.

One general consequence of ethnic awareness is that it strengthens most urban dwellers' close ties to their areas of origin (see chapter 9). Broad ethnic groups or 'tribes' are significant here both in themselves and in providing a context for the kinship groups which may be the really powerful tie. The strong sense of identity with groups based elsewhere naturally reduces the strength of identification with the city, discouraging effective democratic municipal government and 'civic pride'. Yet perhaps in countries where there are great disparities in wealth and welfare between urban and rural areas, and where nation-building is a matter of great concern, it is just as well that people do not think of themselves essentially as Nairobians or Abidjanois. (Most such potential terms are even more unpronounceable!)

It is possible, of course, to exaggerate the importance of ethnicity. If it were all-important, migrants leaving African rural areas would wherever possible move only within their ethnic homeland, and ethnic diversity in the cities would not be as great as it is. The extent to which people of diverse ethnic origins live peacefully together challenges the view of ethnicity as essentially a matter of conflict, and thus something to be resisted. In some cases this view may be justified, but ethnic identity is also a source of strength and assistance to many people for whom life as one of the African urban poor might otherwise be quite intolerable. It is perhaps the sense of still 'belonging' to the ethnic group that has made it possible for many people in Africa to travel so far in response to unevenly distributed economic opportunities, and preserves the less successful among them from the hopelessness and despair found among the urban poor elsewhere. Ethnic identity can thus be an asset as well as a liability, although the Republic of South Africa demonstrates all too clearly how it can be misused.

We certainly cannot resolve the debate as to whether African cities are now functioning as 'melting-pots' in ethnic terms, or whether urban life is intensifying ethnic awareness. Even less can we predict the future, especially since there are some parts of the world where there is a high degree of integration among people of very diverse origins, while there are others where even after centuries of co-existence differences both in physical characteristics and in culture remain profoundly important. Even within tropical Africa it is likely that ethnic divisiveness will intensify in some cities and fade in others. It seems, however, that ethnic identity is generally heightened initially as different groups interact after migration to the cities, and that it then tends to be reduced, at least in second and subsequent generations born and brought up in an urban environment. Rather than thinking only in terms of aggregates we should recognize that in any city at one time there are people for whom ethnic identity is of increasing significance and others for whom the opposite is true. For some people its importance is increasing in some aspects of life while decreasing in others. Certainly for many it is a matter of greater concern than in most other parts of the world.

5 The urban economy

If we are to understand the nature of African cities, we must consider how their inhabitants gain a livelihood. What is the economic basis of city growth in Africa? How is the urban economy structured? How far do indigenous and colonial urban traditions differ in this respect? Is there evidence of convergence in the post-colonial period?

Throughout the world urbanization has normally involved a reduced share of the population gaining a living directly from the land, and expansion of activities more suited to an urban than to a rural location. In general this applies equally to tropical Africa, although many farmers are resident in the indigenous towns of south-western Nigeria. Basically, African towns and cities are centres of administration, trade, and to some extent industry.

The primary motive for rural–urban migration is the wish for increased income (see chapter 3). For many migrants this wish has been fulfilled, and the cities are indeed foci of relatively intense economic activity. They play a vital role in every national economy in terms of both the production and services undertaken within them and also the organization of commercialized rural activities. They thus constitute high peaks on the economic development 'surface' in every country. They are also, of course, concentrated centres of consumption, and may even be more liability than asset for the rural majority (see chapter 9).

However, the cities cannot provide the higher income, or any gainful employment, for all those now seeking it. Their continuing rapid growth is causing concern for many reasons, but the most fundamental is that the urban population is expanding faster than the urban economy, and much faster than employment opportunities. The cities are becoming concentrated centres of poverty, as well as wealth, though this poverty is general to Africa rather than specific to its cities. Urbanization really involves a spatial shift of such poverty rather than providing its cause.

The key problem is sometimes specified as lagging *industrial* employment, but this may be a mis-specification. Urbanization in tropical Africa has not been based on industrialization, the situation differing sharply from that in Europe, and even perhaps Latin America. Roberts (1978: 61), writing on 'Third World' cities, observes that 'urban-based industrialization has become the dominant economic force in Latin America', where manufacturing now contributes more to GDP than agriculture. This is true of very few tropical African countries. Their urban growth still depends largely on tertiary activities. This is often regarded as unhealthy, and even as a deviation from some 'norm': yet throughout the world and over several millennia urbanization has normally been so based, and it is perhaps the 'Western' industrial city, and its partial replica elsewhere, that represents a deviation.

Critical appraisals of the economic basis of African urbanization neglect the fact that many services, from transport to teaching, are meeting more basic needs than many forms of manufacturing. Is the production of cigarettes, or even of furniture or textiles, really of greater benefit to society than medical care? Is not the transfer of goods from areas of surplus to areas of shortage just as valuable as their transformation from one form into another?

Further misunderstanding arises through the assumption that most rural dwellers are engaged only in agriculture, and hence in 'production'. In reality the adults in most African farm families spend much of their time in tertiary activities – teaching, nursing, fetching water and so on. Some of the men are politicians at the local level as much as they are farmers. The balance between 'productive' and other activities may differ little from that in the cities.

Data and definition problems

Precise information on African urban economies is scanty, partly because they are far from self-contained. The urban and rural components of all national economies are inextricably linked. No reliable data exist on the proportion of GDP in any country that can be attributed to each of its cities. At the same time the urban economy is intimately bound up with the world economy. For instance, many highly paid employees in African cities are expatriates who have part of their salaries paid in Europe or North America. The total intensity of economic activity in Abidjan, Kinshasa or Nairobi is therefore extremely difficult to measure, except in the crudest employment terms.

Even the few figures available on employment and unemployment are highly unreliable, due in part to problems of definition
– many people being neither in regular full-time employment nor
entirely without work – and in part to the limited extent of
enumeration. In various countries there are periodic counts of
individuals working in large-scale enterprises, and records of registered unemployed: but neither of these cover the many people who
work in small enterprises, are self-employed, obtain only intermittent casual jobs, or fail to find work yet do not register as unemployed. A few censuses have included questions on employment
status but these also faced problems of definition. Thus many married women who have some minor source of income are uncertain
whether to describe themselves as self-employed or as not in the
labour force, while some individuals are both employees and self-
employed simultaneously, and perhaps also employers – of domestic servants.

Such problems of definition and enumeration arise anywhere in
the world, but even the basic concepts of employment and unemployment can be transferred only very cautiously from Europe or
North America, where working for wages is so much more widespread throughout the national population.

Occupations and urban functions

Geographers have most often discussed the urban economy in
terms of functions (e.g. Vennetier 1976: chapters 7 to 9), and some
attempts have been made to classify African cities on that basis (e.g.
Hance 1970: 259). Within the Copperbelt of Zambia, for example,
one might distinguish between settlements largely dependent on
mining, such as Chililabombwe and Mufulira, and the predominantly commercial city of Ndola. Employment data do not
provide an entirely satisfactory measure of urban functions, as some
activities are more labour intensive than others, but they do show
how people gain a livelihood.

Kenya's annual employment survey (which now attempts some
coverage of self-employment) indicated that in 1979 about 20 per
cent of Nairobi's labour force were in manufacturing, 12 per cent in
construction, almost 30 per cent in commerce and finance, 8 per
cent in transport, and 16 per cent in administration and social
services. The largest remaining category was domestic service,
which may account for almost 10 per cent of wage employment.

Table 10   *Employment by economic activity in selected African cities*

	Total active (hundreds)	Agric/ Fish	Manu- facture	Construc- tion	Com- merce	Trans- port
Nairobi 1979	2608	59	518	353	579	206
Mombasa 1979	927	9	190	51	156	236
Douala 1976	1066	38	253	80	276	145
Yaoundé 1976	727	17	102	70	128	45
Dar es Salaam 1967	906	42	151	68	159	130
Accra 1960	1505	64	194	186	550	109
Accra (men) 1960	1005	60	140	181	185	105

Note: Employment here includes self-employment.
Sources: Census Reports and Employment Surveys.

Rather older data for a selection of other cities are provided in Table 10, most showing a broadly similar structure. One consistent variation, of course, is the higher figure for transport in all the port cities.

Manufacturing has clearly become a major function of all the cities, the industries most widely represented being grain milling, brewing, cigarette manufacture, textiles and clothing, furniture and household utensils, and light engineering. Consumer goods thus predominate over capital goods, even within the large-scale sector, largely supplying domestic markets.

Commercial functions range from export and import handling through wholesaling and large-scale retailing to the activities of street hawkers, and also include banking and insurance. Apart from the large share of trade in agricultural produce, therefore, they differ little from those in cities elsewhere. The same is true of functions such as administration, the law, education and health care.

Awareness of these functions is necessary for an understanding of Lagos, Nairobi or any other city, but since this book focuses on the distinctive features of African cities we shall not examine each activity in detail. They are in any case discussed at length in several existing city studies, such as that of Seck (1970) on Dakar and that of Hinderink and Sterkenburg (1975) on Cape Coast.

A distinction is sometimes made between the 'basic' and 'non-basic' functions of cities, the former being those performed for other areas, such as mining, port activity and national government, and the latter largely internal to the urban economy, such as house building, retail trade and primary education. In industrialized countries the ratio of basic to non-basic activity may be an indicator of the economic health of each city, but this notion is not directly transferable to Africa. Much African urban development has been associated with (basic) externally-oriented activity such as cocoa exports from Ghana or copper exports from Zambia, and most countries are now deliberately expanding the internal exchange economy which involves exchange within the cities as well as between city and countryside. At this level the concept of self-reliance implies some expansion of non-basic activity.

Wherever only ten to twenty per cent of the country's population are urban dwellers many urban activities must be performed largely for people living elsewhere. The fact that so many goods manufactured or services provided in Abidjan or even Dar es Salaam are consumed within those cities reflects less on the health of the urban economy than on the extent of regional and urban–rural disparities within the nation as a whole. The basic/non-basic distinction is important in Africa mainly in relation to this issue, the role of urbanization in national development depending both on the cities' functions and on the range of people for whom they are performed (see chapter 9). Differentiation among African cities must depend mainly on their basic functions. Similar non-basic activities take place in all urban centres: it is basic activities that provide scope for functional specialization within national urban systems. But to what extent has such specialization occurred in tropical Africa?

The degree of functional differentiation

When other fragmentary data are added to the figures given above, it becomes clear that most cities and towns in tropical Africa are multi-functional, serving as central places in a variety of ways. Most administrative centres, from national capitals to district head-quarters, have also become trade foci, and it is in these same centres that industries are developing. In most countries certain towns have one dominant function, but most of these towns are small and rather unimportant in the total urban system.

The functional similarities among many East African towns, large and small, have been demonstrated by O'Connor (1968) and Hirst (1973), and the same characteristic emerged from a study of Ghana's urban system by McNulty (1969). There is also no general differentiation between western and eastern African cities, except with regard to the more extensive market trade in most of the former. Nor do ex-colonial cities necessarily differ from old indigenous cities in respect of the balance between administration, commerce and manufacturing, however much they differ in the character of each of these activities.

Functional differentiation clearly does not offer a suitable basis for producing a typology of African cities, but we might just note some of those which are unusually distinctive.

Functionally specialized cities   Yaoundé in Cameroon is the largest city in which administrative functions predominate, although it is also a major regional commercial centre. Lilongwe in Malawi is now developing on a similar basis, having replaced the even more specialized, but tiny, Zomba as the national capital; and new administrative capitals are being set up in Tanzania and Nigeria (see chapter 8). The likely extent of their other functions is hard to predict. Similarly in Mauritania and Rwanda administration provided the initial impetus for the recent growth of Nouakchott and Kigali. This function is also relatively more important in Harare, Lusaka, Nairobi and Accra than in most African capitals, while it is relatively unimportant in Bulawayo, the Copperbelt cities, Mombasa and Kumasi, as well as in those Nigerian cities which are not State capitals.

While many African towns began as forts, none are primarily military centres today; but some provincial centres such as Kaduna in Nigeria and Gulu in Uganda do have large military barracks. No towns are primarily educational centres, but in some, such as Zaria and Cape Coast, this function is unusually important. Similarly, there are no large towns that are primarily resorts, although tourists make an important contribution to the economy of Mombasa, and are the main source of livelihood in a few smaller centres such as Malindi.

Many towns grew up as transport foci, and Nairobi is one which originated as a railway camp, but in general transport is an even more widespread urban function than administration. Road and rail transport are rather more important in the life of some towns, such as Thiès in Senegal or Kabwe in Zambia, than in others, but most of the urban centres in which transport is the dominant function are ports (Hoyle 1967, 1972), especially those such as Beira, Lobito and Pointe Noire which have an extra-national hinterland. Port activity is also vitally important for cities such as Douala, Mombasa and Takoradi: but these are also major commercial and minor industrial centres, while many of Africa's other ports also serve as national capitals.

The most notable contrast with regions such as Europe and North America is perhaps the lack of 'industrial' towns. The dominance of the tertiary sector in African urbanization reflects this situation more than a lack of manufacturing in the largest cities. Jinja in Uganda is a rare example of a town with a predominantly manufacturing function, as a result of a decision to locate several large enterprises close to its hydro-electric plant. Manufacturing has also become prominent in Kaduna in Nigeria, especially now that it administers only a State rather than the vast former Northern Region. Various other settlements in which manufacturing provides much employment are really the satellites of capital cities, such as Rufisque near Dakar, Thika near Nairobi, and Kafue near Lusaka.

The most specialized urban settlements are mining centres, but many of these are very small. Even the settlements at such large mining enterprises as the iron ore workings in Liberia (Yepeka) and Mauritania (Zouerate) house fewer than 30,000 people each, and might be regarded as mere mining camps. The largest mining-based towns in tropical Africa are those of Zambia and Zaire. On the Zambian Copperbelt mining provides 35 per cent of the large-scale employment in Chingola, Luanshya and Mufulira, and 20 per cent even in the more diversified city of Kitwe. Mining, of course, provides a notoriously precarious economic basis for urban settlement, and while there are as yet no true 'ghost towns' in tropical Africa, the ending of mineral working has severely hit Lunsar in Sierra Leone and several small towns in Ghana.

A final category of functionally distinctive towns comprises those which exist largely to house farmers. All over tropical Africa urban dwellers undertake some cultivation, and it is the main occupation for many in the smaller towns. Among the larger centres, those of south-west Nigeria are unique in their dependence on agriculture. It is impossible to determine what proportion of their population gains a livelihood mainly from the land, both because many combine farming with other activities, and also because so many farmers live part of the time in town and part in a rural settlement: but the 1952 census recorded agriculture as the employment of 60 to 70 per cent of the men in Yoruba towns such as Ilesha, Iwo and Oyo, which then had 50,000 to 100,000 inhabitants. The proportion has now fallen, as people have switched to other activities, but even today these towns remain highly distinctive in terms of occupations.

Quite apart from these towns with many farmers, there is more functional differentiation among Nigeria's urban centres than among those of most African countries (Mabogunje 1968: chapters 5 and 6). However, even there it has recently decreased as a result of the creation of twelve States in 1967. This reduced the role of administration in Enugu, Ibadan and Kaduna, and added it to the commercial activities of Kano, the mining role of Jos and the port function of Port Harcourt. The creation of further States in 1976 extended administrative functions to yet more towns in which trade was previously dominant. Meanwhile, manufacturing has been heavily concentrated in Lagos and in these State capitals rather than in separate industrial towns. However, the creation of a new federal capital at Abuja, leaving Lagos as a commercial-industrial-port city, is a major step in the opposite direction.

Multi-functional cities Nigeria's distinctiveness may be an inevitable result of its sheer size. The pattern of multi-functional cities found elsewhere reflects Africa's political fragmentation, for there is little scope for specialization in Burundi or Togo. Colonial policies are also relevant, for new administrative towns quickly developed transport and other service functions, and trade organized from outside was drawn to these same centres. A major port serving as a capital city inevitably became a focus of commerce. Even inland capitals drew trade to them, as in Kinshasa, Khartoum and Nairobi – though the reverse occurred in Kampala.

Large-scale manufacturing produces mainly consumer goods that were formerly imported, and has been drawn to existing urban centres, often as an outgrowth of trading concerns (O'Connor 1978: 118). These cities offer both the largest markets and the best points for reaching remaining markets. Only a few industries such as cement works, which employ little labour, are located near their raw materials instead. So most national capitals also have the greater part of their countries' factory employment.

This general lack of specialization means that some economies of scale are being lost, but it provides a measure of security for each urban centre. Whereas many national economies are precarious in that they depend heavily on one or two exports, few cities have an economy that is precarious in this sense. The serious employment problems facing them are rarely just a matter of balance among sectors of the economy, as they are in many cities elsewhere.

The structure of the urban economy

Whereas most African cities are very similar in their functions, there are fundamental differences among them in economic organization, notably in terms of the scale of enterprise. All cities have both large- and small-scale enterprise, but the balance between these varies greatly. This variation is closely related to contrasts in urban origins, and again the question of possible convergence between indigenous and colonial cities arises.

It has always been recognized that most people in indigenous Nigerian cities are either self-employed or work in very small enterprises: but only recently have either academics or administrators recognized the growing importance of such activity in ex-colonial, and even ex-'European', cities. This raises problems of terminology, for in discussions of cities such as Ibadan or Kano activities are often labelled 'traditional' or 'modern'. 'Traditional' is hardly appropriate for any enterprise in Lusaka or Nairobi, and prompted by Hart (1973) the ILO has promoted the term 'informal sector'. However, this has remained ill-defined, and so much discussion of it has been in terms of a dependency on the 'formal sector' that it is not really applicable to activities that long pre-dated the colonial impact.

McGee (1973: 138) also recognizes a basic dichotomy, but he brings in yet another terminology, and a link with broader economic analysis, in suggesting that 'the most useful model is that which sees most cities of the Third World as consisting of two juxtaposed systems of production – one derived from capitalist forms of production, the other from the peasant system of production'. He suggests that if the notion of peasants in cities seems too much of a paradox, then those engaged in small-scale activities might be termed the proto-proletariat. Other commentators, such as Moser (1978), prefer to think in terms of petty commodity production, which in Marxist terms implies a particular relationship with large-scale capitalist enterprise.

The problems clearly go far beyond mere terminology, and some writers challenge the whole concept of two sectors, and associated notions of dualism. Some of them, however, notably Santos (1979), then quickly turn to another dichotomy – in his case between 'upper and lower circuits' of the urban economy. In many respects these closely resemble the 'formal and informal sectors' of others, and even the earlier distinction between the 'firm' and 'bazaar' economy made in a South-east Asian context by Geertz (1963).

Useful reviews of some of these issues are presented in collections of papers edited by Bromley (1979) and by Bromley and Gerry (1979). As they point out, no simple dichotomy is likely to sum up satisfactorily the situation even in a single city, much less a wide range of cities. Analysis in terms of two sectors (or circuits) may ignore the intense relationships between them, while intermediate elements always exist.

Nevertheless, some analysis in dualistic terms is appropriate, since there often *are* sharply contrasting economic systems operating side by side in African cities, albeit with many linkages. Furthermore, these relate closely to the juxtaposition and interaction of indigenous and alien elements that provide a recurrent theme in this book, although the labels 'indigenous' and 'alien' would be as unsatisfactory as most others now that national governments have taken charge of many activities that were initiated from outside.

A simple dichotomy is often drawn in respect of manufacturing, as large foreign- or state-owned factories and small local craft establishments are both found. Some craft enterprises have been put out of business as products from footwear to furniture have been produced more cheaply by the large firms, but others have flourished or newly arisen to meet new demands (Peil 1981: 103–9).

In the case of retail trade, there are huge differences between the large foreign-owned concerns in a well-defined Central Business District and the far more numerous and dispersed self-employed market and street traders: but many shops clearly occupy an intermediate position. From the customers' viewpoint the polarization is sharper in the case of financial services, where the highly formal banks co-exist with individual money-lenders or dealers in foreign currency, especially wherever 'informal' exchange rates differ greatly from official rates. On the other hand, numerous financial transactions which are totally irregular do involve the large-scale sector, including the state (e.g. Jenkins 1967).

With regard to many other activities, such as transport, construction, and even medical care, macro- and micro-enterprises operate side by side. In every African city people who are sick have a choice between traditional healers and herbalists or Western-type hospitals, clinics and pharmacies (Maclean 1971, Leeson and

Frankenburg 1977, Katz 1981). Even in respect of administration, there may be two distinct sectors or systems in the sense that local chiefs have jurisdiction over now-suburban areas without being on the payroll of the municipal authorities.

While a two-sector view of the urban economy has been in fashion only since the early 1970s, it is closely related to the older concept of socio-economic dualism, which can be applied to many aspects of African economies (Seidman 1974). Dualistic theories in their extreme form, implying two sectors or systems which function entirely separately, and also versions implying total superiority of one sector, have been rightly criticized. Yet in countries such as Liberia and Zambia two contrasting economic systems have existed side by side throughout this century, one functioning largely on a subsistence basis and the other highly dependent on overseas exports and imports, with little interaction between them except for the movement of labour.

However, there are dangers in associating an urban structural dichotomy with such more general concepts of dualism. At the national level it is often implied that the cities lie clearly within one sector, while the other is almost entirely rural. Thus an urban traditional or small-scale sector is regarded as an anachronism. This view is an extreme over-simplification, for the traditional–modern and rural–urban divisions always cut across each other. Whatever division we make in examining the urban economy, both sectors will have close relationships with rural Africa.

Certainly, in drawing a distinction between large-scale enterprise controlled either from overseas or by the state and smaller-scale local enterprise, we must recognize that in some cities the latter largely pre-dates the colonial intrusion whereas in others it has followed it. There are fundamental differences between pre-colonial cities (or parts of cities), where petty trade and crafts form the historic basis of the urban economy and where the 'formal sector' may even remain peripheral, and those cities where the latter developed first and an 'informal sector' has emerged dependent upon it. Contrasting historical processes in two cities may have produced a similar numerical balance between the sectors, yet the relationships between them will differ greatly.

It may be most appropriate to recognize the much-discussed 'informal sector' as just a part – the newest part – of that broader sector of the African urban economy which also includes more 'traditional' activities (Figure 10).

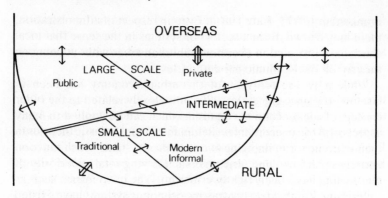

Figure 10   *Sectors of the economy: one approach*

We shall, therefore, examine African urban economies in terms of sectors, using labels which avoid the ambiguities (and even ethnocentrism) of some in common use, and present only the problems of where to draw dividing lines. The basic distinction will be between large-scale and small-scale activities, recognizing that (*a*) there are always strong links between them, though not always links of the same kind, (*b*) the large-scale sector is sub-divided – for instance into public and private components, and that the small-scale sector is also sub-divided – for instance into a component with pre-colonial roots and one growing recently in response to the colonial inheritance, (*c*) the importance of intermediate-scale enterprise may now be increasing.

Even divisions in terms of scale must be arbitrary, and could be based on various criteria. Here the main consideration is employment. Recognizing just two sectors, enterprises with ten or more employees might be distinguished from those with fewer or none. If we identify an intermediate sector, this might cover enterprises employing between, say five and twenty-five people, or even all with one to fifty employees. Perhaps for this discussion a strict definition is not really essential.

The relative sizes of the sectors

In Nairobi, Lusaka and the Copperbelt cities, as well as in Harare and Bulawayo, the large-scale sector still employs most of the workforce, and is totally dominant in terms of the amount of business conducted. In all these ex-'European' cities much small-scale activity has appeared in recent years, but most remains somewhat marginal to the main components of the urban economy.

Conversely, in most Yoruba cities of Nigeria small- and intermediate-scale enterprise still dominates the economy, for both the state and large firms each provide only a small fraction of total employment. Colonial cities such as Kinshasa, Lagos, Lomé and Luanda occupy a midway position, as do the 'dual' cities such as Kano and Khartoum; and all of these have rather more intermediate-scale activities than either of the other types of city.

One basis for comparisons among cities is provided by data from the few censuses which distinguish between those working for wages and the self-employed (Table 11). Data for 1960 showed that self-employment exceeded wage employment by a large margin in Kumasi, and almost matched it in Accra. Unfortunately, comparable data collected in 1970 were never published. A 1965 survey in Kaduna (Lock 1967) indicated that there were about 18,600 people in small-scale (or self-) employment, compared with 13,600 in large-scale private employment and 10,300 working for government bodies. Similarly, a 1974 ILO study of Abidjan (Joshi 1976) estimated that the 'informal sector' employed 44,000 people there, compared with about 100,000 in the 'formal sector' (and also

Table 11 *Employment and self-employment in selected African cities*

	Employees hundreds			Self-employed hundreds			Self-employed per cent		
	Total	m.	f.	Total	m.	f.	Total	m.	f.
Freetown 1963	256	227	29	130	66	64	34	22	69
Accra 1960	787	709	78	646	247	399	45	26	84
Kumasi 1960	323	297	26	488	226	262	60	43	91
Douala 1976	686	621	65	279	178	101	26	20	61
Yaoundé 1976	555	477	78	159	119	40	22	20	34
Brazzaville 1974	334	301	33	205	115	90	37	27	73
Dar es Salaam 1967	792	716	76	159	136	23	17	16	23
Blantyre 1977	590	524	66	124	79	45	17	13	40
Lusaka (Af. pop.) 1969	367	331	36	35	29	6	10	10	14

Source: Census Reports.

suggested that it yielded an average income little below the basic wage for employees in large-scale activity).

Women constitute such a large majority of the self-employed in cities such as Accra and Lagos that meaningful comparisons must take this into account. Table 11 shows that it is this involvement of women in small-scale enterprise which provides the sharpest contrast between, for example, Accra and Dar es Salaam. However, even among men the extent of self-employment is much greater in many West African cities than in those of eastern Africa.

Within each country the employment structure often differs from one urban centre to another. While the ratio of employees to self-employed in 1967 was almost 6:1 in Dar es Salaam, it was only 3:1 in Tanga, while Zanzibar City had almost equal numbers of each. No comparable census data exist for Kenya, but an ILO mission (ILO 1972) estimated that the 'informal sector' accounted for only about 20 per cent of the Nairobi labour force, compared with 35 per cent in Mombasa. In both Tanzania and Kenya the proportions of self-employed, and of employees in small concerns, rose through the 1970s: but no doubt it rose even more sharply in Kampala, where the Amin regime brought the collapse of much large-scale enterprise and its replacement by a highly 'informal' black-market *magendo* economy.

While in other ways the cities of Zambia altered markedly during the 1960s, census figures suggest little change in employment structure. A small-scale sector is growing up in Lusaka, but its African population in 1969 still included only 3500 listed as self-employed, compared with 37,000 in paid jobs. The pattern was very similar on the Copperbelt, as also in Harare. These restrictions on African small enterprise were until recently extremely severe, and the 1969 African population included only just over 2600 stated as self-employed, compared with 123,000 in wage employment. By the early 1980s, however, the situation had changed substantially in Zambia, and had begun to change in Zimbabwe also.

Characteristics of the sectors

The small-scale sector

Even if this sector is not a totally discrete entity, we can indicate the activities embraced by it. Descriptions exist both for the 'Third World' as a whole (McGee 1976, Sethuraman 1976, 1981) and for particular African cities such as Accra (Hart 1973), Nairobi (ILO 1972) and Freetown (Fowler 1981). However, most such discussions relate only to the 'informal' sector which has grown up recently in response to larger-scale activity, whereas the small-scale sector in some cities includes forms of enterprise in existence long before the colonial period. It thus incorporates both the oldest and the newest activities, and some of the most stagnant as well as some of the most dynamic. It may also be seen as the urban counterpart of the small-scale rural activity which still occupies most people in tropical Africa.

Some individuals engage in small-scale activity because they cannot obtain preferred forms of work, but others choose to set up a small business of their own after a period of employment in a large enterprise, using savings and perhaps expertise that they have acquired there. Many are self-employed, such as the great majority of market vendors and hawkers, while others are unpaid workers in small family businesses. However, many enterprises hire two or three employees, and some provide various forms of apprenticeship (Callaway 1967, Peil 1970, King 1977). Many of the tailors sitting at sewing machines on the verandahs outside small shops are employees of the shopkeepers, although others are working on their own account and paying a small rent. The relative importance of one-person enterprises and those with a few paid workers is not really known for any African city.

One near-universal characteristic of this sector is very low capital intensity. Another is dependence on individual rather than institutional resources. Bank loans, for instance, are rarely available for small-scale enterprises. Often no accounts are kept, while most enterprises old and new are informal in the sense that they are nowhere officially registered. Many people are involved only on a part-time or casual basis, but others work very long hours almost every day of the year – often for pitifully small returns.

On average, incomes are much lower than in the large-scale sector, but averages here mask large variations. Skilled craftsmen may earn more than most factory workers, while astute traders can amass great wealth, especially if engaged in such activities as diamond smuggling.

Specific activities

The activities undertaken within the small-scale sector range from farming and fishing through crafts and construction to a host of tertiary occupations. They also range from the provision of essential goods and services to petty crime.

The large numbers of small farmers in most Yoruba towns were noted above. Farming is also the chief activity of many city dwellers elsewhere in West Africa, as in the Upper Volta capital, Ouagadougou (Skinner 1974). Vennetier (1976: 122–8) reviews the situation in various other cities of francophone Africa, noting that most women in Bangui, for instance, find some land to cultivate. Kampala and Blantyre are two other cities in which much land is intensively farmed, mainly by the wives of men who have wage employment. Even on the Copperbelt of Zambia, where small-scale cultivation was not permitted before independence, many city dwellers now have small farms just beyond the urban area. In most cities a few people grow crops for sale, but far more do so just for subsistence. Nevertheless, they are making a vital contribution to the cities' food supplies, and hence to the urban economy.

Traditional Yoruba craft industries, such as weaving and pottery, have been described by Ojo (1966a), and Bray (1969) has provided a case study of Iseyin. However, in most Yoruba cities other types of small-scale manufacturing enterprise, such as tailoring and carpentry, now occupy far more people (Table 12). Both tailoring and furniture-making also figure prominently in surveys of small-scale enterprise in Accra by Steel (1977) and in Kampala by Obbo (1975). Beer brewers are equally numerous in peri-urban Kampala, and this is also one of the main economic activities undertaken within the squatter settlements of Nairobi (Nelson 1979b) and Lusaka.

Table 12 shows that commerce occupies many more people in Ibadan than industry, and figures for the self-employed of Freetown in Table 13 show 65 per cent as traders. Similarly, 63 per cent of the 64,000 self-employed in Accra in 1960 were street or market vendors. In eastern Africa too, many are engaged in street and market trade in food, firewood and charcoal, while others form the final links in the distribution chain for manufactured goods. Markets play a vital role in the economy of all African cities: studies of their operation include those by Garlick (1971) in Ghana, Hodder and Ukwu (1969) in Nigeria, and Beveridge and Oberschall (1979) in Zambia. More informal, and often technically illegal, forms of street trading are also widespread, as vividly described for Nairobi by Hake (1977).

Table 12 *Occupations in Ibadan Province urban centres (1963)*

	Economically active population in hundreds				
	Males		Females		Total
TOTAL	4753		3118		7871
in which:					
Traders	733		2105		2838
Street vendors		660		2091		2751
Farmers	1567		70		1637
Craft/Labourers	1386		164		1550
Tailors		163		11		174
Carpenters		178		2		180
Transport	345		5		350
Clerical	250		36		286
Admin/Professional	244		61		305
Services	190		78		268
Domestic service		44		54		98

Source: Nigeria 1963 Census.

Table 13 *Occupations of the self-employed in Freetown (1963)*

Occupations	Males	Females
TOTAL	6592	6375
in which:		
Commerce	3049	5442
Manufacturing	1705	676
Agric./fishing	502	113
Services	311	131
Transport	312	2
Construction	205	1

Source: Sierra Leone 1963 Census.

The proliferation of such traders creates the impression of an 'unproductive' sector, especially when ten are competing for the demand that two or three could easily satisfy. However, this is too sweeping a dismissal. McGee's (1971: chapter 3) proposition that many people in 'Third World' cities engage in ever-finer divisions of trade as a survival strategy rather than to meet real needs certainly applies to tropical Africa; but many small traders do perform valuable functions both in handling rural produce and in making other goods available where they are needed in appropriate (often minute) quantities. The positive contribution of those in the more specialized cattle or fish trades is even more evident.

Other small-scale activities essential to the urban economy include transport and construction. Although there is no African equivalent of the pedicabs of Singapore or Saigon, scores of taxis are operated by individuals, often without licences, while many self-employed traders must carry their goods long distances. Even in the ex-colonial cities most houses are now being built by individuals with the help of local craftsmen, as was always the case in the indigenous cities, rather than by large firms. Construction within new squatter settlements is in every sense 'informal' enterprise.

The proverbial, and clearly less essential, boot-blacks and car-minders are also found in African cities (Elkan 1982), while gaining a living by queueing on behalf of those without the time or the patience to queue is quite widespread. The list of other occupations is almost endless, the 1963 Nigerian census recording among the urban population of the former Western Region 9000 barbers, 8000 launderers, 8000 herbalists and 6000 actors or musicians. Interestingly, the equivalent figures for herbalists and actors/musicians are equally high for northern Nigerian cities, but far lower for those of the (more 'westernized'?) south-east.

The view that the small-scale, or even the 'informal' sector consists largely of illegal or undesirable activities is thus quite unjustified: but it certainly does include many who make a living by prostitution, smuggling, theft or begging (Hart 1973) – occupations rarely recorded in censuses. One cannot say whether they are more widespread in African cities than in others, but they probably account for a larger share of all small-scale activity in eastern African cities than in those of western Africa because of the greater scope for other small-scale activity in the latter. Furthermore, activities which are technically illegal but not basically anti-social, such as constructing buildings below official minimum standards, are far more widespread in cities of colonial origin than in indigenous cities simply because more rigid regulations exist there.

Other features of the sector

One characteristic of the small-scale sector often noted is its reliance on local rather than external initiatives. However, the term 'local' must not be interpreted too narrowly here, for while many of the local-born are active within it, especially in the indigenous cities, so are many long-distance migrants (Shack and Skinner 1979). Other features commonly attributed to this sector are open to serious question. One is greater ease of entry than into the large-scale sector, while another is a lower level of skill requirements. Control of some activities by particular ethnic groups is often a barrier to entry by others, while for certain trades there is the equivalent of a craft guild; whereas unskilled work in the large-scale sector may only require waiting long enough in a job queue which all are free to join. 'Knowing the right people' is the key to more rapid entry equally in both sectors.

Many small-scale activities actually require much skill, and most require knowledge at least of sources of supply and market conditions. Many illegal activities such as smuggling depend greatly on such expertise. They may also require capital, while activities such as taxi-operating are quite capital-intensive. Indeed, from the individual's viewpoint capital is required for most small-scale enterprise in a way that it is not for wage employment.

Male and female roles   In many parts of the world women play a greater role in this sector than in large-scale enterprise, but within tropical Africa there are sharp regional contrasts. The much greater importance of small-scale urban activity in West Africa than elsewhere is largley due to the fact that most women undertake some form of trading. Census figures for Ghana's cities show far more women than men to be self-employed, and their dominance of the giant Kumasi market is renowned. Both Little (1973) and Peil (1975a) have shown how trading is a normal part of women's life in such cities, as in the surrounding rural areas. They note the low incomes of the majority, but Little indicates how some women have advanced from trading to set up businesses such as bakeries. Accounts of the prosperous market women of Onitsha in Nigeria have been given by both Ukwu (Hodder and Ukwu 1969) and Onyemelukwe (1970). There is diversity even within West Africa, however, and in the cities of northern Nigeria or Mali far fewer women engage in trade, though some gain an income from crafts pursued within their homes.

In most eastern African cities few women have any income from either trade or craft industry. Of the 16,000 people recorded as self-employed in Dar es Salaam by the 1967 census, only 2300 were women, and even in the markets of that city they are outnumbered by men. Studies in the Mathare area of Nairobi by Nelson (1979b) and in peri-urban Kampala by Obbo (1980) show that some women gain a living from prostitution, while women play a larger role than men in making and selling beer; but especially in Kampala far more women contribute to the economy by cultivating any spare land around the houses. As more women settle on a long-term basis in eastern African cities their economic role is beginning to expand within the small-scale sector. Whether it will eventually match that in the southern cities of West Africa must depend in part on the opportunities made available to them in the large-scale sector, to which we now turn.

The large-scale sector

While the recent spate of literature on the small-scale sector of the urban economy represents a reaction to an earlier overemphasis in many quarters on the large-scale sector, few published studies are concerned explicitly with the nature of the large-scale sector in African cities. Most of the writings which do overemphasize it, from academic works to development plans, are concerned with national economies rather than the cities alone.

In some respects it is even more diverse than the small-scale sector, especially since it includes both private and state enterprise, and since it also includes activities under both foreign and local control. For the individual job-seeker these distinctions may not be of great importance, and it is from this perspective that general characteristics may most easily be recognized. In addition to those resulting directly from large scale of organization, they include more impersonal relationships, greater reliance on qualifications and more standardized wage rates than in small-scale enterprise. Incomes tend to be higher, and security greater, than for the majority in the small-scale sector, though the difference may not be sufficient to justify the notion of a 'labour aristocracy' (Arrighi 1973, Hinchcliffe 1974, Peace 1975). Capital-intensive methods are more often adopted in the large-scale sector, ranging from the machinery in a textile mill to the computers in a bank, and this contributes greatly to the sluggish growth of employment.

From other viewpoints we must distinguish between the public and private sub-sectors. The former includes both central and municipal government, together with many semi-autonomous agencies and organizations from marketing boards and housing corporations to airlines and universities. The relative importance of this sub-sector has grown everywhere since independence, but it varies greatly according to the prevailing political philosophy. In Nairobi the public sector, broadly defined, accounted for about 40 per cent of the employment in large-scale enterprise in 1979, and the proportion was similar in Mombasa (Table 14). However, its share is substantially higher in Dar es Salaam, where activities such as banking are no longer in private hands, and no doubt higher still in Conakry and Luanda; while it is rather lower in Kinshasa and in Lagos.

The significance of the distinction between the public and private sub-sectors has increased because it now partly coincides with that between indigenous and alien control, whereas during the colonial period the entire large-scale sector was controlled from overseas.

However, some enterprises established by foreign companies are now partly owned by local individuals or groups, (while the state has taken a share in others). Langdon (1981) and Swainson (1980) have both investigated the patterns in Kenya. Firms ranging from banks to oil distributors have set up partially autonomous subsidiaries in most African countries, but the degree of real local

Table 14 *Wage employment in Nairobi and Mombasa, 1979*

	Public sector	Private sector (large and medium)	Total
Nairobi			
Total (hundreds)	1026	1582	2608
Manufacturing	79	439	518
Construction	128	225	353
Commerce	73	506	579
Transport	112	94	206
Other services	548	302	850
Mombasa			
Total (hundreds)	342	585	927
Manufacturing	33	157	190
Construction	19	31	50
Commerce	9	147	156
Transport	161	75	236
Other services	97	163	260

Source: Kenya, *Employment and Earnings in the Modern Sector 1979* (Nairobi, 1981).

control varies enormously. At the same time, in cities from Dakar to Harare many firms nominally of 'local' origin have been built up by people who retain foreign nationality, whether French, British, Indian or Lebanese.

Despite this growing complexity, there is no doubt that private large-scale enterprise in most African cities is subject to a very large degree of control from overseas, and that this constitutes a major policy problem both for national governments and for municipal authorities. Most large enterprises form part of an international network, and decisions about the operations of banks in Freetown, or oil distributors in Kinshasa are influenced more by the companies' international circumstances than by local needs. Yet even where state intervention is rather limited, the dominance of such direct foreign influence is at last beginning to decrease. In addition to foreign–local partnerships, wholly local firms are emerging in all types of African city (Schatz 1977, Beveridge and Oberschall 1979). These are engaged in a wide range of activities, including manufacturing, trade, transport and construction.

This emergence of these local firms ensures that as the cities grow so does the number of enterprises rather than the average size of each. The total number of firms, and the range of sizes is broadly similar in various capital cities such as Dakar, Accra and Nairobi. The sharpest contrast is provided by those cities on the Zambian Copperbelt where one mining company accounts for the majority of large-scale employment, as it has always done. Paradoxically, something similar is now arising in a very different urban environment as one or two firms establish the first really large enterprises in some of the indigenous Nigerian cities, such as the cigarette factory employing 2000 at Oyo and the steel rolling mills at Oshogbo and Katsina.

Male and female roles in the large-scale sector   While the role of women in African urban economies is often underrated, it is generally small-scale enterprise that is being overlooked. Boserup (1970: 190) has observed that the 'modern' sector in every African country is virtually a male preserve, and this is only a slight exaggeration. In some cities this situation partly results from unbalanced sex-ratios, but it is also one cause of that imbalance.

A useful discussion of the lack of wage-earning opportunities for women has been provided for Zambia by Hansen (1975), while helpful material for Accra has been provided by Pellow (1977). To a large extent it reflects employers' attitudes and policies. Poorer educational facilities for girls than for boys have also been significant, but this situation is now changing rapidly. As elsewhere in the world, family responsibilities impose constraints, and sometimes cause women to prefer casual work in small-scale enterprise, but many families employ domestic servants or have resident relatives who provide domestic help. The prevailing male view on whether the woman's place is in the home rather than in the office or factory may determine both how many jobs are offered to women and how many women can take up the offers. They have been discussed for Uganda by Elkan (1960) and for Ghana by Peil (1972), both authors finding most husbands opposed to the idea of their wives seeking paid employment.

Wider generalization for African cities seems to be possible on this subject than on most others. The ratio of males to females among employees (as against self-employed) in Freetown, Accra and Dar es Salaam during the 1960s, as indicated by census figures, was remarkably similar, ranging only between 8:1 and 10:1. One occupation falling largely within the large-scale sector is clerical work: of those so occupied, women accounted for 20 per cent in Freetown, 18 per cent in Dar es Salaam and 15 per cent in Accra. (The male/female ratio among all employees is much influenced by the fact that men predominate even in domestic service, in total contrast to areas such as Latin America.)

Naturally, there has been some change since the 1960s, but the change seems to have been both gradual and even. Thus in Nairobi the proportion of women recorded in the annual employment surveys rose from 10 per cent in 1960 to 12 per cent in 1968, 14 per cent in 1973 and 16 per cent in 1979. Impressionistic evidence suggests a similar advance elsewhere.

The chief variations among the larger cities are provided by Addis Ababa and by those where strict forms of Islam prevail. The exceptional social system which has brought an excess of females in the population of Addis Ababa has also led to their occupation of about one-third of all paid employment there. Conversely, women's share of wage employment in such predominantly Muslim cities as Bamako, Kano, N'Djamena and Mogadishu remains very small. Women's role in the large-scale sector is even smaller in most provincial towns than in most capital cities, confirming the overall picture of male dominance. How far this can be changed, or how far women in most African cities will have to copy those of Accra and

Lagos in seeking income mainly in small-scale enterprise, remains to be seen.

Intermediate activities

In many African cities an intermediate sector has expanded rapidly in recent years, partly as a direct result of the ending of colonial rule. During the colonial period, both in cities such as Ibadan and in those such as Lusaka, the distinction between activities undertaken on a large scale by the state or by foreign firms and the micro-activities of local individuals was really quite sharp. In a country like Zambia there was little scope for anything in between, but independence has permitted the emergence of many small- to medium-scale local firms (Beveridge and Oberschall 1979). Meanwhile in Ibadan and other cities of indigenous origin the more successful small-scale entrepreneurs are setting up formally as companies and taking on wage employees.

In various other cities medium-scale enterprises have been important over a longer period. These include many set up by individual Europeans in Harare and Bulawayo, and by Asians in the cities of East Africa. Some small French-owned businesses in Dakar and Lebanese enterprises elsewhere in West Africa have played a similar role. In Lagos and Accra some truly indigenous firms existed even before independence, and much expansion has taken place since then (Steel 1977, Kennedy 1980).

Among manufacturing industries, baking and furniture-making are two that are found in many African cities at all scales from the single individual to the factory employing several hundred people (whereas beer-brewing tends to be concentrated at the two extremes). Good opportunities for medium-scale enterprise have been found in various forms of light engineering, while printing is commonly undertaken by firms employing around ten or twelve people.

The construction industry spans all sectors. Often it includes giant foreign firms and a national or municipal housing corporation, each with a very large work-force, while some house-building is undertaken on a subsistence basis by the future occupiers: but many small businesses are also involved, often linked in with both extremes. Much 'self-built' housing actually requires specialist assistance for the more difficult operations, while large organizations are increasingly sub-contracting work to intermediate-scale companies.

Municipal bus companies clearly fall within the large-scale sector, but it is less easy to classify the privately-operated buses and small fleets of mini-buses which are also found in most African cities. It is often uncertain to what extent they are operating not merely informally but illegally, for they are frequently overloaded, and while licensed to ply certain routes they may move elsewhere if business is better there. Road transport is one specific area where the ubiquitous mini-buses of the 1980s reflect some convergence between the earlier patterns of state company dominance in some cities and freelance 'mammy-waggons' in others.

The most extensive intermediate activity is undoubtedly retail trade, and in polarized academic discussions of the 'formal and informal sectors' it is rarely clear how much retailing is included in each. There is in each city a continuous spectrum from street hawkers to foreign-owned motor showrooms, but the largest number of retail establishments are fixed family-owned shops, often with just two or three employees. The Asian enterprises of this type which dominated retailing in Nairobi, Dar es Salaam and Kampala during the colonial period clearly occupied an intermediate position between the outlets of large British firms and African market trade. Today many of their shops have been taken over by African traders, while new shops have been opened both in the city centres and in the expanding suburbs. Similar shops, including both general stores and those specializing in goods such as textiles, are a vital ingredient in the economy of most smaller towns, as well as an obvious feature of the townscape (Larimore 1959, Hjort 1979, Henkel 1979).

Such intermediate-scale activities seem to provide less fertile ground for theoretical formulations than either street and market traders or giant multi-national corporations: but they cannot be ignored in studies of the urban economy. They provide goods and services for each city's inhabitants, they provide a livelihood for many, and they may offer a more appropriate basis for future expansion than either macro- or micro-scale enterprise. Recognition of their importance undermines bold formulations in terms of 'upper and lower circuits' as well as 'formal and informal sectors', but it also offers a prospect of reducing the strains created when there really is a high degree of polarization.

Interaction among the sectors

Even if we accept the notion of distinct sectors or circuits as an aid to understanding the urban economy, it would be quite wrong to think of them as separate and unrelated components. Much recent writing in a general 'Third World' context (e.g. Bromley and Gerry 1979, Santos 1979) directs attention to the linkage between them. Many small-scale activities in ex-colonial cities have arisen in response to needs created by the large-scale sector, and they remain highly dependent upon it. Even where the small-scale enterprise was established first it has always been greatly modified.

Many goods such as tinned milk or enamelware now sold in the traditional markets of Nigerian cities, or on roadside stalls in urban Zambia, have been imported by large trading companies. Others, such as matches and cigarettes, have been produced in local large-scale factories. Traditional crafts such as weaving and dyeing have come to depend on factory-made yarns and dyes, while many blacksmiths are now either working imported metal or repairing imported metal goods. A useful analysis of linkage of this type for Dakar has been made by Gerry (1979).

An interesting example of interaction in many cities is provided by shoemaking. Twenty years ago local leather was often used by self-employed shoemakers, while another part of the market was supplied by importers such as the Bata Company. In several cities this multinational company has now opened a local factory which absorbs the supply of leather from small-scale cattle keeping, while individual shoemakers now depend either upon imported plastic or upon strips of rubber from old imported or factory-produced car tyres.

Many other micro-scale industries arising in every country from Senegal to Malawi depend on raw materials either imported by, or produced in, the large-scale sector, although the system of sub-contracting that is now so widespread in cities such as Hong Kong or Singapore is not yet common in African cities. Others rely on large firms for their equipment, and sometimes for finance, as in the case of all the tailors and dressmakers who have obtained their sewing machines on credit from the Singer Company. Similarly, large importing firms directly or indirectly supply the taxi drivers with their vehicles, while the innumerable bars are providing outlets for the products of large-scale foreign-owned breweries, as well as that epitome of the multinational corporation, Coca Cola.

Among the self-employed who depend on large-scale enterprise in other ways are the cooked food sellers who pitch their stalls at the factory gates or who ply their trade at the railway stations. Yet another case of interdependence is provided by the domestic servants of people employed by governments or large firms. Again, the opportunities for small-scale employment are a direct result of large-scale activity. The two sectors may also be in direct competition, however, not only where large factories have put small craftsmen out of business, but also in respect of services (Bienefeld 1975). Thus the establishment of municipal bus services, the provision of piped water, and the improvement of medical facilities can all undermine the livelihood of small-scale entrepreneurs.

There are other forms of interaction among sectors or circuits of the economy about which little is known for any African city. One is the extent to which they constitute a single labour market, with people moving readily from one sector to another, or even combining a job in one with a job in another. Certainly both of these situations are quite widespread. Many of the self-employed in the newer cities learned their trade as employees in large-scale enterprises, and were able to set up business on their own only when they had accumulated some savings from such employment. King (1979: 221) has observed that 'the origins of the African informal manufacturing and repair sector in a country like Kenya or Tanzania are to be found in the semi-skilled worker who had formerly been employed in an Asian or European company'.

The fact that many people engage in small-scale enterprise while seeking a job in the intermediate or large-scale sector, and then later set up in business on their own account undermines some of the cruder generalizations made in terms of a one-way relationship. It also serves to emphasize that sectors or circuits are more distinct with reference to enterprises than with reference to individuals. In this connection the family or household deserves mention, for some members may be occupied in one sector and some in another. Probably the majority of government employees in Accra and Kumasi are men whose wives engage in petty trade; and even though they keep their domestic budgets more separate than do husbands and wives in many other parts of the world, they can hardly be regarded as belonging to two totally separate economic realms.

If all these links exist between the large-scale and small-scale sectors, there must be just as many between each of these and the intermediate sector. Very often enterprises in this sector are not merely of medium size but also function as intermediaries between the two extremes. Thus a retail store with half a dozen employees may obtain most of its supplies from a very large wholesale firm, and make many of its sales to petty traders who will distribute the goods elsewhere in the city. Swainson (1980: 187–9) has shown how large manufacturing and importing firms in Kenya have set up chains of intermediate-scale distributors both within the cities and in small towns.

The existence of an intermediate sector therefore complicates not only any simple dualistic model of the urban economy but also any analysis in terms of a single set of relationships between two circuits. Even if we disregard it, however, the relationships are far from simple, and would merit far more study in many African cities. The notion of an 'informal' sector subservient to, and dependent upon, the 'formal' sector can be appropriately applied to most small-scale activity in cities such as Lusaka and Nairobi, and perhaps even in those such as Dakar and Dar es Salaam. However, in Ibadan, Kano, Khartoum and Addis Ababa there is much small-scale activity which was not established on the basis of such a dependent relationship. Indeed, when foreign enterprises such as banks were first opened in towns such as Ilesha or Ogbomosho they were dependent upon the pre-existing small-scale economy for their business.

The pre-existing small-scale sector in the cities of indigenous origin is perhaps now becoming increasingly dependent upon the large-scale sector. Perhaps also a few of the more successful 'informal' enterprises in the cities of colonial origin are becoming less dependent in their relationships. This would imply a further instance of the convergence with respect to cities of different types already noted in other contexts.

In terms of policy, therefore, it is important to recognize that contrasting elements are present in most urban economies, but that the relationships as well as the balance among them differ. The potential of each sector for sustaining an increasing population can be assessed only for each city individually, and assessment must be made in the light of current trends which may be diametrically opposed from one city to another.

Well-informed policies are certainly urgently required in view of the fact that one thing common to all the cities is their failure to provide an adequate livelihood for all their inhabitants. Having considered at some length the activities which employ the majority of the labour force, we should now give some explicit attention to those who have no employment at all.

Problems of unemployment

Unemployment is now one of the most serious problems in most African cities. Both national and municipal governments are very aware of the problem, although neither its dimensions nor its causes are fully known. It has also commanded academic attention, most notably from Gutkind, who has suggested (1968: 135) that male unemployment rates for African cities commonly range from 10 per cent to 35 per cent. He quotes a rate of 22 per cent, and a total of 65,000, for Lagos in 1964. Among geographers, Hance (1970: 276) has noted the scale of the problem, and his figure for Lagos in 1965 was 34 per cent.

These figures may have been overestimates, for there are no reliable data and unemployment is hard to define. Gugler (1976: 185) quotes surveys for several cities which revealed rates of 12 to 15 per cent for all adults, and a similar impression is emerging from current ILO studies. These are people who are actively and unsuccessfully seeking work, and are meanwhile largely dependent on others for financial support. In addition, many who have some occupation are seriously underemployed, some working only a few hours each week, others spending long hours – seeking customers, for instance – for pitifully small returns.

Specific country situations

The relatively reliable Ghana 1960 census indicated that 10 per cent of men and 9 per cent of women in Accra were unemployed, while the figures for Kumasi were 10 per cent and 6 per cent. The 1970 census indicated slightly lower rates, averaging 8 per cent in both cities, but many observers suggest that they have risen substantially during the 1970s. Peil's (1972) study of Ghanaian factory workers discusses their experience of unemployment. Many had spent well over a month in town before finding a job, and one in six had known at least one period of over six months without work. The delay in finding work tended to be less in Kumasi than in either Accra or Takoradi.

A survey of Cotonou in 1968 indicated that of the 74,100 males of 15 to 60, resident in the city, 9300 were unemployed, and it is doubtful that the situation there has improved. The ILO (Joshi 1976) study of Abidjan estimated that the labour force there increased by 9.7 per cent a year between 1965 and 1970, while employment rose by 7.5 per cent a year in the formal sector and by 10 per cent a year in the informal sector. As a result, unemployment rose from 9 per cent of the labour force in 1965 to almost 20 per cent in 1970, or to an absolute figure of about 35,000.

The situation in Nigeria's cities can only be guessed, but there is probably much variation. A series of unpublished studies by Doxiadis Associates in the early 1970s suggested an unemployment rate of 20 to 25 per cent in several cities, including both indigenous cities such as Ibadan and Sokoto and colonial cities such as Enugu and Kaduna. Such consistency seems rather implausible, especially since true unemployment hardly existed until recently in the indigenous cities.

The ILO 1972 report on Kenya estimated male unemployment at 14 per cent in Mombasa, 10 per cent in Nairobi and 8 per cent in Kisumu, and while stressing the hazardous nature of estimating female unemployment indicated that this might be closer to 20 per cent. The 1967 Tanzania census implied a much brighter situation, recording as wholly unemployed only 4 per cent of men and 2 per cent of women in Dar es Salaam. Strangely, the rates in most provincial towns were considerably higher – around 6 to 9 per cent. Sabot (1979: 151) suggests 8 to 12 per cent, depending on definition, for all Tanzania urban centres together and contradicts the census by indicating a much higher rate for women than for men.

Further south, the 1969 census figure for Harare was only 5700 unemployed out of an African adult male population of 180,000, i.e. 3 per cent. The rate was long kept down there by tight migration control, thus bottling up in the rural areas the pressures which give rise to urban unemployment.

The nature of the unemployment

Unemployment results largely from the failure of the urban economy to provide jobs, or self-employment opportunities, fast enough to match the increase of the labour force. More specifically, a great increase in the number of school leavers has coincided with a reduction in vacancies in many cities, as a result of greater stabilization of the urban population. The problem is exacerbated by the adoption of capital-intensive rather than labour-intensive techniques in the most rapidly expanding activities, from manufacturing to banking. As wage rates rise, concerns such as the railways are increasingly reluctant to maintain an unduly large labour force.

The nature of unemployment may differ among African cities more than its magnitude. The problems of graduate unemployment faced by some Asian countries have not reached tropical Africa, but in her Ghana survey Peil found that workers with a middle school education had experienced more unemployment than those with little or no education, due to their higher aspirations. The level was higher among people of urban origin and migrants from the south than among migrants from the poorer north and from Upper Volta, who were more willing to do unskilled low-paid work – often in a rural setting. By contrast, the ILO mission to Kenya found the incidence of unemployment in Nairobi to be highest among the least educated.

The fullest study so far of African urban unemployment is that undertaken by Hutton (1973) in Uganda, largely based on interviews with job-seekers at factory gates in Kampala and Jinja. She found that in terms of origins, age and education the unemployed differed little from those who had found work. Since most were migrants from rural areas, she concluded that the roots of the problem lay there. Rural unemployment may hardly exist, but the countryside cannot offer the type of work to which many now aspire.

Both Gugler (1976) and Elkan (1970) have referred to urban unemployment as only the tip of an iceberg, pointing to a vast rural pool of potential urban labour which would flood into the cities if employment prospects there were to improve. This has led many observers to insist that creating more urban jobs will not solve the problem, and may only exacerbate it, and to argue that action within the rural areas is at least equally important.

It is unfortunate that inquiries on unemployment have been largely confined to the major cities, for the levels may be just as high in most provincial towns. While these attract fewer migrants, their local economies are often growing even more slowly, and the range of job opportunities which they offer to school-leavers is very restricted. There may also be fewer opportunities for self-employment, though there is greater scope for people to undertake some peri-urban cultivation.

Gutkind (1969 etc) has noted that the unemployed in African cities have largely failed to become a powerful political force. Actions such as the 1969 'sans travail' demonstration in Abidjan are still quite rare. The main explanation may lie in the extent to which kinsfolk support those without work. In most parts of the world so many people simply could not survive for so long without earnings or social security benefits. However, this willingness to provide board and lodging for indefinite periods is now decreasing, as costs of living rise and as social structures change.

The scale of unemployment and underemployment was rising in most African cities throughout the 1970s, and there is an urgent need for more study of the problem in the context of each city's own circumstances: but meanwhile immediate efforts to tackle it are required everywhere, by action both within the cities and within the rural areas.

Conclusions

For the purposes of analysis, this chapter has isolated the urban economy, and examined the related issues of employment, organizational structure and urban functions. We have not really addressed the basic issue of poverty, for that is a feature of Africa as a whole rather than of its cities in particular: but the fact that the great majority of the urban population survives on incomes that are extremely low by any international standards must never be forgotten. All policies for urban management in Africa must have among their aims a general improvement in the economic well-being of this majority. We have also not explored the many ways in which the economy is closely linked to that of the rich world, and its fortunes largely determined by decisions made in New York, London, Paris or Zurich. This theme lies beyond the scope of this book, but again the situation must constantly be borne in mind in any discussion of cities from Dakar to Dar es Salaam.

We have seen how the growth of the urban population throughout tropical Africa is tending to outpace the growth of the urban economy, creating a serious employment problem everywhere. More and more people are unable to find any sort of work, and have to depend for long periods on their kinsmen. Many of those seeking wage employment unsuccessfully do manage to engage in some activity, legal or otherwise, in the small-scale sector: but this is not as easy to enter as is sometimes suggested, and income is generally very low, even for long hours of work.

Fortunately, in every city the majority of those wishing to find work have succeeded: and so, despite the increasingly serious employment problem, the cities do constitute intense concentrations of economic activity. Indeed, their economic condition is in many ways far healthier than that of most rural areas, and it is for this reason above all that they continue to attract vast streams of migrants.

Most tropical African cities, and indeed most provincial towns also, are very similar in their functions. There is much less functional specialization than in some other parts of the world, so that most administrative capitals, for example, are also centres of trade and now also of manufacturing. Contrasts are greater with regard to organizational structure, for in some cities the vast majority gain their livelihood working for the state or for large companies, while in others there is much small-scale enterprise.

These contrasts are less marked today, however, than they were twenty years ago, and this is one respect in which clear convergence has taken place between different types of African city. While the predominantly small-scale enterprise of Ibadan and other indigenous cities has increasingly been supplemented by new large-scale enterprise in the period since independence, a new 'informal' small-scale sector has rapidly developed in cities such as Lusaka and Nairobi. This is by no means identical to the more traditional trading and craft activity that remains in the cities of indigenous origin, but it does share many features with it. The main difference is, of course, that it has grown up highly dependent upon the pre-existing large-scale sector.

As long as such distinctions are made, a two-sector model is of value for the understanding of African urban economies. It is, however, an extreme simplification of reality, and it is helpful to recognize an intermediate sector. Indeed, some of the activities that are growing most rapidly in many cities can best be regarded as falling within that sector, and it may be here that governments can do most to boost the economy. On the other hand, the emergence of local capitalism in this fashion may be ideologically so unwelcome in some countries that the maintenance of a sharp division between large-scale state enterprise and small-scale individual enterprise would be preferred.

6 Housing

Housing is a key problem of rapid urban growth throughout tropical Africa, where both poverty and inequality are all too clearly reflected in housing patterns. Housing is one of man's most basic needs, yet it is grossly deficient in both quantity and quality in every African city. By any standards, 'Western' or otherwise, many people are living in appalling conditions. The quality of the physical fabric and access to amenities such as water supply may be better than in most rural areas, but that does not make them remotely adequate; and the urban environment presents additional problems through overcrowding, which is intensified year by year.

Several entire books have been devoted to urban housing in a 'Third World' context (Dwyer 1975, Payne 1977, Murison and Lea 1979, Drakakis-Smith 1981, UNCHS 1981, Ward 1982), and a few specialized studies exist on individual African cities (Stren 1975, 1978, Vernière 1977, Pasteur 1979). This discussion in a single chapter must be superficial by comparison, but perhaps housing is sometimes given disproportionate attention in urban studies. Odongo (1979) has even suggested that the housing crisis in poor countries may often be overstated, and further studies are required of just how far residents themselves see housing as a major problem. Peil (1981: 135) considers 'a case can be made that housing is a less important factor in the standard of living and self-image of a West African than of an Englishman or American'. In many African urban situations other things do indeed seem to worry people more.

To some extent there is a distinctively African viewpoint here, influenced by the nature of African family and social life, by the tropical climate, and by comparison with the rural dwellings from which so many have recently come. Circular processes are also at work. Dwellings too small and crowded, especially for entertaining others, cause people to rely on 'hotels' and bars, and then preference for these diverts at least the men's attention away from their houses. Women's priorities may, of course, differ, but their views rarely prevail. Preference for undertaking many activities out of doors is also part cause and part effect of poor housing.

Throughout tropical Africa attachment to land, and indeed to 'home', is particularly strong, but many who are investing in a house are doing this in their rural homeland rather than in the city. This applies even to the increasing numbers now settling semi-permanently in the cities, while there are still many who think only of a very temporary home there.

Nevertheless, housing does present a severe challenge in every city (Abiodun 1976, Brand 1976, UN 1976). Particular forms of urban settlement, notably squatting, may be seen more acutely as a 'problem' by the municipal authorities than by the residents themselves, but as long as this is so other problems will arise for the residents. It may even lead to demolition of their dwellings; more generally it will mean lack of infrastructure and services. Indeed, housing merits attention as one area where conflicts of interest are readily apparent, underlying the nature of the city as a complex entity. Furthermore, for most households, whatever their priorities, rent is a large and rising item of expenditure. Housing needs are fast increasing as migration continues, as many settle more permanently, and as an urban-born generation reaches adulthood; and in many cities housing provision is not keeping pace, so that average conditions are deteriorating. How far it is governments' responsibility to meet this need is open to debate, but it must be a cause for concern.

The distinction between indigenous and colonial cities is at least as relevant to housing as to other aspects of the urban scene, but once again a simple dichotomy may be of limited value as both local and alien ingredients are present in most cities. Intermediate forms are more common than either those described for Ibadan's core by Schwerdtfeger (1982) or those described for Harare by Smout (Kay and Smout 1977), and even between these cities some convergence is now occurring. Yet in other ways the total diversity within the African urban housing situation is increasing.

Diversity in housing patterns

One of the main limitations of the existing literature is that it overstresses certain elements in the total picture at the expense of others. It is easy to gain the impression that almost everyone lives either in government housing or in squatter settlements. Generally this is far from the truth. Whether in Dakar, in Accra, or in Kampala, most houses are privately built by individuals who have some form of right of occupancy. Many are used as homes by these owners, but often some of their rooms are let to tenants. Others are occupied entirely by tenants, some at extortionate rents but others at very low rents – especially the shacks erected by small farmers around the city margins as an alternative land use to growing crops. Most urban dwellers are thus renting accommodation from private landlords rather than either squatting or depending on the state for housing.

A widespread housing pattern inherited from the colonial period involved official laying out of plots on which individuals could build their own houses on payment of a small plot rent. Often all were originally quite similar, but some have since been enlarged or improved while others have decayed. Meanwhile, this form of part-government and part-individual housing has been re-discovered since independence in the form of site and service schemes in cities from Ouagadougou to Lusaka.

In every city, whatever its origins, there are areas of close-packed houses and areas occupied at very low density, there is high quality housing and there are areas of the crudest shacks. Variations in patterns of ownership often cut right across these other variables to complicate the total picture immensely. For instance, dwellings built by private companies for their employees range from exclusive properties for oil company managers to squalid 'labour lines' for factory workers. In face of this complexity we shall consider certain aspects one by one and then examine several housing types more fully.

Housing density and quality

Nowhere in tropical Africa do residential densities yet match those in parts of some Asian cities, and often overall densities are no higher than in cities in Europe. This is partly due to the existence of both spacious elite suburbs and peri-urban areas where low-income housing is interspersed with cultivation, and partly because most dwellings are of only one storey. Everywhere from Dakar to Harare high-rise flat dwelling is repugnant to most people, as well as too costly, and is rejected even when alternatives involve long journeys on inadequate public transport. Of course, none of the cities yet match in population the larger Asian and Latin American metropoli, but even now that Lagos and Kinshasa have passed 3 million their residential growth continues to be horizontal.

While single-storey development precludes exceptionally high densities per hectare, it is conducive to high densities per room – almost the world's highest in some cases. Most households occupy only one room, with access to communal cooking and toilet areas. The proportions indicated by a 1970 Nigeria government survey were 64 per cent for Kaduna, 69 per cent for Kano and 72 per cent for Lagos. Some of these households comprise only one person, but others are large families, and by 1976 Lagos dwellings averaged 4.1 persons per room (Ayeni 1981). Similarly in Dar es Salaam the 1967 census indicated that 70 per cent of the dwellings consisted of only one room, many occupied by families of five or six people. In Lusaka overcrowding is less severe, but even there most families have only two rooms.

This is clearly one respect in which generalizations can be made for all tropical African cities, regardless of their different origins. Indeed, in so far as any cities have lower average densities of occupation of dwellings these include both the extreme 'European' cities, Harare and Bulawayo, where severe overcrowding co-exists with spacious living for large numbers, and those indigenous cities least affected by colonial economic change, which have only slow-growing populations.

In respect of densities per hectare, however, the contrasts are much greater, and they do reflect contrasting urban traditions. It is hardly practicable to compare whole cities in terms of average residential density per hectare, since this is profoundly affected by the limits adopted for the urban area. (Figures for houses per hectare would be even more meaningless, since a 'house' in one city implies a single family dwelling while in another it may be a structure occupied by many families.) However, we may compare the seventy people per hectare indicated by the 1962 census for the combined residential areas of Nairobi with the 200 to 500 per hectare indicated by the 1963 census for most parts of Ibadan.

Around that time densities per hectare were much higher in most indigenous cities, including the indigenous cores of Accra and Lagos, than in the 'European' cities. However, the contrasts are now being reduced as cities such as Ibadan acquire new low-density suburbs while those such as Nairobi acquire close-packed squatter settlements. This, of course, is pointing to the sharp contrasts *within* cities, discussed in chapter 7.

All discussions of housing quality are bound to be highly subjective: there can be no single yardstick, since priorities are much influenced by both environment and culture. The word 'slum' is therefore avoided here, though many would apply it to most African urban housing. With respect to building materials and physical comfort most deficiencies apply equally to rural Africa, however aesthetically pleasing some rural housing may be (Denyer 1978). Like inadequacies in educational provision or health care, they are manifestations of the general material poverty of tropical Africa.

The provision of specific services such as piped water and electricity is, of course, far better in the cities than in most rural areas: yet they often fall short of people's aspirations to a greater extent than in the countryside. Levels of provision differ markedly from one locality to another within each city, and those who lack these services are well aware that others have them. In certain cities water is provided by private entrepreneurs to poor residential areas, but at charges higher than those set for municipal supplies in the elite areas. Many outside observers would suggest that improved sewerage systems are the most urgent of all needs in overcrowded cities, even if this is not the view of most urban dwellers themselves.

Surveys of Nigerian cities show great contrasts in the level of provision of water and electricity. A 1970 government inquiry indicated that 75 per cent of all dwellings in Port Harcourt and 72 per cent of those in Lagos had piped water, compared with only 33 per cent in Ibadan, 26 per cent in Kano and 25 per cent in Benin (Nigeria 1975: 307). Such contrasts might be expected between cities which long pre-date the arrival of 'Western' technology and those which have arisen more recently, but the failure to bring this technology into many parts of the old cities is notable. In cities such as Kano the dualistic physical structure is clearly reflected in features such as this. However, there are also new housing areas, such as Ajeromi on the western edge of Lagos, where most landlords have been unwilling to meet the costs of water installations.

Moving across to East Africa, the great majority of houses in Dar es Salaam have neither piped water nor electricity. The 1967 census showed that of the 83,000 households there only 10,000 had piped water within the house, while 32,000 had no access to piped water at all. Variations within the city were enormous, as demonstrated by Figure 22 and Table 16 in the next chapter.

In both respects the 1969 Zambia census indicated that Lusaka was rather better placed, though this partly reflected a tightly-drawn city boundary. Of the 36,000 dwellings within it, 30 per cent had electricity, 37 per cent had private piped water, and 80 per cent had at least access to piped water. the Copperbelt towns were even better provided than Lusaka, partly because they had less spontaneous housing. In Kitwe, for instance, just half the dwellings had electricity, and virtually all had access to piped water.

More information is needed on the present availability of such amenities in African cities, and on the reasons for variations among them, but the greatest need is for investigation into how the deficiencies can be remedied, especially where the funds available both to individuals and to municipal authorities are much lower than in Zambia. In some cities the proportion of the population lacking basic amenities is steadily rising. In Dar es Salaam an extensive 1976 government survey indicated that the proportion of dwellings built in 'permanent materials' had fallen since the 1967 census from 35 per cent to 27 per cent, and that the proportion with electricity and with piped water had also fallen. Almost everywhere the absolute numbers inadequately served are rising rapidly (Hardoy and Satterthwaite 1981: 176–85). Despite the problems of subjectivity mentioned above, there is little doubt that the overall quality of housing is deteriorating in many African cities, just as the quantity is lagging behind the growing demand.

House ownership and occupancy

It is not normal in rural Africa for individuals or even families to own land, since this belongs to the whole community: but houses are normally private property. Similarly in the cities most houses are privately owned, though standing on plots leased from either a municipal or a traditional authority – or occupied illegally. It is often unrealistic in Africa to consider whether the buildings are owner-occupied or rented, for frequently they are both. Since so many city dwellers occupy only one or two rooms rather than entire houses discussion must often be in terms of dwelling-units or households. Table 15 indicates how the cities vary in the proportion who rent. More data on this subject would be valuable, especially since Barnes (1979) and others have indicated a strong correlation between house-owning and commitment to long-term urban residence. A further variation is how far the renting is from resident landlords, absentee landlords, private employees – or from the state, which has become far more involved in housing in some cities than in others.

Table 15 *Dwelling ownership in selected African cities*

| | Percentage of households | |
	owning	renting
Brazzaville 1974	55	45
Douala 1976	53	47
Blantyre 1972	40	60
Lusaka 1969	39	61
Dar es Salaam 1967	24	76
Kitwe 1969	17	83

Note: (a) Renting here includes lodging. (b) Many renters own a dwelling in their rural homeland.

Sources: Census Reports.

Two categories of occupancy are not always sufficient, since many people are lodging with kinsmen. Some surveys record 20 to 40 per cent of all adults as lodgers (e.g. Parkin 1978: 90), and while some of these may live as part of the main household others may have a room of their own and make some financial contribution.

A further complication is provided by an increasing number of tenant-purchase schemes on government-built housing estates: in these some families will have become owners while their neighbours still have many payments to make.

Western Africa

In West African cities of indigenous origin most households occupy dwellings which belong either to them or to their extended families, they or their forefathers having built the houses on family land. In places such as Ogbomosho, Ilorin and Maiduguri few households pay rent because few need to do so. Even in Ibadan owner-occupation predominates throughout the core area and the eastern suburbs, although to the south-west many houses have been built either by Ibadan families or by the more prosperous migrants, for letting to poorer migrants.

At one time most houses in Kano and Zaria were owned by the families that occupied them, but the addition of new sectors outside the old walls has brought great change, and there are now sharp contrasts among their component parts. In Zaria in 1974 (Bedawi 1976) 93 per cent of households in the old city owned their dwellings, whereas this applied to only 15 per cent in Tudun Wada and only 5 per cent in Sabon Gari. There, as in Kano, each compound in the old city is occupied by one extended family, whereas each Sabon Gari house is occupied by several unrelated families or individuals. Trevallion's (1966) Kano survey indicated over 5 households per house in Sabon Gari, compared with 1.6 in the old city.

In Lagos and Accra most families now live in rented rooms, but the house owners are often also resident, while some traditional family-owned properties remain. In Cape Coast (Ghana) Hinderink and Sterkenburg (1975) found 60 per cent of households renting, 10 per cent owning houses individually, and over 20 per cent living in large *abusua* houses belonging to extended families. In the cities of more recent colonial origin, such as Abidjan or Enugu, more than 80 per cent of households live in rented accommodation – government-built or privately owned.

In Kinshasa too, La Fontaine (1970) found that most households had to rent rooms despite a huge spread of self-built housing in the early 1960s. Many are committed to long-term urban residence and would like to own houses, but most cannot afford to do so. La Fontaine's study examines in depth tenant/proprietor relationships, and the patterns revealed are similar to those in many other African cities, such as Dar es Salaam.

Eastern Africa

In Dar es Salaam in 1967 there were 18,000 households in their own dwellings and 58,000 in rented accommodation. Most of this is privately owned, with many resident landlords letting out parts of their modest property. The extent of municipal housing is very limited. In Kampala the structure is broadly similar, a small minority living on municipal estates such as Nakawa and Naguru (Parkin 1969a) but far more renting privately-owned dwellings, many of which originally lay outside the city boundary.

In Nairobi too most households are paying rent, but since colonial policy opposed African private house-building many more are in city council housing than in most cities (Stren 1972, Ross 1975). A 1969 survey revealed 36 per cent in such housing, 13 per cent in central government housing, 17 per cent in accommodation provided by other employers, and only 34 per cent in privately-owned houses – as tenants or owners. The proportion living in privately-owned houses has since risen to over 50 per cent, but most house-holds are renting rooms within these.

In Lusaka 1969 census data indicated that 8000 dwelling-units were rented from the city council, 5800 from central government bodies, 2100 from private employers and 5500 from individual landlords, while a further 14,200 were occupied by their owners. On the Copperbelt there is much less private ownership, but also less government housing, as many workers are housed by the mining companies.

Until very recently the pattern in Harare and Bulawayo was very largely a matter of race. Many Europeans owned their homes, as they still do, but Africans were not permitted to do so within the cities. The majority of the population thus had to be housed by their employers (often not paying rent, but with wages reduced accord-ingly) or rent accommodation provided by the city council. Policies began to change in the 1960s, with some limited tenant-purchase schemes, and a rapid increase in African house ownership can be expected in the 1980s, but it is as yet still confined to a small minority.

Owner-occupation thus characterized both pre-colonial African cities and communities of European settlers, while it is also found in some of the squatter settlements that have recently developed. On the other hand the colonial city in Africa involved far more people in renting accommodation, and this is still the norm. One result has been a great deal of legislation to control levels of rents, and government policy must influence future trends; but these will also be affected by a host of other factors such as prevailing economic structure and income distribution, and attitudes towards permanent settlement in the city or continued attachment to a rural homeland.

While it is very clear that renting will remain the norm for most African urban dwellers in the foreseeable future, it is also clear that this depends on the existence of a house-owning minority who have a critical role to play in the growth of the cities. Studies of Lagos (Barnes 1979), Kinshasa (La Fontaine 1970), and Nairobi (Clark 1978) all identify this group, most of whom are only a little more prosperous than the majority and depend upon their rents for a substantial share of their income. A high proportion are from the local ethnic group in each case, and they have an obvious commit-ment to the city. They may join their tenants in retiring eventually to their rural areas of origin, but they expect their children to take over their urban property so that the family will continue to have a firm urban base. They are often keen to involve themselves in urban politics to protect their interests, and in many ways the future of African cities will depend on them as well as on the bureaucrats and the proto-proletariat – if that is what the majority should be termed.

Some housing types

The housing in African cities is so diverse that various types will be considered in turn, though any division must be somewhat arbitrary. Turner's (1976) threefold division into public, private and popular housing must be modified in the African context. There is no clear distinction between private and popular, for while large private building firms and real self-help both exist, there are many small building enterprises and much 'self-help' involves hiring skilled craftsmen for the more difficult tasks. There has also been much activity on the borders between public and popular in the form of self-building on serviced plots; and housing provided by employers often occupies the third borderland between public and private.

Certain types of housing are largely absent from tropical Africa. Few of the colonial cities are old enough to have inner-city tenement slums of the type discussed for other regions by Gilbert and Ward (1978) or Drakakis-Smith (1981). There are also few of the new high-rise flats such as Dwyer (1975) has examined in Singapore, Hong Kong and Caracas. Thankfully, few have to sleep on the streets as in Calcutta, though appalling conditions have existed in camps for refugees from political conflict or drought, for instance in Nouakchott (Mauritania) and Mogadishu (Somalia). The widespread forms of housing considered here are firstly government housing, then employer housing, legal and illegal private housing at all scales, and squatter settlement, the last involving illegal occupation of *land* – which people care about so much in Africa.

High-quality government housing

In all African cities there are some large well-built houses maintained by government bodies for their own personnel. This is partly a legacy of colonial rule, for all the colonial authorities assumed responsibility for housing administrators and professionals such as teachers or doctors arriving from Europe. Some of these houses are over fifty years old, and located near the city centres, adjacent to the main administrative zone, but often the majority of those inherited at independence dated only from the 1950s.

Similar houses occupy a substantial section of most provincial towns across the continent. In Nigeria each town that served any colonial administrative function has its Government Residential Area, known by most townspeople as the GRA. Its character differs little whether it is part of a colonial town such as Jos or Enugu, or an appendage to an indigenous centre such as Ilorin or Sokoto. Outliers of similar housing are often attached to places of employment such as university campuses, boarding schools and hospitals. In Ibadan, for instance, there are more government houses on such sites than in the old GRA.

The attainment of independence brought little immediate change in policy on housing for high-ranking government employees. As Africanization took place it was rarely thought appropriate to discriminate between expatriates and local personnel, and once the local elite have the privilege of highly subsidized housing of high quality they are reluctant to give it up. In some cities further construction of such housing has occurred, though its share of all housing has generally fallen rapidly. In this respect there is more variation from one city to another, often reflecting national priorities. Thus in Dar es Salaam the stock of high-quality government housing has not increased greatly, whereas in Abidjan the main government housing corporation, SICOGI, has devoted much of its effort to high-quality housing (Cohen 1974). While the provision of low-cost dwellings in Abidjan has fallen far behind both needs and official plans, over half the new houses in the exclusive quarters of Cocody and Marcory have been bult by SICOGI.

Lower-quality government housing

African cities differ very greatly in the extent of government housing provision for the low-income majority. Far more has been done in eastern than in western Africa, for example. In this context eastern Africa includes Zambia and Zimbabwe, but not Ethiopia where the public sector's role has been very small.

Until recently Africans in Harare and Bulawayo were not permitted to build houses for themselves there, nor to rent European-owned dwellings, so all who were not accommodated by their employers had to live in government housing (Moller 1978). In the 1950s most consisted of hostels for single men, but from the early

1960s new construction was mainly of two-room units for families. In Bulawayo there was no increase between 1960 and 1975 in the 25,000 'single units', but a rise from 6000 to 16,000 family units, the latter often having to accommodate eight or ten people. This housing is sturdily built, though often drab and monotonous in appearance, but it is low-quality housing in terms of living space, especially in comparison with the luxury suburban homes of the Europeans.

One of the worst features of most government housing in Harare is its distance from places of work, as also in Lusaka, where public transport is even more inadequate. The same progression from one tiny room to two-room family units occurred there, but considerably earlier as the 1930s estates of Old Kabwata and Kamwala were supplemented by Chilenje in the 1940s and Matero in the 1950s (Figure 20).

In Nairobi low-quality government housing in the 1920s and 1930s was largely confined to the 'labour lines' for such organizations as the railways or the police, but official thinking then changed and between 1945 and 1952 the city council built 12,000 dwellings (Stren 1972: 71). Further municipal housing estates followed and by 1963 almost half Nairobi's population lived in government housing. Many dwellings in Bahati and Shauri Moyo are only single rooms, but on the later estates most are two-room units. Single-storey buildings predominate, but by the late 1960s there were also some three- or four-storey blocks of flats, as at Kariokor (Ross 1975). Building of such council estates continued through the 1970s, though at a slower pace. As in other cities, all this housing is too costly to meet the needs of the poorest (Stren 1979, Temple 1980), partly due to presidential insistence on 'decent' standards, but there has been no shortage of demand for everything built.

In Dar es Salaam there were only around 2000 dwellings on government housing estates in 1960, but after independence the National Housing Corporation's 'heroic effort' (Bienefeld and Binhammer 1972: 186) added over 6000 in five years. While not disputing the effort, other writers (e.g. Stren 1975) emphasize the modest performance in relation to needs, due to shortage both of funds and of professional expertise: and these constraints remained in the 1970s.

In most Nigerian cities little low-income housing has been built by the state, apart from institutional housing such as railway quarters and police barracks, the most notable exception being that built at Surulere in the 1950s for people moved out of central Lagos. In Ghana much the most extensive programme has been that in the new town of Tema, on the fringe of Accra, where the government undertook to house most of the workers both in the new port and in the associated industries.

Variations in the extent of government housing provision reflect in part the funds available, but other factors have been more significant. Some city administrations have regarded housing as largely their responsibility, while others give the impression that they hardly care how most people are housed. A third group have given serious attention to the matter, but have decided to take little action themselves.

It is sometimes felt that allocating large sums to urban housing will encourage accelerated rural–urban migration. Some governments consider that house-building is best left to private enterprise. A third issue arises from comparison with the rural areas: as governments rarely provide rural housing perhaps large investments in urban housing would be seen as bias. In some cities uncertain land tenure situations have hindered municipal house-building, while political rivalries may also have an impact, as Stren (1978) has shown for Mombasa.

Recognizing that rents for government housing are bound to be beyond the means of many people, emphasis has shifted in some cities to the site and service schemes and squatter upgrading programmes noted below. A third response, which has not yet found favour, is to accept that many urban dwellers cannot afford any individual houses or flats, and to build six- or eight-room houses on the understanding that the tenants will sub-let most of the rooms. A city council might provide shelter for more people in this way than by using the same funds for twice as many two-room dwellings. The appropriateness of such an approach depends critically on whether large numbers of city dwellers will continue to regard a village elsewhere as their real 'home' – a theme explored later.

Private employer housing

In the 'European' cities, where it was official policy at least up to the 1940s to keep the African population to a minimum, housing for the essential work-force was seen as the employers' responsibility. Even today, many private companies continue to provide housing for their employees, notable examples being the mining companies on the Zambian Copperbelt. Over 40 per cent of all dwellings in Kitwe are company-owned, and the proportion is even higher in Chingola, Luanshya and Mufulira. The company housing is physically separate from the municipal housing, and includes a range of quality matching that of incomes. At first most 'quarters' were designed for men without families, and changed company housing policies in the 1950s contributed greatly to changing migration patterns (Heisler 1974).

Elsewhere in Africa similar company housing can be found, as in the BP estates in Port Harcourt and Warri in Nigeria. Even more commonly firms build or buy houses in the best residential areas for their senior staff, and lease private or government-built medium quality housing for staff in intermediate grades. Many of the Tudor estate flats in Mombasa, for instance, are leased to Shell or to East African Breweries (Stren 1978).

Another form of employer housing is the provision of servants' quarters close to the main house in high-quality residential areas. These are just as cramped as other low-income housing, but they often have water on tap, adequate sanitation and even electricity. One consequence of this widespread arrangement is that residential separation of income groups is undermined.

The extent of employer housing reflects the fact that neither high-level expatriates nor low-paid local workers were expected to settle permanently in these cities. Now that expatriates are being replaced, and ever more employees are city-based at least for their working life, it is becoming an anachronism. It heightens workers' dependency on their employers, and makes loss of a job a double disaster. Even apart from such special cases as the Copperbelt it remains a major component in the urban housing scene, but its relative importance is now decreasing. Paternalism remains in evidence when employees are given a housing allowance rather than a suitably adjusted wage, but this does mean that employees of large private companies are now increasingly part of the general housing markets – as renters, as owner-occupiers, or even as squatters.

High-quality private housing

While some high-quality houses are owned by government or by large firms, others are owned by affluent individuals. This reaches its extreme in Harare and Bulawayo, where large areas are divided into quarter-acre or half-acre plots which were bought freehold by

European families (Kay and Smout 1977: 35–7). Seen from the air a distinctive feature is the blue-tiled swimming pool in almost every garden. Today the African elite are gradually moving in, and this may bring sub-division of the plots and the building of additional dwellings on them, as has begun to happen in Lusaka and Nairobi.

In various cities a few wealthy Indian or Lebanese businessmen have built themselves quite palatial houses. In Nairobi many people of Asian origin have rather more modest privately-owned houses, while successful local businessmen are now building luxury houses on private plots on the outskirts. In West African cities too, a few local people have amassed fortunes through trade, and while some have remained in very humble dwellings others have built large and even ostentatious houses. Much depends on custom within each ethnic group, as well as on individual personality.

Since independence the wealthy traders have been joined as builders and owners of large houses by the new bureaucratic and professional elite. In Lagos or in Freetown some of these doctors, lawyers and politicians have built several such houses which are let to firms or foreign embassies at astronomical rents, while they continue to occupy government housing. In some other cities, such as Dar es Salaam, this is now prohibited. Whether owner-occupied or rented, this high-quality housing is very demanding on both land and municipal services while giving shelter to very few people. Its construction benefits the poor majority only in so far as it provides employment, for such houses are normally built by contractors using fairly labour-intensive methods – whereas nearly all the lower-quality private housing involves a large measure of 'self-help'.

Low-quality private housing: traditional systems

There is no sharp division between high- and low-quality private housing, but most clearly occupies the lower end of the spectrum. Eurocentric value judgements may be involved here, but on most criteria this must apply to housing that pre-dates colonial rule as well as to that built during this century.

Several writers have described traditional housing in the Yoruba cities of south-west Nigeria (Ojo 1966a; Krapf-Askari 1969; Schwerdtfeger 1982), although it is not always clear how far traditional patterns survive. Each extended family has a compound, but these vary greatly in size, and Schwab (1965) found in Oshogbo that they could house anything from fifteen to 450 people. They often

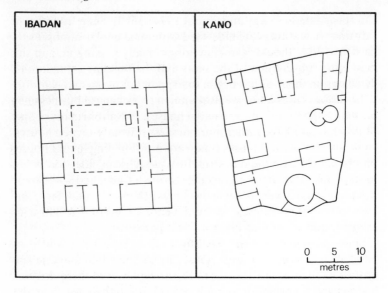

Figure 11   *'Traditional' compounds in Nigerian cities*

comprise a single-storey building occupying all four sides of a rectangle (Figure 11), with only one doorway breaking the outer wall, but with many doorways of individual rooms opening on to a large central space (Ojo 1966a: 147–51). Many such structures remain, but even in the cities least affected by colonial impact a two-storey house has sometimes replaced one section, built by a family member who once went to make his fortune elsewhere.

In Ibadan most old compounds are disintegrating through what Mabogunje (1968: 226) terms 'growth by fission'. As families expand, individual dwellings not only replace parts of the compound building, but also fill up the open area within it, leading to appalling overcrowding. As more children now survive, not all can remain as adults within the same site, and some usually acquire land and build houses on the edge of the city. Meanwhile living conditions are deteriorating in the inner areas, but customary rights largely prevent any policies of urban renewal.

In the Hausa cities, including the old parts of Kano and Zaria, compounds are larger and architectural styles are quite different. The ten to twenty-five rooms may be in several separate buildings, which often occupy less than a third of the compound area

(Schwerdtfeger 1982: 32). But the basic system of several related households sharing an inherited compound is comparable to that in Yoruba cities.

In southern Ghana the traditional urban dwellings are more often single structures than compounds, but these houses are commonly quite large, each being occupied by several households. A clear account of this *abusua* system in Cape Coast has been provided by Hinderink and Sterkenburg (1975: 278). There most of the older houses have eight to twelve rooms, and provide homes for four to five related households. Cape Coast is a relatively slow-growing town, from which many of the younger generation have moved to Accra. There a bustling modern city has grown up around the old Ga settlements of James Town and Ussher Town. Although these also did not contain compounds of the sort found in Yoruba towns, Brand (1972, 1976) suggests that a process of growth by fission similar to that described by Mabogunje has taken place. Population has increased inexorably in these areas which are now hemmed in by other forms of development, so that rooms have been subdivided and shacks have been built in courtyards and alleys.

In many respects this situation is repeated in the heart of Lagos, for although largely a colonial city its core includes land occupied by old-established Yoruba families under customary tenure. Many of the buildings in which these families live are now both dilapidated and overcrowded, but attempts at 'slum-clearance' operations have met with stiff resistance over three decades (Marris 1961). The urban authorities wish to convert this central area to non-residential uses, but the occupants have objected in the strongest terms. They regard the area not merely as their home which should not be subject to interference by outsiders, but as their ancestral land which it is their duty to defend.

Both in Lagos and in Accra increased land prices all around have had remarkably little impact, though how far this is due to a lack of commercial orientation or to realization that land is the best investment is unclear. The residents know that large-scale redevelopment would break up the complex set of community relationships which they value; and they wish to stay near their places of work, whether this be in a paid job or in self-employment. Brand (1976) notes how the political power of the Ga community has blocked renewal schemes in Accra, while Baker (1974) observes an increasing dominance of the residents of the inner city core in the local politics of Lagos.

Particularly outspoken views on these inner city areas are offered by Ajaegbu (1976: 41–2): 'unfortunately, the government and urban planning authorities do not dare impose their will on the indigenous people' who 'are largely unequipped' for urban life, and who 'constitute a major barrier to urban planning'. A more conciliatory approach is advocated by El-Shakhs and Salau (1979: 22), for whom a goal is 'to minimize disturbances and abrupt changes in the structure of traditional quarters in order to preserve highly held cultural and social values'. Certainly a distinctively African solution will have to be found to this problem.

Low-quality private housing from the colonial period

Even though they are extremely overcrowded, traditional dwellings house only a small proportion of all residents in Accra. Many more live in dwellings built within the past fifty years by private individuals on plots, often of 300 to 400 square metres, laid out by the municipal authorities. Comparable housing is found in other cities from Dakar in the west to Dar es Salaam in the east (Figure 12). Most residential growth in Dar es Salaam has occurred as people

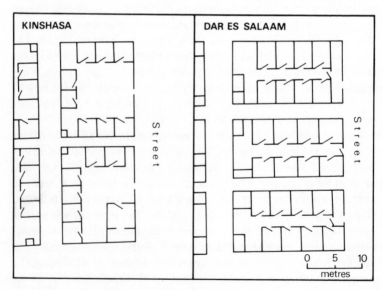

Figure 12   *Typical forms of rental housing*

have leased plots at a nominal charge, and built on these either themselves or aided by local craftsmen. The conventional 'Swahili' house is a rectangular single-storey building with a central passage leading back from the main doorway and three or four rooms leading off it on each side. Individual rooms can easily be let out to tenants, and more rooms can later be added at the rear.

The Medina area of Dakar has a comparable planned layout, dating from early in this century. Densities have risen to over 300 people per hectare and many buildings are now deteriorating rapidly. Similar densities prevail over the inner areas of Kinshasa, where most *parcelles* have the owner living in one or two rooms and about six tenants occupying one room each; and the same system of private building on leased plots extends over vast areas occupied at lower density. Another very extensive tract of self-built housing on officially leased plots is that of the New Diems in Khartoum.

Nigeria has its full share of such housing. In parts of Lagos, in the Sabon Gari sections of the northern cities, and in cities of the south-east such as Aba and Enugu most people rent rooms in houses privately built on plots laid out by the municipal authorities. Two-storey structures are more common than in most countries, and landlords owning several of these can now obtain a large income from them.

Peri-urban housing

This category is even more imprecise than most, since areas once marginal to a city may now be fully incorporated within it, and since settlement may thin out very gradually on the present urban fringe. It is, however, very substantial if it is taken to cover all housing functionally related to the city but built outside its jurisdiction in accordance with customary law. The extent and nature of such peri-urban settlement around each city depend on factors ranging from the general density of population to changes in the location of the city boundaries.

Up to 1966 the Kampala city boundary excluded the area occupied by the old Ganda capital, and half the people working within the city lived outside it. Here a form of private land ownership existed, and the owners not only constituted a peri-urban population themselves but also put up buildings to house migrants. Kisenyi, close to the old boundary and now an 'inner' area, was once described as 'a disgraceful slum in which profiteering landlords extort excessive rents for substandard accommodation' (Southall and Gutkind 1957: 43). Unfortunately, it has not improved.

In Lagos also the city boundary was still tightly drawn in the 1950s, and many people were then being housed in areas such as Mushin which lay outside it. The land was occupied perfectly legally, though haphazardly, and the buildings did not have to satisfy any municipal regulations (Abiodun 1974). Neither Kisenyi nor Mushin are therefore squatter areas, though they present many legal problems now that city boundaries encompass them. They are also peri-urban more in origin than in present character, as are some once rural settlements that have been engulfed by the expanding cities. Lagos provides few examples since its swampy surroundings were sparsely settled, but cities such as Enugu are gradually absorbing many substantial villages. Similarly, many people in Yaoundé, Bangui and Blantyre have become urban dwellers without moving from their formerly rural dwellings.

Peri-urban housing has also been established further away from both city boundaries and pre-existing villages, as small farmers find that they can increase their income by erecting shacks on their land to house city workers. For several kilometres around Kampala there are rather grand landowners' villas, with cars parked beneath the banana trees, but there are also many simple structures of mud and wattle or rusty metal sheets which are somehow divided up into several 'bedspaces' for the poorest migrants to the city (Muench 1978). To the northwest of Nairobi, there has been much housebuilding of equally diverse standards in the formerly rural area of Dagoretti, which is now within the city boundary, and in adjacent parts of Kiambu District (Memon 1982).

At prevailing income levels such settlement may be more satisfactory than any alternative. Most houses lack services such as piped water or electricity, and sanitation is of the crudest form, but at least densities are lower than in the city proper, while one member of the family can often grow some food while others are in – or seeking – urban employment. The scope for such housing systems is, of course, greatest around the smaller towns, where a population as large as that housed within the towns can live within walking distance. Unfortunately, around the larger cities either densities or travelling distances are likely to become intolerable without careful planning. Furthermore, it is in some areas of this type that the most acute forms of poverty and deprivation are found. There is therefore an urgent need for urban administrations to pay heed to the peri-urban areas, without imposing unattainable housing standards which force people to act illegally.

Squatter settlements and government responses

Squatter settlements, involving illegal occupation of land, figure prominently in the literature on 'Third World' urban housing, some writers seeing them as a problem for planners while others stress their positive features. However, few of these discussions relate specifically to tropical Africa, for until recently little squatter housing existed there.

In many cities, especially in West Africa, this is still so (Peil 1976), as it has been possible for much 'spontaneous' settlement to take place quite legally. Those wanting to acquire land can often do this through the traditional chiefs who control it everywhere except in the city centres. Furthermore, far more urban dwellers than in Latin America or South-east Asia prefer to rent accommodation, because they do not intend to stay permanently, and because entrepreneurs have made this available, sometimes at very low rents.

In most eastern African cities land could not be acquired so easily during the colonial period, but government powers were strong enough to prevent squatting. This became impossible after independence, and in cities such as Lusaka and Nairobi squatter housing has developed rapidly (Figures 13 and 20). Peil suggests stronger commitment to urban life than in West Africa as a reason, but the evidence on this is inconclusive. The lack of private rental accommodation, and continuing scarcity of land for those who might seek a livelihood by providing this, may be more significant.

Even in Lusaka and Nairobi squatter settlement differs from that in many cities elsewhere in the world, for by no means all residents are owner-occupiers. Many are tenants, who may not even know that the owner has occupied the land illegally. So although almost half Lusaka's inhabitants now live in squatter housing, many are not really 'squatters'. The proportion of owner-occupiers is probably even smaller in Nairobi, where 1600 structures with 7600 rooms had been built by 1971, housing over 35,000 people, in the Mathare valley (Etherton 1971, Ross 1973, Hake 1977). In the late 1970s a further huge area of rental rooms was established at Kibera by landlords whose legal claim to the land is highly dubious.

Stren (1975, 1982) has provided useful accounts of squatter

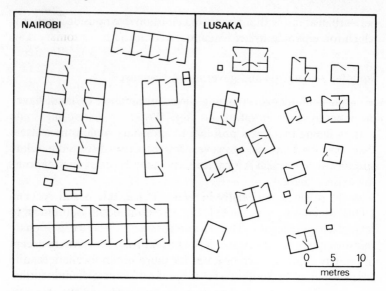

Figure 13   *Patterns of squatter housing*

housing in Dar es Salaam, where in-migration in the 1960s out-paced the municipality's capacity to provide even surveyed building plots. By 1972 some 28,000 squatter dwellings housed about 220,000 people, and by 1980 these figures had doubled. Building quality differs little between squatter and many non-squatter areas, but provision of services such as water supply and road access is much poorer in the former. Another example is the Ndirande area of Blantyre (Norwood 1972), which includes both ex-rural dwellings engulfed by the city and houses built illegally since it was incorporated within an enlarged boundary.

In Kinshasa the desire for one's own plot is widespread, but the extent of squatting, as defined here, is not easily determined. Many householders consider that they have obtained land in the suburbs in a proper manner from the local chiefs, but these arrangements have often had no government approval, and are supported by no documents (Kayitenkore 1967). Similarly in Luanda and Maputo there are large 'unauthorized' housing areas known as *musseques* or *caniços*, which contrast sharply with the very solid buildings erected by the Portuguese (Guedes 1971).

Even in West Africa some squatter settlements involving illegal land occupancy do exist. Vast areas of spontaneous housing have arisen around Abidjan, and while much conforms to customary law there are plenty of exceptions. In his study of Dakar, Vernière (1977) points not only to the relatively effective illegal settlements of Pikine Irrégulière, but also to the *bidonvilles* of central Dakar from which many Pikine residents have come. However, these have never been very extensive.

Discussions of squatter housing do not always note its diversity, though a few (e.g. Schlyter 1980, on Lusaka) present a much fuller picture than can be provided here. Some dwellings are crude shacks made from cardboard boxes; some make ingenious use of scrap metal and plastic; some depend on more traditional materials such as wooden poles, reeds and straw. Many have no water supply within easy reach, and some have no form of sanitation. Other squatter houses are as substantial as those of most urban dwellers (or rural dwellers), have at least pit latrines, and may even have an illegal hook-up to an electricity supply. However, there is little evidence of the consolidation, without government aid, that is widely reported from Latin America (Turner 1969, Ward 1978); and even the best provided of tropical African squatter settlements do not sprout a host of television aerials such as can be seen in Latin American *barrios* and even North African *bidonvilles*.

The residents   There has been much debate elsewhere on how far the squatters are new migrants or long-term urban residents moving out of inner areas. Many African cities have no inner city tenements which could provide reception areas as in Latin America, yet any notion of hordes of new rural migrants squatting in the cities would be quite false – except in times of war or drought. Most migrants go initially to wherever their kinsfolk are to be found, and many stay for several months. In new squatter areas, therefore, nearly all the residents have come from elsewhere in the city; but later on these areas may have rather more new arrivals, living as lodgers. Few adult residents are city-born, but that is true of the whole urban population.

In other respects too the residents differ little from most urban dwellers. The myth of squatter settlements as the hotbeds of crime and violence has been largely dispelled: one that persists is that they can be largely equated with the 'informal' sector of the economy. This is often not so, for many of the residents have jobs in the large-scale sector. However, many 'informal' activities are undertaken within these areas, often by the women. These range from rearing chickens to elaborately-organized beer-brewing enterprises (Nelson 1979b). Some illegal activities, such as extremely unhygienic production of stronger beverages, can be pursued more easily down these winding paths than in a government housing estate: but they are equally common in some legal peri-urban settlements, while in some squatter areas quite rigorous policing is undertaken by the local community, or – as in Lusaka – by local political party branches.

Negative and positive responses

The official colonial response to squatter settlements was often to ignore them, but if they threatened to grow rapidly they were demolished. This policy was generally maintained after independence, and Hake (1977) has shown the extent of the demolitions in Nairobi around 1968 to 1972. There were similar instances in Lusaka, while the authorities in Harare made short work of most attempts at squatting there up to the late 1970s.

These policies brought increasing criticism (e.g. Van Velsen 1975) as being both inhumane and ineffective. Rarely was alternative accommodation offered, so those evicted hastened to set up even flimsier shelters, in even more unhygienic conditions, on another patch of land. The view commonly expressed in newspaper editorials that they should return to their rural homes ignored the fact that some were long-established urban dwellers in regular wage employment. Reducing the housing stock must aggravate a situation of severe housing shortage; and such productive self-help activities as house-building merit encouragement. Pleas have been put forward around the world (Dwyer 1975, McGee 1976) for more positive approaches, and in Africa as elsewhere they have eventually been heeded.

In several cities housing areas that began through squatting are now so extensive and well established that the authorities have had to recognize them as permanent. In Dar es Salaam legal rights have been granted to many who built illegally in the 1960s (Stren 1979: 196), and basic services have been provided for 70,000 people in the Manzese area. Lusaka has also embarked upon a massive programme of 'squatter upgrading' (Pasteur 1979), which involves first the granting of legal occupancy rights and then provision of services such as roads, water supplies, schools and clinics. Such schemes, in

Lusaka and elsewhere, have been criticized from both ends of the political spectrum, either as condoning anti-social behaviour or as forestalling the revolutionary force of the poor. Criticism from the left has intensified following World Bank involvement (Seymour 1975). However, these projects have achieved some success (Martin 1982), and provide one of the most hopeful features in the African urban scene today.

Legalizing squatter housing tends to have a double impact in terms of amenity. Government can proceed with service provision, while residents have more incentive to make house and neighbourhood improvements, knowing that these will not be destroyed by city council bulldozers. It also enables strong community spirit to be preserved, and indeed mobilized.

This does not mean, however, that squatter upgrading provides an ideal form of housing provision. Squatter occupation is often clearly against the interests of the populace in general, and it undermines the rule of law. It is also more costly to bring public utilities to areas of irregular housing than to provide them in advance in new housing areas. Ways have to be found to accept existing settlements as assets without encouraging further squatting, and alternative solutions must be included in plans to overcome the housing deficit.

Site and service schemes

In many African countries governments have recognized that they cannot build enough houses for the growing urban population, yet they cannot permit totally uncontrolled settlement. Site and service schemes offer a compromise, and two laudable principles lie behind them. One is that something should be provided for many people, rather than everything for just a few. The other is that self-help initiatives should be encouraged, while the state concentrates on whatever individuals cannot do for themselves.

Generally government determines the location of the scheme, lays out individual plots, and provides access roads, piped water and sewerage, while the new residents undertake the actual house construction at whatever pace they can manage. In some schemes government has also constructed the core of each house in the form of a toilet and shower, and provided a concrete foundation for two or three rooms.

This approach has been adopted extensively in Lusaka (Martin

1974, 1975), where dwellings built in this way over the previous ten years accounted for 12 per cent of the total housing stock in 1973, and has continued alongside the squatter upgrading programme. It became the main low-cost housing strategy in Nairobi in the late 1970s (Muwonge 1980): a vast 6000-unit World Bank scheme at Dandora on the eastern outskirts was nearing completion in 1982, and more are planned. Harare has now also turned to 'core housing'. Its main limitation has been that it suits those aspiring to middle-class status rather than the very poorest, and Weisner (1976) has shown how many sites on Nairobi's scheme at Kariobangi were taken up not by the homeless but by entrepreneurs building in order to let rooms at extortionate rents. Nevertheless, in all these cities site and service schemes have eased the housing problem more than similar expenditure on conventional house-building, even where most of the occupants are now tenants of the plot-holders.

These schemes are not confined to eastern Africa. Despite the more flourishing commercial market in low-income housing in many West African cities, governments have intervened there also in order to accelerate housing provision or to make it more orderly. A well-documented case is the Cissin project in Ouagadougou, the Upper Volta capital (Bricker and Traore 1979). Some housing schemes within the vast Pikine suburb of Dakar (Vernière 1977) are also similar.

A strange feature of these recent site and service programmes is the frequency with which they are regarded as innovations, when comparable forms of residential development have occurred in many cities over several decades – as indicated earlier. Stren (1978) has described in some detail the 'village layouts' introduced by the British in Mombasa; and site and service schemes through which 6000 to 7000 plots a year were provided in Dar es Salaam in the early 1970s represent a continuation of a similar colonial pattern there. Systems of management are now, of course, very different, but the principle of individual enterprise within a basic planned framework is as relevant to the housing question now as it was then.

Conclusions

This chapter has indicated the complexity of the housing situation in African cities. Many components are involved everywhere, but the balance among them differs greatly from one city to another. Some have much government housing, others have little. In some squatter settlements are extensive, in others they are not. There are a few widespread features, however, in addition to those which simply reflect Africa's poverty.

One is the way in which new arrivals everywhere are able to lodge with kinsmen, even as complete families and sometimes for weeks or months. Another is the preponderance of renting rather than owner-occupation, and the frequency with which large households are renting only one room each rather than entire houses. Some landlords are wealthy, but most own only one or two buildings, and some are just as poor as their tenants. In Dakar, in Lagos, in Kinshasa and in Kampala housing for the majority combines features imported from Europe with features inherent to Africa. Even today the cities of indigenous origin are rather different, as are the cities where European interests were once totally dominant, but both are becoming less distinctive in housing patterns as in other respects.

Fortunately, Africa does not have many destitute pavement-dwellers such as are found in Calcutta and Djakarta. The unemployed are given shelter by kinsfolk, and will normally return to a rural home if they have outstayed their welcome before finding work. As regards the majority, the optimistic view is that while governments are largely failing to meet their needs, 'the system' is just managing to do so, whether through the private housing market or by a squatting process. To some extent this is true, and the literature largely neglects some widespread forms of housing because they are not seen to pose major problems. However, increasingly inadequate and expensive housing creates serious hardship for many people, while much exploitation can occur within apparently viable systems.

How far it is the state's responsibility to provide housing is a matter for debate worldwide, but all African national and municipal governments face severe challenges in respect of urban housing. More action is often required, but a large share of state funds cannot be allocated to housing the urban minority while rural dwellers are left to their own devices. The need for basic services is greater when people are living at urban densities, and there is much merit in both site and service and squatter upgrading schemes. These spread limited funds as widely as possible, using them for investments best undertaken on a large scale, and leaving individuals free to do those things which they can do for themselves. They will not produce very comfortable houses, especially if they aim at the most needy: but the eradication of poverty cannot be achieved by any housing policy.

The level of poverty is such that for the foreseeable future many urban families will see their housing need in terms of a room to rent rather than a house of their own. This is greatly reinforced by the widespread practice of building a house in the rural area to which one plans to return, though not all can afford to do this and in the future fewer may wish to do so. Housing is thus another issue which is, and will be, much affected in Africa by the nature of urban–rural relationships. This is the theme of a later chapter: meanwhile we shall examine the spatial structure of the cities, including some further aspects of residential patterns.

7 Spatial structures

The diversity of people, economic activities and types of housing in African cities are all reflected in their physical forms and spatial structures. Just as there are many differences among cities, so also within each there are contrasts from one locality to another. Knowledge of one neighbourhood or 'quarter' may give a very false impression of the city as a whole. Yet the extent of such internal contrasts itself varies greatly from city to city.

The physical form of the cities

One important set of factors is provided by the physical environment. The spatial structure of many cities has been influenced by a seaboard location, while others such as Khartoum (Figure 5) or Kinshasa (Figure 19) lie astride or beside a major river. The site of Lagos (Figure 14), originating on an island surrounded by lagoons and swamps, has severely constrained its physical growth, and created severe traffic problems. Freetown, strung along a narrow strip between mountains and the sea, faces a different set of constraints (Figure 23). Further examples are mentioned later.

However, these environmental factors are often particular to individual localities, and few generalizations about their consequences can be made even for groups of cities. They must be given close attention in planning decisions for each city, but in this overview emphasis is placed on those recurring spatial patterns which reflect ideas and attitudes – and the contrasting urban traditions outlined in chapter 2.

The greatest differences in physical structure, as in most respects, are between the pre-colonial cities and those which we have designated 'European' in origin. The Yoruba cities of Nigeria all share many features, while they differ hugely from cities such as Harare and Nairobi. They were designed by very different people, with very different aims and preconceptions. Among the contrasts in

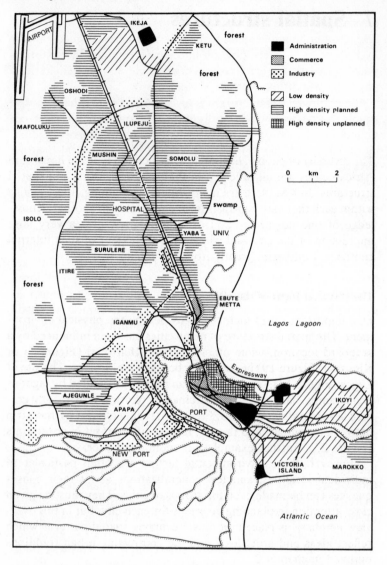

Figure 14   *Site and form of Lagos*

physical form is the fact that internally the Yoruba cities are in many respects more homogeneous than those that were designed entirely by Europeans – where division into zones occupied by particular people or particular activities was at one time sharper than in cities anywhere else in the world.

Some colonial and hybrid cities such as Accra or Kinshasa occupy simply a mid-way position, with contrasting zones but less clear-cut boundaries. However, we might again recognize a category of 'dual' cities, such as Kano (Figure 17), in which the physical contrast between the predominantly indigenous sector and the colonial addition has been so stark that these have often been regarded as two quite separate entities, each with its own internal structure, and almost functioning as separate systems.

These once sharply contrasting spatial structures may now be converging somewhat. There is increasing differentiation within Ibadan and a blurring of divisions in Nairobi, so that both are becoming more like Accra or Kinshasa in their physical form. Similarly, the components of the 'dual' cities are no longer as distinct in physical terms as in the past. Yet the contrasts are still such that we might begin by considering in turn each of the main urban traditions.

Morphology of pre-colonial cities

Yoruba cities   The physical form of Yoruba towns and cities has been described by several writers, notably Lloyd (1962), Ojo (1966a) and Krapf-Askari (1969). Naturally there are variations among them, for example, between the larger and the smaller, between the more northerly and the more southerly, and between those more or less affected by colonial rule; but many features are shared by most of them. Some are features considered by Sjoberg (1960) to be characteristic of pre-industrial cities in general.

Each city is very compact, with a high density of single-storey settlement and a relatively abrupt edge (Figure 2). This was traditionally marked by a wall, but often little of this survives. Krapf-Askari (1969: 39) likens their plan to a wheel, with the palace of the *Oba*, or king, at the centre, with the wall as the rim, and with roads radiating like spokes and dividing the city into several quarters or wards – each with its own identity but all very similar in appearance. Beyond the wall lie the farm plots (first *oko etile* and then *oko egan*) tended by the city-dwelling population.

The palace (or *afin*) generally provides the focal point of the city, especially when an adjacent market serves as a social centre as well as a trading place under the eye of the king. The palaces themselves vary greatly in nature (Ojo 1966b), some having very extensive grounds, and some having a range of administrative buildings within these. Many are built in the same local materials as other houses, and they normally rise only one storey higher than these.

To outside observers these cities may seem to be amorphous masses, for while each has an ordered structure this is based on kinship and lineage ties, and hence is not visible. All the quarters surrounding the palace tend to have a comparable density of settlement, compounds having gradually filled up with dwellings as families have expanded. Building styles and materials were once similar throughout, and although these are beginning to change, 'improved' houses are fairly evenly scattered. Trading and crafts are also widely dispersed, so that there are no distinct functional and residential zones.

This century has brought some change everywhere. Space has often been found near the centre for post offices and banks, while schools and hospitals have generally been located on the periphery. Whereas in the past there was little residential separation based on status or income, there is now usually an outlying zone of new houses occupied by people with education or wealth. Meanwhile, the older parts of each city remain little altered, so that the whole is much more diverse than in the past.

In Ibadan the colonial and post-colonial sectors are as extensive as the traditional sectors, though housing far fewer people (Figure 15). Some would now regard it as a dual or hybrid city in physical terms, since its compound structure has largely broken down and since so much has now been appended to the indigenous core (Mabogunje 1967b, 1968: chapter 9; Oyelese 1971; Aronson 1975).

Hausa cities   Much less has been written on the structure of the Islamic Hausa cities of northern Nigeria than on their Yoruba counterparts, though Dihoff (1970) has examined Katsina (Figure 2), and Urquhart (1977) has compared the physical form of Zaria with that of other northern cities. Traditional Hausa cities also have a clearly identified focal centre, a bounding wall, and buildings of fairly uniform character occupying most of the land in between. There is usually a triple focus, for in addition to the *Emir*'s palace

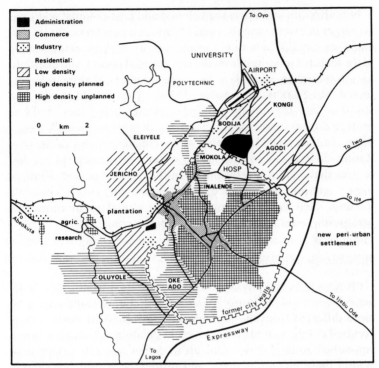

Figure 15   *Physical structure of Ibadan*

and the main city market there is the Grand Mosque, often an imposing building rising high above the generally even skyline.

Again, the city is divided into wards or quarters, and further subdivided into compounds, in each of which rights of occupation are passed down within a family. All compounds once included some cultivated land, though most families also had fields within and outside the city wall: but as the population has grown, ever more dwellings have been built within each compound. Narrow winding paths run between the compound walls, which often remain intact, broken only by a single doorway (Moughtin 1964, Schwerdtfeger 1982).

Minor markets and small mosques are spread through the various wards, and craft industries are also widely scattered, so that for many people residence and workplace are the same. Often, however, the colonial additions are physically even more separate than in most Yoruba cities.

In both Kano and Zaria the colonial and post-colonial additions are larger in extent than the original city, and now houses at least as many people, But in both places the old city or *Birni*, retains many of the features inherited from the pre-colonial period, and decisions have to be taken about how far these should be deliberately preserved (El-Shakhs and Salau 1979). They could simply be absorbed into the rapidly growing agglomerations; they could be protected from most types of change, with growth channelled elsewhere; or they could be adapted while remaining highly distinctive. Rather different decisions must be made in respect of smaller centres that were not rejuvenated in the colonial period. Some of these might now be expanded, either maintaining as far as possible the traditional framework, or creating new 'dual' urban centres by juxtaposing a set of very different urban forms.

Morphology of colonial and 'European' cities

With respect to the physical structure inherited from the colonial period cities such as Nairobi, Lusaka and Harare could hardly be more different from the pre-colonial cities of West Africa. They occupy far larger areas for a given population, although a broad peri-urban zone makes it difficult to define the truly urban area. Within these cities functional and residential sectors are sharply differentiated, and are themselves clearly subdivided. Distinct administrative, commercial and industrial zones can be recognized, while separate residential areas were originally established for each race. A further sharp division is now that between officially planned development and the spontaneous settlement which has sprung up since independence.

These are not 'dual' cities in terms of origin or overall layout, and all types of people converge on the same places of work, but the contrasting residential areas constitute distinct sub-systems within each city. Sections of Harare (Figure 4) and Nairobi, and also of Abidjan and Dakar (Figure 3), both appear and function much like high-class suburbs in Europe, while other sections have buildings and amenities comparable to those in many African rural areas. Forms of social organization within these areas also have more in common with the rural areas than with the elite section of the city. Recently, of course, increasing numbers have begun to earn their living within the low-income housing areas, so that in a sense these are increasingly becoming 'dual' cities (Hake 1977).

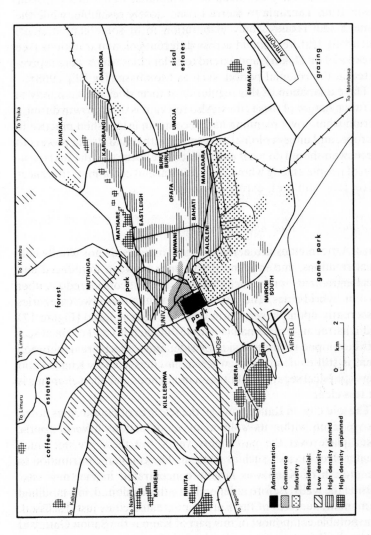

Figure 16 *Physical structure of Nairobi*

Many of these aspects of internal differentiation are found both in the larger cities such as Nairobi (Figure 16) and Lusaka (Figure 20), and in the smaller provincial towns (McMaster 1968). A model of a colonial up-country town can be formulated which many specific towns from Tanzania to Sierra Leone closely resemble, while the same model requires only elaboration to fit some capital cities. Recurring features extend across different colonial traditions (see Seck 1970 on Dakar), and extend to older cities which were rejuvenated in the colonial period, such as Mombasa (De Blij 1968).

The explanation of this regularity of form does not lie purely in the alien nature of these cities. Also relevant is their growth during a period when town planning had become an established practice in Europe, and under colonial governments that had strong powers to direct who should do what and where. It reflects, too, the juxtaposition of people among whom both cultural and economic differences were, (and still are), extremely wide.

Morphology of dual and hybrid cities

Most African cities are neither wholly indigenous nor wholly colonial creations, and in many the balance between introduced and local ingredients is now such that they are best considered as either dual or hybrid cities. The distinction between these two categories rests partly upon physical form. In cities such as Kano (Figure 17) and Khartoum–Omdurman (Figure 5) indigenous and colonial sectors developed separately side by side, and a sharp break between them is still evident today, whereas in cities such as Kumasi and Lagos physical separation between indigenous and alien elements is far less clear.

The 'old city' in Kano shows all the features of Hausa cities noted above. Even within its walls many modifications have of course taken place over the past eighty years, but these are not much greater than in cities such as Katsina. The colonial contribution to the growth of Kano was largely concentrated in the 'new city' outside the walls. Before independence this exhibited, in a modified form, many features of the European-created cities just discussed. One notable component of this part of Kano is the Sabon Gari, laid out by the British as the residential area for migrants from southern Nigeria. Much has now changed in such cities, but their form still makes it impossible to use such a term as 'the city centre'.

Some francophone capitals might also be considered dual cities in

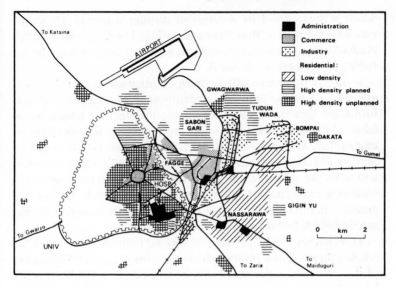

Figure 17   *Physical structure of Kano*

terms of physical structure, even when they were of colonial origin and never had an indigenous sector as independent as in Kano or Khartoum. The clear distinction between 'ville blanche' and 'ville noire' in such cities as Bamako, Brazzaville, N'Djamena and Niamey, often with an open space separating the two, has been emphasized by Vennetier (1976: 101), though he notes a blurring of the distinction since independence. It has been expressed even more vividly (for northern as well as tropical Africa) by Fanon (1967: 30).

The physical form of Lagos is more complex, and cannot be simplified into just two or three components. The original Yoruba settlement provides the historic core (Figure 14), but the ex-colonial administrative and commerical focus is immediately adjacent on Lagos Island, while all around there are diverse zones, some owing much to colonial initiatives and others owing rather more to indigenous enterprise.

As another hybrid city, Ouagadougou does not show a clear division between 'ville blanche' and 'ville noire', but has a somewhat cellular structure. The physical elements of the old Mossi capital have been absorbed within the 'modern' city, the centre of which is surrounded by a series of distinct 'quarters' set up by various groups of settlers (Skinner 1974). The Ethiopian capital, Addis Ababa, also has such a cellular structure, and alien influences there are very evenly diffused.

Today, in other basically indigenous cities the small European-created zone is becoming less evidently an appendage as 'Western' forms are infiltrating more and more through the whole urban fabric. Meanwhile, distinct zones are becoming less clear-cut in cities which were once essentially colonial. From Dakar to Dar es Salaam physical structures are becoming steadily more complex; and with the growth of large spontaneous settlements since the 1960s the same trend is apparent even in cities such as Lusaka and Nairobi. In physical terms most African cities are increasingly taking on hybrid forms.

This chapter will therefore now take up individual topics for the whole range of cities, rather than considering at greater length each of the particular types that could be so clearly recognized twenty years ago.

Patterns of land use

We have already seen that the extent of separation between land used for functional activities such as commerce or industry and land used for residential purposes varies greatly from one city to another. In general it is far greater in the cities of colonial origin than in those of indigenous origin, while in most cities some areas are entirely 'functional', some are entirely residential, and some are mixed. In every city most of the built-up area is either entirely or predominantly residential, but other categories of land use will be examined first.

Land use: administration

In the traditional towns of both south-western and northern Nigeria the palace is not only the ruler's home but also the seat of his administration. Similarly, there is a clearly marked zone of government offices in the centre of most African colonial cities and towns. Whereas this zone has changed little since independence in most provincial towns, it has altered greatly in most capital cities with the construction of new ministerial headquarters, and sometimes new parliament buildings. In many capitals, such as Nairobi, the administrative zone remains very clear-cut, for there was room for some horizontal expansion while vertical growth has also taken place. In others, such as Lagos, the extension of this zone has made it less clearly separated from the main commercial area. In others again, such as Freetown, lacking the space of horizontal growth and the funds for vertical growth, the old administrative area has been supplemented by another, far from the centre. In Lusaka a new administrative zone was established in the 1930s well away from the older commercial zone when it became Northern Rhodesia's capital (Davies 1969), and was planned in a spacious way which has allowed much recent growth.

A common recent development has been an expansion of the administrative zone into an adjacent area occupied by the houses of the former colonial officials. Some of these have been used as they stand for government offices, while others have been demolished to make way for new office blocks. Abidjan and Dar es Salaam both provide clear examples of such sequent occupancy (Figure 18).

The most interesting situations are those in the dual cities. Should they maintain two quite distinct administrative zones? Sometimes, of course, this reflects the much wider issue of whether to maintain two distinct urban (or regional) administrations. Generally the trend is towards greater integration, and physical separation of the two zones represents a minor stumbling-block in this. In some cities it may prove appropriate to consider total reorganization, and to use the pre-colonial administrative area for the integrated municipal government while the former municipal offices are taken over for national or regional administration.

Land use: commerce

In all cities commerce is diffused much more widely than administration, and in some African cities it seems to be taking place almost everywhere – and at most hours of day and night. A concentrated central business district can often be recognized, but there are many houses of which one room has become a shop. The diversity of commercial activity indicated in chapter 5 is often reflected in its spatial pattern. Thus dualistic structures arising out of the meeting of indigenous and alien cultures have often produced two distinct commercial foci, and even two distinct sets of subsidiary centres.

A large central market is a notable feature of most indigenous cities, and such markets are focal points even in highly modified

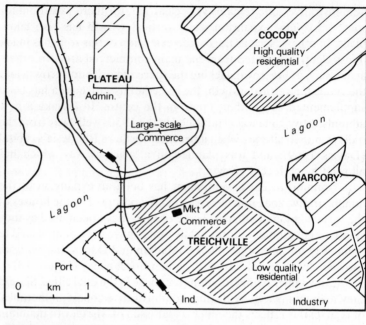

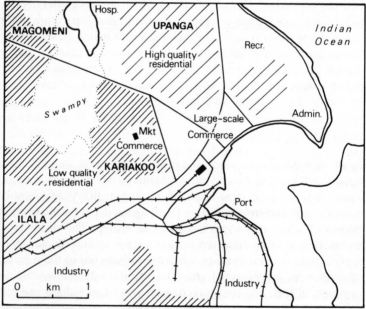

Figure 18   *Central area of Abidjan (above) and Dar es Salaam (below)*

cities such as Ibadan and Kano. However, these cities have a separate commercial zone in which most large firms (especially European and Asian firms) are located. In some places, such as Ilorin, this zone is almost on the edge of the city.

In many ex-colonial cities the same two elements are present but their locations are reversed. Foreign banks, commercial offices and shops occupy the heart of the city, forming a zone comparable to the 'CBD' identified in many studies of European and American cities. Often a small market within this zone serves the elite, but larger markets have been set up elsewhere. The Medina 'grand marché' in Dakar, and those at Treichville in Abidjan and at Kariakoo in Dar es Salaam are each within one of the earliest low-income residential areas (Figure 18). Originally they all lay well away from the 'city centre', but since independence the commercial centre of gravity has shifted towards these expanded and rebuilt markets, with new shops and even bank branches opening in the adjacent streets.

Kano is distinctive in having three commercial foci, for in addition to the traditional Kurmi central market in the old city and the largely alien business district outside it, there is the large Sabon Gari market in the area set aside for migrants from southern Nigeria. By the early 1960s this had overhauled the Kurmi market in number of stallholders and volume of business (Trevallion 1966). Kumasi in Ghana provides a clear contrast, for although it has one of Africa's largest markets, with 10,000 stalls on ten hectares (Garlick 1971), this lies very close to the large-scale business area.

Detailed studies of the central business district of three very different African cities have been provided by Smout (Kay and Smout 1977), De Blij (1963) and Mabogunje (1964). Smout shows how an elongated central business district has emerged in Harare, with specialized retailing around the peak land value area, more commercial and financial offices a little to the north, and wholesaling nearer the railway to the south. He also distinguishes a concentration of Asian-owned retail stores catering to a lower-income market in the Kopje area to the west.

De Blij demonstrates at greater length the way in which the commercial centre of Dar es Salaam grew up with an even clearer division between European enterprises in the east, towards the administrative area, and Asian enterprises in the west, towards the main African residential areas. This contrast is still evident today, although it has been somewhat blurred by changes since independence such as the nationalization of some formerly European-controlled enterprises. A similar contrast is quite evident in Nairobi, between the airline offices and motor showrooms on some streets and the Asian retail shops on others. A useful comparison of Dar es Salaam and Nairobi has been provided by Tiwari (1979).

In Lagos the role of traders of Asian origin has always been far smaller, but there too subdivisions of the main business district can be recognized. For instance, the financial centre lies to the south-east of the retail core, while wholesale establishments are concentrated to the north-west. In sharp contrast to Harare, the cramped nature of the central business district, the presence of many middle-income customers, and the existence for many years of an indigenous business class, have all encouraged the extension of retail trade in a belt along the main axis leading inland from Ebute Metta to Ikeja. This is far more helpful for shoppers, but it has greatly exacerbated the traffic problems discussed below.

In the cities of indigenous origin the main market is usually only the central feature of an extensive area given over to commercial activities. It is sometimes said that the largest of all such markets is that in Addis Ababa (De Young 1967), but there it is particularly hard to say where the market ends and the zone of 'shops' begins. In Ibadan commercial enterprises line all the roads radiating from the Oja Iba market, while at the same time there are numerous other markets scattered around the city (Hodder 1969). An account of the various markets within the indigenous half of greater Khartoum (i.e. Omdurman) has been provided by Kuhn (1970).

Even within cities such as Lusaka and Nairobi there is now a whole series of markets, some quite specialized and some meeting the general requirements of scattered residential areas. In Kampala there was by the 1960s a single system of markets that spanned both the largely indigenous and the largely colonial parts of the city (Temple 1969).

As indicated in chapter 5, attention can be unduly focused on two contrasting commercial systems – large-scale enterprises and market trade – at the expense of the rapidly-growing intermediate sector of small shops. These are catering not for a car-owning elite but for the daily needs of the broad mass of the people, and they must therefore be scattered through the residential areas even if this means more middlemen and thus higher prices. A most impressive mapping of their distribution in Kinshasa is included in the work of Pain (1979). There some concentration in the inner suburbs persists, so that many people in the new outer suburbs must walk far to make essential purchases. In Lusaka the 1968 legislation protecting African traders outside the central area from non-African competition has aided a particularly rapid dispersal of retail trade there. Most new neighbourhood traders are also already known to their clientele, and can feel assured of their custom, especially if they demonstrate their friendship by offering credit.

This spread of commercial activities away from the central area and a fixed set of market places reflects not only new needs as the cities have expanded but also new attitudes on the part of the municipal authorities. Policies of keeping residential and commercial areas quite separate are now seen to be inappropriate and impracticable. Even today many small shops are infringing planning regulations, but more and more often this is condoned, and in various cities restrictions are gradually being lifted. In many cases, of course, the new residential areas in which the shops are located are themselves illegal squatter areas: but in localities such as Mathare Valley in Nairobi the fact that many buildings are used as shops helps to produce genuine communities which the municipal authorities must accept as integral parts of the city.

While much information is now available on the spatial pattern of shops and markets in African cities, little is known on the extent to which the present distribution suits the needs of the city dwellers. There is much scope for studies of who uses which shops and why, whether in Nairobi or in Ibadan. Are the Sabon Gari areas of Kano and Zaria largely self-reliant in this respect, or is there much interaction with other quarters? Do shops in Omdurman draw many customers from Khartoum proper, and vice versa? Indeed, what are the spatial patterns of goods and cash flows from one trader to another? Answers to these questions will be necessary for a full understanding of African cities not just as static spatial structures but also as dynamic spatial systems.

Land use: industry

In the ex-colonial cities manufacturing is often highly concentrated within one zone, often known as 'the industrial area'. In Nairobi this extends southwards from the railway station, and in 1970 it occupied about 300 hectares (Ogendo 1972). In Dar es Salaam nearly all manufacturing is concentrated in a zone running inland beside the railway, apart from a group of factories at Ubungo and

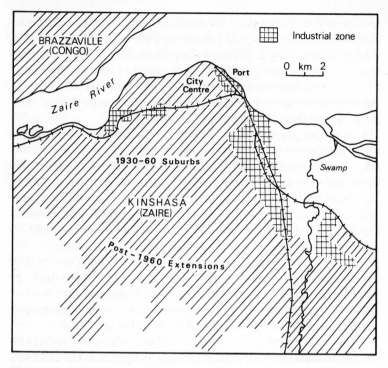

Figure 19   *Industrial zone of Kinshasa*

the oil refinery at Kigamboni. Kinshasa (Pain 1979) and Dakar (Seck 1970) each have one zone within which over 80 per cent of the city's industrial activity takes place (Figures 3 and 19), at least in terms of gross output. In each case, of course, manufacturing within the rapidly-growing small-scale sector is much more widely dispersed.

The separation of large-scale industry from other land uses reflects both its recent arrival and the existence of strong municipal planning powers at this level in such cities. Where manufacturing has provided a foundation for urban growth, as in Europe, it may be widely scattered through the urban area; but in these African cities it represents an addition to an existing urban structure, which has been channelled in a desired direction.

The establishment of new industrial towns as satellites of capital cities, as at Tema near Accra, Thika near Nairobi, and Kafue near

Lusaka, represents an extension of the same principle, though it does also enable more of the workforce to live within easy reach of the factories. Rapid urban growth may soon make other forms of industrial dispersion essential, for while a single zone may be accessible from most housing areas in a city of half a million people, it cannot be so in a city of several million.

Any plans to bring industrial employment closer to where people live would certainly accord with traditional African urban forms, for in the pre-colonial towns craft industry is even more widely dispersed than commerce. There is no industrial equivalent to the central market (or palace, or mosque), nearly all manufacturing taking place within or just outside people's homes. Bray's (1969) study of Iseyin in Nigeria illustrates this, for she mapped the distribution of various crafts. In all such towns certain industries are concentrated in specific quarters, either because they are the preserve of one group, or because, like dyepits, they depend on particular environmental features; but collectively they are highly scattered.

Once again, extreme cases have been presented to highlight contrasts. In several of the larger Yoruba cities there is now a 'modern' industrial zone as well as much dispersed 'traditional' manufacturing, while many people are engaged in tailoring or carpentry beside their homes in Accra and Freetown. Furthermore, such activities are now expanding in the new spontaneous housing areas within Lusaka and Nairobi. As ever, the distinction is really between two urban traditions rather than between two discrete sets of cities. The two patterns therefore exist side by side in Kano and in Khartoum–Omdurman, and the general trend is towards a blend between the two. Lagos, for example, has a highly complex pattern (including one industrial zone at Ikeja set up just outside its boundary by the former Western Region government).

The special case of the Copperbelt towns of Zambia and Zaire should be mentioned. Here vast areas are occupied by the mining companies for the mines themselves, for waste dumps, and for ancillary services such as railway sidings. The area occupied is increased by the fact that much mining is open-cast. The implications for the future spatial pattern of urban growth are very substantial, but are not discussed here since they are similar to those in mining towns anywhere in the world.

Other functional land use

Land is set aside in every city in Africa, as elsewhere, for other specific uses ranging from religious observance, health care and education to transport facilities. Many of the larger cities are ports, and much land is always needed for port operations. In contrast to many colonial cities in India, those in Africa generally did not have a large 'cantonment' for the army, but military barracks form an important component of some cities, especially where the military have seized power.

In view of the critical food shortages experienced in many cities, and the extent of unemployment, preservation of the maximum possible amount of intensive cultivation within the metropolitan area must be considered. The fields of Yoruba city families generally lie far outside, but most of the Hausa cities still have much farm land within the city walls. The situation is similar in some colonial cities such as Blantyre and Kampala, as well as indigenous Addis Ababa, much of the space between their clusters of houses being cultivated. In all types of city, patches of swampy ground, unsuitable for building, are used to grow high-yielding crops such as sweet potatoes, and almost everywhere scattered plots awaiting 'development' are used to produce a quick crop of maize. Furthermore, around most cities there is a peri-urban zone where dwellings are set among land that has long been used for food-crop cultivation, though some land has become so worn out that only cassava – many people's food of last resort – will grow on it.

Residential patterns

In nearly all cities, in Africa as elsewhere, most land comprises plots used primarily for dwellings, though with some private open space also. In most pre-colonial cities the home was also the workplace for many people, but over tropical Africa as a whole most of those 'gainfully employed' now work elsewhere. Large tracts can thus be regarded as residential areas, even though some small-scale trade, or other activities from craft industry to prostitution, may take place in some houses, and even though a little cultivation is undertaken around some of them.

Many questions might be asked about urban residential patterns. How great are the variations within cities in the density of housing and occupancy? How far do neighbourhoods differ in the provision of amenities? To what extent is owner-occupation, or renting, or squatting, concentrated in particular areas? How far are different ethnic or income groups separated? No Africa-wide surveys exist, but on each issue fragmentary evidence is available from individual cities.

The diversity in housing type, quality and tenure stressed in the last chapter does not necessarily imply spatial separation. Sharply contrasting types are sometimes found side by side in each area. In most cities, however, there is a high degree of spatial differentiation, often the result of deliberate colonial planning, but sometimes due more to spontaneous forces – or even an unintended result of environmental influences. In many cities low-, medium-, and high-density residential areas are officially designated, while often the location of the city boundary (present or past) has been a critical factor affecting residential patterns.

Each of the forms of housing discussed in chapter 6 tends to occupy a distinct zone, as was noted there with reference to the GRA in Nigerian cities. Dakar, Abidjan, Kinshasa and Dar es Salaam all provide examples of high-quality government housing close to the main administrative zone, and similar housing occupies much of Ikoyi Island in Lagos. The city council housing estates in Nairobi are all in a solid block in the east, and in Harare such government housing was highly concentrated in the south-western sector (Figure 4) until some more scattered estates were built in the 1960s.

Private employer housing is sometimes widely distributed, but on the Zambian Copperbelt mining company housing has been built on company land, so far removed from municipal housing that 'twin towns' have been created (Kay 1967a: 91). It is only since independence that Kitwe-Nkana or Chingola-Nchanga have really become single entities, and even now they remain sharply divided in many ways.

The spatial pattern of squatter settlement varies greatly from one city to another. In Nairobi it is highly concentrated in the Mathare Valley (Figure 16), partly because this offered the most suitable vacant site and partly because most pockets of squatter housing elsewhere have been demolished, whereas in Dar es Salaam it is highly dispersed. Lusaka provides an intermediate situation, for most squatter housing there is within about six to eight concentrated tracts around the edges of the city (Figure 20).

The data for renting and owning given in the last chapter (Table

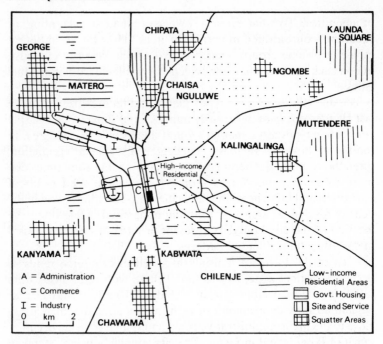

Figure 20   *Low-income housing areas in Lusaka*

15) mask great spatial variations within each city. In 1973 the majority of households in Khartoum City were renting accommodation, while the majority in Omdurman were owner-occupiers.

Before they were subject to strong European influence both the indigenous Yoruba towns and the Islamic Hausa towns of Nigeria were notable for their relative homogeneity in residential densities. In some cases dwellings were evenly spread throughout the town or city and ended abruptly at its walls. In other cases there were farmlands within the walls, but buildings ended just as abruptly at the edge of these. In towns such as Ife and Katsina the situation over much of the built-up area has still not changed drastically, although increasing numbers of 'strangers' do now live in areas of lower-density housing on their peripheries. In cities such as Kano, Zaria and Ibadan, however, there have been greater changes.

A survey in Kano in the 1960s (Trevallion 1966) indicated the lack of any marked density gradient within the old city from its centre to its edges, and average densities in its four main wards ranged only from about 300 to about 500 people per hectare. However, densities were twice as high in some of the areas outside the walls occupied by immigrant groups, while they were less than fifteen per hectare in the extensive tracts to the east originally built for the Europeans and known as the 'township'. In most parts of the old city Muslim families with their own land, reserving as far as possible a room for the husband and a room for each wife, lived at 1.2 to 1.6 per room, while the southerners renting accommodation in the Sabon Gari outside the old city lived at six to seven per room (perhaps a larger room?).

In Zaria, also in northern Nigeria, a later survey by Bedawi (1976) showed that the immigrant areas of Tudun Wada and Sabon Gari each had both more dwellings per hectare and a higher occupancy rate than the old city, so that their average densities of 600 and 850 people per hectare respectively compared with little over 100 for the old city. Within the old city many families still have large compounds, with gardens for food crops, whereas in the in-migrant areas landlords have used their land to house as many tenants as possible.

In cities such as Harare and Nairobi stark contrasts in residential density (and housing quality) have existed since their foundation. In Nairobi the 1962 census recorded 32,000 people living in the western sector, at only three dwellings and fifteen people per hectare. The Parklands-Eastleigh sector had some 80,000 people, with eleven dwellings and 120 people per hectare. Finally, the eastern sector housed 110,000 people, with sixty-five dwellings and 320 people per hectare. These contrasts persist today (Figure 21), and have become even more extreme with over 1000 people per hectare in the new squatter areas of Mathare Valley and Kibera yet little increase in density in some of the elite suburbs. Patterns have become more complex, however, especially as densities have increased in formerly rural areas beyond these western suburbs.

Lagos is quite representative of the colonial/hybrid cities. Sada (1972) has shown how densities rise there from 200 people per hectare on the northern outskirts, through 500 in Surulere and 700 in Ebute Metta, to over 1100 in the old core area on Lagos Island, but then drop sharply to under 200 per hectare on adjacent Ikoyi Island (Figure 14).

In tropical Africa as elsewhere densities tend to fall away from city centres, in line with land values and accessibility to jobs, but other factors have everywhere intervened to distort gravely any

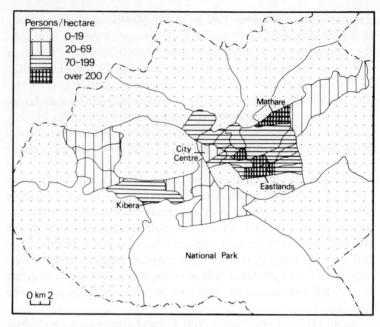

Figure 21   *Residential densities in Nairobi*

regular density gradient. Low-density housing is by no means confined to the fringes: it often occupies a wedge such as that running north-eastwards out of Accra, or that extending north-wards through Upanga to Oyster Bay in Dar es Salaam, in each case coinciding closely with the zone originally set aside for European occupation.

The housing in these zones is of high quality as well as low density, and in most cities there are sharp contrasts among neighbourhoods with regard to housing quality. The general picture for Dar es Salaam is presented in Table 16 and Figure 22. In Azania and Upanga most dwellings comprise at least three rooms, are sturdily built and have a full range of amenities. In some other wards over 70 per cent of dwellings comprise only one room, and many of even the five- and six-member households are living in such dwellings – with no piped water or electricity. Ayeni (1981: 134–6) demonstrates similar contrasts within Lagos.

The concentration of superior housing in certain parts of the city is naturally linked to a similar concentration of the high-income

Table 16 *Housing quality in the wards of Dar es Salaam*

Ward	Households (1967)	% with 2 or more rooms	With piped water	% with electricity	% with 'permanent' houses
Azania	1214	90	87	84	85
Commercial	2615	88	99	95	92
Upanga	2603	77	87	79	76
Kurasini	1329	65	70	43	52
Oyster Bay	2521	50	92	48	53
Kinondoni	7541	42	79	31	38
Temeke E	5342	40	47	8	28
Temeke W	9406	31	70	5	9
Changombe	5949	31	54	13	16
Magomeni S	9646	30	67	30	71
Magomeni N	6409	27	23	19	45
Ilala E	6801	25	63	38	47
Ilala W	9522	24	41	3	4
Kariakoo S	5046	23	50	37	14
Kariakoo C	4442	23	97	37	23
Kariakoo N	3042	13	92	28	11

Source: Tanzania 1967 Population Census, Volume 2, Dar es Salaam, 1970.

population. No specific data are available on this subject for any African city, but there is ample evidence to suggest that separation according to income is greater in eastern than in western Africa, and greatest of all in the 'European' cities. Peil (1981: 115) suggests that 'segregation by income appears to be much less prevalent in West Africa than in Europe', and that 'spatially separate housing is generally not highly valued by the wealthy'. Such remarks could not be made for Nairobi or Harare.

Residential separation of racial groups

In all tropical African cities there is some degree of residential separation of different races, although there is a wide range from the compulsory separation prevailing until recently in the cities of Zimbabwe to the much less clear-cut situation in Addis Ababa and Khartoum. Not only are the non-Africans in general localized, but where there are large numbers of both Europeans and Asians they tend to be concentrated in different areas. In East and Central

Africa this was official policy in the early years of this century, and it was only gradually that restrictions were lifted first in one country and then in another. In Nairobi they persisted until the 1950s, and in Kinshasa legal separation into European and African quarters remained until 1956.

This legislation partly reflected choices that people would have made in any case, and its abolition rarely brought sudden change. Even in West African countries where no restrictions existed there was a large measure of separation, both in the cities of indigenous origin and in those that were colonial creations. While cultural preference clearly contributed to this, it was massively reinforced by the consistently high economic status of the Europeans, which ensured that they were concentrated in areas of high-standard housing.

The trend everywhere since independence has been for reduced separation between Europeans and Africans as the new African elite has penetrated the former European residential areas, though the Europeans remain confined almost entirely to those areas. With regard to people of Asian origin in the cities of East Africa change is occurring more slowly, and they remain a clear majority in some districts. The families concerned have sometimes lived there for two or three generations, and often own the houses individually, while the local Hindu temple or Gujerati-language institutions provide no attraction for the new African middle class.

By the 1970s Harare and Bulawayo were exceptional in the way that they remained rigidly divided along racial lines (Kay and Smout 1977: 45–7). Up to that time Africans were not permitted to own property in most parts of the city, and were only permitted to live in the European residential areas if they were domestic servants. There were sufficient of these to ensure a substantial African population in every district, but over most of the city in 1969 Europeans formed a clear majority and there were virtually no Africans other than in servants' quarters. A total contrast was provided by Harari, Highfields and other 'townships', which were entirely African-occupied (Figure 4). The small Asian population was heavily concentrated in the central area, where some lived above their shops, and in the early post-war suburb of Arcadia. Even by 1980 the changes in this pattern were still slight.

In Lusaka and on the Copperbelt the divisions were once equally sharp, although the European areas were not quite so extensive and they have now been penetrated by Africans to a much higher degree. Similarly in Nairobi residential areas were specifically designated in racial terms throughout the colonial period, thus contributing to the marked compartmentalization of the city (Halliman and Morgan 1967). As late as the 1950s well over half the residential land was exclusively for Europeans (and their domestic servants), about a quarter for Asians, and a little over 10 per cent for the African population. Today Africans form a clear majority in all the former European areas, but the substantial European population is still found almost exclusively in this half of the city. The much larger number of Asians are even more concentrated, and in areas such as Parklands they still form a clear majority of the residents, though there has been a considerable African take-over further east in Juja and Eastleigh. A much higher proportion of the Asians than of the other groups are private land holders, and the heavy concentration of their holdings in Parklands, Ngara and Juja was clearly shown in a study by Kimani (1972).

In most West African cities the degree of racial residential separation is almost as great, though it is less important since the numbers of non-Africans are so much smaller. Europeans are almost entirely confined to the high-quality housing areas discussed above, though often divided between an old area close to the city centre and new sea-front or hill-top areas on the periphery. In Abidjan in 1975 Europeans formed 25 per cent of the population in the old Plateau zone and 14 per cent in Cocody, compared with 2.5 per cent in the whole city.

Rather than reviewing the pattern in city after city we shall conclude the section by considering one country rather more closely as a case study.

Table 17 *Racial residential separation in Dar es Salaam*

Households by ethnic origin of the head of household, 1967

Ward	Total	African	Asian	European	Arab
Ilala W	9151	9118	6	2	25
Magomeni S	9493	9414	21	5	53
Oyster Bay	2443	1945	66	408	24
Azania	1147	447	425	261	14
Commercial	2555	96	2421	12	26

Source: Tanzania 1967 Census.

The 1967 census of Tanzania gave a clear picture of the situation in Dar es Salaam, and it is doubtful if this has changed fundamentally since then (Table 17 and Figure 22). Eight wards were occupied almost entirely by African households, while nine had substantial numbers of non-Africans. Europeans were concentrated in four wards, but formed only a minority in each of these; while Asians were heavily concentrated in two central wards, and constituted over 90 per cent of the households in each. A comparison with figures for housing types, or a visit to the areas in question,

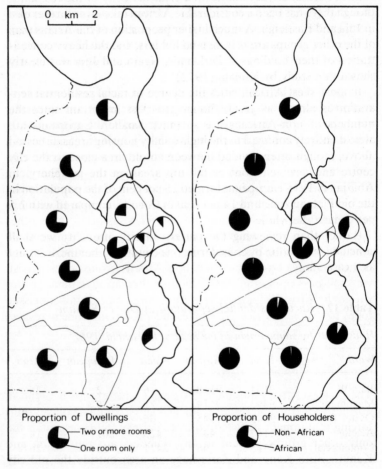

Figure 22   *Housing patterns in Dar es Salaam*

shows that the commercial zone incorporates a very homogeneous area of relatively large and solid Asian-occupied dwellings. Oyster Bay includes the highest class, largely post 1950, residential area with a very mixed population today, while Azania is an older area near the centre where both Europeans and Africans in government quarters live close to Africans in very poor quality private dwellings.

Similar patterns are repeated in the provincial towns of Tanzania. Mwanza and Morogoro each had one ward in which Asians were in a clear majority in 1967, while Moshi had one in which there were almost equal numbers of Asians and Africans (really a ward span-ning two different residential areas), and another in which most of the Europeans were concentrated, although only as a minority. Perhaps the most striking pattern is that in Zanzibar, where Asians formed a clear majority in two wards in 1967, Africans formed a clear majority in the other four, and Arabs were a sizeable minority in five of the six wards.

There would be no great difficulty in documenting the degree of racial residential separation in various other cities, or in investi-gating how far colonial legislation contributed to this in the past. It would be very much harder to establish how far its continuance is a function of mere inertia, of choice, or of other circumstances. Do affluent Europeans occupy certain areas because they are European or because they are affluent? Are Asians in East African cities strongly represented in some central districts because their shops are located there, or because they prefer to associate with other Asians? In the absence of any recent research on such subjects we could do no more than speculate. So, having noted that a high degree of concentration of such non-African groups does persist, we shall pass on to the distribution of the various ethnic groups within the African majority. This is possibly a more significant issue today for tropical Africa as a whole, and it is certainly one in respect of which even the basic facts are not easily established.

Residential separation of 'tribal' groups

The greatest separation among African ethnic groups is found in northern Nigeria, and results from distinctive colonial policies rein-forcing traditional practice. In the old parts of the Hausa cities the only other groups present in any numbers are the Fulani and Kanuri. Both Kano and Zaria have an area outside the old city known as Tudun Wada, which is also occupied almost exclusively by northerners, and another area known as Sabon Gari established early in this century explicitly for migrants of other ethnic groups. The separation in Kano in the mid 1950s was so sharp that Ibo accounted for 60 per cent of the population in Sabon Gari, and Hausa for less than 1 per cent (Paden 1971: 120). Since the Ibo exodus in 1966 each Sabon Gari has become much more mixed, but the distinction between Hausa and non-Hausa areas remains almost as sharp as ever. In Kano, for instance, they are really intermingled only in the newer suburb of Gwagwarwa and in the low-density ex-colonial 'township'.

In the Yoruba cities the few non-Yoruba tend to be highly concentrated, and here too government policy has contributed. Cohen (1969) has made an intensive study of Sabo, the Hausa quarter of Ibadan, which was set aside for this group in 1917 by the municipal authorities. The city council revoked recognition of Sabo as a specifically Hausa area in 1952 since this was seen as encouraging tribalism rather than national unity, and some recent Hausa migrants have had to seek accommodation with Yoruba landlords elsewhere, but this is generally in adjacent Mokola or Ekotedo.

This separation of Hausa, notable in cities such as Oshogbo also (Schwab 1965: 90), is encouraged by their sharp cultural differentiation from the Yoruba, and by their distinctive role as traders in kola nuts and cattle, while religious fervour also plays a part. No other group has such a distinct quarter in these cities, but there is some concentration even of Yoruba sub-groups, such as Ijebu in Ibadan (Aronson 1978: 31). Strong ethnic clustering is also found in Benin City (Onokerhoraye 1977).

A sharp contrast is provided by the ex-colonial city of Port Harcourt, where Wolpe (1974: 29) found 'an absence of communally segregated residential areas' despite a very mixed population. Even Lagos is more of a 'melting-pot' in this respect than the indigenous cities, though some concentrations are found there (Mabogunje 1968: 292–306). In 1952 Yoruba accounted for 92 per cent of the population on Lagos Island, and 83 per cent in Ebute Metta, but for only half in Apapa and Yaba. In Ikoyi only one-third were Yoruba, and slightly more were Ibo. Among the more recent suburbs Mushin and Agege have large Yoruba majorities, while Ajegunle is much more mixed (Peil 1981: 26). This indicates that ethnic separation is not just a matter of when each residential area developed; and in Lagos no legislation has been involved.

Ethnic identity has influenced where people live within the cities of Ghana also. In Accra there is still a high concentration of Ga people in the old central districts (Kilson 1974), and far more northerners are still found in the Zongo area that was set aside for them in the 1920s (Dinan 1975). The Zongo is even more distinct in Kumasi, where it has been intensively studied by Schildkrout (1978), though even there the degree of separation between local Asante and various stranger groups has steadily declined.

In Monrovia, Fraenkel (1964) estimated that about a quarter of the population lived in strongly segregated ethnic communities such as Vai Town and New Kru Town, leaving the great majority in ethnically mixed areas. There is some evidence of gradual increase of mixing, and it is notable that in Old Kru Town groups such as the Vai, Mandingo and Fante together now outnumber the Kru.

Among the major West African cities, Dakar seems to be that in which ethnic origin has least influence on where people live. The local Lebou are more numerous in the old Medina area than else-where, while the Toucouleur are best represented in the newer parts of Pikine: but that reflects time of arrival in the city rather than area of origin *per se*. The Wolof, who constitute about half the total city population, account for about half in almost every individual district also.

Some of the most detailed studies of ethnic patterns in African cities have been made in Zaire. A notable example is that under-taken in Kisangani (when it was still Stanleyville) by Pons (1969: chapter 4). He mapped the distribution of nine distinct groups in one part of the city, finding some highly dispersed and others far more concentrated in particular areas.

Possibly to a greater degree than anywhere else, the layout of Addis Ababa is based upon quarters (*sefer*) originally allocated to specific ethnic groups or sub-groups. Even today the city 'is a collection of ethnic *sefers*' (Shack 1973: 260), with some neigh-bourhoods occupied largely by people from one rural locality.

In the cities of eastern Africa where race used to influence resi-dential patterns so profoundly, ethnic differences within the Afri-can population have tended to be less significant than in at least parts of western Africa. In Nairobi many localities have a mixture of Kikuyu, Luo, Luhya, Kamba and other inhabitants fairly rep-resentative of the city as a whole (Ross 1975: 21). However, the decrease in the proportion living in government housing and the increase in both squatter settlement and other forms of private housing has brought some increased differentiation. Some parts of

Mathare Valley have a very mixed population, but other parts are occupied almost entirely by Kikuyu, as are many of the peri-urban areas west of the city.

Among the Nairobi housing estates, Kaloleni is often regarded as a Luo area and serves in many ways as a focus for Luo social and political activity (Parkin 1978: 36–42). The Luo do not in fact form a majority there, but in 1969 they accounted for 39 per cent of the total, while a further 26 per cent were Luhya and only 14 per cent Kikuyu. The concentration there of both Luo and Luhya is largely explained by the fact that the estate was built in the late 1940s, just before the exclusion of Kikuyu from the city during the Emergency.

Hirst (1975) examined the distribution of migrants in Kampala on the basis of 1969 census birthplace data, and found a remarkably complex picture. Again there is some concentration of Luo, here in the eastern parts of the city both on the housing estates and in private peri-urban settlement as at Namuwongo. The main differentiation in Kampala, however, is between all the areas which have long lain within the municipal boundary, and which have an ethnically very mixed population, and the areas around the former Buganda capital which lay outside the boundary until 1966 and which are overwhelmingly occupied by Ganda.

The unusually small significance of ethnicity both in Dar es Salaam and in the cities of Zambia, noted in chapter 4, is reflected in residential patterns, for in none of these cities are there any marked concentrations of people according to ethnic group. The similarities of language and custom among most groups no doubt contributes to this, but in Zambia the nature of the residential areas is also an important factor. As long as most people were accommodated in mining company housing or on city council housing estates they simply took what was offered. This seems to have influenced attitudes subsequently, for the diversity of ethnic groups seems almost equally great within each of the recent squatter settlements. The early squatters in each area seem to have been so mixed that even the common tendency for later settlers to join kinsmen has not brought any marked concentrations. In residential patterns as in other ways Lusaka certainly seems to be more of an ethnic melting-pot than most African cities.

In Harare the vast majority of Zimbabweans are Shona but there are substantial numbers of other groups who have come in from Malawi and Mozambique. It is notable that these accounted for 28 per cent of the African population in the 'European' areas of the city in 1969, but for only 9 per cent in Highfields township (Kay and Smout 1977: 43). It would be interesting to know how the greater mixture of Shona and Ndebele in Bulawayo are arranging themselves but no information is readily available on this.

Throughout this discussion the emphasis has been on ethnic clustering on a fairly broad scale. It is important to note that it is sometimes more evident on a very local scale, especially within large ethnically-mixed spontaneous settlements, where a family from one area often attracts others to the immediate vicinity. On the other hand several studies indicate that multi-ethnic occupation of individual buildings is much more common in many cities than might be expected (Schildkrout 1978: 129–33, Peil 1981: 116). A probable reason for that is the hesitation people may feel about extracting rent from members of the same group. Tenants from other groups may be taken in preference so that the maximum rent can be charged.

Even on a wider scale the clustering may not always be entirely the result of personal preference. We have noted certain cases where it was encouraged by government policy, and others where a concentration of one group simply reflects their presence there as a community before the city grew up around them. Many factors other than sheer sentiment are also relevant, such as the difficulties of living where one's own language is not understood, and more specifically a wish to live where one's own language is used in the local primary schools. Conversely many areas are ethnically mixed not because this issue is of less concern to their inhabitants but simply because they are government housing estates where ethnicity is not a factor in the order of allocation, or where people must accept whichever house falls vacant.

Problems of people and land

Closely related to the spatial structures of the cities are the links between man and land within them, and some specific mention must be made of four issues that would demand close attention in a truly comprehensive review of African urbanization. These are land ownership; the provision of physical infrastructure such as water supply and sewerage; circulation within the cities; and the general significance of the natural environment.

Each is only briefly discussed here since none is peculiar to cities. The physical environment impinges even more directly on the life of most rural dwellers; problems of communication and access are even greater for them; and services such as safe drinking water and electricity are available to even fewer people in the rural areas than in the cities. There is indeed no discussion in this book of some of the very real problems of African urban dwellers, such as inadequate education facilities and the high incidence of disease, since these are in no way specifically urban problems, nor in general are they problems exacerbated by urbanization. Certain environmental problems perhaps differ somewhat in that they are intensified in the urban situation. Thus whereas most farmers in Africa live close beside their fields, many urban dwellers must make long daily journeys to work, sometimes because accommodation in the vicinity of major employment foci is too expensive: and the way in which high-density living intensifies the problems of lack of effective sewage disposal is all too evident.

Land ownership or tenure is also an issue of increasing significance in rural Africa, but rarely is the situation as complex as in most cities. It is to that topic that we turn first.

Land ownership

Very little has been written on land ownership in African cities as a factor influencing urban structures. The subject is strangely neglected in most sociological as well as geographical studies. Most published work concerned with urban land is of a technical nature, relating to the legal procedures involved in land transactions. A rare exception is Lloyd's (1962) monograph on the structure of land holding in Yoruba towns. A sharply contrasting situation is examined by Kimani (1972), whose work on Nairobi covered both land tenure and spatial patterns of land values. Further discussions for eastern Africa are provided in a symposium volume edited by Kanyeihamba and MacAuslan (1978), and, returning to West Africa, Haeringer (1969, 1973) has provided useful studies of Abidjan and Douala. These, however, are mere fragments in relation to the enormity of the subject.

Patterns of land ownership are often extremely complicated within each city, as well as differing markedly from one city to another. Many complications arise as a further consequence of the meeting of local and alien cultures, for systems transplanted from Europe have often been superimposed on indigenous systems. This means that there are frequently two claimants to each tract of land;

and in some cases national government, the municipality, traditional authorities and private individuals all lay claim to the same tract.

In most traditional African tenure systems land is not owned by individuals, but is held in trust for the community by local chiefs, who allocate it to families for their use. Normally this means for farming, but the same principle may apply to tiny plots on the city margins sought largely for a dwelling place. Houses are regarded as personal property, and may be bought and sold, but this does not extend to the land on which they stand.

Such traditional systems are now changing in many areas, even where they have not been totally replaced by imported systems based on private land ownership. Thus much land within Lagos and Accra is held in small blocks by individual families, who now consider that they may sell it as private property even though they may have no documents to support their claim to it (Barnes 1979). Yet in the core of both these cities whole communities retain a strong group attachment to land, inhibiting individual sales, and creating great problems for attempted 'slum-clearance' schemes. Outright individual ownership is more common away from the centre, with a highly competitive land market developing and many businessmen now engaging in land speculation.

Various forms of leasehold were established by the British as the norm in northern Nigerian cities, partly because this matched reasonably closely the customary view of individuals having just rights of occupancy. Some land could be leased from the local authorities for up to thirty years, and other land leased from the central government for up to ninety-nine years: but there were also tracts over which both authorities claimed jurisdiction, and a planning report on Kaduna (Lock 1967) described the situation there as a 'thick legal jungle'.

An unusual situation is that in Monrovia (Fraenkel 1964), where almost all land within the city limits is owned freehold by individuals. The original settlers from America were allocated 'town lots' 150 years ago, and many remain in the hands of the same families. Some had small Vai villages on them, so that these villagers have had to pay rent ever since, while others have been used for commercial and even government buildings, thus bringing handsome incomes to the landlords. Such features of Liberian life led to the 1980 coup, and the land tenure pattern in Monrovia may now be changed drastically.

The only country where an indigenous tenure system put large urban tracts firmly into the hands of private individuals is Ethiopia. Such landowners played a large part in the growth of Addis Ababa, amassing much wealth from rents, until all urban land was nationalized in 1975 after the revolution. The former owners were then each given only usufruct rights over 500 square metres, with no compensation payments.

In various other countries traditional tenure systems were totally displaced within the emerging urban areas when colonial rule was imposed. Sometimes the government became the owner of the land, much of which was then leased out to individuals or companies for both commercial and residential use. This pattern prevailed in most of the 'Colonial' cities such as Dakar and Kinshasa, and continues to operate today.

In the 'European' cities, however, much land passed into private freehold ownership. Kimani's study in Nairobi (1972) covered just over half of the pre-1963 city area. He found that 23 per cent of the land was in government ownership, 20 per cent was owned by business organizations, 9 per cent by other organizations, 22 per cent by individual Europeans, 22 per cent by individual Asians, and just 4 per cent by individual Africans. Much of the remaining city land is probably in some form of public ownership, but even so the large share of the total in private non-indigenous ownership presents a serious dilemma for policy makers.

The complexities of the land market in two African cities are demonstrated in theses by Bobo (1974) and by Muench (1978). Muench shows how two largely separate systems operate side by side in Kampala. About 20 per cent of transactions are officially recorded and fully documented while about 80 per cent take the form of verbal agreements, all technically illegal, which initially save both time and money but which often lead later to disputes. Bobo shows how the prevalence of customary land law in the central Ussher Town and James Town areas of Accra has made it almost impossible for large-scale commercial enterprises which operate in the neighbouring central business district to acquire land there. He suggests that over much of the city uncertainty about property rights has discouraged investment in construction and thus aggravated the housing shortage. It is quite clear that in both Kampala and Accra, as in many other cities, government would like to control all transactions in land but has nothing like the administrative capacity to do so.

It is also clear that land ownership is a difficult and delicate subject to study in most African cities, not only because so much is unrecorded but also because the widespread illegality makes people reluctant to discuss it and because the frequent disputes can arouse so much hostility. Yet further study is essential as a basis for policy decisions, whether these incline towards increased regulation or towards increased recognition that informal systems must inevitably continue to operate over large areas. Meanwhile we must recognize that discussion of topics ranging from squatter settlements to industrial zoning in African cities requires very careful thought about any assumptions that are being made in respect of land tenure.

Provision of basic services

The availability of an adequate water supply has been a factor affecting the location of all types of towns all around the world, and has certainly been important for both pre-colonial and colonial town building in Africa. More recently it has had to be taken into account in selecting the sites for the new capital cities of Nigeria and Tanzania, though neither site is ideal in this regard.

There are many cases, however, where urban growth has far out-run the capacity of local sources of water, and where large capital investments have had to be made in alternative sources. In Zimbabwe a dam completed in 1954 on the Hunyani River has created the large Lake McIlwaine mainly to supply water for Harare. In Sierra Leone the very high rainfall experienced by Freetown is so concentrated in part of the year that severe seasonal water shortage was a regular occurrence until the building of the Guma Dam. A useful review of the urban water supply situation in Nigeria has been provided by Oyebande (1978), who notes the serious deficiencies that remain in spite of substantial government expenditures.

If the provision of an adequate supply of water to each city is one dimension of the problem, another is its distribution to the potential consumers. Large-scale industrial enterprises and institutions such as hospitals and schools are generally linked into the municipal distribution network without great difficulty, but the situation is very different for the great majority of individual households. Even in cities where there is an ample supply in macro terms, as in Kinshasa beside the great Zaire River, many households have either to use highly polluted local streams or to make long journeys to the nearest municipal standpipe. Some indication of the small proportion of houses in various cities that have their own water supply was given in the last chapter. An extremely useful discussion of the alternative sources used in a number of East African towns and cities is provided in White *et al.* (1972):

The very poor toilet facilities, and even their total absence, in many houses were mentioned in the last chapter, since they constitute a very real part of the 'housing problem'. However, the subject must also be raised here since sewage disposal constitutes a major problem for each city as a whole, and since there are generally marked contrasts from area to area within each city. This is one field where 'Western' technology has very clear advantages over indigenous systems, which are adequate enough in a rural environment but quite unsuited to high-density living. Every city has therefore established some form of water-borne sewerage system: but whereas in Harare and Nairobi it extends through the greater part of the urban area, in Ibadan it serves only a minority of the population and in some other Nigerian cities it serves less than 20 per cent of the inhabitants (Sada 1977). Such a system is costly to establish anywhere, but it is particularly difficult in an area of pre-existing unplanned settlement, where installation would cause much upheaval.

In view of the continuing rapid growth of the population of most cities the prospects of providing a water-borne sewerage system for all are very dim, yet the existing pit latrines (or bushes) constitute a serious health hazard (Onyemelukwe 1981). There is thus an urgent need for the application of intermediate technology in this field, and also for selection of the best among the methods used in the indigenous cities for use elsewhere.

A further health hazard, and a further contributor to the stench in many areas, is provided by household refuse for which there are no disposal arrangements. The dimensions of this problem in parts of Lagos have been outlined by Sule (1979). As in many other cities, refuse lorries regularly visit the central administrative and business zones, and the high-quality residential areas, but very little effort is made to clear refuse from the areas where most people live – even those areas which have reasonable road access.

Circulation within the cities

In the cities of the richer nations one of the most critical physical problems is that of intra-city transport, and its improvement is normally one of the main preoccupations of the planners. In most African cities its relative importance is rather less, and priority should be given to other issues such as water supplies. None the less some effort and funds must be devoted everywhere to transport, and the needs tend to increase in geometrical progression as the cities expand.

In the indigenous cities from Nigeria to Ethiopia movement took place almost entirely on foot. Both the compact nature of these cities and the fact that most people's home was also their workplace kept to a minimum the amount of walking that had to be done. Most urban growth resulting from European initiatives has occurred in the context of the availability of motor transport, at least for those who could afford it. This has been a major factor in the sprawling nature of such cities as Harare and Lusaka, and even of the colonial extensions of such cities as Ibadan and Zaria. In many cities, from Abidjan to Nairobi, a satisfactory road system has been perceived by the administrators as a priority issue, even though the majority of urban dwellers may not have shared this view, and adequate provisions have been made. The outstanding exception is Lagos, which has become infamous for its traffic congestion, especially since the proliferation of private cars that has followed the oil boom (Adefolalu 1977, Ayeni 1981). There even the elite are suffering, as a ten-kilometre journey to work often takes over two hours, and more people must miss their flights from Lagos airport than from any other airport in the world!

In a survey of traffic conditions in many cities Thomson (1978: 234–43) suggested that in Lagos 'the situation must rank among the worst in the world', as a result of a difficult site, rapid physical growth, and lack of both the finance and the planning machinery to respond. Until 1970 only a single bridge linked Lagos Island to the mainland, and while a second bridge and a new road linking the docks to the new industrial areas and the hinterland have provided some relief, huge problems remain. Among the 'human problems' listed in a discussion by Sada and Adefolalu (1975: 103) are reckless driving, obstructions caused by breakdowns of poorly-maintained vehicles, dubious ways of obtaining driving licences, and the failure of the police to deal with offenders. These problems are, of course, not peculiar to Lagos, and may soon become serious elsewhere too.

Large sums are now being spent on new roads to relieve traffic congestion in Lagos, but perhaps equally valuable would be investment in ferry services and in making better use of the railway. Furthermore, a given road network could be far more efficiently used with the help of an appropriately expanded and improved bus system than with unlimited use of private cars. The issue of public versus private transport is one faced in cities throughout the world: in Lagos, as in all African cities where only a small minority can afford private cars, the case for an emphasis on public transport is overwhelming. Whether the politicians and planners together accept this remains to be seen.

However, the problems of circulation within the cities do not depend just on how efficiently people and goods can be moved over given distances. They depend also on the layout of the cities, and the needs for movement which this layout generates. In African cities which have still to experience most of their physical growth it is especially important to adopt this wider perspective.

In most cities the chief problems are arising from the combination of African income levels and European ideas on separation of home and workplace. In some cases people have been shifted out of homes near the city centre and have been offered, or have just been expected to find, alternative homes on the outskirts, while employment opportunities have remained highly concentrated. In Dakar severe transport problems are felt not by the elite who drive to work from residential areas such as Fann, but by the masses who have to travel over fifteen kilometres from the vast low-income areas of Dagoudane–Pikine (Vernière 1977). Large numbers of private mini-buses as well as some municipal buses make this possible, but transport accounts for almost 20 per cent of the income of some workers. The situation is similar for workers travelling into central Abidjan from such suburbs as Abobo, and into central Kinshasa from Ndjili and Kimbanseke.

Even in these cities many more people make nearly all their journeys on foot, as in the indigenous cities a hundred years ago. On the outskirts of cities from Ouagadougou to Kampala, the flood of crowded buses and taxis between 7 and 8 a.m. is preceded by processions of people trudging in along the roadsides, many having left their homes in the peri-urban zone before 6 a.m. In addition to those coming in to work there are the children and teenagers coming in to school; and in Ouagadougou there are also many people carrying loads of fuel to city markets.

In some of the cities of the Sahel animal carts are widely used for moving goods within the cities and between the cities and their rural hinterlands, and in a few places donkeys are either ridden or used for carrying loads. Over tropical Africa as a whole, however, the bicycle is now far more important as a mode of transport intermediate between motor vehicles and movement on foot. It seems that no study has ever been made of bicycle movements in African cities (nor indeed in African rural areas), and such study is long overdue. It is clear from casual observation that the cities differ remarkably in the extent of bicycle use. For example, within West Africa they are most prolific in the francophone capitals, while few are used in Monrovia or Accra. It is also clear that the availability of more bicycles at lower cost would greatly improve the quality of life for many people.

The most effective way of reducing transport problems is often not investment in improved transport facilities, but the location of homes, workplaces, shops and schools in such a manner that essential movements are reduced to a minimum. From this point of view both the proliferation of local shops and the growth of small-scale employment within spontaneous housing areas are to be welcomed. Modification of the colonial pattern whereby most manufacturing was concentrated into a single zone would bring such employment within easier reach of new and scattered suburbs.

Lengthy commuter journeys should then be necessary only for those who choose to maintain a semi-rural home with sufficient land for food production. Others, living closer to their place of work, should be able to save their transport expenditure for the periodic visits to a home area which most are so keen to make. Africa's future cities could involve less wasted time, effort and expense in personal travel than cities elsewhere: they could also build on their citizens' evident willingness to travel in order to preserve valued urban–rural linkages (chapter 9). Both notions imply deliberate planning of spatial patterns rather than simply allowing market forces to operate from the basis of existing structures.

Problems of the natural environment

Throughout the world cities are places where the direct impact of the natural environment on people's lives is reduced, as the built environment assumes so much significance. This was brutally demonstrated in the Sahel zone of West Africa in the 1970s, when thousands of people flocked into the towns to escape the threat of starvation brought by extreme drought. Indeed, the relationship of African farmers and pastoralists with the natural environment is so intense that it might be argued that environment affects the cities largely through the rural component of the rural–urban system upon which attention is focused elsewhere in this book. For example, not only drought but also soil erosion and degradation may force farmers to seek alternative sources of livelihood in the cities, while favourable environments in such areas as the Kenya highlands encourage successful city dwellers to invest in farms for their later years.

Nevertheless, there are numerous ways in which the natural environment is of direct concern for life in the cities, ranging from permanent features such as coastal forms suitable for port construction to periodic events such as earthquakes and floods which may cause far greater loss of life where people are concentrated than in thinly settled rural areas. Some of these are in no way peculiar to Africa, so that, for example, geomorphological conditions favouring port development or geological conditions affecting water supplies, will not be discussed here.

Several cities face severe problems as a result of their location on a site that was entirely suitable for a small settlement but is highly unsatisfactory for a metropolis (Figure 23). The most obvious example of this is Lagos, the core of which lies on an island largely surrounded by lagoons and swamps (Figure 14). Throughout this century expansion has been taking place on to other islands and on to the mainland, but the terrain has severely constrained the directions of this expansion. One result has been the development of a major axis of growth northwards to Ikeja, and gradual intensification of the most appalling traffic congestion along this axis. The swampy land to the east and west provides scope for the construction of alternative highways – but only at enormous cost.

The problems posed by the natural environment at Lagos have been sufficiently severe for this to be a major contributory factor to the decision to build a new capital city elsewhere. This decision will not prevent further physical growth in Lagos, but it will reduce the rate of growth and allow rather more times in which to tackle some of these problems.

The site of Abidjan is in some respects similar to that of Lagos, and

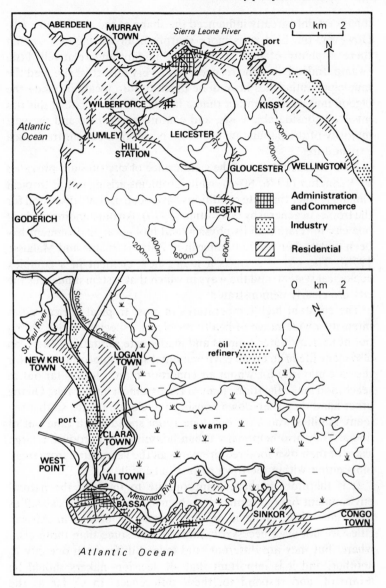

Figure 23   *Sites of Freetown (above) and Monrovia (below)*

it has certainly greatly influenced the shape of the city (Figure 18). However, the land rises more sharply from the lagoon, so that there is plenty of firm ground for building and relatively little swamp. Indeed, in some respects it is a very attractive site, and the municipal authorities have done much to turn location beside the lagoon into an asset rather than a liability. Unfortunately, this has involved considerable costs, and continues to do so, and the vast majority of the population are in no position to benefit from such expenditure.

Further illustrations of the significance of city sites are provided by Vennetier (1976: 80–5), while problems arising out of tropical climates rather than site conditions have been usefully discussed for the tropics in general by Giacottino (1979). An outstanding study of one city in relation to its physical and biological environment has been undertaken for Lubumbashi in Zaire (Leblanc and Malaisse 1978). The city is seen as a major new element in a complex ecological system, and the ways in which that system influences the city are clearly demonstrated.

The constant high temperatures in most tropical African cities intensify a wide range of health problems, especially those arising out of unclean water sources and inadequate sanitation. They can also make life in an urban environment distinctly uncomfortable for the vast majority for whom air conditioning is a luxury far out of reach, and make the traffic jams of Lagos almost intolerable. On the other hand they keep down housing and clothing costs, so that the many families who have only one room spend much time out of doors. They also help many urban households to produce a large share of their own food requirements all the year round from small plots either within the town or just outside it.

It is therefore perhaps inappropriate to think of the natural environment only in terms of problems. It sustains life as well as sometimes threatening it. Environmental conditions in African cities are not even necessarily more troublesome than those elsewhere: but they are different, and indeed differ from one city to another, and it is important that all decision-makers should be aware of, and respond to, these differences. In so far as the decision-makers are the inhabitants themselves there is normally no lack of awareness, though people may lack the technical knowledge to respond in the most effective way, especially when the circumstances of urban life are new to them. This awareness is not always so evident among those drawing up plans for the cities, whether they be expatriates from Europe and America or even government officials from another part of the same country. It is critically important that housing schemes, health services, and even policies with regard to employment and incomes (as well as the more obvious water supplies, sewerage schemes, etc.) take into account particular local natural environmental conditions. The rapidity of urban growth, the lack of financial resources, the acute problems of poverty facing so many people, all increase the need for the pattern of urban development to be one that is in harmony with these conditions to the greatest extent possible.

Physical planning

The present physical form of the cities results from the interactions among a wide range of decision-makers – colonial governments, independent governments, municipal authorities, private firms, local communities and millions of individuals. All have made plans and have attempted to implement them: so it could be said that a great deal of planning has taken place everywhere. However, there are immense differences between cities such as Nairobi, where the whole layout has resulted from governmental plans for the entire city ever since it was first established, and cities such as Ibadan, where the decisions of individual families have always had a major influence, and government plans have produced only modifications of the resulting structure.

This is another respect in which there are signs of some convergence between cities of different traditions. In Ibadan and some other indigenous cities increasing efforts have been made since independence to institute effective large-scale planning, albeit with limited success (Onibokun 1970, Green 1979), while in most of the cities of European and colonial origin comprehensive planning has had to be abandoned, and replaced with a combination of outline plans for the whole city and detailed planning for selected parts of it. This latter situation is clearly exemplified by Abidjan, where the response to the surge of growth that far exceeds what the authorities can handle has been to maintain colonial building standards and to provide a correspondingly high level of services in certain areas while the people of other areas are left largely to their own devices. A rather different policy has been adopted in Dar es Salaam, where there is a measure of control throughout but not at the same intensity as in the colonial period (Segal 1979).

Accra is particularly interesting in this context, for it is in some ways quite typical of African cities and in other ways unique. It occupies a representative intermediate situation in the extent to which government planning has influenced its total physical form. It is also fairly typical in that the colonial government prepared several physical plans for the city, but within the broad structure thus established there were always various areas where development was largely spontaneous, and the extent of (officially) unplanned growth increased after independence.

One of the more distinctive features in comparison with many colonial capitals is the existence of an indigenous core area very close to the main business centre where local community opinion has prevailed over the ideas of the government planners. In other words a number of Ga families have had their own 'plans' for this area, generally involving a minimum of change, in the same way that much larger numbers of local residents have resisted official plans for redevelopment in Ibadan. The most distinctive feature of all, on the other hand, is the establishment within greater Accra of the 'new town' of Tema, where government planning has been more intense and comprehensive than anywhere else in West Africa. There is a widespread tendency in the social science literature to label all such government schemes as failures, but although life is far from perfect for the residents of Tema, and although there is little to be said in its favour aesthetically, this large-scale government initiative has achieved a good measure of success. In the context of the broad outlines of city structure the success has been in establishing a large community within 20 kilometres of the centre of Accra which is not a dormitory suburb involving commuting on a massive scale, but which rather has provided both homes and jobs within easy reach of each other.

The very rapid rate of urban growth, the very limited resources of all municipal authorities, and the basic human wish for freedom combine to rule out comprehensive government planning of who does what where in the cities of tropical Africa. But the same considerations make the determination of some broad guidelines for the spatial pattern of physical growth absolutely essential. The limited resources increase the need for people to live in areas where services can be provided at reasonable cost and for economic activities to be located in such a way that transport and other costs are minimized. The rapidity of the growth puts extra strain on these resources, causes great pressures from competing interests which may require adjudication, and means that unsatisfactory patterns may very quickly be consolidated to such an extent that they will be very difficult to alter. Even the wish for freedom on the part of numerous individuals may be better satisfied with the aid of some indicative planning, for otherwise people may be trapped in conditions that are far from what they would choose.

Some of these issues are common to many parts of the world, but the specific circumstances of tropical Africa, and often of individual cities, require distinctive planning responses – and planning mechanisms. Existing mechanisms are in fact extremely diverse, and there is an urgent need for a comparative study of these, building upon fragments such as have been provided by Safier (1967) and Green (1979), as well as for publications indicating possible lines of advance.

However, we must also note the very limited capacity for urban planning in most African countries, the difficulties of just establishing – not to mention reconciling – the views of all the interested parties, and the very limited resources for implementing even those programmes which all might agree to be desirable. The physical form or spatial structure of each city is therefore being influenced to a very large extent by the planning decisions of a few foreign firms and thousands of local individuals or families, rather than by officials of any town planning department.

Conclusions

African cities remain highly diverse in their spatial structures, this diversity reflecting contrasting indigenous and alien urban traditions. The separation of residence and workplace, for instance, is much more extreme in some cities than in others. In many respects, however, convergence is now taking place, as new distinctive land-use zones emerge in the cities of indigenous origin, or are attached to their fringes, and as formerly sharp dividing lines are blurred in the cities designed by Europeans. Even within what were once very clearly 'dual' cities the indigenous sector is now being 'Westernized' while the sectors laid out by the colonial authorities are being Africanized.

Physical planning policies must respond both to the contrasts and to the convergence. The most distinctive problems facing all those involved in determining the future form of tropical African cities probably lie in the historical legacies (El-Shakhs and Salau 1979).

Each type of city presents its own challenge. Neither the form of the indigenous cities nor that of the cities designed by Europeans primarily for Europeans is well suited to the needs of African countries in the 1980s. However, there are widely differing views on how far the physical structure of Ibadan needs to be changed, with many residents of the core area resisting any suggestion that this area requires wholesale 'redevelopment'; and there are also widely differing views on whether steps should be taken as rapidly as possible to break down the rigid divisions built into the spatial structure of Harare.

Particularly interesting cases are presented by those cities which still retain a dual structure. Should this be preserved? Does it have merits in offering people a choice of environments in which to live and work? Or should greater integration be sought even at the risk of replacing diversity with drab uniformity? Can physical planning for each part of such cities, and for their new quarters, provide 'the best of both worlds'? Urgent decisions must be made in view of the speed of urban growth, and these must tie in with decisions regarding in-migration, the urban economy, housing systems and so on for each city as a whole.

The greatest challenge of all is presented by the new cities that are being built as a result of planned change in the national urban system. The most ambitious of these developments is at Abuja where a new capital for Nigeria is rapidly taking shape without even a small town as a nucleus. The hope is that its spatial structure will offer the ideal blend of Nigerian and imported elements.

The plans for Abuja prepared for the Nigerian government by an international consortium of consultants are too complex to be summarized here. They may in any case be greatly altered as construction proceeds, for spatial structures will always reflect evolving social and economic structures. Since these cannot be predicted with any precision, subject as they are to forces ranging from the global economy to individual whim, there is little chance that any 'Master Plan' could, or should, be closely followed. For any student of African urbanization, however, the spatial structures that do emerge at Abuja should be of immense interest.

The decision to create such a new city was, of course, also an exercise in spatial planning, though at a very different scale. Spatial structures at that scale are the concern of the next chapter.

8 Urban systems

Earlier chapters have considered cities as individual entities, but all cities and towns form part of an urban system, involving much interaction. Chapter 2 did discuss the distribution of urban centres, and the issue of primacy within national urban systems was mentioned there, but linkages among cities were not considered. These merit a chapter of their own, even though very little information on interaction among African cities is available from published sources, and little research has been undertaken on the subject. Expositions of the general theme of urban systems have been provided by Berry (1964) and others, and patterns in 'advanced economies' have been reviewed by Pred (1977). The most valuable contributions for less-developed countries in general have been those of Friedmann (1973), while Obudho and El-Shakhs (1979) have brought together a set of papers which begin to explore the African situation.

Three sub-themes must be taken up in any discussion of this subject. Firstly, the notion of an urban system extends to a variety of scales, from local through national to international and intercontinental. Our concern here is primarily with national systems of cities, but there is much scope for study of local systems of small urban places, and also for work on the links of African cities with those elsewhere. Secondly, all urban systems are constantly changing, and in tropical Africa there were dramatic changes as colonial structures were superimposed on pre-colonial systems. After a relatively stable phase as colonial rule was consolidated, independence has brought renewed change. Thirdly, all urban systems involve diverse elements, the links ranging from flows of people and goods to the transmission of messages and the spread of ideas. Some linkages are basically economic, while others are cultural or political.

One notion present in much discussion of urban systems in developed countries and equally applicable in Africa is that of an urban hierarchy. Its application in Nigeria has been demonstrated by Abiodun (1967) and more briefly by Ajaegbu (1976: 55–7). It involves recognition of many small centres which perform a similar limited range of functions, and which depend on fewer larger centres for more specialized functions. These are often district or provincial headquarters, which in turn depend on the capital city at the top of the national hierarchy. For colonial urbanization the principle clearly extended to the position of the metropolis above the African capitals; and it remains highly relevant at this inter-continental scale even today. At all levels, of course, such hierarchical spatial structures are reflecting hierarchical power structures.

The notion of dualism is also relevant in this context, since the new urban system set up by the Europeans did not always obliterate indigenous systems of central places. In some areas the two have co-existed, only partly integrated, for decades. They can still represent spatial forces pulling in opposite directions, one dispersed and tied to the local soil, the other highly concentrated and tied more closely to London or Paris.

Countries such as Burundi and Gambia have the simplest systems, with just one city and a series of local centres that are barely urban. Others, such as Senegal and Tanzania (Figure 25), have a fuller hierarchy, with at least two levels of urban centre below the capital city. Some have distinctive systems due to particular local circumstances, such as Zambia with its Copperbelt cities forming a counterbalance to Lusaka. Finally, there are the more complex systems developing out of the dualistic situations just mentioned, Mali providing one example but Nigeria constituting much the most complex case of all (Figure 26).

Before these national systems are examined more closely, they should be placed in their international context.

The international urban system

Most aspects of life in Africa are still profoundly influenced by decisions made far away in Europe and North America. There is now a massive literature on such dependency, past and present, much focused on Latin America but some concerned explicitly with Africa (Amin 1973, Arrighi and Saul 1973, Gutkind and Wallerstein 1976, Ake 1981). The influence of Europe on Africa throughout the colonial period was of course exerted largely through the cities of London, Paris, Brussels and Lisbon. Indeed much of the influence could be narrowed down to Whitehall and the

Quai d'Orsay, though some operated through business firms based not only in other parts of London and Paris but also in Liverpool and Marseilles. Within the colonial territories too, the influence was channelled largely through urban centres despite the low level of urbanization. In some cases pre-existing urban centres served the purpose, but more often a new urban system was created specifically for the exercise of colonial authority. So not only are African urban systems closely linked into the international system, but to some extent they were established as a deliberate extension of it. Adams has dealt with this theme in a thesis which unfortunately remains unpublished, and summed up the situation in a brief paper by observing (1972a: 116): 'West Africa, at the present time, has two primate cities, London and Paris.'

The nature of the influence exerted from Europe through the international urban system has, of course, changed since independence. There is no longer a chain of command from Colonial Office officials in London through subordinates in Dar es Salaam to even lower subordinates in Mwanza or Tabora. Nevertheless, the influence remains substantial, even in the political realm; and in some economic affairs there has been little change, as exemplified by the continued operation of London-based banks in Sierra Leone or Zambia. No African countries have as yet opted out of the world capitalist system to the same extent as Cuba or Kampuchea. Contrary to popular belief in some quarters, Dar es Salaam retains strong ties with London, while both Luanda and Maputo retain even stronger ties with Lisbon.

One widespread change has been a widening of the range of international contacts from the ex-metropolis to other parts of the 'developed world', which may be seen as African countries exercising freedom or merely as external control of African affairs passing to other European countries, to the USA, and to the USSR. However, this in no way reduces the urban orientation of the relationships, for it means that Lagos, Kinshasa and Nairobi have much increased interaction with New York, Washington, Moscow and Zurich. As Kinshasa diverts some contacts away from Brussels as ex-colonial capital, other African cities increasingly look towards it as EEC headquarters. Even wider networks have been newly established, especially by the larger African countries, in the field of international diplomacy, and again this operates entirely through urban centres. Links with the United Nations and its agencies are likewise links with New York, Geneva and Rome.

Within each African country the movements of people, goods, money, messages and ideas involved in these international contacts are still channelled through the towns and cities as strongly as ever. Furthermore, the role of the capital cities as compared to that of the smaller towns is now greater than ever. In the past, London had many direct dealings with both Kaduna and Kano: by the 1970s nearly all Nigeria–UK relationships were channelled through Lagos. Similarly, Lusaka's role in the international transactions of the Zambian copper industry has increased since independence. The numerous foreign embassies naturally congregate in the national capitals, and negotiations even on rural projects with FAO or the World Bank are conducted there.

Africa's international relations are therefore highly relevant to the extent and rate of urbanization in each country, to its nature, and even to its spatial distribution. 'Urban' implications can be readily seen in discussions such as that by Mazrui (1977). Yet little research has been undertaken on these implications, and virtually nothing has been written about them. One deterrent is perhaps that the research would have to be a large-scale comparative operation. It would be extremely hard to determine just how international relationships were influencing urban development in Kenya, Tanzania, Ivory Coast or Mali as individual cases; but comparisons might be much more revealing.

The international links are, of course, not all with the 'developed world'. There are weak links with Latin American cities, and rather stronger links with various Asian cities, as well as the intra-African ties that will be considered shortly. Each connection in the vast interlocking global system is of potential interest. To what extent do the activities of Indian traders create an urban sub-system extending from Kisumu through Nairobi and Mombasa to Bombay? How strong are the connections now between Khartoum and Kuwait? Tanzania and China may share many ideas about rural-based development, but actual relationships may be characterized by a deal made in Peking to supply bicycles made in Shanghai and shipped to Dar es Salaam for eventual use in both city and countryside. However, for tropical Africa as a whole such relationships with Asian cities are far weaker than those with cities in Europe and North America.

Intra-African relationships

While many cities in Europe have the important links with African cities mentioned above, they have even closer ties with cities in neighbouring countries. A notable feature of the African scene is that such intra-continental links are often very weak. While Abidjan and Accra do have some relationships with each other, those with Paris and London respectively are far more intense, despite the vastly greater distance involved. Adams documented the international telephone network in West Africa in the early 1960s, and found that many cities could only link up through London and Paris. This was still being quoted in the late 1970s when it was in fact no longer true, especially following the advent of satellite communications: but the general point remains, that many African cities remain better connected in various ways to cities in Europe than to cities elsewhere in Africa.

This is, of course, not just failure to modify the colonial inheritance: nor is it just perversity. There is little evidence of a large unsatisfied demand for better communications among African cities. The matter really runs much deeper than mere physical links, for it reflects the whole orientation of African economies, as well as the distribution of economic and political power. In terms of a crude gravity model, the fact that Abidjan interacts so much more with Paris than with Accra, ten times smaller but a hundred times nearer, might appear an anomaly: but if wealth is also taken into account the anomaly largely disappears. With respect to more widely separated African cities, such as Freetown and Lusaka, there is little reason to expect much interaction.

There are dangers of exaggeration with regard to the lack of linkages among African cities. In some cases where the more easily measured connections such as telephone calls and airline flights are less than might be expected, other important channels of communications do exist. Many of the goods sold in Banjul have come from Dakar, but not all have passed through the border customs posts, for overland links within the 'informal sector' are quite strong. A dramatic case is provided by Brazzaville and Kinshasa, which face each other across the Congo/Zaire River (Figure 19). Ever since independence formal relations between the two countries, and therefore the two capital cities, have been strained: but one cannot gain a full understanding of the city of Brazzaville without paying heed to its many, often clandestine, relationships with Kinshasa.

Furthermore, while there clearly is no closely integrated 'African' urban system, various regional systems have been inherited from the colonial period. The French administered their West African territories very largely as a single entity, through the city of Dakar, reducing direct links between Paris and cities such as Abidjan, Bamako, Conakry or Cotonou. Independence weakened the bonds within this West African urban system, though to sharply varying degrees. There is now very little interaction between Conakry and Abidjan, or even Conakry and Dakar, but Bamako and Dakar remain closely tied, as do Ouagadougou and Abidjan. A similar mixture of continuity and change may be seen in links among the cities of the former French Equatorial Africa.

Comparable situations were created by the British in East and Central Africa. While Dar es Salaam and Kampala were each at the apex of a territorial urban hierarchy, both were subservient in many respects to Nairobi. The growth of both Nairobi and Mombasa during the colonial period owed much to the existence of an integrated East African urban system, though they have survived its recent collapse remarkably well. This is another instance where continuing links may be stronger than is officially recognized. Nairobi may no longer perform administrative functions for East Africa as a whole, or even house an East African head office for many commercial and financial enterprises, but purely personal ties ensure that Dar es Salaam and Kampala are still influenced by all that happens there.

The pattern of urban development in Zimbabwe, Zambia and Malawi has been influenced by their common administration as the Federation of Rhodesia and Nyasaland from 1953 to 1963, as well as by subsequent political changes. It remains to be seen whether Harare, Bulawayo, Lusaka and the Copperbelt will once again become closely linked in the 1980s. The Malawi situation is especially complex, not only because it lacks a single dominant capital city, but also because its urban centres have strong ties with those in both Mozambique and South Africa as well as those in Zambia and Zimbabwe.

The lower levels of the urban hierarchy

Relationships among the major towns and cities within each African country are influenced not only by the international urban systems of which they are components, but also by the national

settlement systems which they dominate. There is a dearth of literature on the numerous very small urban centres in Africa, but rather
more exists than is sometimes suggested. Some publications are
case studies of a particular issue such as local political processes in a
small-town setting (Hopkins 1972, Vincent 1971), but others consider the towns' role as central places and as intermediaries between
the cities and the countryside. Three East African examples are the
early study in Uganda by Larimore (1959), and the more recent
studies in Kenya by Henkel (1979) and by Hjort (1979). Useful
papers have been provided by McMaster (1968), Taylor (1974) and
Funnell (1976), while further material for Kenya has been provided
by Obudho and Waller (1976). In francophone Africa Auger
(1968) has explored this subject in Congo, while a collection of
papers has been produced on the very small towns of Ivory Coast
(ORSTOM 1969). Most recently, a symposium volume and a
special issue of the journal *Africa* (Southall 1979) have been devoted to the subject.

The impression gained from these studies, and from travelling
around the countries concerned, is that substantial efforts were
made by the colonial authorities to extend their urban systems into
the African countryside, and to provide central places for administration and trade within reach of the majority of the population.
There is, of course, scope for debate as to whether this was a
basically benevolent or malevolent process. Both administrative
posts and trading centres may be seen either as providing valuable
services or as aiding exploitation and extraction of surplus, whether
by government tax-collectors or by pernicious businessmen. It is
quite clear to this writer that both sets of processes have operated,
and totally unclear as to which has predominated even in given
areas, let alone in tropical Africa as a whole.

Another general impression is that these systems of small central
places were often established with little reference to pre-existing
patterns of settlement and pre-existing political and economic systems. The colonial decision-makers were sometimes unaware of
these, sometimes simply ignored them, and sometimes deliberately
avoided getting involved in them. Case studies of the processes
involved are provided for western Kenya by Obudho (1976) and for
Sierra Leone by Howard (1975). The result is often a dualistic
situation, whereby, for example, a pattern of trading centres has
been superimposed upon a pattern of traditional markets which
has continued to operate within its own spatial framework. These

market systems, on which there is a substantial literature (e.g. Bohanan and Dalton 1962, Hodder and Ukwu 1969, Meillassoux 1971) are normally wholly indigenous in origin and in operation, while outsiders have not only planned, but also largely operated, the superimposed system. Throughout East Africa, for example, the businessmen who set up shop in the small trading centres, bought local produce, and brought manufactured goods from the towns, were largely Asians (Ghai 1965, Bharati 1972). In parts of West Africa people of Syrian or Lebanese origin performed the same role (Van der Laan 1975), often penetrating far into the countryside.

A further element in the situation in most parts of Africa has been provided by the missionary societies, for their dispersed mission stations have also become focal points within local settlement systems. Being concerned not only to spread the Christian faith but also to provide education and medical facilities, they have been major agents of the types of social change often associated with urbanization. In some countries their medical and educational functions have now been taken over by the national governments, but in others they continue as in the past. A common intermediate situation is that in which the state has taken responsibility in the major cities, but the missions are still critically important in service provision in many rural areas. In this way they function quite explicitly as a link between the cities and the mass of the rural population.

A major planning decision now facing many governments is how much effort should be made to integrate these various elements in the spatial systems of rural Africa, thereby establishing a more coherent network of central places rather than separate systems of markets, trading centres and mission stations. New opportunities to achieve integration are being provided by changes such as increased government involvement in educational and medical provision, the forced departure of alien traders from certain countries, and their voluntary withdrawal from the small trading centres to the larger towns in others. The departure of Asian traders from many rural areas in East Africa might be ending the dualism of traditional and superimposed trading systems, though it is unclear how far they have been replaced by local people or by entrepreneurs from elsewhere in the country. Also of potential importance is the 'localization' of churches, and the addition of new elements in the field of social service provision, such as the Harambee schools of Kenya.

Kenya is the country which has given most attention to the lower end of the urban hierarchy in its published development plans. The

1970–4 plan stated that 'the Government recognizes that the concentration of all economic, social and political life in the two main
cities carries dangers of an economic and cultural gulf being created
between them and the rest of the economy' (Kenya 1969: 85).
Included in the plan document was a list of over 800 places designated as urban, rural, market and local centres, the aim being to
provide a local centre for every 5000 rural population, a market
centre for every 15,000, a rural centre for every 40,000, and an
urban centre for every 120,000. This policy remained prominent in
the 1974–8 and 1979–83 plans, each of which included a revised
schedule of these service centres.

While Kenya was planning this extension of the urban system
downwards from the capital city, Tanzania was engaged in its
renowned transformation of the structure of rural settlement. Soon
after the Arusha Declaration of 1967 rural dwellers were encouraged
to abandon their customary highly dispersed pattern of settlement
and to congregate in villages, and in the early 1970s encouragement gave way to persuasion, and then for a while force. By 1976 the
majority of the rural population were living in designated 'villages',
and although not all had actually moved their homes at least 6 million
had done so.

These planned villages vary greatly in size, but the largest house
over 10,000 people, far more than the smaller urban centres
identified in the Kenya programme, and rather more than Tanzania's own long-established minor towns and trading centres.
However, because they were seen as part of a 'rural' development
strategy very little attention was given to their potential role in
providing services for the people of smaller villages, and equally
little to their relationships with these existing minor towns and
trading centres. In contrast to the massive involvement of government in re-planning rural settlement, and some clearly stated aims
for the larger urban centres, the neglect of the elements in between
the two is remarkable.

For a third case study we turn to Ghana, where a comprehensive
survey of the urban hierarchy down to the smallest local service
centres was undertaken in the early 1960s by Grove and Huszar
(1964). The situation there differs from that in both Kenya and
Tanzania because of the existence of much more nucleated settlement that pre-dates colonial rule. In some areas traditional settlements were large enough (including traders and craftsmen) to be
considered small towns, a notable example being provided by the

ridge-top settlements of Akwapim, twenty-five to forty kilometres north of Accra (Brokensha 1966, Middleton 1979). Each of these now has a resident population of a few thousand, but each has also provided many migrants to the cities who always refer to them as their 'home-towns'. Policies for the lower levels of the urban hierarchy in Ghana must distinguish between these indigenous settlements and others of similar size but of colonial origin and thus quite distinct character.

National urban systems and urban primacy

The facts that African cities have close links with cities elsewhere in the world, and that no sharp distinctions can be made between the smaller urban centres and 'rural' central places, do not undermine the proposition that clear national urban systems have now emerged. In some countries these incorporate sub-systems that were already well established before the colonial period, Nigeria providing the most obvious example. Elsewhere the whole system was created by the colonial authorities. In every case the system has been reinforced in a variety of ways by the attainment of independence, and it now plays a vital role in the processes of nation-building and national integration – which are priority issues wherever disparate peoples co-exist within the arbitrarily defined boundaries of ex-colonial states.

The question of urban primacy was introduced in chapter 2. We noted that in most African countries the urban system is dominated by a single primate city (Table 4), though the idea that this is in some way abnormal was rejected. It was also suggested that the extent of such primacy is increasing, even in simple population terms, and that it is probably much greater in respect of phenomena other than population numbers: but evidence on these points was left to this chapter.

Twenty years ago *Nigeria* was notable as a country without a dominant primate city in simple population terms, but Lagos has rapidly assumed that position since independence. Its population is now probably three times higher than that of any other Nigerian city (Table 2). The lack of reliable census data increases the need for other indicators, and these all tell the same story. Even by 1963 manufacturing employment in Lagos was 21,000, compared with 6000 each in Kano and Kaduna, and only 3000 in Ibadan, out of a national total of 68,000. By 1970 Lagos accounted for 58,000 of the

Nigerian total of 130,000. The capital's share of national electricity consumption also increased during the 1960s from 41 per cent in 1960/1 to 47 per cent in 1971/2.

Widening disparities are even clearer in the case of telephones. Working lines in Nigeria increased from 24,000 in 1962 to 45,000 in 1972, and increases in many cities were of around 50 per cent (Ibadan 2610–3650, Kano 1560–2550, Enugu 1290–1740, Kaduna 1080–1480); but in Lagos the number rose from 5860 to 20,540, and even this did not satisfy the demand. Finally, an increase of bank branches in Nigeria from 173 in 1960 to 301 in 1972 involved some diffusion of facilities to areas formerly without them, but the largest share represented a proliferation of new branches in Lagos, where the number rose from 34 to 83. The value of cheques cleared at the Lagos clearing house in 1971 was £1316 million, compared with £182 million at Kano, £177 million at Ibadan, and under £100 million at the others.

The 1967–70 civil war contributed to the increasing economic dominance of Lagos, especially since the city lay outside the areas of conflict. For instance, the war was one factor encouraging the international oil companies to shift their Nigerian headquarters from Port Harcourt to Lagos (another was the development of the mid-west oilfield). The division of the country into twelve States may also have contributed, for while some powers were thereby further decentralized, others became more concentrated in Lagos as the co-ordinating centre. Both processes were carried further when some of these States were subdivided in 1976.

In *Ghana* the capital city had in 1970 only just over twice as many inhabitants as the second city, which in turn had twice as many as the

Table 18 *Growth of urban centres in Ghana, 1960–70*

Urban agglomeration	Population (thousands) 1960	Population (thousands) 1970	Percentage increase
Accra–Tema	415	739	78
Kumasi	218	345	59
Sekondi–Takoradi	123	161	31
Tamale	58	99	71
Cape Coast	57	71	25
Koforidua	54	70	30

Source: Ghana 1960 and 1970 Censuses.

third, but as Table 18 indicates, this represented increased primacy compared with 1960. The 78 per cent rise in population for Greater Accra during the 1960s includes the development of the new port and industrial centres at Tema (Hilling 1966), which is functionally part of the capital city, lies within the same administrative authority, and will soon be part of a continuously built-up area.

Most other measures indicated both a higher degree of primacy and its increasing intensity. For example, in 1960 there were sixteen bank branches in Accra, eight in Kumasi and seven in Sekondi–Takoradi, but by 1968 the number in Accra had risen to thirty-eight, compared with a modest rise to twelve in Kumasi and to eight in Sekondi–Takoradi. In several provincial towns there were two or three branches at both dates.

Accra's dominant position was comparable with regard to electricity consumption in 1960, when it accounted for 54 million kwh of the national total of 105 million. This compared with 19 million for Kumasi and 22 million for Takoradi. Partly due to the opening of the very power-intensive aluminium smelting industry at Tema, the figure for Accra had risen by 1970 to 360 million of a national total of 522 million, while consumption in the other centres had risen more slowly to 57 and 59 million kwh respectively.

Information on telephones in use is available only for 1963 and 1968, but even over this short period the same trend towards concentration is evident. The number rose by 35 per cent in Accra, but by only 15 to 25 per cent in Kumasi and Takoradi, as also in several smaller towns. More significant as an indicator of the pressures for concentration, however, was the existence in 1968 of 11,600 unsatisfied applications in Accra, compared with 960 in Kumasi and under 250 in every other town.

In *Kenya* there is not a totally dominant primate city in terms of population, for Mombasa has almost half as many inhabitants as Nairobi: the real gap is between these two cities and the rest of the urban centres. Crude population figures suggest that between 1962 and 1969 Nairobi grew much faster than both Mombasa and most of the provincial towns: but between 1969 and 1979 Nairobi's growth slowed, that of Mombasa slowed even further, and many smaller towns began to expand rapidly. To some extent, however, this reflects intercensal boundary changes, and other types of data should also be considered, some of which are presented in Table 19.

The gap between Nairobi and Mombasa, and that between both of these and all other towns, is much wider for wage employment

Table 19 *Some measures of urban primacy in Kenya*

	Wage employment (hundreds) 1970	1980	Wage earnings (£K million) 1970	1980	Municipal expenditure (£K million) 1970	1979	Private buildings completed 1975–80 (thousand m²)
All towns	3036	5233	111	459	13.4	39.4	2015
Nairobi	1640	2742	74	288	9.1	26.7	1377
Mombasa	571	947	19	74	1.9	4.6	409
Nakuru	143	197	4	15	0.8	2.2	38
Kisumu	130	176	4	12	0.8	1.6	28
Eldoret	94	153	2	9	0.3	1.3	41
Thika	62	140	2	10	0.5	1.0	89

Source: Kenya Statistical Abstract (annual).

than for population, and for annual earnings it is wider still. Furthermore such employment and earnings rose much faster between 1970 and 1979 in these cities than in towns such as Nakuru and Kisumu. The same trends are evident with respect to annual municipal expenditures, except that here Mombasa lags remarkably far behind Nairobi. Official data on buildings completed for private ownership indicate an even greater contrast in current dynamism between Nairobi and other centres, though these perhaps distort the picture slightly through the nature of the coverage.

The 1979–83 development plan recognized the trend towards increasing primacy, and indicated a 'government policy to spread urbanization around the country rather than to permit excessive concentration in Nairobi and Mombasa' (1979: 47). This will require much effort, however, for pressures in the opposite direction remain very strong, not least because of the dominant role of the Kikuyu in the most dynamic sectors of the economy.

Tanzania has an urban system dominated by a single primate city to a much greater extent than Kenya (Mascarenhas 1973), and in population terms the supremacy of Dar es Salaam has been steadily increasing (Table 20). 1967 census figures revealed an even greater concentration in Dar es Salaam of certain types of people, such as those with a relatively high level of education. It accounted for 54 per cent of the Tanzanian citizens with nine or more years of full-time education in all mainland towns, and for 65 per cent of those with a

Table 20   Growth of urban centres in Tanzania, 1948–78

| | Population (thousands) | | | | Percentage increase | | |
	1948	1957	1967	1978	1948–78	1957–78	1967–78
Dar es Salaam	69	129	273	757	997	487	177
Zanzibar	47	63	81	111	136	76	37
Next 9 towns*	85	138	247	643	656	366	160

* i.e. Those over 50,000 in 1978 (Mwanza, Tanga, Mbeya, Tabora, Morogoro, Iringa, Arusha, Moshi, Kigoma)

Source: Censuses.

university degree. Throughout the 1970s the level of wage employment was around six times larger than in the second town, and electricity consumption was around eight times larger.

A similar picture of increasing primacy is presented by the majority of other African countries, even in terms of simple population figures. Thus in *Ethiopia*, official estimates of the urban population for 1966 and 1978 indicate a rise from 489,000 to 1,125,000 (130 per cent) in Addis Ababa and a much slower increase from 364,000 to 752,000 (107 per cent) in the next seven towns together. Similarly in *Sudan* the population of Greater Khartoum rose by 79 per cent between 1965 and 1973, from 439,000 to 784,000, while that of the next four towns rose only by 56 per cent, from 254,000 to 396,000.

In *Zaire* the population of Kinshasa and that of the next six towns together were both about 1.7 million in 1975, but this represented a rise from 370,000 since 1956 in the capital city compared with a rise from 560,000 in the other towns. Increasing primacy has been even more marked in most of the francophone states of West Africa. In *Mali* the population of Bamako rose from 68,000 in 1955 to 404,000 in 1976 while that of the next four towns rose from 64,000 to 210,000; in *Niger* there was an increase in Niamey between 1963 and 1977 from 44,000 to 225,000 but only one from 67,000 to 155,000 in the next four towns; and in *Ivory Coast* the expansion of Abidjan from 285,000 in 1963 to 920,000 in 1975 constituted a 220 per cent increase, compared with a 130 per cent increase from 160,000 to 360,000 in the next five towns.

In every case supplementary data for other phenomena also indicate an intensification of urban primacy, with the capital city increasing its pre-eminence, even though individual provincial towns have sometimes received a boost through an elevation of their administrative status or the opening of a new factory.

A rare exception is provided by *Sierra Leone*, where a generally stagnant economy, a shift of the economic centre of gravity towards the diamond-mining area, and perhaps also the declining influence of the Creole group, have led to a reduction in the primacy of Freetown, with Koidu growing far faster between the 1963 and 1974 censuses (Gleave 1981).

It is clear that in most African countries the degree of urban primacy has tended to increase in recent years, with the capital city growing rather faster than the majority of urban centres in each country, and accounting for an increasing share of the total urban population and economic activity. If the phenomenon is associated with colonial rule, we have to say that political independence has not brought a reversal of a well-entrenched process. On the other hand, there are ways in which the attainment of independence has itself intensified it, at least in the short term.

The range of external political and economic relationships has been somewhat widened, but they are channelled through the capital city and major port to a greater extent than ever. The political parties which strove for independence and which now hold power are firmly based in the capital cities: there have been built not only party headquarters, but also national parliaments, new offices for government departments, and a range of foreign embassies, as a direct result of the new political status (Mascarenhas 1967). There has been no necessity for any equivalent change in the various provincial headquarters, and in many small district headquarters the only consequence of independence has been the replacement of expatriates by local officials. The dissolution of empire has brought some shift of urban functions from London and Paris to the national capitals, but not necessarily any further dispersal. This situation has clear policy implications, especially if it can be shown that a less concentrated pattern of urban growth would be in the general interest.

Future conurbations?

The rapid physical expansion of neighbouring cities and towns within a national urban system can lead to the emergence of continuous urban areas with several nuclei, commonly known as conurbations. Coalescence in this fashion may reduce the number of distinct entities within the urban system. However, although reference to emerging conurbations in tropical Africa have been made by a number of writers (e.g. Ajaegbu 1967: 56–9), this is perhaps premature. There is really nothing in tropical Africa comparable to the West Midlands in Britain, the Ruhr in West Germany, or the Witwatersrand in South Africa, now or even in prospect.

The nearest example is probably the Copperbelt of Zambia, where the majority of the country's large towns lie within a very small part of the national territory (Kay 1967a). Nevertheless, they are mostly twenty to thirty kilometres apart, and are still separated by extensive tracts of savanna woodland (Figure 24). Most of Ajaegbu's examples from Nigeria are simply groups of towns that lie relatively close together, interacting strongly with each other,

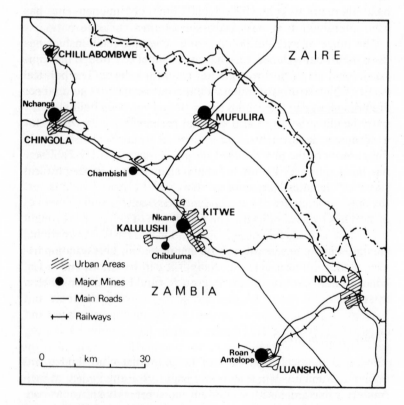

Figure 24   *The Copperbelt of Zambia*

and forming sub-systems within the national urban system. Kano, Zaria and Kaduna form one such group, and Benin, Sapele and Warri form another, but large tracts of farmland separate these towns (Figure 26). A more spatially compact grouping comprises Port Harcourt, Aba, Owerri and Umuahia, which are growing towards each other much faster than equally compact groups of Yoruba towns, and where the thirty kilometres separating them is occupied by a very dense rural population.

Elsewhere there are cities which are expanding so rapidly that they are linking up with much smaller towns which were once quite separate, as in the case of Dakar and Rufisque, or which were designed as industrial satellites, as in the case of Tema within greater Accra, Ikeja within greater Lagos, and Thika still not quite within Nairobi. (Some might regard greater Khartoum as a conurbation, but since its component parts have been adjacent from the start it is probably better viewed as a dual, or triple, city.)

In general, there seems good reason to regard the conurbation as a form of the Western industrial city not likely to be widely replicated in tropical Africa, for it often arose out of the concentration of urban growth on the coalfields. As we have indicated earlier, the pattern of urban growth in Africa has depended mainly on the role of towns as administrative and commercial centres rather than on resource-based industrialization, and the result has been a relatively even spacing. Interest in most African countries is more likely to be concentrated on the evolving relationships of cities with their rural hinterlands, discussed in the next chapter, than on the physical fusion of the cities themselves.

Linkages and flows within the national urban systems

Many discussions of urban systems confine themselves to comparisons of the individual centres, to rank–size distributions and so on, failing to give attention to the links, flows and relationships within these systems. Between Kumasi and Accra, between Mombasa and Nairobi, there are flows of people, goods, money, messages and ideas that reflect the relationships which have evolved over the years. All these flows could not be documented here, even if data on them were available: but in fact for most flows no figures are available. Numbers of rail and air passengers are recorded, though nowhere published, but most inter-city movements take place by road, and only a very few local surveys indicate the patterns of these.

Rail transport accounts for a larger share of goods movements, and records of these have been examined in Nigeria by Hay and Smith (1970), but only for 1964. Even for goods, road transport is accounting for an ever greater share of internal movements in most countries, leaving the railways to handle bulky export crops and minerals. More must be known about inter-city flows of money than about movements of people or goods, but little information on this is revealed by the banks, and even they could only guess at the large sums that are carried in cash rather than transmitted through the banking system.

As with international linkages, much the best documented form of interaction is telephone traffic, although the advent of STD has led to fewer records of inter-city calls. Several papers have appeared making use of such information, and some of the findings are presented below. Naturally, too many conclusions about the urban system should not be drawn from telephone statistics in a continent where so few people have direct access to a telephone, but outright rejection of this indicator as 'Eurocentric' seems unjustified. Telephones are often used by a few people on behalf of a large number, and the pattern of calls reflects patterns of interaction in many spheres of national life, from administration and political party organization to commerce and industry.

In order to understand the overall pattern of national spatial relationships, we should really know much more than we usually do about the spatial distribution of power (Friedmann 1973) and the lines of authority and command that follow from this. In most African countries power and authority is highly concentrated in one city, and it is perhaps in this respect that the primacy of Abidjan or Kinshasa is most significant. In this respect too Nigeria has always been exceptional, for cities such as Kano and Ibadan have never been totally subservient to Lagos. By contrast, power within Kenya is concentrated in Nairobi rather than Mombasa to a far greater extent than population or even employment or income. An interesting feature of the pattern of telephone calls, repeated in almost every country and perhaps related to the distribution of power, is that calls from the provincial towns to the capital city far exceed calls in the reverse direction. This might indicate rather more neglect of the rest of the country than exploitation on the part of the capital city.

In discussing actual patterns of interaction among urban centres, we shall focus upon Tanzania and Nigeria. Studies of telephone traffic by both Hirst (1973) and this author indicate that from the majority of Regional capitals in Tanzania far more calls are made to Dar es Salaam than to any other place. There are just two types of exception to this uniform orientation towards the capital city. In the far south-east Lindi and Mtwara lie close together, and interact more with each other than with Dar es Salaam; and the same applies to Arusha and Moshi in the north (Figure 25). For all these four towns, however, Dar es Salaam ranks second in terms of telephone links. The second type of exception is provided by Bukoba and Musoma, which interact most strongly with Mwanza in what is clearly a sub-system around Lake Victoria. Mwanza is here serving as an intermediary, as most Regional headquarters do in respect of neighbouring smaller towns.

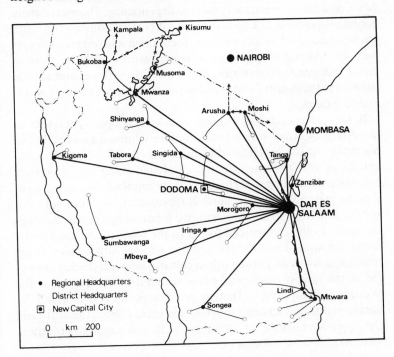

Figure 25 *The urban system of Tanzania*

In general this clear-cut hierarchical system in Tanzania differs little from that prevailing in the colonial period. The main change relates to the four towns already mentioned. Before independence Moshi, Arusha and Musoma had strong links with the Kenya urban system, and especially with Mombasa, Nairobi and Kisumu respectively, while Bukoba had close ties to Kampala in Uganda. This was reflected not only in telephone traffic, but in the sources of supply used by most traders and even in export routes for local produce. Independence itself, the break-up of the East African community, the Tanzania–Uganda conflict during the Amin period, and the prolonged Tanzania–Kenya border closure have all contributed to reorientation and close integration into the national system.

The situation in Nigeria is far more complex than that in Tanzania, and has changed more since independence. The increasingly dominant position of Lagos in terms of comparisons among cities has been matched by an increasing focus upon it in terms of interaction. In addition to the centralizing pressures common to most newly independent countries, three years of civil war and several changes in the country's administrative structure have had a considerable influence.

Before independence, Nigeria was a very loose federation of three Regions over which Lagos had only limited powers. In the north the indigenous Hausa–Fulani cities of Sokoto, Katsina, Kano and Zaria were to some extent integrated in a single urban system before the British arrived (Figure 26). When Kaduna was set up as the colonial capital for the north it represented an addition to this system, and became its administrative focus though never challenging Kano as the commercial focus. In the south-west, the Yoruba towns constituted another pre-colonial system, with Ife seen as the traditional focus of Yoruba urban culture, but with Ibadan emerging as the largest centre and being selected by the British as the Western Region capital. There is great scope for research into the nature of linkages among the towns and cities of both the north and the south-west before the arrival of the British, and into how these were modified by colonial rule.

In the south-east, where there was no such well-established tradition of urban life, the British set up a network of urban centres, and these soon constituted a third sub-system, focused upon the Eastern Region capital of Enugu and to a lesser extent upon Port Harcourt. Towns such as Aba and Onitsha were less self-reliant than the traditional Hausa and Yoruba towns, and the extent of interaction

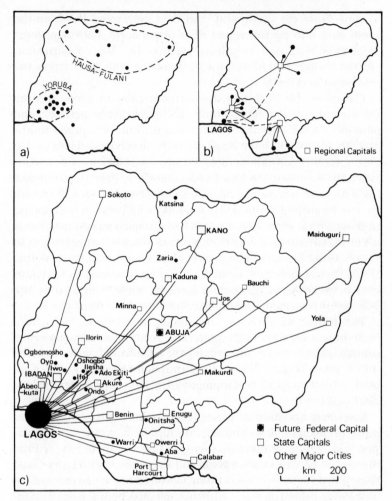

Figure 26 *The urban system of Nigeria*

among the towns of this eastern sub-system was therefore even greater.

Colonial rule did more than just modify the two major existing urban systems and add a third to them. It connected them all together by placing a boundary around them, by introducing roads and railways, and by promoting new patterns of inter-regional migration. This is most clearly exemplified by the spread of first

Yoruba, from the south-west, and then even more Ibo from the south-east, into the towns and cities of the north, both as government employees and as private traders. The Ibo, in particular, created a complex trading network involving both the towns of the south-east and the north.

The massacres of Ibo in the northern cities in 1966, and the subsequent civil war, largely broke up this particular network; and on a more local scale the war broke some links within the southeast. Meanwhile the large Regions had been subdivided into twelve States, each directly answerable to Lagos, whose powers were considerably increased. By the 1970s, therefore, Port Harcourt and Calabar were interacting far more closely with Lagos than with Enugu. Benin had developed closer links with Lagos at the expense of those with Ibadan. Ilorin, which had occupied an odd position as a Yoruba city administered from Kaduna, likewise turned largely to Lagos, as did Jos as the new capital of Benue–Plateau State. Within the far north, however, interaction remained almost as strong as ever between Kano, Zaria and Kaduna, while both Sokoto and Maiduguri remained closely linked in with these three cities.

The further subdivisions into nineteen States in 1976 have brought new changes in the pattern of relationships among urban centres, and are further intensifying the nodality of Lagos within the urban system (Figure 26); but this in turn must be greatly influenced in the 1980s by the development of a new capital city, briefly discussed later.

Elsewhere also the dominance of the capital city is even greater in terms of linkages, flows and relationships than in terms of population size, wealth or service provision. In Zaire there is very little interaction between Lubumbashi and Kisangani, and in Ivory Coast there is little between the northern provincial towns and those of the west. Where there do seem to be stronger links between one provincial town and another this is generally because one is on the route between the other and the capital. Thus all road traffic from Tamale to Accra passes through Kumasi, and all from Korhogo to Abidjan passes through Bouaké.

There are, of course, a number of special cases where a group of towns form a local sub-system, interacting more with each other than with the capital city. Two sharply contrasting examples are provided by the Islamic cities of the middle Niger valley in Mali, such as Ségou, Djenné and Mopti, and by the Copperbelt towns of Zambia, such as Kitwe, Ndola and Luanshya, which really form a single urban region. However, for nine out of every ten major provincial towns the strongest links are those with the capital city. Most of the national urban systems therefore show a high degree of integration, but of a type that conforms very clearly to Friedmann's (1973) 'centre–periphery' model, with only very weak connections within the periphery.

Planned changes in national urban systems

While most African governments have devoted much effort over the past twenty years to development planning, very little of this effort has been directed to their urban systems. In some countries there is no evidence of any attention having been given to the matter: in others there has been discussion but very little action (Salau 1979). A symposium volume edited by Mabogunje and Faniran (1977) confirms that impression, for several contributors refer to the neglect of planning for the urban system, and few can report on much that has actually happened.

Kudiabor (1977) indicates that planners in Ghana have thought of Tamale as a growth centre and thirty-nine smaller towns as growth points, drawing on the earlier work of Grove and Huszar (1964), but little has been done there. In Ivory Coast efforts at diverting urban growth from Abidjan have been largely concentrated on the establishment of the new port of San Pedro in the south-west. In some respects this has proved a successful venture, but its impact on the urban system as a whole is not great.

In Zaire, no steps have been taken to constrain the growth of Kinshasa, and nothing has been published to indicate that the government has a clear strategy for the distribution of future urban growth. The situation is similar in Sudan, in spite of the extreme primacy of the Khartoum agglomeration, except that after years of north–south conflict the plans for southern development have involved much government investment in the regional capital, Juba. Ethiopia provides a third case of extreme primacy advancing unchecked. Another regional conflict is highly relevant there, causing economic stagnation in the second city and Eritrean regional capital, Asmara.

Three countries which have made, or are making, one major change in their urban system are those shifting the location of the capital city (Malawi, Tanzania and Nigeria) all discussed in the next section. In Nigeria, further deliberate changes have arisen through the division of the country into first twelve, and then nineteen States. While these decisions did not arise from any reappraisal of the national urban system, it was recognized that the selection of State capitals would have implications for this system, and those such as Akure and Owerri (Nwaka 1980) have diverted some urban growth from other larger centres.

However, it is Kenya that has the most comprehensive programme for modifying the urban system, for as indicated above its development plans pay heed to the whole urban hierarchy, down to tiny local centres (Richardson 1980). In an effort to divert some urban growth from Nairobi and Mombasa, eleven towns were selected in the 1974–8 plan as centres for rapid development, including both the largest provincial towns, Nakuru and Kisumu, and smaller ones such as Kakamega and Meru. The 1979–83 plan (1979: 49–50) identified nine other towns meriting special attention: Bungoma, Kericho and Kisii to support the regional development effort for western Kenya; Garissa, Isiolo, Kapenguria and Narok as gateway towns for the semi-arid areas; and Machakos and Malindi as towns able to attract industries away from Nairobi and Mombasa respectively. The chief measures proposed for implementation of these plans are the provision of government funds for infrastructure and special investment allowances for industrial development.

The situation in Zimbabwe should be particularly interesting in the years ahead. The government in power up to the late 1970s restricted the rate of urbanization, but paid little heed to its distribution. Now rapid urban growth is expected in the 1980s and its location could greatly affect national integration. As in Kenya the inherited structure comprises two large cities, with Harare now tending to forge ahead of Bulawayo, and small provincial towns: but the latter are even smaller and fewer than in Kenya, and most rural dwellers live far from any urban centre, since even small towns were confined to the European-occupied areas. Davies (1981) has outlined a possible strategy for a more appropriate national urban system.

In various countries there has been much talk of growth poles, growth centres and growth points (Mabogunje 1978 for Nigeria; Zambia 1979: 81–4), but as has been amply demonstrated by other writers (Darwent 1969, Friedmann and Weaver 1979) there is confusion as to the real meaning of these phrases. Suggestions that they are points through which economic growth can be generated in surrounding rural areas raise wider issues taken up in the next chapter.

In most African official plans the terms are used in the narrower sense of places considered suitable for urban growth. The identification of such places, as done in Kenya, may prove in the long run a valuable exercise, but only if it really does influence location decisions. As yet it has rarely done so, and both the spatial pattern of urban growth and linkages among urban centres have depended on a combination of unco-ordinated governmental decisions and market forces.

New capital cities

While most African countries have taken few deliberate steps to modify the urban system inherited at independence, there are notable exceptions. In both Mauritania and Rwanda there was really no urban system during the colonial period. Only embryonic urban centres existed, and both countries were administered from outside their borders – Mauritania from Saint-Louis in Senegal, and Rwanda from Bujumbura in present-day Burundi. In Mauritania a brand new settlement forms the new capital city of Nouakchott (Pitte 1977), while in Rwanda the tiny provincial town of Kigali was elevated to the status of national capital (Nwafor 1981). In three other countries a decision has been made to shift the national capital. In Tanzania it is to be moved from Dar es Salaam to the provincial town of Dodoma during the course of the 1980s. In Nigeria it is being moved more rapidly from Lagos to a totally new urban centre in the vicinity of Abuja. In Malawi the shift took place during the 1970s, the provincial town of Lilongwe taking over some functions from the tiny administrative capital of Zomba and some from the primate city and commercial capital of Blantyre. In most respects, whether one considers size, location, level of prosperity or ideological stance, these three countries form a very motley group. The most significant feature that they shared at independence was a lower level of vested interest in an all-dominant capital city than in many other countries.

Malawi is one of the least urbanized, as well as one of the poorest, countries in Africa. At the 1966 census, its only major city, Blantyre, had a population of 110,000, while Zomba and Lilongwe each had just under 20,000 inhabitants. There had been various proposals during the colonial period to shift the seat of administration from Zomba to Blantyre, and some ministries were already located in Blantyre when, in 1965, it was announced that the shift would instead be to Lilongwe. It was essentially a presidential decision, and a controversial one, especially in view of the costs involved and the fact that only South Africa offered funds. The main arguments in support of the policy were that the expenditure would be required for urban growth in the 1970s wherever it might be located, that Blantyre already had sufficient impetus for growth, and that a move to Lilongwe would counteract the excessive concentration of development in the extreme south of the country.

Mlia (1975) notes that both national pride and President Banda's Central Region origins may have been relevant, but suggests that regional development goals and the identification of most of the elite with areas other than the south were more important. As Blantyre was not the administrative capital, independence had brought less immediate change there than in most African primate cities, and expatriate interests remained particularly dominant there. Foreign firms see no objection to the concentration of urban growth in the south; but many Malawians see things differently. Perhaps also those viewing the matter from within have a longer-term perspective, for Malawi has to an exceptional degree only an urban system 'in the making' even now. Not only is a shift to a central capital easier now than it would be once the south had become totally dominant, but the expansion of various district headquarters may be better achieved from a Lilongwe focus than from a Zomba/Blantyre focus.

The development of Lilongwe proceeded steadily throughout the 1970s, most ministries moving there by 1975. To what extent commerce and industry also shifts largely remains to be seen, but evidence to date suggests continued growth of Blantyre's commercial and industrial activities. Zomba is now moribund, but Blantyre's population probably rose between 1966 and 1980 at about 7 per cent a year, to some 270,000, even while that of Lilongwe was rising at 15 per cent a year, to about 140,000.

Tanzania is just as poor as Malawi, and there too few of the elite identify closely with the largest city, Dar es Salaam, which is much the most concentrated centre of foreign interests in the country. Thus, while the two countries are far apart ideologically, it is perhaps their shared ardent nationalism that is most relevant here. One major difference is that throughout the colonial period, German and British, Dar es Salaam was both commercial and administrative capital, and another is that it headed a much fuller hierarchy of provincial towns than in Malawi. Rather than the embryonic urban system found in that country, Tanzania had in the 1960s a firmly established system (Hirst 1973, Mascarenhas 1973). This, as well as lack of funds, is now contributing to the slow progress in implementing the 1973 decision to shift the capital to Dodoma (Figure 25).

A combination of poverty and policy curbed vested interests in Dar es Salaam sufficiently to permit the decision, but the same combination means few resources for urban investments, whether on the existing pattern or striking out in new directions. In the short term it would have been cheaper to concentrate such government spending in Dar es Salaam, but as in Malawi a long-term view must also be taken (Hoyle 1979). It is believed that Tanzania will be better served by an urban system focused on the twin poles of Dodoma and Dar es Salaam than on a single alien-dominated centre: and while economic development was certainly not concentrated in one area as in Malawi, it was moving in that direction, especially in respect of the secondary and tertiary sectors. It is also felt that national integration will be best served by a central capital which is equally accessible (or more realistically, equally inaccessible!) from most regions. Regional equity goals should also be served in that the Dodoma Region is one of the poorest in the country; while other national ideals may be served by the nature of the new urban centre that eventually arises beside the unassuming provincial town that had a population of 46,000 at the 1978 census, comparable to that of a dozen other such towns.

The Nigerian situation differs in almost every respect from both those just considered. The country has a far larger population, is more urbanized, with diverse urban traditions, and has substantial government revenues from its oil exports, even if these hardly – as some observers suggest – make it a rich country. Its capital city of Lagos is vastly larger than Dar es Salaam or Blantyre, with a population passing the 2 million mark sometime in the 1970s; and in this case problems of congestion and actual diseconomies of scale on a highly unsatisfactory physical site come into play (Adejuyigbe 1970). As in the other two countries, the capital is seen as peripherally located, and the rapid expansion of foreign influence there is seen as a threat to national integrity, but in Nigeria ethnicity also assumes greater proportions. Lagos has grown around a Yoruba nucleus, is dominated numerically by that group, and has always interacted more strongly with the Yoruba urban sub-system than with the rest of the country. In so far as its links with other urban centres have been increasing recently, as discussed above, these are often seen by both northerners and easterners as representing domination; and by the late 1970s the pressures to use oil revenues to arrest this trend before it became irreversible became so strong that a decision on a shift was made by the outgoing federal military government.

Neither an indigenous city associated with one ethnic group, nor a provincial town of colonial origin, was considered an appropriate nucleus for a new capital city, and therefore a largely unoccupied site was selected in the vicinity of Abuja (Salau 1977). Not only is this in the very heart of the country (Figure 26), but it is in the territory of peoples whose role in Nigerian political life is minimal, and is therefore equally acceptable to each of the major ethnic groups. Regional development considerations also affected the choice of the new site – within the 'Middle Belt' which has been largely bypassed by economic change in twentieth-century Nigeria.

Although a later decision than in Tanzania, it is being implemented much more speedily, and Abuja may well be the site of a large city by 1990. Just how large must depend on a host of factors, some entirely beyond Nigeria's control, others an outcome of its own policies. It is not yet clear, for instance, how far Abuja will become a multi-functional metropolis rather than a largely administrative city comparable to Canberra or Brasilia. Whatever policy in that respect emerges, much will depend on attitudes both in Lagos and in Nigeria's other cities. Paradoxically, perhaps, the very size and complexity of Nigeria's urban system increase the possibility of the new capital city having a major impact on that system. The citizens of Zaria, Jos and Ilorin have always had some degree of choice as to whether their contacts up the urban hierarchy are with Kano and Kaduna or with Lagos, and they will now exercise that choice with regard to Abuja also. Together with the citizens of Kano and Kaduna themselves, and those of Ibadan, Enugu, Port Harcourt and many other cities, they could probably over-ride the local and foreign influences favouring the continued dominance of Lagos, and so bring about far greater change in the Nigerian space economy than has occurred, for example, in Brazil.

Conclusions

The building of new capital cities is the most exciting aspect of the urban systems of Africa, but the operation of such systems is important even where governments have decided to maintain the status quo and to proceed with the urban framework inherited from the colonial period. No doubt these governments will watch with interest progress in Malawi, Tanzania and Nigeria, but meanwhile their own urban systems will be consolidated. These systems differ greatly from one country to another, but a notable feature common to all is that they link into both the international urban system and the local arrangement of rural settlement.

Another feature of most national urban systems in Africa is a high and increasing level of primacy, and we might consider to what extent this matters. In a small and poor country one major urban centre may be enough. Togo would probably benefit little from any attempt to develop an inland city rivalling Lomé. Yet increasing primacy may be very inappropriate in larger countries, especially where the dominant city lies within the most prosperous region. Primacy certainly matters wherever it is much more extreme on other criteria than simple population numbers, for this implies that the leading city enjoys a disproportionate share of jobs, wage income, medical facilities, or whatever. Policy should therefore perhaps be directed more to these issues than to the sheer size of each urban centre.

Another highly relevant factor in tropical Africa is ethnicity. Where people from all parts of a country can identify with the capital city equally well, and can be assimilated there equally easily, little social injustice need result from a concentration of job opportunities there: but in most African countries such concentration in one city means advantage for one ethnic group. It is often mainly for reasons of political cohesion and national integration that increasing urban primacy should be resisted.

Social and cultural issues are relevant in other ways also. The greater the dispersal of urban growth, the larger the number of urban dwellers remaining within easy reach of their rural homeland. Much therefore depends on how the maintenance of close links with rural home and kinsfolk is valued (chapter 9). It may be considered preferable to the aping of foreign life-styles which generally reaches its peak in the capital city. The choice is often between increasing cultural dependency if the urban population is concentrated there, and reinforcing ethnic rather than national identity if most people move only to towns in their home region. In most African countries these issues are more important than issues of economic efficiency, especially since diseconomies from absolute city size are as yet only slight.

Roberts (1978: 47–9) stresses the pressures for centralization in Latin America, noting the lack of any power base for regional counterbalance. In tropical Africa ethnic affiliation could still provide this, if governments chose to mobilize it. Most Luba and Ngala, including the most influential members of these groups, would prefer increased dispersal of urban development in Zaire to increased concentration in Kinshasa: and if the Kenya government increased its efforts to divert some urban growth from Nairobi to Kisumu all strata of Luo society would warmly support this.

Economic issues are also relevant, for intense urban primacy is likely to mean severe regional income and welfare inequalities, and the importance of these is heightened by the way in which most people identify more strongly with their home region than the country as a whole. One argument for deflecting urban growth to medium-sized provincial towns is that these should be more effective in promoting rural development. A full exposition of this view for poor countries in general has been provided by Johnson (1970), and it has been applied to West Africa by Harison Church (1972).

It is argued that more dispersed urbanization would bring urban amenities nearer to most rural dwellers, would provide more local markets for surplus farm produce, and would benefit the rural population through the diffusion of various ideas and innovations. However, other observers (e.g. Soja and Weaver 1976) see African rural–urban relationships as essentially harmful to the rural population, and see the towns as agents of underdevelopment. So any evaluation of the benefits of more dispersed urban growth for regional and rural development must depend on our assessment of all urban–rural interaction.

Many governments have so far given little attention to the distribution of urban growth, but greater efforts to plan this may be made in the 1980s. There is growing concern about ever-increasing urban primacy, about possible future diseconomies in congested capital cities, about regional development disparities, and about the alienation of ethnic groups who feel neglected. The disastrous agricultural situation in many countries is now acknowledged, and it is widely accepted, rightly or wrongly, that more dispersed urban growth will assist rural development. The most pressing consideration, however, may be the political threat presented by masses of people without work or housing in the largest cities, and the hope that by deflecting some migration to smaller centres this will be diminished.

In Malawi, Tanzania and Nigeria a major decision about the national urban system has been taken, but in each case its outcome will depend on many other decisions made both within and outside the country. What level of funds will be invested in the new capitals, and over what period? Will these be funds diverted from other urban centres? What adjustments will people elsewhere in the country, and abroad, be prepared to make? Will each provincial town look more to the new capital or the old? A fundamental question is how far decisions on economic links are controlled or left to market forces, national and international. Elsewhere, no such dramatic step has been taken, yet many decisions still have to be made that will influence the urban system. Planning for every city must consider its linkages with others, as well as with the surrounding rural areas.

9 Urban–rural relationships

While this book is concerned essentially with the *cities* of tropical Africa, they cannot be considered in isolation from the predominantly rural societies within which they are placed. Not only is each city part of a national and an international urban system, as shown in the last chapter, but each also has numerous close links with the surrounding rural area. Furthermore, the great majority of adults in most cities have a rural background: they were born and brought up in the countryside.

The importance of these bonds is heightened by the fact that only a small proportion of the population in most African countries are urban dwellers. In Argentina or Japan decisions made in cities on behalf of the whole nation are in large measure decisions on behalf of city people: in Ethiopia or Zaire this is not so – or at least should not be so if 'the nation' has real meaning. African cities have much responsibility for organizing and managing countries that are predominantly rural.

Contrasts can be drawn in both time and space. In most of pre-colonial Africa the rulers and the ruled were both rural, while in much of the world both are predominantly urban. In Africa today there is no doubt that the city rules over the countryside, though views differ widely as to how much benevolence or oppression is involved. If African cities are bound up in many ways with the world capitalist system, they are bound up in other ways with peasant societies deeply rooted in the African soil. Indeed, while the terms 'urban' and 'rural' present few major problems as applied to settlements, their use for sections of society in Africa is far more problematical.

These generalizations may seem very sweeping in view of the diversity of urban traditions in Africa. While ties between indigenous cities and their hinterlands were particularly close, colonial cities arose on a quite different basis, more closely tied to the metropoles in Europe than to the local rural economy. Yet the growth of most cities of colonial origin has depended on the production of surplus goods in the rural areas, and on the provision of some services for these areas. Furthermore, many economic and social changes associated with the 'alien town' have profoundly affected rural Africa also. The nature of contemporary urban–rural links differs considerably from place to place, but they are of profound importance everywhere.

One set of links comprises the migration flows considered earlier. Many of these are long-term shifts, and were discussed in relation to the city growth. Others, however, are seasonal movements or other forms of short-term circulation, which may not contribute at all to city growth, but which do much to bind city and country together. In many cities an important additional element is provided by daily or weekly movement to and from the rural area immediately around.

Links closely related to the migration flows include visits home by the migrants and visits to the city by their rural-based relatives, letters sent each way, and often cash remittances, as well as the transmission of ideas and values. Relationships arising more from the cities' economic and political functions include the movements of traders and their customers, of farm produce and manufactured goods, and of cash exchanged in the transactions, and also the chains of command and pathways of power involved in any political structure.

Such urban–rural relationships are of course universal, but the personal links are more complex and intense in tropical Africa than anywhere else. More than in any other region people belong to a combined rural–urban system of social and economic relationships. Many individuals have one foot in each world, and many families have at any given time some members in the city and some in the country. Much temporary migration continues, while even the long-term migrant normally intends to retire back 'home' and maintains close links, often using any savings to build a house there. Even people born and brought up in the city can generally identify such a 'home' area, and young men commonly seek a wife there.

Hanna and Hanna (1981: 51) observe that 'the personal urbanization of most townsmen is far from complete' and that 'most town dwellers sooner or later return home permanently'. Gugler (1971: 405) says that 'the majority of urban dwellers in subsaharan Africa are an integral part both of the towns they live in and of the villages they have come from', and writes of 'life in a dual system'. Numerous studies of individual cities make the same point. Thus in Nairobi 'if one asks residents of the city "Where is your home?" very few name a location in Nairobi' (Ross 1975: 44). Around Dar es Salaam 'the village is a base to which the city Zaramo return and most often refer to as *kwetu* (our home) even if they have moved away more or less permanently' (Swantz 1970: 159). Similarly 'one can sit in a Ghanaian town discussing rural life, and find that most participants preface nearly every observation with "In my village . . ."' (Caldwell 1969: 140).

An example from francophone Africa is provided by Cotten and Marguerat (1977: 352), who observe: 'le plus grand nombre des gens durant toute leur vie font la navette entre la campagne et la ville'. They also say: 'le but de l'exode rural, c'est le retour à la terre'. Most village communities can readily provide full details of what in West African English are often termed 'sons abroad', even though some left for the city thirty years ago. Tangible reminders of them exist in the form of the half-built houses which have puzzled many an outsider travelling in rural Africa. As noted when discussing the limited extent of owner-occupation of city houses, many urban dwellers are putting their savings into building a retirement home in their area of origin. In Ghana, Caldwell (1969: 147) found that 80 per cent of urban migrants either owned a house in a rural area or planned to do so; while in Kampala, Odongo and Lea (1977: 65) found that 46 per cent of migrants had built such a house while a further 29 per cent planned to do so.

The strength of family and kinship feeling, and the wish to retain land rights and thus a measure of social security, are reasons for maintaining links between town and country. Since both types of attachment are deeply engrained in African culture, this may not be just a temporary anomaly as Africa passes through a transition to Western-style urbanism, but may persist in a distinctive African form of urbanism (Dike 1979).

This intensity of social links between city and country is one of the few features shared by all types of tropical African city. It is also shared by all classes or income groups among the urban population. The new elite of Nairobi retain just as great an interest in their rural home area as the urban poor, though some have also bought up ex-European farms in other areas.

Urban–rural links are in fact so strong and so diverse that any book devoted to African urbanization may be in various respects misleading. Some scholars have even suggested total abandonment of a rural–urban dichotomy in the study of Africa, and much work which cuts across it is certainly needed; but since the physical distinction between rural and urban settlement is as clear as anywhere else, some writing focused on the urban areas is surely justified. The point that must be emphasized is that 'there is no clear division between urban and rural population' (Caldwell 1969: 140) in any tropical African country. This has important implications for any discussions of whether resources are unfairly distributed between town and country. It also means that explanations of urban patterns must often be sought in the rural areas. These rural–urban linkages are matters on which very few precise data are available. No one knows how much rural produce is brought in for sale in the urban markets of Abidjan or Addis Ababa, or how many letters move each way annually between Lusaka and Zambia's rural districts. Such flows could in theory be regularly recorded, but no African government has the resources to do this. Other relationships such as the transmission of ideas and the pattern of political domination are hardly susceptible to measurement at all.

However, linkages have been the subject of research in specific areas. For instance, some migration studies have investigated remittances and visits, while several case studies of local food supplies to francophone African cities have been undertaken. Such studies provide us with many insights into the nature of urban–rural relationships: but they do not provide clear answers to the question which concerns so many social scientists – whether the urban centres bring benefits to rural dwellers or instead prosper at their expense. On this question we can still only speculate.

This chapter will therefore be highly selective, discussing just a few forms of urban–rural linkage – involving movements of people, transmission of ideas, flows of goods, and finally transfers of cash. Before considering the first of these for rural areas in general, we shall consider daily or very short-term movements to and from the areas immediately surrounding the cities. In Europe or North America these would include much short-distance movement for recreation, but that is very slight indeed around African cities. Most movements are either for work or relate to the provision of urban services.

Daily commuting from rural homes

When rural dwellers shift into urban occupations this generally involves a change of residence, but there is a zone around each city from which people can travel in daily for work, returning each evening. Such patterns of daily commuting have been extensively studied in more industrialized regions: we know for instance that daily travel from the traditional family home in the countryside is more common in France and Germany than in Britain. Very little attention has been given to the phenomenon in tropical Africa, although it occurs in every country. It is particularly widespread in East Africa, and helps to explain the apparently low level of urbanization in that region. There are even some such movements in south-western Nigeria, though there they are outnumbered by the reverse movements of town-dwelling farmers discussed briefly in chapter 5 and more fully by Goddard (1965) and Ojo (1970).

There are, of course, no data on this subject for any city, and any attempt to quantify is hindered by the difficulty of defining rural and urban homes, since most African cities are fringed by peri-urban tracts in which houses stand within small plots of intensively cultivated land. Here our concern is rather with truly rural areas, in which the economy is primarily agricultural, but from which some people travel daily for work: but no sharp division between these and the peri-urban zone can be made.

The flow of daily commuters can be seen each morning on any of the roads leading into Kampala, starting with those moving on foot, followed by those on bicycles, who do not need to set off so early, and finally by those travelling either by bus or crammed twelve at a time in taxis. Those on foot commonly come from homes seven or eight kilometres from the edge of the city or twelve kilometres from its centre, the others from places up to thirty kilometres distant.

The pattern is repeated around Jinja, the second town of Uganda, and Brandt (1972: 81) reports that of 2800 employees in Jinja factories 83 per cent then lived outside the rather tightly-drawn town boundary. Many lived in peri-urban settlements, but 25 per cent stated that they lived on their own family farms. The same phenomenon was discussed in Elkan's (1960) study of workers in Kampala and Jinja, and noted as an advantage of such relatively small urban centres compared with giant metropoli. Indeed, throughout East Africa the proportion of the urban workforce commuting from rural homes seems even higher in provincial towns than in the cities. Many travel daily from Kiambu District into Nairobi, but proportionately more commute into Kisumu, Nyeri and Machakos.

Clearly the extent of such movement around each urban centre depends in part on the density of the rural population. There is little on the Zambian Copperbelt, where urban centres grew up in almost uninhabited country, and not much in Lusaka, where the surrounding land is mainly under large farms. Within Nigeria, such commuting is most common in the south-east, where rural population densities around most towns are very high, while some also takes place from what Hill (1977) insists are essentially rural communities in the close-settled zone around Kano. Mortimore (1972) indicates a substantial flow into Kano from over ninety villages. Throughout northern Nigeria, and indeed the whole Sahel region, the intensity of such flows varies greatly with the seasons, and in the dry season people moving into the towns daily from their own farms may be joined by others from further afield who are temporarily settled in the vicinity.

Some academics are highly critical of this system of commuting in the African context, since they regard it as a case of the countryside subsidizing the town, where foreign firms and local big businessmen can pay shockingly low wages to employees whose costs of living are relatively low. Certainly, the operation of the system provides no excuse whatever for intolerably low wage rates: but from the individual's viewpoint the system makes much sense. Travelling involves expenditure of either effort or cash, but it also offers clear economic advantages over residence in town, especially in societies in which urban employment is predominantly for men while women customarily undertake most farming work. Not only is there a saving of rent, but few basic foodstuffs have to be bought either. It represents fuller employment for the family as a whole than would be possible with urban residence, provides a higher standard of living, and offers much greater security in the event of the man losing his job.

There are many advantages in non-economic terms too, for the situation is one in which rural dwellers can benefit from urban employment without either the upheaval of moving from a familiar social setting to an unfamiliar one, or the prolonged separation of husbands and wives. If maintaining a small farm is a burden on the wives, it may be no greater than for women farming beyond commuting distance, and should be eased if some labour-saving devices can be afforded: it is also one which most do not appear to resent.

Since the advantages to the municipal authorities are also great, in that pressure on their own housing and service provision is reduced, there seems every reason to encourage this well-established pattern of daily movement as long as it is not used to justify exploitative practices or sexist job discrimination. The dispersal of secondary and tertiary economic activity into these near-by rural areas may be even more advantageous, if Africa can succeed in doing this where others have failed; while the considerable possibilities of low-density peri-urban settlements for migrant families were indicated in chapter 6. However, the intermediate situation of rural families remaining on their own land but entering the urban economy by means of commuting to the cities, and especially the smaller towns, has an important part to play in tropical African countries in the 1980s and 1990s.

Journeys for urban services

Studies of urban–rural links in more developed regions are dominated by the role of cities as service centres for the rural population, who travel in for shopping, entertainment, medical treatment and so on. To judge from the literature on African urbanization one might imagine that such relationships were non-existent there. This is utterly untrue, and the neglect of the subject is quite inexplicable, except perhaps that it is not seen as constituting a grave problem. Critical problems do lie to a greater extent within the cities themselves, and especially in the rural areas remote from them, but the existence of rural areas with reasonable access to urban services should not be totally ignored.

Medical facilities might be taken as a specific example. These are highly concentrated in the urban areas, though not to the same extent as, say, in Latin America, mainly due to the large and continuing involvement of the missions. However, such concentration is universal and reflects the function of cities as central places for service provision, though there are certainly distortions arising from the distance many people live from any facilities, from inequitable provision among regions, and often from excessive stress on a few well-equipped institutions rather than on widespread facilities at a more modest level (Gish 1975).

Hopefully, many countries will follow Tanzania's lead in changing priorities in medical provision, but meanwhile it should be understood that urban hospitals do not receive only urban dwellers as patients. The zone from which people can commute for urban employment also has the advantage of access to these hospitals, and many people take this opportunity when the need arises. Medical treatment ranks very high on the list of what many people feel that the city offers, and a remarkably high proportion of journeys to the cities are made either for treatment or for visiting relatives in hospital. Most rural dwellers attending city hospitals as either out- or in-patients come from the immediate hinterland, and improved access for those from further away is an urgent need: but already a few are referred as in-patients, and there are more who come to stay in town with relatives while seeking treatment.

Another common purpose for travelling to town is to do business in a government office. Obtaining a licence, or scholarship, often requires a personal visit – or indeed several. In many cases it also requires a bribe which must be handed over personally, though the extent of this varies considerably across Africa. So also do attitudes towards it, for in some cities most officials regard it as a proper compromise between traditional and modern ways of operating, while in others it is agreed to be one of the worst consequences of culture contact. Even where no bribe has to be handed over, attempts to conduct such business by post are likely to result in inordinate delays.

The number of journeys made for purposes such as this have increased enormously since independence, and so have journeys for many other purposes, from political rallies to football matches. Among the various factors causing this, beyond simple population growth, three might be singled out. In the rural areas just around the cities transport facilities have improved greatly, often a matter of a dozen people crammed in a Peugeot van rather than a regular bus service. In these areas most of the younger generation have now had at least primary school education, and as well as being aware of what the city has to offer they feel quite able to cope with its challenges. Finally, even the older generation now find that the cities are not such alien places as in the past.

The use of the towns for shopping has increased more slowly, partly because of the great expansion of small-scale trading establishments in the more accessible type of rural areas. Incomes are still generally too low to allow many purchases beyond those things that can be obtained locally. In the major cities nearly all the customers of the larger retail stores are urban dwellers, as they always have been. But often there is a set of shops around the country bus station or the lorry park which rely more heavily on rural customers, some of whom have brought in rural produce for the city markets. In some cities this trade has expanded greatly in recent years. Furthermore, many of those who have opened small shops in the neighbouring rural areas, with very little capital, must travel into the city at very frequent intervals to obtain their supplies. These points all apply to the provincial towns as well as the major cities, and in general the smaller they are the higher the proportion of rural-dwelling customers in their shops.

There is much scope for study of such relationships between African towns, large and small, and their immediate rural hinterlands: and there is a need for more discrimination between these rural areas and those more distant from the cities than has been customary in discussions of urban–rural relationships.

Visits to and from rural homes

The large numbers of migrants in most cities, and continuing close attachment to their areas of origin give rise to many periodic visits. In any city the long-distance bus terminal is often thronged with people about to depart on visits 'home', and with rural dwellers arriving to visit town-based kinsfolk. Even those born in the city may regularly visit the rural area occupied by other branches of their family.

These visits now represent a far greater volume of personal movement each year than the migrations themselves. However, we cannot draw a really sharp distinction between them. In northern Nigeria, for example, much seasonal movement into and out of the cities could be regarded either as short-term migration or as rather lengthy visits. The same applies to the journeys made by many women from western Kenya in the agricultural slack season to join their husbands in Nairobi.

No comprehensive data on visiting could ever be compiled, but various sample surveys indicate its extent. In Tanzania a 1971 survey, analysed by Sabot (1979: 194–7), showed that 70 per cent of all male urban migrants had made at least one visit home, those who had not done so being mainly the most recent arrivals. The great majority make home visits at least once a year, including even those who have migrated to Dar es Salaam from as far away as West Lake and Mara Regions. In Arusha and Moshi towns, Mlay (1974) found that 80 per cent of migrants make some home visits, most from the surrounding district doing so at least once a month. The proportions receiving visits from rural relatives at various frequencies are very similar.

Caldwell (1969: 140–2) found that about 80 per cent of migrants in Ghana's cities make visits home at least once a year, and that many do so much more frequently, however long the interval since the original migration. The Ghanaian 'mammy waggons' also carry many people on visits in the reverse direction, so that (p. 120) 'nearly half the rural population have at least seen and had brief experience of the larger urban centres'.

Such visiting is not confined to the urban centres which grew largely through colonial contact. In a survey of migrant heads of households in two old Yoruba towns, Ife and Oshogbo, Adepoju (1974) found that all but 7 per cent visit their home areas on occasion, and that 40 per cent do so more than seven times a year. Writing of the Ijebu people in Ibadan, Mabogunje (1967a: 92) suggests that many return to their home areas most week-ends, so that it is hard to say to what extent they are really 'resident' in the city at all, even though they are fully integrated in its economy. They clearly occupy a mid-way position between the long-distance migrants who predominate in most African cities and the non-migrant Yoruba who have homes in both city and country and are constantly moving between the two.

Most migrants in Adepoju's surveys came from within south-western Nigeria, and he found that distance had little effect on the frequency or nature of the visits, but in respect of most African cities distinctions between short-distance and long-distance migrants are highly relevant. In Ghana and Ivory Coast, in Kenya and Tanzania, people who have come to the city from far away can afford to make only one or two home visits a year, often lasting about two weeks, whereas those from the surrounding region can make, and receive, frequent and briefer visits. In Kampala, Gutkind (1965: 54) found a far greater intensity of visiting in both directions among the local Ganda than among groups from further afield. In many areas the frequency of visiting has increased as more and more vehicles have been introduced on an expanding road network; and as migration patterns in eastern and central Africa have moved closer to the long-term family migration previously more common in West Africa, so short visits have tended to replace the longer periods of residence back home that were characteristic of circulatory labour migration.

Another variable that requires further investigation is the nature of employment. Those working in government offices in Abidjan or the copper mines of Zambia do their home visiting as far as possible during paid holidays, but for workers in small enterprises and for the self-employed the position is less straightforward. Many of these people face very difficult decisions, when social pressures for visiting conflict with the economic losses which this may cause. Perhaps the further growth of such self-employment will lead to a greater proportion of rural–to–urban visiting, or perhaps it will basically militate against this type of urban–rural link and encourage a sharper separation between urban and rural society. Again, the extent to which people come from the region just around the city may prove particularly significant.

The motives for the visits in each direction are as varied as those for migration itself, and often just as mixed in respect of each individual. Since there are still many men in the cities without their families, visits home are for them rare chances to spend a while with wives and children. For those in town as families the visits home may be for weddings or funerals, or just to keep in touch with parents and other relatives who certainly expect this: but a whole range of other matters from land disputes to religious festivals may be involved. The rural dwellers travelling to town may be just relatives keeping in touch, but they may also be kinsfolk requesting funds or favours, coming in search of a school place, or investigating job possibilities.

As Ross (1975) has demonstrated for Nairobi, such visiting is found in all income groups. While the poor may have the greatest need to maintain rural ties for security, the more affluent may have invested in land which they must supervise from time to time. They can, of course, more easily afford to make visits (and may even have their own private cars), while they also provide more attractive targets for rural visitors.

One deficiency of most surveys is their focus on male migrants, and their assumption that 'home' is the man's area of origin. Little is known about urban–rural visits by either single or married women, or of how far wives make separate journeys to their own ancestral homes rather than accompanying their husbands. In some areas wives commonly return to stay with their mothers for childbirth, but patterns differ greatly from place to place. Indeed, research in a variety of cities is particularly necessary with respect to movements by women since these differ from city to city according to local social and kinship structure even more than those of men.

Within each city there is more variation among women than among men in the pattern of visiting. In Nairobi and Kampala some migrant women never return to their area of origin because it was either acute dissatisfaction with rural society or being treated as a social outcast that drove them into town (Obbo 1980). Others spend their time so evenly divided between town and country that it is hard to say which journeys constitute the visits. These are often wives who are not in wage employment, and who are sent by their husbands – willingly in some cases, less willingly in others – to maintain the family farm. If they go for several months at a time, this perhaps represents constantly recurring short-term migration; if they go just for a few weeks at critical planting and harvest times to supervise relatives or labourers, they might be regarded as visiting. The terms used are not important, but recognition of the ways in which large numbers of women maintain this mobility between urban and rural homes is vital.

So also is the fact that young children often travel with their mothers on these occasions, while many other children move between town and country with school terms and holidays. Remarkably few researchers seem to have bothered about movements of children (Gould 1975) even though in African countries the under-sixteens constitute half the population, and though their present life-style must greatly influence their future attitudes as adults. The fact that so many are growing up as 'a child of two worlds' greatly increases the plausibility of the proposition that strong urban–rural interaction may remain a lasting and valued African phenomenon, rather than representing a temporary maladjustment.

Discussions of future prospects, of children, and of the limitations of current research leads to the issue of the rural ties of the urban-born children of migrants. Surprisingly little is known of these, even with respect to something as specific as visits.

In so far as various writers give some impression of the patterns, this varies from place to place. Gibbal (1974: 288, 309, 314) suggests that most people born in Abidjan have much weaker links with any rural home community than those who have themselves migrated, with few visits in either direction. Peil (1972: 215) says of Ghana that 'second-generation city dwellers who do not go home regularly with parents during childhood will lose all but vague emotional attachment to "home"', but she does not speculate on what proportion do not do so. Caldwell hints that even many of the urban-born in Ghana will visit their ancestral home area, and Gugler (1971: 405) suggests the same for south-eastern Nigeria. In

Dar es Salaam, Leslie (1963: 254) found that while the urban-born of some ethnic groups had a few rural links, those of other groups had strong ties, involving many visits. The fullest study of the second generation is that undertaken in Kumasi by Schildkrout (1978), but the Mossi on whom it was focused are unusual in that even the first generation visit home less often than comparable groups elsewhere.

The transmission of ideas and innovation

The exchange of visits between urban and rural dwellers is not merely an important aspect of life for millions of people, but is also highly significant for the spread of ideas and attitudes from one area to another. We tend to think first of a spread from city to countryside, but transmission to the cities of changing ideas in the countryside is also involved. Perhaps innovations do flow predominantly in one direction, but information of various types is constantly flowing both ways. These processes are, of course, not peculiar to tropical Africa, but they are especially important there because of the extreme contrasts between some aspects of city life and some aspects of rural life, especially where the city still largely reflects alien cultures. In countries where most people are still rural dwellers, the national role of the cities as the meeting ground of cultures depends heavily on these flows of ideas and information to and from the rural areas.

In addition to people just making visits, the migrants themselves are bringing ideas, attitudes and knowledge with them, which must influence the longer-settled townsfolk whom they are joining. Likewise, those who return to their rural homelands, whether after a city career or after six months' unsuccessful job search, are often extremely important agents of change there. Influential roles are also played by other groups, such as itinerant traders or city-trained schoolteachers and nurses working in rural schools and health centres, not to mention Ministry of Agriculture extension workers. Supplementing all these direct movements of people there is the flow of letters, and now the almost ubiquitous radio. It is nonsense to suggest that almost every rural family has a radio, as some writers have done, but there is at least one in the great majority of villages in rural Africa today.

The theme of the city as the centre of change in what are sometimes termed 'traditional societies', made explicit for parts of Asia by Dwyer (1972), also permeates much writing on Africa. Thus

Gutkind (1962: 185) writes that cities are 'centres in which a major restructuring of African society as a whole is taking place, a restructuring which is reaching deep into the countryside'. Miner (1967: 1) observes that 'the emergence of national cultures in Africa is overwhelmingly an urban phenomenon'. Similarly, Hanna and Hanna (1981: 2) claim that African cities 'are the forgers of new national communities' and that 'in the post-independence period, most of the ideas for nation-building, economic development and even revolution have been born in towns'. Other presentations of this view of the cities as catalysts are provided in the studies by Gould (1970), Riddell (1970) and Soja (1968) on the geography of modernization, and in a volume on regional planning edited by Mabogunje and Faniran (1977). Gould's study of Tanzania clearly indicated how the type of changes that he was tracing were concentrated in the towns, and rather less clearly suggested that they diffused from them. Soja found proximity to, and linkage with, Nairobi to be a key variable in his analysis of spatial patterns of modernization in Kenya, though contrasting rates of change among Kikuyu and Masai show that proximity alone may be less significant than the types of relationship established.

Riddell's proposition that innovations have cascaded down the urban hierarchy was noted in the last chapter, and like Gould he suggested that many types of change spread eventually from small towns into the rural areas. This undoubtedly happens, but through actual interaction among people rather than in any mechanistic way. The role of the urban hierarchy as a whole is such that no clear contrasts in terms of social or economic change are apparent between the rural areas fairly close to Freetown and those further away. Likewise in Tanzania, proximity to Dar es Salaam has had few marked effects on the rural districts of the Coast Region. On the other hand, Abidjan in Ivory Coast and Kampala in Uganda do appear to influence particularly strongly the rural areas surrounding them. The importance of sheer distance can easily be exaggerated: that of differences in circumstances from one area to another cannot.

We might be more specific about the types of ideas or innovation that are diffused from the cities when migrants return either on a visit or permanently. As they relate their experiences, either accurately or with some embroidery, they clearly increase the villagers' awareness of the city and of differences between life in the two places. They may also contribute to the nation-building process by increasing people's awareness of the new nation-state; and they may contribute to the gradual change in the rural dwellers' world-view, lending credence to what has been heard in primary school or over the radio.

Some of the new ideas and information transmitted from the cities to the countryside are clearly beneficial, such as ways of improving health. Others, including new consumption patterns ranging from the use of baby food which requires mixing with water to the smoking of cigarettes, are much more open to question. Some changes of diet are harmful in nutritional terms and lead to increased dependence on imports, but others provide a real improvement in the quality of life. Many changes in material culture, concerning dress, furniture and house-building materials for example, involve increased convenience but also the loss of cultural distinctiveness. Perhaps more important, however, are all the changes in respect of attitudes, aspirations, behaviour and personal relationships, which we shall have to leave to the anthropologists and sociologists such as Lloyd (1967), and Peil (1977). They are summarized for Ghana by Caldwell (1969: 206) thus: 'Rural Ghanaians look upon the large towns as the sources from which the new patterns of living will come to an extent that would astonish rural residents in many developed countries.'

The reverse flows are not necessarily less important, but they have an impact in different ways. The rural dwellers are not informing existing urban dwellers of a world of which the latter were only dimly aware, but are merely reminding them of things and keeping them up to date. Their contribution is often to reinforce cultural traits which might otherwise be rapidly weakened in the cosmopolitan city. Within the realm of ideas, rural–urban flows will generally represent forces for preservation rather than for change, and this may be even more true in respect of attitudes.

However, in another sense, migrants from the rural areas, and even visitors, are changing the cities by the sets of ideas, attitudes and behaviour that they bring with them. This is particularly relevant in the post-colonial era and in those cities where colonial expatriates had the strongest influences. An obvious example is the rapid spread in cities such as Lusaka of housing which shares many characteristics with rural housing: slightly less obvious are the expansion of indigenous forms of medicine within the urban environment (Leeson and Frankenberg 1977) and the prevalence of witchcraft (La Fontaine 1970: 182–6).

Such features may be seen as the 'ruralization' of the cities, but in general they represent only the addition of elements brought from the rural environment, rather than substantial change of what already existed. The latter can also happen however, language providing one example. The substantial shift from English to Swahili in Dar es Salaam results from a wide range of factors, but these certainly include the in-migration of many people who know no English, as well as governmental (perhaps presidential) aware-ness of the value of using Swahili for effective contact between the city and the country's rural majority. Even in other cities increasing use of, and respect for, indigenous languages may be seen today.

There is some debate about how far cities in tropical Africa are really the sources of ideas and of changes which are now permeating the countryside, or are merely agents through which ideas from other parts of the world are being channelled (Little 1974: 103).

The cities may at present be primarily transmitters rather than generators of information, innovations and ideas. Some of these are in reality being imposed on rural Africa from Europe and North America through neo-colonial relationships in which the cities play a critical role: but such a negative view is not always appropriate, for the people of rural Africa are making their own desires for change perfectly clear. Furthermore, the process considerably pre-dates the colonial period, as exemplified by the role of towns in the spread of Islam through the Sahel. It also extends far beyond changes directly attributable to colonial status, such as the gradual spread of familiarity with European languages (though rarely fluent use of them), to aspects of 'Westernization' such as division of the year into fifty-two weeks, the week into seven days, and the day into twenty-four hours. (We might note in passing that such aspects of 'Westernization' often actually originated in China!)

Flows of goods

Even in pre-colonial Africa trade played a vital role in urban growth. Kano supplied manufactured goods to places far away, and many of these were produced in the surrounding villages rather than in the city itself. At the same time, this and other cities provided some consumer goods for the rural population in exchange for food. In Uganda much agricultural produce was brought into the Buganda capital as tribute (Gutkind 1963).

Then during the colonial period one of the main purposes of establishing towns throughout tropical Africa was to assist extraction of rural produce to supply growing demands in Europe, first for palm oil, then for groundnuts, cotton, coffee and cocoa. In some countries the pattern was extremely simple, for a single urban centre constituted the organizational focus, the collecting point, and the port for shipment of the produce overseas. Examples include Banjul in the Gambia, and Lomé in Togo, where the basic pattern remains unchanged to this day. Dakar in Senegal and Abidjan in Ivory Coast fulfilled similar functions, though with more assistance from subsidiary towns. Even in Uganda the initial spread of cotton growing was organized from Kampala, but soon the bulk of the crop was being sent across Lake Victoria to Kisumu railhead, and shipped overseas through Mombasa. Later coffee overtook cotton in importance, and the coffee trade was more firmly centred on Kampala, but Mombasa remained the export port, and Nairobi played some role also. Meanwhile cotton cultivation had largely shifted to the east and north, so that most of the cotton crop passed through Mbale and Tororo rather than either Kampala or Jinja, while towns like Soroti and Gulu had become local collecting centres.

The more productive parts of rural Africa were seen in Britain, France and Belgium not only as sources of primary products, but also as potential markets for manufactures. Some imports into African countries have always been destined largely for the towns themselves, but others, such as textiles or simple household utensils, as well as farm implements, have been widely distributed among the rural population. And whereas in countries such as Uganda crop exports may now bypass the cities to some extent, nearly all imports pass through them. Flows of commodities to and from the ports, often via provincial towns, thus formed an essential part of the rural–urban system built up during the colonial period, and remain extremely important today.

A recent change, much encouraged by the attainment of political independence, has been the growth of manufacturing in the cities, largely on the basis of import substitution. In some cases this has merely meant that imports have been of basic products such as crude oil or wheat rather than refined petroleum products or flour, but in many others it has provided a local market for cash crops such as cotton and groundnuts. Import-substitution policies have incurred much criticism but in terms of the national economy the use of local cottom to produce textiles or local groundnuts to produce cooking oil seems eminently appropriate. It also represents a structural change in the economy, but it may have little effect on the spatial pattern of rural–urban and urban–rural commodity flows. Groundnuts are still brought into Kano city from rural northern Nigeria as in the past, but mainly for use in the city's oil mills. Cotton textiles are still distributed through rural Mali from Bamako, but most are now produced in factories there.

There is not the place for a comprehensive survey of such movements of goods throughout tropical Africa. We shall merely note three ways in which the situation differs from one country to another. One concerns the intensity of such flows. For many years in southern Ghana, and now to an even greater extent in Ivory Coast, the countryside has been penetrated by numerous vehicles collecting crops and distributing consumer goods, whereas in Upper Volta, and even in northern Ghana they are still few and far between. The same contrasts are apparent on a local scale in every country. Another variation is in the modes of transport employed. Railways remain important for some flows, such as that of sisal to the ports in Tanzania, but elsewhere road transport has taken over even bulk long-distance movements. At the local level, the bicycle is of immense importance for moving goods in some areas, such as most parts of Uganda and south-eastern Nigeria, while it is very little used in others, such as south-western Nigeria and most parts of Sierra Leone. The reasons for these variations merit research.

A third variation is in the nature of the organization of such flows. Five structures that are all represented in one country or another are continuing control by European trading companies, control of a large part of the trade by Lebanese or Indian merchants, an almost complete takeover by local private entrepreneurs, management by co-operative societies, and control even down to the village level by the state.

The type of rural–urban commodity flow that has received most attention in the academic literature is the flow of basic foodstuffs to meet the needs of the increasing urban population. This is a fundamental element in the process of urbanization in most places at most times; it is one of the ways in which African economies can be shifted from dependence on the twin pillars of a subsistence sector and an export/import sector; and it is one way in which city growth should surely be of direct benefit to sections of the rural population.

Much of the work on this subject has been undertaken under the auspices of the Centre d'Etudes de Géographie Tropicale in Bordeaux. Three volumes of case studies have been published (CEGET 1972, CNRS 1976, CEGET 1977), while Vennetier provided an overview in the first of these. The studies ranged over ten countries, and indicated wide diversity in farmers' responses to the increasing demand for foodstuffs and other rural produce. Some of the smaller cities such as N'Djamena have not yet had much impact, since many of the townspeople have their own plots of land in the vicinity; and in some rather larger cities, such as Bangui, requirements are satisfied partly by supplies from rural relatives: but the needs of cities such as Abidjan and Douala are increasingly being met commercially by farmers and traders.

Supplies of meat, often on the hoof, are more completely commercialized, and often involve movements of cattle over long distances, especially to cities in the tsetse infested regions, such as Douala and Brazzaville. Ouagadougou is one of a number of cities where a basic need which few people can provide for themselves is fuelwood. A flourishing rural–urban trade in this commodity was already well established in the 1960s, and this has expanded there and elsewhere in the 1970s as kerosine prices have risen.

Patterns of fuelwood supplies to Kano have been mapped by Mortimore (1972), who pointed out that the donkeys which bring most of it often take back loads of manure gathered from animals kept in urban compounds. Studies of food supplies to town markets elsewhere in Nigeria have been undertaken by Hodder and Ukwu (1969) and by Onyemelukwe (1972). In the case of Uganda the supply of basic foodstuffs to Jinja in the 1960s has been analysed by Brandt and Schubert (1972).

The prices paid to the farmers for these food crops often seem extremely low. In part this reflects real transport costs, the risks of handling perishable commodities, and so on: but in part it reflects the profit margin of the urban-based middlemen. In some countries deliberate government policies also keep down food prices for the urban population. None the less, this flow of produce is bringing some extra income to farmers, and in some of the more fertile areas such as southern Uganda it is providing an outlet for surplus food crops that would otherwise just go to waste. In other areas, such as the West African Sahel, the cities usefully absorb a seasonal surplus of basic foodstuffs, though too often farmers then have to buy food at exorbitant prices later in the year, so that the real need is for better rural storage facilities.

Transfers of money

It should not be too difficult to discover much more about transfers of goods between city and countryside. The problems would lie largely in the effort and cost of conducting traffic counts and so on, and analysing the results. The situation with regard to transfers of money is altogether more complex, yet this is a critically important aspect of urban–rural relations. The claims that the cities are often parasitic and exploitative cannot be evaluated without some reference to these flows: but no data exist on most of them, and none could easily be gathered.

The problems are conceptual as well as practical. Direct money flows include payments for the rural produce supplied to the cities, and for that shipped directly overseas, and equivalent payments for the goods and services provided for the rural population by or through the cities. For a real evaluation, however, we should know how far these money flows fairly reflect the value of the goods and services in question. If trade is organized from the cities some funds must remain there, as profits if it is in private hands, or to cover administrative costs if it is undertaken by the state. Who is to say whether the rural dwellers are getting a fair deal or whether these profits or administrative costs are excessive?

Other direct flows are cash remittances made by those living in the towns, on which some data have been gathered, but while some of these are made to kinsmen who are rural dwellers others remain within the immediate family and may be used for such purposes as building a house for the remitter's own use later in life. Are we then considering transfers between urban and rural people, or best between urban and rural areas?

Possibly more significant in relation to suspected parasitic relationships are flows within government channels, arising from tax collection and public expenditure. No one has yet succeeded in determining for any African country how much of the total tax burden falls on the rural population, especially since much comes from import duties on commodities such as petroleum; and efforts to determine the allocation of expenditure between rural and urban areas have been no more successful. We can ascertain what proportion of spending has gone into agriculture, or into urban infrastructure; but who is deemed to benefit from new roads which traverse rural areas but are used by much inter-city traffic? How should we allocate disturbingly high military expenditure – by the location of the barracks, the origins of the soldiers, or the life-style of the commanders?

There is thus no possibility of establishing for any country, much less for tropical Africa as a whole, to what extent the cities extract a surplus from the countryside, which may then in part be passed on through the international urban system to the rich world. Nor in the much less likely event of a net subsidy of the rural areas anywhere could we determine the extent of that. All that can be done here is to review certain types of cash transaction, and to demonstrate spatial variations with respect to these.

Personal remittances

One set of transactions that force us to reject any suggestions that African cities are totally parasitic upon the rural areas are the cash remittances made by migrants to their rural relatives. Several surveys indicate that these far outweigh personal transfers of cash in the opposite direction, and represent a far higher proportion of urban earnings than in most parts of the world.

The most extreme case is provided by a survey of Nairobi working men, undertaken by Johnson and Whitelaw (1974). They found that 89 per cent made regular remittances, and that these averaged 21 per cent of their earnings. In his study of two Nairobi housing estates, Ross (1975: 46) found more than 80 per cent of households making regular remittances. Stren (1978: 268) reports a similar finding in a Mombasa municipal housing estate, with a rather lower figure for the Majengo area of traditional housing. In Tanzania (Sabot 1979: 194–7) a major national survey found that 61 per cent of male migrants make remittances to their home areas, and that 72 per cent of those who have been in town for over a year do so. In Harare also, Moller (1978: 243–6) found a clear majority making remittances to the rural areas, often amounting to 15 or 20 per cent of income.

West African examples are provided by Caldwell (1969: 153–63), Plotnicov (1970: 70–3) and Adepoju (1974: 132–6). Caldwell found that rather more than half the households in Ghana cities send cash to rural relatives, and that almost two-thirds of migrant households do so – generally once a month. The dependence of many rural households on these cash flows emerged clearly from his parallel rural survey. Adepoju found that among the migrants in the Yoruba town of Oshogbo, 60 per cent made remittances, in half the cases about once a month, and he asserts (p. 136) that 'a substantial part of the migrants' income flows out in the form of remittances, gifts, goods and savings to the migrants' home communities'.

Plotnicov spells out particularly clearly the uses to which remittances are put, but others tell a similar story. Some is spent on consumer goods by the rural kinsfolk, some is used for school fees and medical treatment, a little is injected into agriculture. Larger sums may be needed for special crises or ceremonies. In parts of Nigeria some funds are sent on behalf of village improvement unions for the building of churches, schools or dispensaries. Some funds are sent to pay for the construction of the retirement homes mentioned earlier, and wherever rural land is increasingly being bought and sold remittances are also used for land purchase. Yet another use of increasing importance, especially where urban dwellers have either bought or inherited land, is the payment of one or two farm labourers.

It is extremely difficult to say how much of this flow is to the ultimate benefit of these who have remained in the rural areas. Money invested in schooling may result in the loss of those children to the city, but meanwhile the funds have been used mainly to pay rural teachers. Money invested in a retirement house is largely for the ultimate benefit of the urban dweller, but it has provided employment for village people. Those who see nothing good in the urbanization process argue that direct gifts to rural relatives merely create a taste for luxury consumer goods supplied from the cities, and cause local inflation in the process. Yet Adepoju (p. 135) suggests that 'the remittance system has made it possible for a large number of people in the rural areas to benefit from the development and growth of the urban economy'. Caldwell (p. 216) concludes that the cash flow 'is a demonstration that the development of the urban economy directly benefits very large numbers of people who do not take up residence in the towns', while 'the effect of cash remittances on rural areas is a good deal more important in causing fundamental economic change than is suggested merely by a rise in consumption levels'.

Gugler and Flanagan (1978: 70) also accept that urban–rural transfers 'provide a means of mitigating the serious inequalities that exist between urban and rural areas' despite their critical view of current rural–urban migration. With respect to Zambia, Bates (1976: 253) has expressed the matter even more strongly: 'migration has served as a means whereby rural dwellers extract wealth from the towns and transfer it to the village communities', using the mechanism of family ties to manipulate the labour market.

There are, of course, considerable differences from one rural area to another in these respects – perhaps greater than the differences from one city to another. In parts of northern Ghana and western Kenya, where there is severe population pressure on limited resources, some people are now partly dependent on remittances for sheer survival. One can regard that either as clear benefit, or as shoring up socio-economic structures that need drastic reform. In more affluent parts of southern Ghana and central Kenya, some remittances are used to expand the size of farms that already bring in a good income, or to develop small trading concerns. One can regard that either as stimulating the rural economy, or as the pernicious spread of capitalist enterprise. Agreement on the extent of real benefit resulting from remittances will never be reached, but without doubt they play a large part in ensuring that urban dwellers and many rural dwellers remain part of a single interlocking system.

Two types of money flow which are very important in other continents do not loom so large in tropical Africa. Firstly, few rural dwellers pay rents to big landowners who live in the cities and spend their money there, as so many do in Latin America. Most land is held under customary tenure, while the remainder is mainly owner-occupied. Until the 1970s parts of Ethiopia constituted the sole exception, and even there the situation has changed since the revolution brought expropriation of the aristocracy's private estates. On the other hand, the new elite in many countries are buying large blocks of rural land, not always in their home areas. These are normally worked by wage labourers rather than occupied by tenants, but part of the farm profits is no doubt transmitted to the cities. Vennetier (1976: 172) notes this new phenomenon in Zaire, the Central African Republic and elsewhere, while it is spreading rapidly in Kenya and Nigeria also.

Secondly, rural dwellers in most parts of tropical Africa are not paying interest to moneylenders to the same extent as, for instance, in India. Lack of capital is certainly a problem throughout rural Africa, and much borrowing takes place, but there are not many people in the towns who make handsome profit from money-lending as a full-time activity. However, there are disturbing signs of increasing numbers of people falling into debt, and having to pay high interest charges, especially to traders from whom they have made purchases on credit.

Flows handled by government

With respect to flows of money reaching the government through taxation, the rural population contributed a very large share in most territories during the colonial period. The level of personal or poll tax may seem to have been small in absolute terms, but it often represented a high proportion of people's cash income, while the graduated income tax levied on the urban population was often quite modest. Furthermore, much government revenue in such countries as Ghana and Uganda came from taxes on export crops and thus essentially from the rural population.

Since independence the importance of both flat-rate personal tax and export taxes on cash crops has declined in many countries, while that of both graduated income tax and taxes on urban-based commerce and industry has increased. In Nigeria change has been particularly drastic, for the advent of oil as a source of government revenue has permitted the abolition of taxes on cash crops. It has also made the distinction between urban and rural sources of revenue almost meaningless, especially as the greater part of the oil comes from off-shore. If the national economy has to be divided into rural and urban sectors, we surely must say that the latter is contributing most to government revenue in Nigeria, but we might do better to use this example to underline the unrealistic nature of such a clear-cut dichotomy.

With respect to government expenditure, examples of spending which could not be allocated as either urban or rural were given above. A few further observations may be in order since several writers have presented a rather misleading picture on this subject. The very small share set aside for agriculture in the expenditure projected by many African development plans is often quoted as evidence of urban bias. Sometimes, however, only direct central government expenditures have been considered when there are also Regional programmes, as in Zambia, or State plans, as in Nigeria, with much more planned rural investment.

The general picture for tropical Africa is of a pattern of government spending not far out of line with the pattern of government revenues in so far as any realistic distinctions between rural and urban can be made. In many countries there is evidence of a net flow of funds from rural to urban areas, but this is perhaps quite appropriate in a situation where there is also a rapid shift of population so that the extra requirements for housing, schools or whatever are heavily concentrated in the cities. On the other hand, a reverse flow could be justified in terms of rectifying inequities inherited from the past, and perhaps also to slow down the rate of rural–urban migration over the next decade.

Any general picture must mask substantial national variations. Tanzania is widely known for its policies of increasing the rural share of government spending. It is often sharply contrasted with Kenya, but by the late 1970s moves in the same direction were also taking place there. In Zambia the government has found great difficulty in shifting its expenditure away from the urban sector, but this sector is responsible for a particularly large proportion of revenues there (Bates 1976: chapter 6). In Nigeria there is much evidence of a flow of government funds from rural to urban areas in the past (Olatunbosun 1975), but the shift to oil as the main source of revenue has been followed by some genuine efforts to allocate more funds to rural development. The most outstanding example of urban concentration of present government spending is probably Zaire, but the state of the rural economy there is such that the government cannot be obtaining very much tax revenue from it. Certainly, it is the mining sector which contributes the largest share of such revenue.

Everywhere, however, the picture is blurred by the way in which urban and rural components are integrated into an even more closely interlocking single system in respect of government revenues and expenditure than in respect of most other aspects of life.

Power and authority

The spatial distribution of power is another aspect of urban–rural relationships (Friedmann 1975), but it is impossible to do justice here to a subject so complex that it really merits a book to itself. In most eras and in most parts of the world cities have tended to be centres of power and authority, whether sacred (Wheatley 1969) or secular. In this respect tropical Africa today is no exception.

The old indigenous towns of south-western Nigeria have an intimate set of relationships with the surrounding areas that largely depend on their role as the seat of the *Oba* or king, to whom all people equally owe allegiance wherever they normally reside (Krapf-Askari 1969: 25). The rise of Ibadan and other new Yoruba towns in the nineteenth century, the advent of colonial rule, and changing administrative structures since independence have all modified this structure, but they have by no means swept it away. In northern Nigeria change over the past hundred years has been more drastic, but the Emirs of Kano, Katsina, Sokoto and other cities still exercise strong powers over the people living in the surrounding villages, which once were really part of a city-state, and rather weaker powers over the people of rural areas far beyond.

Elsewhere, both capital cities and provincial towns were set up by the colonial authorities for the specific purpose of controlling the people of the surrounding areas, and that spatial pattern of control has been inherited by the post-colonial states. In every country the basic administrative apparatus of the state is organized from a city, with government departments located there responsible for the country as a whole, and with a series of regional, provincial or district offices invariably located in other urban centres. Structures for the administration of particular sectors such as education and health are normally very similar to those for general administration, and the same applies to the police and the judiciary. Even agriculture is controlled through a similar town-based network of offices.

There is now a gradual progression from power exercised through government departments, and that exercised through parastatal organizations such as crop marketing boards and transport authorities, to that held by private organizations such as banks and trading companies which use exactly the same urban network to control what goes on in the country as a whole. In such ways the towns and cities play a huge role in the organization of space, and it is there that major decisions are taken that influence the lives of all citizens, urban and rural dwellers alike.

To what extent does tropical Africa differ in this respect from other parts of the world? One difference is that in most of Africa this structure was imposed from outside, very suddenly, and still relatively recently. Whereas the concentration of power in Moscow and Madrid, or even Kano and Kumasi, was a fairly gradual process, it was concentrated almost overnight in Kinshasa, Nairobi, Abidjan and Freetown, which had in no way previously constituted a focus for the surrounding areas. It was a traumatic change for farming communities which had for generations done whatever they thought fit, to be sternly required, or even gently advised, by someone from a new urban centre, to do something different. However, we need not summarize the nature of colonial rule here: nor perhaps do more than suggest that the replacement of a white face by a black one in the district offices makes very little difference. For many rural communities, control from a distant town still seems something new, something irksome in many ways, but something rather unreal in others.

Another somewhat distinctive feature of tropical Africa is the limited and spatially concentrated nature of the state apparatus. Contrary to popular belief the bureaucracies are extremely small in relation to the total national population, and power lies largely in the hands of a very few people – often the president and a small circle around him. Very little lies with ordinary members of parliament, most of whom represent mainly rural constituencies; and local government is generally very weak, especially in the rural areas. The fact that in most countries government business is conducted in a language understood by few rural dwellers accentuates this concentration. The towns may have played a major role in incorporating the farmers into the world economy, but the rural majority are incorporated to only a very limited extent into the political process of the modern state.

Even most political parties are much more firmly established in the cities than elsewhere, and in all those countries which experienced a peaceful transition to independence the process largely involved taking over control there. As Miner (1967: 10) has said, 'small groups of powerful men in a few African cities work to create the sort of modern society which they require'. Once any group has control of the towns it can claim to represent the state, even if those towns house only 10 per cent of the country's population. The significance of such control was made clear in the lengthy conflicts in Zaire and southern Sudan, and in both the rule and the eventual overthrow of Idi Amin in Uganda. It is equally relevant today in Ethiopia's efforts to retain control in Eritrea.

A third feature of tropical Africa, however, is that the power of the state is far from all-pervasive. While urban-based government officials are still constantly telling rural dwellers what to do, just as during the colonial period, they often have little effect, as Hyden (1980) has clearly demonstrated for Tanzania. The spatial concentration of power is reflected in the ease with which coups have been achieved; its limited extent is shown by the small effect that most of these have had on the rural population, and the difficulty that many new leaders have had in consolidating their position. At one level decision-making in, say, Congo is highly concentrated in Brazzaville, but at another level it is widely distributed among the peasants, who take very little notice of what is decided there. The present Congo government may enunciate Marxist principles, but Brazzaville does not have the powers to operate a command economy throughout the country. Furthermore, there have been many cases of rural rebellion in post-colonial Africa, when those holding power have attempted to exert it.

The concentration of state power, and indeed private sector economic power, in the urban centres would be deeply disturbing if this meant concentration in the hands of a few elite families who were wholly identified with those centres; but as explained elsewhere, this is not so. At present the concentration is essentially geographical, and those who exercise power from the towns almost invariably have rural roots. Resentment at the concentration may increase if this situation changes over the next one or two generations; but by then various countries may have experimented with new decentralized administrative structures.

In countries which experience a peaceful transfer of power from a colonial government which has ruled through a totally urban-based structure, it is hardly surprising that this structure at first remains intact: but it may in due course be rejected in the same way as the 'Westminster-style' party system. It is the ex-Portuguese territories that are leading the way in this direction. They did not experience a peaceful transfer of power, and the parties now in control had several years' experience of administering large areas from rural bases. Yet even in Mozambique and Guinea–Bissau it will be some years before it is clear whether lasting decentralized structures have been established, or whether Maputo and Bissau will rule. Meanwhile, Tanzania is having some success in spreading power within the CCM party from a few city dwellers to large sections of the rural population, but is making less progress with the decentralization of power in other channels. In many other countries, such as Ivory Coast and Zaire, no serious attempts have been made to check a totally one-way 'flow' of authority, though of course some would argue that control there is really exercised from Paris or New York/Washington.

Conclusions

This chapter has investigated only a few of the innumerable relationships between African cities and the rural areas, but it should have indicated their intensity and importance, as well as their complexity. For the urban dwellers themselves these relationships are both more intense and more important than anywhere else in the world. For the outside observer the usual baffling complexity of urban–rural economic links is compounded by the social networks which continue to tie together the urban and rural members of extended families and kinship groups. This has much relevance for the worldwide debates on the generative or parasitic role of cities, and on urban/rural disparities in welfare, but study of the tropical African situation provides no simple answers.

The main problems arise from perception of the cities and the rural areas as totally discrete and separate entities, and from failure to distinguish between people and place. In physical terms the cities are indeed relatively discrete entities, although around each there is a peri-urban zone within which it is hard to say where 'urban' ends and 'rural' begins. We can certainly identify small totally urban tracts and extensive totally rural tracts. Yet it is not reasonable to speak of areas either assisting or exploiting other areas: only people can do these things, and people can be identified with place to only a limited and variable degree.

The debates must therefore be about whether the urban dwellers do or do not exploit the rural dwellers; and the special difficulty in Africa lies in the identification of these two groups. Most adults now resident in the cities were born and brought up in a rural environment, retain strong links with it, and probably intend to end their days there, while many are living in the city only temporarily with their main attachment still being to the farm. Conversely, a substantial, but largely unknown, proportion of those resident in the rural areas have some experience of city life. Some are only on temporary visits from homes in the city, and probably the majority have some members of their families away there. It is thus hard to accept for tropical Africa Lipton's (1977: 13) proposition that 'the most important class conflict in the poor countries of the world today is . . . between the rural classes and the urban classes'.

An example of the difficulty in distinguishing urban and rural populations is presented by the question of comparative educational opportunities. Do Nairobi or Abidjan children have far greater opportunities than their rural counterparts? The question is not so simple. A few children have been born and brought up in the city; others have moved in as part of a family migration and then attended city schools; others have remained with the rural-based branch of the family for schooling away from the harmful influences of the city; yet others have moved into the city specifically for better schooling. One cannot even distinguish clearly between urban and rural schools in countries like Kenya and Uganda, where some of the most prestigious secondary schools are boarding schools located at a discrete distance from the cities.

Another difficulty in accepting or rejecting general statements such as Lipton's lies in the diversity of urban traditions. In so far as recent writings on tropical African urban bias have differentiated between indigenous and colonial cities, they have tended to assume that the latter have been the more parasitic. Some have even quoted Mabogunje's (1965) paper on Nigerian urbanization as a constraint on economic development as substantiation of this, whereas that paper actually suggested that some of the indigenous cities were the most parasitic.

The same view is expressed in his book (1968: 315–16), and it is with reference to cities established or rejuvenated during colonial rule that he says (p. 324) 'policy must be based on the realization of the crucial role of urban centres for generating economic development within a given region'. Similarly, just after a discussion of indigenous towns bypassed by colonial transport routes. Ajaegbu (1976: 44) suggests that 'it is to some of these towns today that the adjective "parasitic" is still apt'.

Part of the problem lies in the imprecision of these terms, and in the widespread acceptance of the parasitic/generative dichotomy put forward by Hoselitz (1957), when the latter must mean generative *of* some*thing* while the former must mean parasitic *upon* some*one*. Possibly the colonial cities have been both more generative and more parasitic than the indigenous cities, the real query being with what has been generated.

There is little doubt that city dwellers benefit from most urban–rural relationships. Some have jobs which depend almost entirely on rural activities, such as those engaged in the cocoa trade in Ghana or the coffee trade in Kenya. Many more have jobs which depend on providing goods or services for the whole population, urban and rural, whether in a textile factory or a government ministry. There would not be such a large concentration of jobs, of physical infrastructure or of social amenities in Abidjan, or even in Dar es Salaam, if these cities did not have large, predominantly rural, hinterlands to support them. More specific links such as the supply of food and fuel also benefit the urban dwellers, while the security provided by a rural homeland where even the more committed townsman would always find a welcome and to which he could retire represents a benefit of a rather different kind.

For those who see most of life as a zero-sum-game, in which one person's gain must be another's loss, these benefits for people in the city must be at the expense of people in the rural areas; but that is not the view offered here. It seems quite possible that many of these relationships also benefit most rural dwellers although it is very unlikely that the gains are equally distributed.

Unless one believes that it would have been better for the farmers of southern Ghana never to have grown any cocoa, and that the smallholders in Kenya are ill-advised to grow coffee or tea, then clearly these groups benefit from the activities of the port workers in Takoradi and Mombasa. Unless it can be shown that cottage indus-try is a viable alternative, then surely a textile factory in Dar es Salaam aids both Tanzanian cotton growers and the rural consum-ers of the products. Even most government ministries surely per-form some services of value to the rural population!

The supply of food to the cities illustrates perhaps the most common situation, i.e. of links which do aid the rural population but which should aid them more – and in some places are beginning to do so. In those districts which can produce a surplus of such food-stuffs there is little local demand, since most families meet their own needs, while there is often no prospect of overseas sales. An expand-ing pool of urban consumers is therefore just what is required. However, the prices paid in the past were often unjustifiably low, and recent sharp rises in food prices in many cities are quite approp-riate, provided that most of the increase does reach the farmers.

In purely material terms there is little evidence that any African city is parasitic in the sense that the rural population would be materially better-off if it did not exist. Yet most city dwellers are enjoying somewhat better material standards of living than the majority of the rural population; and they are probably gaining disproportionately from relationships between the two groups. The actual extent of the disequilibrium varies not only from city to city, but also from one rural community to another; any policy proposals would have to pay much heed to this. Just as some of the less developed countries would benefit more than others from a trim-ming of their links with the rich world, so also some African rural areas would benefit much more than others from an equivalent policy in respect of links with the cities.

So research on the ways in which African rural and urban

dwellers gain and lose from the relationships between them will be of most value if comparisons are made, for instance between rural areas close to the cities and those further away, or between those with local population pressure on the land and those where land is superabundant. This might well reveal that even if urbanization is not really taking place at the expense of those remaining in the rural areas throughout tropical Africa, particular rural communities are suffering not just from the effects of out-migration by their liveliest members, but also from their ongoing relationships with people in the cities.

This is not just another plea for less generalization and more study of specific cases. In respect of ongoing urban–rural relationships, as in respect of migration, there are clear similarities between southern Ghana and southern Uganda, arising from the possibility of frequent contact with the major cities. In Kenya, both the Kikuyu areas close to Nairobi and the Mijikenda areas around Mombasa show similar features. Conversely, there are similarities between northern Ghana, western Kenya, and northern Uganda in the nature of their relationships with the cities. One could therefore think in terms of a model distinguishing these two types of urban–rural relationship; or perhaps one distinguishing rural areas within commuting distance, those within reach for weekly to monthly visits, those with links to be maintained even though visits can rarely be more than annual, and those which still have very weak links with the cities. However, even the application of this model to specific countries would require consideration of other factors, such as the degree to which one ethnic group is dominant in each city, the social structure of the rural groups concerned, and the agricultural resources available to them, as well as the position of the city on the alien/indigenous continuum.

If it is hard to be precise about the material consequences of urban–rural relationships, it is even harder in respect of other consequences. Yet a full assessment of the impact of urbanization on rural communities, and of the gains and losses to them from contact with the cities, would involve consideration of a much wider range of issues. Many concern the spread of ideas and values, both through personal contact and through new forms of communication such as radio. This is to a large extent a one-way process throughout tropical Africa, with ideas on everything from dress and diet to political systems spreading from city to countryside rather than the reverse. While new migrants bring various notions and life-styles from the rural areas into the cities there is little evidence of these spreading among the existing urban population. In countries such as Tanzania genuine attempts have been made by urban-based decision-makers to pay heed to the views of rural dwellers, but the extent of such rural–to–urban influence is very small. Even the very idea of the Tanzanian (or Kenyan or Nigerian) nation is being diffused from the cities.

The consequences of continuing urbanization for the rural population may be far greater in terms of the spread of notions and attitudes, either generated in the cities or brought through them from overseas, than in terms of material changes. However, analysis of these consequences is beyond the scope of this book, while any assessment of whether they constitute gains or losses would have to be even more subjective than in relation to material well-being. Study of both variation from place to place and change over time in the urban–rural spread of ideas in Africa is a task for the future. Are the effects on the rural population in Senegal similar to those in Zambia, or quite different? Are urban influences generally increasing or is the widespread shift from short-term circulation to long-term migration reducing the non-material impact of the cities on the rural population? Discussion of these questions must await such study.

10 Conclusions

Rapid urbanization is undoubtedly one of the most important changes now occurring in tropical Africa, with implications for every aspect of life throughout the region. The situation today is vastly different from that of a hundred, or even twenty, years ago; and it will be very different again in twenty years' time, so that immense challenges face today's decision-makers.

Urbanism is by no means totally alien to tropical Africa, but its present extent clearly owes much to the colonial experience. Specifically, cities and towns played a critical role in colonial penetration, and more generally they have grown up here, as in many other regions, largely as points of contact between local populations and outsiders. Indeed, most African cities reflect the meeting of cultures to such an extent that many of their features, from employment structures to housing systems, may be viewed in dualistic terms. Yet there has generally been sufficient integration to produce urban forms far more complex than in either purely indigenous cities or cities directly transplanted from one continent to another. Many dual structures remain, but distinctions are now becoming more and more blurred.

The momentum of rapid urbanization has been fully maintained into the post-colonial period, the cities still serving as points of contact between the rural majority and the outside world, but also assuming a major role in the nation-building process and associated internal social and economic change. In some countries urbanization now shows signs of slowing, but exceptionally high rates of urban growth persist as each country's total population continues to increase rapidly. The present Abidjan, Kinshasa and Nairobi thus constitute only a small part of the probable future Abidjan, Kinshasa and Nairobi.

Views differ widely on the merits or demerits of this rapid urbanization, though there is some consensus that its speed and its spatial concentration are both excessive, and also that there is no humane way in which it could be halted. Policies are needed to reduce the rates of urban growth, and to divert some from the primate cities to smaller centres; but policies to cope with inevitable city expansion are also required. These must profoundly influence the character of the greater part of the future cities – the part yet to be built – though no doubt many forces will also operate irrespective of policy formulation.

There is also, of course, a desperate need for effective policies to overcome the poverty and the inequality that are characteristic of all African cities: but it is suggested here that these are national, rather than specifically urban, problems. They are in some ways intensified by urbanization, but it is doubtful whether they are direct results of it. Solutions must therefore be sought in a broader context than that of the city alone.

Various more specific realms requiring decisions have been reviewed, with emphasis placed on the co-existence of internal and external forces, and on the diversity from place to place in the balance between these. While all are so closely inter-related that they should ideally be considered together, they involve such a wide range of issues that treatment topic by topic has been unavoidable.

Not only are matters such as rural–urban migration, urban economies and housing all closely inter-related, but each is also affected by variables ranging from the physical environment and levels of technology to religious belief and political ideology. Geographers have sometimes been challenged by other social scientists for failing to stress that 'Third World' cities reflect the wider political, social and economic systems of which they are a part. However, while others are often prepared to generalize wildly about such systems, the geographers' concern with how these differ from place to place makes it impossible to do full justice to their influence in a continent-wide review. We can only acknowledge that all processes at work in any city will be profoundly affected by a complex set of environmental, economic, social and political structures and systems operating at local, national and international scales.

'Urban' and 'rural'

One conclusion that has emerged from writing this book is that 'urban' and 'rural' are categories that should be used with great caution, and perhaps rather sparingly, in tropical Africa. In much of the Middle East, in southern and eastern Europe and in Latin

America one can distinguish fairly clearly not only rural and urban places but also rural and urban people. Such a distinction is less clear-cut in the United States or north-west Europe, and in a very different cultural and economic context it is equally blurred in tropical Africa.

Even in pre-colonial Africa many Yoruba people lived in very large nucleated settlements, but there is much dispute about how far these were really 'urban'. Some certainly had urban attributes, but no sharp division could be drawn between these and others which were surely exceptionally large rural settlements. There is still in many respects more in common between Yoruba urban society and Yoruba rural society than between each of these and its Hausa equivalent. And still today, as in the past, many Yoruba families have houses both in the town and in the country, with family members constantly moving to and fro between them. Thus even a census conducted honestly and efficiently could not give an 'accurate' population figure for each town in south-west Nigeria, since there is no clearly-defined town population.

In the much larger tracts of Africa where towns are largely colonial creations urban–rural relationships are quite different, but often equally close. Earlier chapters have indicated how many of those living in the cities have migrated from the countryside, and the range of contacts that they maintain with what most still regard as their 'home'. We have suggested that the concepts of 'urban bias' and of cities exploiting the countryside lose much of their meaning when so many families have members resident in both types of place, and so many individuals still feel very much a part of both. A few people are totally committed to city life, and many more have always lived in a wholly rural environment: but increasing numbers, and the great majority of those currently living in the cities, do not fall into either category.

If so many people are, as is sometimes said, 'living in two worlds', then can these really be regarded as 'two worlds'? To some extent they can, and this justifies writing devoted specifically to African cities: but in many respects they cannot, and this is why most topics and issues discussed here should also be considered from other viewpoints. More studies are needed of particular cities, and there is an even greater need for more comparative studies; but further studies must also be made of relationships and transactions between city and countryside without special reference to either end. Furthermore, topics such as housing or small-scale enterprise and must not always be investigated exclusively in an urban context, or even just separately for urban and rural areas. The viewpoint of the whole rural–urban system must sometimes be adopted. This 'urban' book contributes something on such subjects, but it represents only a partial view, from one perspective.

There are some signs of increasing separation today between town and country, even between townsmen and countrymen, in Africa. That perhaps provides another valid reason for adopting the cities as the spatial framework for some studies, especially those focusing upon post-colonial change. It is also a reason for suggesting that there are urbanization processes taking place over and above the increase in the proportion of the population residing in the cities. Whether these are universal processes, and whether the urban–rural distinction will in future become as sharp in tropical Africa as elsewhere, is extremely hard to say.

The situation will certainly vary from country to country. A sharp dichotomy may perhaps emerge in Zambia while the distinction remains much more blurred in Kenya, as well as in Nigeria. To some extent the future lies in the hands of the people involved, for despite many pressures upon them, they still retain some freedom of choice. Millions of individuals, including of course the few who can exert so much influence over the majority, therefore have to decide how far city and countryside *should* be separated and how far closely integrated rural–urban systems should be retained. Even if a divisive trend is clearly apparent, and cannot be reversed, it can certainly be either encouraged or resisted.

Cities in context

If one conclusion is that an understanding of Africa's cities requires an understanding of its rural societies – in all their diversity – another is that each city must be seen in its total national context. The role of the cities in national economic and political change, and indeed in nation-building, has been great but by no means all-pervasive; and therefore the reverse relationship – the influence on the cities of change in national economies, national political structures and national ideologies – also requires study. Another notable aspect of African urbanization is of course the immense colonial influence upon it, most cities emerging through decisions made in London or Paris: and the continuing close relationship of Africa with Europe is also part of the context in which African urbaniza-

tion should be studied. Whether these relationships are predominantly beneficial to Africa or largely exploitative – a debate that can
hardly be resolved here – they are undoubtedly highly relevant.
Their continuing influence on urban development is a priority area
for future research.

More specifically, it was shown in chapter 8 that cities and towns
in Africa are not only linked to each other in national urban systems, but are in turn tied into an international urban system, with
generally weak links among African capitals but much stronger
links with cities in Europe. This pattern can be viewed either as a
simple nested hierarchy common to spatial organization everywhere, or as a set of metropolis-satellite relationships at various
levels in the manner of the Latin American based 'dependency'
writings. Thus relationships between capital cities and provincial
towns are sometimes seen as just a link in a chain of exploitation and
dependency which extends from London and Paris to the most
'peripheral' rural areas of Africa.

There is undoubtedly some truth in this proposition, but the total
situation is far too complex to be reduced to such a simple formula.
The links are not only in a single chain, for while some forms of
interaction between capital cities and rural hinterlands pass through
provincial towns, others do not: and especially since independence
the links outward from the capital cities are not only to the former
metropoles but increasingly to New York, Zurich and even Moscow. Furthermore, the links are of many different types, and the
patterns in respect of economic relationships may not be the same as
those in respect of cultural ties. Perhaps one of the key paradoxes of
African urbanization is that while socially the cities are essentially
bound up with the rural areas (in networks which are encouraging
accelerated in-migration), they are economically more intimately
bound up with other cities, especially in the rich world (in networks
which are not encouraging increased employment opportunities).

The paragraphs above have indicated how African cities lie
within highly complex systems of relationships, which pose a vast
range of geographical, historical, economic, sociological and political questions. Three further sets of questions remain, some of which
have been partially answered in this book.

Contrasts and convergence

The first set of questions are explicitly geographical, and might be termed 'academic': and it is these which have underlain much of the book. We have investigated how far it is possible to generalize about the cities of tropical Africa, and in so far as we can generalize, we have been concerned with how far the African situation is distinctive.

We have noted the diversity of urban traditions present within tropical Africa, and how, at least until recently, cities such as Ibadan and Harare have been as different as cities anywhere in the world. Yoruba urbanism is perhaps particularly distinctive, with roots firmly in the local soil, physical forms showing many features characteristic of the 'pre-industrial' city, and outward movements of people to work on the land. At the other extreme has lain not just the 'colonial' city, but the 'European' city in Africa. The initiatives behind the growth and structuring of Harare, Lusaka and Nairobi over the first sixty years of this century came almost entirely from Europe: and the combination of wide social and economic disparities among the population and authoritarian governments interested in 'planning' produced cities that in matters such as land-use separation were almost more 'European' than those in Europe. They were certainly even further removed than most British cities from classic 'pre-industrial' forms.

These of course represent the extreme cases of contrast among tropical African cities, and their existence might not prevent generalization about the majority of such cities which lie at neither extreme. However, we have noted a tendency to group all African cities into one of two contrasting types: an old, indigenous type most often found in West Africa, and a new, colonial-inspired type more characteristic of East and Central Africa. As suggested in chapter 2, this is an excessively crude dichotomy, and it is far more realistic to think in terms of four, or even six, types of African city. This reduces the scope of any generalization, but it does not mean that every city is in every way unique, since those within one category, such as Kinshasa and Abidjan, or Nairobi and Lusaka, may have much in common.

It is possible to take this issue further, in two directions. One conclusion emerging from this study is that however diverse African cities may be, similar *elements* are present in almost all of them, though often in widely differing proportions. Examples include large-scale 'formal' and small-scale 'informal' sectors of the economy, one originally largely under alien control and the other almost entirely indigenous; and areas of high-quality, low-density housing juxtaposed with areas of densely-packed, shanty dwellings. These may be seen as manifestations of cultural and economic 'dualism', though some writers are unhappy with that term and prefer alternative notions such as 'upper and lower circuits'. They certainly reflect the fact that however diverse their origins, the rapid growth of most African cities during this century has resulted from *interaction* between local populations and outsiders of one type or another. Therefore the study of most cities requires an understanding of traditional indigenous settlement, the colonial impact, the local response to this, and the continuing neo-colonial influences.

Another conclusion which was not so apparent when the writing of this book began, and is not really evident from most existing literature on African urbanization, is that the contrasts among various types of city are less striking today than they were twenty years ago. The issue of convergence or divergence in world urbanization will be mentioned below, but the argument put forward here is that marked convergence has been taking place within tropical Africa.

In respect of demographic structures, urban economies, and physical form, cities such as Lusaka, and to a lesser extent Nairobi, have become far more similar to Lagos or Accra than they used to be. In such formerly 'European' cities various processes of indigenization have been taking place, either replacing or supplementing the elements inherited from the colonial period. Meanwhile in cities such as Ibadan or Sokoto, and even Abeokuta or Katsina, processes of 'Westernization' are continuing and perhaps accelerating, with populations becoming ethnically more heterogeneous and new physical structures from petrol stations to hospitals intruding into the traditional urban fabric. Most Yoruba cities remain very distinctive in many respects, but with steadily fewer inhabitants engaged in farming and more having contacts with other cities, Yoruba urban society is tending to diverge from Yoruba rural society and to converge with other urban societies.

Thus in terms of the typology offered in chapter 2 so many cities are shifting towards the 'hybrid' category that the value of that typology might now be questioned. This even applies to the 'dual' cities, where the processes of 'Westernization' and indigenization have been taking place within the respective components. There are still differences between Khartoum proper and Omdurman, and between old and new Kano, but these are becoming progressively less marked. Around the time of independence one really could distinguish six types of city in tropical Africa, but this is hardly so today. The value of the typology now therefore lies largely in terms of urban traditions and the urban inheritance of the newly-independent states. On the basis of this inheritance further urbanization has produced by the 1980s a range of cities which still differ markedly at the extremes, but which defy any satisfactory form of classification. Increasingly the differences, whether in demography or economy, in migration patterns or in male/female roles, are differences of degree rather than of kind.

A critical factor in this convergence is of course the character of the people who are making the key decisions. At one time these were traditional African rulers in some cities, and Europeans who had neither much understanding of, nor much interest in, the African population in others. Today more and more decisions are being made by a 'Westernized' African elite whose ideas and attitudes are often very similar whether they are in Nigeria or Zambia.

With respect to the broad question of how far we can generalize about African cities and African urbanization, we must note that convergence among cities of contrasting origins normally results from contrasting, and sometimes directly opposite, *processes*. In some cities the large-scale sector is accounting for an increasing share of economic activity, in others for a decreasing share. In some cities housing is increasingly seen as government's responsibility, in others self-help is becoming ever more important. The processes at work then in turn affect relationships within each city. Thus Lusaka and Ibadan are converging in terms of the proportion of the inhabitants occupied in the large-scale and small-scale sectors of the economy, and soon they may be statistically quite similar in this respect: but the relationships between the two sectors cannot be the same when in Ibadan the small-scale sector is of much longer standing than the large-scale, while in Lusaka the former is a recent addition that has grown up dependent on the latter.

Meanwhile there are other processes common to nearly all the cities, notably rapid population growth resulting from relatively consistent rates of natural increase combined with varying amounts of in-migration which ensures continued close social relationships between city and countryside. Evidence of increasing unemployment and underemployment was unfortunately also to be found almost everywhere in the 1970s, as the urban economies failed to expand as rapidly as the urban population, but this has to be seen in the context of stagnation or even decline in the rural economies of all too many countries. Another very widespread process of the 1960s and 1970s has been increasing concentration of urban growth in the national capitals, intensifying their primacy within the national urban systems, though the official response to this has varied from country to country.

The city in tropical Africa and elsewhere

In so far as some generalization about tropical African cities is possible, we might consider how far they resemble, or differ from, those elsewhere in the world. And if there is evidence of convergence among different types of African city, we might consider whether this also constitutes convergence towards urban forms found elsewhere.

A widespread view is that in various superficial ways all cities are becoming more alike, but that in a number of fundamental respects 'Third World' cities and urbanization processes differ from those of the more developed world, East and West. Thus Berry (1973) speaks of 'divergent paths' at this level of analysis. Other writers have implied that 'Third World' cities constitute a distinct category by taking these as their unit of study, and while noting spatial variations they still feel able to generalize extensively across three continents. Dwyer (1975), Friedmann and Wulff (1976), Lloyd (1979), Santos (1979) and Drakakis Smith (1980) all project this viewpoint. McGee has written about 'The Urbanization Process in the Third World' (1971) largely from South-east Asian experience; Roberts (1978) claims to analyse 'Third World' processes while freely acknowledging his dependence on Latin American experience; and Mabogunje (1980) suggests that his observations apply equally widely although they are firmly rooted in Africa. The recent study by Gilbert and Gugler (1982) pays more heed to spatial variations, but even this suggests that much generalization is possible, and indicates increasing similarity rather than increasing differentiation.

Such a general consensus is very persuasive, yet this writer is inclined to dissent, and considers that much existing literature is positively misleading. Most cities in tropical Africa differ substantially not only from those of Europe and North America but also from those of the Middle East and Latin America. Certain forces encourage increasing similarities, but others have the opposite effect.

The cities of tropical Africa have more in common with those of South Asia than those of any other major world region. In India one finds the same range from old indigenous cities to those established by the colonial power, and the same mixture of local and alien elements within most urban centres. Much of the discussion in King's (1976) study of colonial urbanization in India appears very relevant to Africa. In both areas many contemporary processes reflect the recency of independence, while many urgent decisions concern appropriate responses to colonial legacies.

Furthermore, South Asia, unlike most of the Middle East or Latin America, shares with tropical Africa a low level of urbanization. There too, most people are rural dwellers, and agriculture is the mainstay of the economy. The two regions are also similar in the extent of their poverty in both national and specifically urban contexts, though perhaps some Asian cities show an even greater range from the very wealthy to the utterly destitute.

One major difference is that for some years South Asia has experienced less rapid urban growth than tropical Africa, largely due to a lower level of rural–urban migration. The reasons have never been fully explained, but contributory factors are a less intense set of relationships between town and country, and more rigid social stratification exemplified by the caste system. The Asian urban population includes more members of long-established urban families whose links with the rural areas are very weak. Conversely, most rural dwellers have contacts with the cities only through middle-men; and if any members of their families have migrated to the cities they are more certain to be numbered among the urban poor rather than on a real or imaginary ladder to fame and fortune. Kinship ties are generally weaker than in Africa, so migrants are less assured of hospitality on arrival in town. This contrast in the degree of separation between town and country is perhaps one reason why Lipton's (1977) India-based thesis blaming rural poverty on 'urban bias' fails to ring completely true for tropical Africa.

Other differences arise out of the stronger European orientation of most African economies. Dependence on exports and imports is far greater in African than South Asian countries, and so handling these looms larger in the urban economies, while expatriates from

Europe play a much larger role in most African capitals than in Bombay, Calcutta, Delhi or Dacca. This influences the character of each city in many ways, from house types to language use. This factor also combines with political fragmentation to cause a lower degree of inter-city integration in tropical Africa, though the contrast with Bangladesh and Sri Lanka is less than that with India.

Many features shared by tropical Africa and South Asia are shared by South-east Asia also, although generalization about that region is difficult when it includes both Singapore and Kampuchea. The concept of cultural dualism, widely employed in this book, came into 'Western' social science literature largely through studies in Indonesia, and many themes considered in McGee's (1967) book on the South-east Asian city are echoed in the present volume.

Once the discussion is widened to all 'developing countries' or the 'Third World' our concern is no longer essentially with cities in predominantly rural societies, or with cities in newly independent countries. In both the Middle East and Latin America over half the population are now urban dwellers, and in several countries the proportion is as high as in Europe. It is hard to believe that the urbanization process in countries where 75 per cent are city dwellers is similar to that where the figure is 10 per cent. The role of the cities in national, economic and political life is bound to be vastly different, as are most urban–rural relationships. Contrasts in migration patterns have been clearly shown by Nelson (1979a: chapter 2). Similarly, contrasts in political history mean that cities in Colombia, Chile, Iran or even Egypt are not involved in a 'nation-building' process in the same way as Lagos or Nairobi.

Most Latin American cities are considerably older than most in tropical Africa, nearly all the national capitals dating from the sixteenth century. Many in the Middle East are older still, and there is something distinctly ahistoric about the proposition that Kinshasa and Harare are fundamentally similar phenomena to Damascus and Baghdad. In many cities in both Latin America and the Middle East power lies in the hands of long-established local elite families. These families are part of a very rigid class structure, and much analysis of these cities is appropriately presented in class terms.

The African urban elite, by contrast, have largely come from elsewhere, and have rural-based extended families, most branches of which consist of poor peasant farmers. Most are, often reluctantly, much involved with this extended family, and feel strong responsibility towards them. The poorer members feel in turn that they can make claims on those who have prospered. Class is therefore not the overriding basis of social structure in these cities. Furthermore, the key decision-makers not only at municipal level but also at national level, in most countries from Mexico to Argentina, identify entirely with the capital city, and may be little aware of things outside it. Plans for Ghana or Uganda do not (yet) represent just the view from Accra or Kampala to the same extent.

Without doubt the trend in this respect is towards greater similarity, as a new African urban-based elite begins to dig itself into a position of political and economic power. But in most countries foreign interests are too strong to allow this to happen really rapidly – and might thus be regarded by some as a blessing in disguise. In many countries political instability has also had its effect here, while ethnicity acts against the solidarity of this emerging group. This means that options are still to some extent open, and it is still to be determined how far Lima or Teheran are models for the future cities of Africa.

A most important difference between tropical African and Latin American cities lies in their economic base. Thus Roberts (1979: 6) writes that 'in underdeveloped countries' an 'emphasis on urbanization without industrialization is misleading', arguing this 'by taking the example of Latin America where, in almost every country by 1970, industry contributed a greater share of the gross national product than did agriculture'. Roberts is clearly right in challenging this notion for Latin American, but not for 'the underdeveloped countries' in general. In tropical Africa industry plays a far smaller role in the national economy than does agriculture, especially when a true valuation is placed on subsistence production; and within the urban economy manufacturing contributes far less than services.

This may be just a temporary phase in Africa, and urban economies there may in due course follow the Latin American path: but this is by no means certain, and without major changes in the structure of the global economy it is unlikely. An alternative suggestion is that on a global scale manufacturing-based urbanization was a temporary phenomenon, characteristic of Europe and North America in the nineteenth century, of the USSR and Japan in the early twentieth century, and of various middle income countries from Brazil to South Korea today; and that this wave will have exhausted itself before it washes onto tropical Africa or South Asia.

The constant references to rapid and extensive industrialization are vital to Roberts's main arguments, and so are references to substantial consumer spending power. 'Thus, in most Latin American cities, it is common to find radios, televisions and refrigerators even in the poorest squatter settlements' (p. 138). This does not apply in Africa, and by his focus on Latin American circumstances Roberts really provides a powerful antidote to current generalizations about the world's cities. Our query must be basically with his opening sentence – 'The theme of this book is the contemporary urban problems of underdeveloped countries'.

Another basic distinction between tropical African cities and those in both Latin America and the Middle East lies in the cultural realm, as exemplified by language use. The theme of culture contact essential to any discussion of African cities is also relevant in most Middle Eastern countries, but one cultural tradition dominates most individuals' lives. English or French are occasionally used in Baghdad, Cairo and Damascus, but almost all interaction takes place through the medium of Arabic. There are important issues of culture contact in most Latin American cities also, sometimes relating to the contribution of indigenous pre-Hispanic cultures and sometimes to United States influence; but neither is more than marginally reflected in language use. All official business is conducted in Portuguese in Brazil, and in Spanish elsewhere, and it is assumed that everyone can understand this. In most cities, either Portuguese or Spanish is the home language of the great majority of the residents. The contrasting African situation, in which indigenous and alien languages co-exist, is not merely of interest in itself, but highly relevant to all issues of relationships, control and power, both within the cities and nationally.

It seems that a progressively narrower range of generalization is possible as one proceeds up the spatial scale. Most efforts to understand 'the Third World city' may thus be misplaced. Although the cities in question do have features in common, many of these are near-universal. 'Bidonvilles' are found in France as well as in both Senegal and Tunisia; and increasing attention is being given to 'the informal sector' in British cities. Rather than either crudely applying 'Western' models to African cities, or attempting to create alternative models for all the cities of the less developed countries, we might recognize that urbanization involves a whole series of paths, sometimes converging and sometimes diverging, with no city ever exactly following in the footsteps of another but with many having a general orientation in common.

Urbanization and development

This brief comparison of tropical Africa with other regions, some enjoying more material prosperity, leads us on to a second set of questions. These concern the role of African cities in 'development', whatever that term may be taken to mean, and also in related changes, such as those sometimes grouped together as 'modernization' and those which constitute an intensification of 'dependency'. These issues can be considered in broad national terms, levels of urbanization being compared with levels of development, modernization or dependency; or attention can be focused on their geographical dimension, stressing the role of urban centres in regional development, in the spatial diffusion of modernization, or in the extension of dependency relationships throughout each national territory.

Even at the national level, little research has been undertaken on these issues. Assertions are frequently made, either to the effect that urban growth greatly assists economic development in largely rural countries, or conversely to the effect that urban growth is taking place at the expense of the rural majority, thus hampering rather than aiding true development. Few of these assertions are supported by firm evidence, and many depend on a particular view of what constitutes development.

A very favourable view of urbanization in the less developed countries was taken in the early 1970s by Friedmann (1973). At that time he clearly saw cities as sources of beneficial economic and political changes, though he has since revised his views. As he explicitly stated (p. 154): 'the point of view adopted in the present volume' is that 'urbanization is no longer regarded as an unfortunate by-product of planned industrialization whose consequences governments should learn how to constrain, but as a set of powerful developmental forces in its own right'. A similar attitude was implicit in much development literature of the 1960s.

Hance (1970) clearly regards urbanization as contributing to development in Africa, while recognizing many problems that it poses. Ajaegbu (1976: 63) states that 'planners should also recognize the role of the urban centres in diffusing development impulses to the rural areas' and that 'vast rural areas in Nigeria are still far away from the existing growth-generating urban centres, so that planning should be concerned also with creating and developing such centres'. Another very positive view is presented in a paper by

Gellar (1967) entitled 'West African capital cities as motors for development'.

Mabogunje has always been more ambivalent on the matter. His 1968 study of Nigeria looked favourably on urbanization, but saw some forms of traditional urbanism as a constraint upon development. His more general 1980 study is more critical of the impact of colonial and post-colonial urban growth (especially pp. 154–65), but then concludes (p. 173) that the effects on 'overall development . . . cannot be answered unambiguously'.

An example of more negative views is provided by Gugler and Flanagan (1977), who argue that resources are disproportionately allocated to the cities, and that people are moving out of productive occupations in the rural areas to unproductive activities in the cities. Undoubtedly some are doing so, but how many? And for how many is the opposite true? How long do they remain unproductive in the city, and would they have remained productive as pressures increase in the rural areas? How do we determine what constitutes 'being productive' anyway? Certainly many in the cities are providing services rather than producing goods, but surely they may be contributing to welfare equally by doing so.

In their book on West African urbanization, Gugler and Flanagan (1978: 26) suggest that the process there 'must be viewed as overurbanization', and also that a 'problem is presented by a number of cities growing beyond what may be considered an optimal city size'. Yet neither they nor anyone else have demonstrated that there is an optimal size below the 2 to 3 million now attained by Lagos and Kinshasa. The issue is not clearly resolved even for Mexico City, with its 14 million.

The negative view sometimes extends beyond bias and inefficiency in resource allocation, argued for poor countries in general by Lipton (1977), to more active and purposeful exploitation. Urban centres are seen as having been agents in colonial exploitation, and as continuing to assist the rich world to exploit rural Africa, as well as extracting surplus for their own benefit. According to Williams (1976: 236) in colonial Nigeria 'the city itself engaged in the parasitical exactions of a surplus from the countryside', while both Doherty (1977) with reference to Tanzania and Magubane (1979) for Africa in general insist that the role of cities has so far been overwhelmingly exploitative.

These negative views are highly relevant to any policies regarding the *spatial* pattern of urbanization and national urban systems. If urban centres are basically exploitative at the national level, they must be so at the regional level also, and so decentralization of urban growth will not assist regional development programmes. The same argument may be applied even to the growth of small market centres so strongly advocated for poor countries in general by Johnson (1970), and for tropical Africa by Harrison Church (1972), Taylor (1974), and others.

Southall has directed a group of scholars in the United States to the role of small towns in African development, but in introducing a resulting set of papers he states (1979: 213) that 'most small towns appear as the lowest rung of systems for the oppression and exploitation of rural peoples'. Kabwegyere (1979: 314) concludes that 'if the experience in Kenya is any indication, the growth of small urban centres is in many ways an intensification of dependence relationships and underdevelopment – this time extended to incorporate the rural areas – and in no way concerned with development'.

In reality of course any views of urbanization either just as an agent of development or as wholly inimical to the real interests of the people of Africa are gross oversimplifications. The cities are playing a major role in most nationwide processes, beneficial and otherwise, and urban centres can play both positive and negative roles simultaneously in respect of regional development. The establishment of a new town in a formerly isolated region, like the construction of a new transport route, is likely to assist some people, to harm the interests of others, and to bring a mixture of changes to the majority.

Future research on these issues would benefit from more disaggregation than has been customary. This might be in terms of the impact of urbanization on different income-groups, or on different age-groups, or on women as against men. It might also involve distinguishing the consequences for (a) the existing urban population, (b) those moving to the cities, (c) those remaining in rural areas nearby, (d) those remaining in distant rural areas with much out-migration, and (e) those inhabiting distant rural areas which provide few migrants. Thus the effects of further growth of Nairobi on neighbouring Kiambu will differ from those on distant Kakamega, while the effects on the people of the coastal zone will be different again. No wonder there are no simple answers on whether urbanization is or is not contributing to Kenyan development.

In addition, the research that is required on the developmental impact of African urbanization must recognize that at present the urban–rural split is less sharp than in many parts of the world. It is unrealistic to think of relationships as simply urban dwellers exploiting rural dwellers when so many individuals have a foot in both worlds and when so many families have members resident in both town and country. Of course, members of a family can exploit each other, even in Africa, but the strength and nature of family ties complicates the picture everywhere from Mauritania to Mozambique.

We might note again here how tropical Africa differs from other regions in that most of the key decision-makers in the cities are not members of long-established urban families totally out of touch with the needs of the rural majority. Most of them were born in a rural area, and still have parents and other close relatives living there. It is particularly important that these people should ensure that urbanization does benefit the nation as a whole now, rather than waiting for benefits to emerge in time, since the next generation of urban-based decision-makers may well not have such deep rural roots.

Urbanization policies

A third series of questions regarding urbanization in tropical Africa is less academic in nature, and relates to policy. Every African government is faced with a wide range of decisions that will affect the extent, pace and nature of urban growth, and anyone concerned with Africa should have some appreciation of these. Decisions of direct importance at the national level include legislation aiding or discouraging migration, the adoption of various employment policies, and the allocation of central government funds for urban housing and infrastructure. Decisions indirectly affecting urbanization range from those on alternative sources of tax revenue to those on the role of foreign private investment. It is notable that some national development plans devote chapters specifically to urbanization while others make only scattered references to it. In some countries policy decisions have been made specifically concerned with the spatial pattern of urban growth, such as the relocation of the administrative capital in Malawi, Tanzania and Nigeria, whereas in others little government attention has been given to the matter.

Many vital decisions also face those in municipal authorities, businessmen who may have alternative urban and rural locations for their investments, trade union or community leaders, and of course every individual citizen. The size and shape of Africa's cities is to a large extent determined by their inhabitants, all of whom have some option on where to live, what type of employment to seek, what ties to retain with their rural kinsfolk, and so on; and also by innumerable rural dwellers, including both those who decide to migrate and, equally important but much less studied, those who decide not to do so. An appreciation of the choices facing all these people, and of the factors affecting their decisions, is necessary for an understanding of African urbanization.

Yet more decisions affecting African urban development are constantly being made by people far away in other continents, some of whom may have never even heard of Accra or Kinshasa. Such is the interdependent nature of national economies, and the particularly dependent nature of most in Africa. African governments are frequently faced with circumstances beyond their control, and the choices open to individuals are often highly constrained, as a result of these decisions that outsiders take in their own self-interests. Whether a greater awareness of the African situation would alter many of these decisions can only be a matter of speculation, and perhaps of hope.

It often seems to be expected that books such as this will have policy recommendations to offer to governments, though apparently not to individuals. That is not, however, the intention of this author. To make general policy recommendations for African cities would be quite impractical, and indeed illogical in so far as a major concern of the book has been the diversity of urban situations in Africa. Appropriate policies may be quite different for each government, each municipal authority, each group of urban dwellers, and each potential migrant. For example, the case for checking the rate of rural–urban migration is greater in some countries than in others, and within each country such migration is more appropriate from some rural areas than from others. A brief book like this could not spell out the perhaps contrasting urban policies appropriate for Gabon and for Somalia.

Since we have been concerned with the juxtaposition of indigenous and alien ingredients in African urbanization, we can at least assert that in no country are solutions to urban planning problems likely to be either wholly indigenous or wholly imported. Whether in the designing of a new capital city, or in the humbler tasks of existing municipalities, advantage must be taken of international technological breakthroughs while local cultural values are retained and respected. The quest must often be for 'the best of both worlds'.

Similarly, solutions to problems of employment, of housing, or whatever, rarely lie either wholly in government initiatives or wholly in the spontaneous responses made by poor families and individuals. As Mabogunje has said (1980: 198), 'the urban crisis of underdevelopment is . . . how to integrate the indigenous solutions' into the strategies adopted by the state. However, the form of such integration, as well as the balance between individual and corporate initiatives, must differ from one city to another.

Furthermore, policy must depend on ultimate *goals* – of African governments, groups and individuals – and it would be highly presumptuous for an outsider to specify these. They certainly cannot just be taken as given, for far too little is known about people's priorities, and how these differ from place to place. The relative importance that people attach to current income, future economic prospects, congenial employment, environmental issues, political rights, personal security, family relationships, and so on, must all profoundly affect what both individuals and governments should do. It is therefore the hopes and the fears of the people of Ethiopia, Nigeria and Zaire that must largely determine policies in these countries, both towards specific issues such as unemployment or squatter settlement, and towards the general issues of whether the majority of the population should in due course become urban dwellers.

In a sense the proposition that each African country should determine its own urban future is a recommendation, though hardly a novel one; and so is the assertion that each decision must reflect a host of locally varying factors rather than depending on theoretical models and worldwide, or even Africa-wide, generalizations. At the same time those making policy decisions for any African city could learn much from experience elsewhere in Africa, something from that in Asia and Latin America, and a little – notably regarding mistakes to avoid – from that in Europe and North America. So a further plea is for more comparative study of urbanization processes.

In so far as we *can* generalize about many of the cities of tropical Africa it seems clear that their circumstances are quite unlike those of Europe past or present. Perhaps for countries which combine an economy still highly dependent on subsistence farming with access to the latest forms of satellite communications some quite new settlement patterns would be appropriate.

At present many African families live within integrated rural–urban social systems, and there is no sharp division between urban dwellers and rural dwellers. Decision-makers at all levels should certainly consider how far this might be preserved. Perhaps intense spatial concentrations of population are increasingly an anachronism worldwide, and Africa's delayed urbanization gives it some opportunity to avoid them. Perhaps the mobility which is a widespread feature of African societies, (albeit combined with a long-term attachment to land and home), together with late-twentieth-century technology, will permit large numbers to move to and fro between rural and urban settlements into any foreseeable future even if the physical growth of the latter continues unabated.

Certainly African urbanization need not follow, and probably should not follow, paths trodden elsewhere in different circumstances. The planners and the people at large should at least experiment with new forms of physically dispersed city, with some commuting but with dispersal of employment also. Meanwhile more might be done to permeate the countryside with some of those social, economic and political elements which so powerfully attract people to the cities, as Tanzania has tried to do perhaps on an over-ambitious time scale. There might also be more deliberate planning for a distinctively African pattern of living involving periodic movement between town and country, especially where environmental conditions favour relatively dense rural settlement within fifty to a hundred kilometres of moderate-sized urban centres. Yet it must be stressed that no single path is suitable for all parts of tropical Africa – so one should not be sought.

The final 'policy recommendation' is that African planners should be cautious about asking academics to make policy recommendations, and especially about seizing upon the latest academic fashions as guidelines for policy. A clear illustration is provided by the widespread tendency towards polarization of discussion. There may be analytical value in attempting to distinguish between generative and parasitic cities, but in reality all cities are both in some degree. Attention needed to be drawn to the co-existence of formal and informal sectors or upper and lower circuits in the urban economy, but in reality much activity lies in between the two. Every dichotomy, from more and less developed countries to urban and rural, can be grossly misleading if crudely used as a basis for policy. The same applies to concepts such as central place theory which are obviously relevant to settlement policies but which are too idealized to determine them. Such academic constructs must remain the planners' servants and not become the masters.

It is thus not the business of a British academic to propose what ought to be done with respect to the city in tropical Africa. The people directly involved must decide how much urbanization should take place, what form it should take, and how it should be distributed over space. I merely hope that a review such as this may be of value as a source of information and ideas to some of those decision-makers, as well as helping students in Africa and elsewhere to understand the diversity of African cities, some of the processes at work in them, and some of the decisions that are already being made.

Bibliography

Thirty suggestions for deeper or wider reading are indicated by asterisks.

Abiodun, J. O. (1967) 'Urban hierarchy in a developing country.' *Economic Geography*, 43, 347–67.

Abiodun, J. O. (1974) 'Urban growth and problems in metropolitan Lagos.' *Urban Studies*, 11, 341–7.

Abiodun, J. O. (1976) 'Housing problems in Nigerian cities.' *Town Planning Review*, 47, 339–47.

Abu Lughod, J. and Hay, R. (eds.) (1977) *Third World Urbanization*. Chicago: Maaroufa Press.

Adams, J. G. U. (1972a) 'External linkages of national economies in West Africa.' *African Urban Notes*, 6 (3), 97–116.

Adams, J. G. U. (1972b) 'The measurement and interpretation of change in West African urban hierarchies.' *African Urban Notes*, 6 (3), 43–55.

Adedeji, A. (ed.) (1981) *The Indigenization of African Economies*. London: Hutchinson.

Adefolalu, A. A. (1977) 'Traffic congestion in the city of Lagos.' *Nigerian Geographical Journal*, 20, 123–44.

Adejuyigbe, O. (1970) 'The case for a new federal capital in Nigeria.' *Journal of Modern African Studies*, 8, 301–6.

Adepoju, A. (1974) 'Migration and socio-economic links between urban migrants and their home communities in Nigeria.' *Africa*, 44, 383–95.

Ajaegbu, H. I. (1976) *Urban and Rural Development in Nigeria*. London: Heinemann.

Ake, C. (1981) *A Political Economy of Africa*. London: Longman.

Amin, S. (1973) *Neo-Colonialism in West Africa*. London: Penguin.

*Amin, S. (ed.) (1974) *Modern Migrations in Western Africa*. London: Oxford University Press.

Aronson, D. R. (1975) 'Residential growth in Ibadan, 1966–1972.' *Journal of Tropical Geography*, 40, 8–17.

Aronson, D. R. (1978) *The City is our Farm: seven migrant Ijebu Yoruba families*. Cambridge, Mass.: Schenkmann.

Arrighi, G. and Saul, J. (1973) *Essays on the Political Economy of Africa*. New York: Monthly Review Press.

Auger, A. (1968) 'Notes sur les centres urbains secondaires au Congo–Brazzaville.' *Cahiers d'Outre-Mer*, 21, 29–55.

Ayeni, B. (1979) *Concepts and Techniques in Urban Analysis*. London: Croom Helm.

Ayeni, B. (1981) 'Lagos.' In Pacione, M. (ed.), *Problems and Planning in Third World Cities*, London: Croom Helm.

Baeck, L. (1961) 'An expenditure study of the Congolese "évolués" of Leopoldville.' In Southall, A. (ed.), *Social Change in Modern Africa*, London: Oxford University Press.

Baker, P. H. (1974) *Urbanization and Political Change: the politics of Lagos 1917–1967*. Berkeley: University of California Press.

Banton, M. P. (1957) *West African City: a study of tribal life in Freetown*. London: Oxford University Press.

Banton, M. P. (1965) 'Social alignment and identity in a West African city.' In Kuper, H. (ed.) *Urbanization and Migration in West Africa*, Berkeley: University of California Press.

Barber, W. J. (1967) 'Urbanisation and economic growth: the cases of two white settler territories.' In Miner, H. (ed.), *The City in Modern Africa*, New York: Praeger.

Barclay, H. B. (1964) *Buurri al Lamaab: a suburban village in the Sudan*. Ithaca, N.Y.: Cornell University Press.

Barnes, S. T. (1979) 'Migration and land acquisition: the new landowners of Lagos.' *African Urban Studies*, 4, 59–70.

Bascom, W. R. (1962) 'Some aspects of Yoruba urbanism.' *American Anthropologist*, 64, 699–709.

Bascom, W. R. (1968) 'The urban African and his world.' In Fava, S. F. (ed.), *Urbanism in World Perspective*, New York: Crowell.

Bates, R. H. (1976) *Rural Responses to Industrialization: a study of village Zambia*. New Haven: Yale University Press.

Becker, C. (1969) *Kano: eine afrikanische Gorsstadt*. Hamburg: Deutsches Institut für Afrika–Forschung.

Bedawi, H. Y. (1976) 'Variation in residential space standards in Zaria.' *Savanna*, 5, 75–9.

Bender, D. R. (1971) 'De facto families and de jure households in Ondo.' *American Anthropologist*, 73, 223–41.

Bernus, S. (1969) *Particularismes Ethniques en Milieu Urbain: l'exemple de Niamey*. Paris: Musée de l'Homme.

Berry, B. J. L. (1961) 'City-size distributions and economic development.' *Economic Development and Cultural Change*, 9, 573–87.

Berry, B. J. L. (1964) 'Cities as systems within systems of cities.' *Papers of the Regional Science Association*, 13, 147–63.

*Berry, B. J. L. (1973) *The Human Consequences of Urbanisation*. London: Macmillan.

Berry, S. S. (1975) *Cocoa, Custom and Socio-Economic Change in Rural Western Nigeria*. Oxford: Clarendon Press.

Beveridge, A. A. and Oberschall, A. R. (1979) *African Businessmen and Development in Zambia*. Princeton, N.J.: Princeton University Press.

Bharati, A. (1972) *The Asians in East Africa*. Chicago: Nelson-Hall.

Bienefeld, M. A. (1975) 'The informal sector and peripheral capitalism: the case of Tanzania.' *Institute of Development Studies Bulletin*, 6 (3), 53–73.

Bienefeld, M. A. and Binhammer, H. (1972) 'Tanzanian housing finance and housing policy.' In Hutton, J. (ed.), *Urban Challenge in East Africa*, Nairobi: East African Publishing House.

Blake, G. H. and Lawless, R. I. (eds.) (1980) *The Changing Middle Eastern City*. London: Croom Helm.

Bobo, B. F. (1974) *Economic Factors Influencing Migration and Urban Growth and Structure: Accra, Ghana*. Ph.D. thesis, University of California, Los Angeles.

Bohanan, P. and Dalton, G. (eds.) (1962) *Markets in Africa*. Evanston: Northwestern University Press.

Boserup, E. (1970) *Women's Role in Economic Development*. London: Geroge Allen and Unwin.

Brand, R. (1972) 'The spatial organization of residential areas in Accra.' *Economic Geography*, 48, 284–96.

Brand, R. (1976) 'The urban housing challenge.' In Knight, C. G. and Newman, J. L. (eds.), *Contemporary Africa*. Englewood Cliffs, N.J.: Prentice-Hall.

Brandt, H. *et al.* (1972) *The Industrial Town as a Factor of Economic and Social Development: the example of Jinja, Uganda*. Munich: Weltforum.

Brass, W. *et al.* (1968) *The Demography of Tropical Africa*. Princeton, N.J.: Princeton University Press.

Brasseur, G. (1968) *Les Etablissements Humains au Mali*. Dakar: IFAN.

Bray, J. M. (1969) 'The craft structure of a traditional Yoruba town.' *Transactions, Institute of British Geographers*, 46, 179–93.

Breese, G. (1966) *Urbanization in Newly Developing Countries*. Englewood Cliffs, N.J.: Prentice-Hall.

Breese, G. (ed.) (1969) *The City in Newly Developing Countries*. Englewood Cliffs, N.J.: Prentice-Hall.

Bricker, G, and Traore, S. (1979) 'Transitional urbanization in Upper Volta.' In Obudho, R. A. and El-Shakhs, S. (eds.), *Development of Urban Systems in Africa*. New York: Praeger.

Brokensha, D. (1966) *Social Change at Larteh, Ghana*. Oxford: Clarendon Press.

Bromley, R. (ed.) (1979) *The Urban Informal Sector*. Oxford: Pergamon.

Bromley, R. and Gerry, C. (eds.) (1979) *Casual Work and Poverty in Third World Cities*. Chichester: Wiley.

Brookfield, H. C. (1975) *Interdependent Development*. London: Methuen.

Byerlee, D. (1974) 'Rural–urban migration in Africa.' *International Migration Review*, 8, 543–66.

*Caldwell, J. C. (1969) *African Rural–Urban Migration: the movement to Ghana's towns*. London: C. Hurst.

Caldwell, J. C. (ed.) (1975) *Population Growth and Socio-Economic Change in West Africa*. New York: Columbia University Press.

Callaway, A. (1967) 'Traditional crafts to modern industry.' In Lloyd, P. C. *et al.*, *The City of Ibadan*. Cambridge: Cambridge University Press.

CEGET (1972) *Dix Etudes sur l'Approvisionnement des Villes*. Bordeaux: Centre d'Etudes de Géographie Tropicale.

CEGET (1977) *Nouvelles Recherches sur l'Approvisionnement des Villes*. Bordeaux: Centre d'Etudes de Géographie Tropicale.

Chilivumbo, A. B. (1975) 'The ecology of social types in Blantyre.' In Parkin, D. J. (ed.), *Town and Country in Central and Eastern Africa*, London: Oxford University Press.

Claeson, C. F. and Egero, B. (1971) *Population Movement in Tanzania: movement to towns*. Dar es Salaam: University of Dar es Salaam, BRALUP.

Clark, D. (1978) 'Unregulated housing, vested interest and the development of community identity in Nairobi.' *African Urban Studies*, 3, 33–46.

Clarke, J. I. (1972) 'Urban primacy in tropical Africa.' In *La Croissance Urbaine en Afrique Noire et à Madagascar*, Paris: CNRS.

Clarke, J. I. (1975) *An Advanced Geography of Africa*, Chapter 8. Amersham: Hulton.

Clarke, J. I. and Kosiński, L. A. (eds.) (1982) *Redistribution of Population in Africa*. London: Heinemann.

*CNRS (1972) *La Croissance Urbaine en Afrique Noire et à Madagascar*. Paris: Centre National de la Recherche Scientifique.

CNRS (1976) *Recherches sur l'Approvisionnement des Villes*. Paris: Centre National de la Recherche Scientifique.

Cohen, A. (1967) 'The Hausa.' In Lloyd, P. C. *et al.*, *The City of Ibadan*. Cambridge: Cambridge University Press.

Cohen, A. (1969) *Custom and Politics in Urban Africa*. London: Routledge and Kegan Paul.

Cohen, A. (ed.) (1974) *Urban Ethnicity*. London: Tavistock.

Cohen, A. (1981) *The Politics of Elite Culture*. Berkeley: University of California Press.

Cohen, M. A. (1974) *Urban Policy and Political Conflict in Africa: a study of the Ivory Coast*. Chicago: University of Chicago Press.

Cole, P. (1975) *Modern and Traditional Elites in the Politics of Lagos*. Cambridge: Cambridge University Press.

Cooper, R. L. and Horvath, R. J. (1976) 'Language, migration and urbanization.' In Bender, M. L. (ed.), *Language in Ethiopia*, London: Oxford University Press.

Costello, V. F. (1977) *Urbanization in the Middle East*. Cambridge: Cambridge University Press.

Cotten, A. M. and Marguerat, Y. (1976/7) 'Deux réseaux urbains africains: Cameroun et Côte d'Ivoire.' *Cahiers d'Outre-Mer*, 29, 348–85 and 30, 348–82.

Crowder, M. (1962) *Senegal*. London: Oxford University Press.

Cruise O'Brien, R. (1972) *White Society in Black Africa: the French of Senegal*. London: Faber.

Darwent, D. F. (1969) 'Growth poles and growth centres in regional planning: a review.' *Environment and Planning*, 1, 5–32.

Davies, D. H. (1969) *Lusaka: some town planning problems of an African city*. Lusaka: University of Zambia.

Davies, D. H. (1981) 'Towards an urbanization strategy for Zimbabwe.' *Geojournal*, Supplement 2, 73–84.

De Blij, H. J. (1963) *Dar es Salaam*. Evanston: Northwestern University Press.

De Blij, H. J. (1968) *Mombasa*. Evanston: Northwestern University Press.

Deniel, R. (1968) *De la Savane á la Ville: essai sur la migration des Mossi vers Abidjan*. Paris: Aubier-Montaigne.

Denyer, S. (1978) *African Traditional Architecture*. London: Heinemann.

De Saint Moulin, L. (1977) 'Perspectives de la croissance urbaine au Zaire.' *Zaire-Afrique*, 111, 35–52.

De Young, M. (1967) 'An African emporium: the Addis Markato.' *Journal of Ethiopian Studies*, 5 (2), 103–22.

Dihoff, G. (1970) *Katsina*. New York: Praeger.

Dike, A. A. (1979) 'Misconceptions of African urbanism.' In Obudho, R. A. and El-Shakhs, S. (ed.) *Development of Urban Systems in Africa*. New York: Praeger.

Dinan, C. (1975) 'Socialization in an Accra suburb.' In Oppong, C. (ed.) *Changing Family Studies*. Accra: University of Ghana.

Doherty, J. (1977) 'Urban places and Third World development: the case of Tanzania.' *Antipode*, 9 (3), 32–42.

Dongmo, J.-L. (1982) 'The competitive migration fields of Douala and Yaoundé, Cameroon.' In Clarke, J. I. and Kosiński, L. A. (eds.), *Redistribution of Population in Africa*. London: Heinemann.

Drakakis-Smith, D. (1981) *Urbanization, Housing and the Development Process*. London: Croom Helm.

Dwyer, D. J. (ed.) (1972) *The City as a Centre of Change in Asia*. Hong Kong: Hong Kong University Press.

Dwyer, D. J. (ed.) (1974) *The City in the Third World*. London: Macmillan.

Dwyer, D. J. (1975) *People and Housing in Third World Cities*. London: Longman.

Eades, J. S. (1979) 'Kinship and entrepreneurship among Yoruba in northern Ghana.' In Shack, W. A. and Skinner, E. P. (eds.), *Strangers in African Societies*, Berkeley: University of California Press.

El-Bushra, El-S. (1976) *An Atlas of Khartoum Conurbation*. Khartoum: Khartoum University Press.

Elkan, W. (1960) *Migrants and Proletarians*. London: Oxford University Press.

Elkan, W. (1967) 'Circular migration and the growth of towns in East Africa.' *International Labour Review*, 96, 581–9.

Elkan, W. (1970) 'Urban unemployment in East Africa.' *International Affairs*, 46, 517–28.

Elkan, W. (1976) 'Is a proletariat emerging in Nairobi?' *Economic Development and Cultural Change*, 24, 695–706.

Elkan, W., Ryan, T. and Mukui, J. T. (1982) 'The economics of shoe shining in Nairobi.' *African Affairs*, 81, 247–56.

Elliott, C. (1975) *Patterns of Poverty in the Third World*. New York: Praeger.

El-Shakhs, S. (1972) 'Development, primacy and systems of cities.' *Journal of Developing Areas*, 7, 11–36.

El-Shakhs, S. and Obudho, R. A. (eds.) (1974) *Urbanization, National Development and Regional Planning in Africa*. New York: Praeger.

El-Shakhs, S. and Salau, A. T. (1979) 'Modernization and the planning of cities in Africa: implications for internal structure.' *African Urban Studies*, 4, 15–26.

Etherton, D. (1971) *Mathare Valley: a case study of uncontrolled settlement in Nairobi*. Nairobi: University of Nairobi, HRDU.

Fanon, F. (1967) *The Wretched of the Earth*. London: Penguin.

Ferraro, G. (1973) 'Tradition or transition? Rural and urban kinsmen in East Africa.' *Urban Anthropology*, 2, 214–31.

Ferraro, G. (1978) 'Nairobi: overview of an East African city.' *African Urban Studies*, 3, 1–13.

Forde, D. (1956) 'Introductory Survey.' In *Social Implications of Industrialization and Urbanization in Africa South of the Sahara*. Paris: UNESCO.

Fowler, D. A. (1981) 'The informal sector in Freetown.' In Sethuraman, S. V. (ed.) *The Urban Informal Sector in Developing Countries*. Geneva: ILO.

Fraenkel, M. (1964) *Tribe and Class in Monrovia*. London: Oxford University Press.

* Friedmann, J. (1973) *Urbanization, Planning and National Development*. Beverly Hills: Sage.

Friedmann, J. (1975) 'The spatial organization of power in the development of urban systems.' In Friedmann, J. and Alonso, W. (eds.) *Regional Policy*. Cambridge, Mass.: MIT Press.

Friedmann, J. and Weaver, C. (1979) *Territory and Function: the evolution of regional planning*. London: E. Arnold.

Friedmann, J. and Wulff, R. (1975) *The Urban Transition*. London: E. Arnold.

Funnell, D. C. (1976) 'The role of small service centres in regional and rural development, with special reference to Eastern Africa.' In Gilbert, A. (ed.) *Development Planning and Spatial Structure*. London: Wiley.

Fyfe, C. and Jones, E. (eds.) (1968) *Freetown*. London: Oxford University Press.

Garbett, G. K. (1975) 'Circulatory migration in Rhodesia: towards a decision model.' In Parkin, D. J. (ed.) *Town and Country in Central and Eastern Africa*. London: Oxford University Press.

Garlick, P. C. (1971) *African Traders and Economic Development in Ghana*. London: Oxford University Press.

Geertz, C. (1963) *Peddlers and Princes*. Chicago: University of Chicago Press.

Gellar, S. (1967) 'West African cities as motors for development.' *Civilisations* 17, 254–62.

Gerry, C. (1979) 'Small-scale manufacturing and repairs in Dakar.' In Bromley, R. and Gerry, C. (eds.) *Casual Work and Poverty in Third World Cities*. Chichester: Wiley.

Ghai, D. P. (ed.) (1965) *Portrait of a Minority: Asians in East Africa*. Nairobi: Oxford University Press.

Giacottino, J.-C. (1979) 'La ville tropicale et ses problèmes d'environnement.' *Cahiers d'Outre-Mer*, 32, 22–38.

Gibbal, J.-M. (1974) *Citadins et Villageois dans la Ville Africaine: l'exemple d'Abidjan*. Paris: Maspero.

* Gilbert, A. and Gugler, J. (1982) *Cities, Poverty and Development: urbanization in the Third World*. London: Oxford University Press.

Gilbert, A. and Ward, P. M. (1978) 'Housing in Latin American cities.' In Herbert, D. T. and Johnston, R. J. (eds.), *Geography and the Urban Environment*, vol. 1. Chichester: Wiley.

Ginsburg, N. (1955) 'The great city in Southeast Asia.' *American Journal of Sociology*, 60, 455–62.

Gish, O. (1975) *Planning the Health Sector: the Tanzanian experience*. London: Croom Helm.

Gleave, M. B. (1981) 'Urban growth, urbanization and development in Sierra Leone, 1963–1974.' *Malaysian Journal of Tropical Geography*, 3, 7–17.

Gluckman, M. (1961) 'Anthropological problems arising from the African industrial revolution.' In Southall, A. (ed.) *Social Change in Modern Africa*. London: Oxford University Press.

Goddard, S. (1965) 'Town–farm relations in Yoruba land.' *Africa*, 35, 21–9.

Gouellain, R. (1975) *Douala: ville et histoire*. Paris: Institut d'Ethnologie.

Gould, P. (1970) 'Tanzania 1920–63: the spatial impress of the modernization process.' *World Politics*, 22, 149–70.

Gould, W. T. S. (1975) 'Movements of schoolchildren and provision of secondary schools in Uganda.' In Parkin, D. J. (ed.) *Town and Country in Central and Eastern Africa*. London: Oxford University Press.

Gould, W. T. S. and Prothero, R. M. (1975) 'Space and time in African population mobility.' In Kosiński, L. and Prothero, R. M. (ed.) *People on the Move*. London: Methuen.

Green, H. A. (1979) 'Urban planning in Nigeria.' *Journal of Administration Overseas*, 18, 22–33.

Green, L. (1974) 'Migration, urbanization and national development in Nigeria.' In Amin, S. (ed.) *Modern Migrations in Western Africa*. London: Oxford University Press.

Gregory, J. W. (1974) 'Development and in-migration in Upper Volta.' In Amin, S. (ed.), *Modern Migrations in Western Africa*. London: Oxford University Press.

Grillo, R. D. (1973) *African Railwaymen*. Cambridge: Cambridge University Press.

Grove, D. and Huszar, L. (1964) *The Towns of Ghana: the role of service centres in regional planning*. Accra: Ghana Universities Press.

Guedes, A. (1971) 'The caniços of Mozambique.' In Oliver, P. (ed.), *Shelter in Africa*. London: Barrie and Jenkins.

Gugler, J. (1969) 'On the theory of rural–urban migration: the case of sub-Saharan Africa.' In Jackson, J. A. (ed.), *Migration*. Cambridge: Cambridge University Press.

Gugler, J. (1971) 'Life in a dual system: Eastern Nigerians in town.' *Cahiers d'Etudes Africaines*, 11, 400–21.

Gugler, J. (1975) 'Migration and ethnicity in sub-Saharan Africa.' In Safa, H. I. and Du Toit, B. M. (eds.) *Migration and Development*. The Hague: Mouton.

Gugler, J. (1976) 'Migrating to urban centres of unemployment in tropical Africa. In Richmond, A. H. and Kubat, D. (eds.), *Internal Migration*. Beverly Hills: Sage.

Gugler, J. and Flanagan, W. (1977) 'On the political economy of urbanization in the Third World: the case of West Africa.' *International Journal of Urban and Regional Research*, 1, 272–92.

* Gugler, J. and Flanagan, W. (1978) *Urbanization and Social Change in West Africa*. Cambridge: Cambridge University Press.

Gutkind, P. C. W. (1962) 'The African urban milieu: a force in rapid change.' *Civilisations*, 12, 167–91.

Gutkind, P. C. W. (1963) *The Royal Capital of Buganda.* The Hague: Mouton.

Gutkind, P. C. W. (1965) 'African urbanism, mobility and the social network.' *International Journal of Comparative Sociology*, 6, 48–60.

Gutkind, P. C. W. (1968) 'African urban studies: past accomplishments, future trends and needs.' *Canadian Journal of African Studies*, 2, 63–80.

Gutkind, P. C. W. (1969) 'Tradition, migration, urbanization, modernity and unemployment in Africa.' *Canadian Journal of African Studies*, 3, 343–66.

Gutkind, P. C. W. (1974) *Urban Anthropology.* Assen: Van Gorcum.

Gutkind, P. C. W. and Wallerstein, I. (eds.) (1976) *The Political Economy of Contemporary Africa.* Beverly Hills: Sage.

Haeringer, P. (1969) 'Structures foncières et création urbaine à Abidjan. *Cahiers d'Etudes Africaines*, 9, 219–70.

Haeringer, P. (1973) 'Propriétés foncières et politiques urbaines à Douala.' *Cahiers d'Etudes Africaines*, 13, 469–96.

*Hake, A. (1977) *African Metropolis: Nairobi's self-help city.* London: Chatto and Windus.

Halliman, D. M. and Morgan, W. T. W. (1967) 'The city of Nairobi.' In Morgan, W. T. W. (ed.), *Nairobi: city and region.* Nairobi: Oxford University Press.

Halpenny, P. (1975) 'Three styles of ethnic migration in Kisenyi, Kampala.' In Parkin, D. J. (ed.) *Town and Country in Central and Eastern Africa.* London: Oxford University Press.

*Hance, W. A. (1970) *Population, Migration and Urbanization in Africa.* New York: Columbia University Press.

*Hanna, W. J. and Hanna, J. L. (1981) *Urban Dynamics in Black Africa,* second edition. New York: Aldine.

Hannerz, U. (1980) *Exploring the City.* New York: Columbia University Press.

Hansen, K. T. (1975) 'Married women and work.' *African Social Research*, 20, 777–99.

Hardoy, J. E. and Satterthwaite, D. (1981) *Shelter: need and response.* Chichester: Wiley.

Harrell-Bond, B. E., Howard, A. M. and Skinner, D. E. (1978) *Community Leadership and the Transformation of Freetown, 1801–1976.* The Hague: Mouton.

Harrison Church, R. J. (1972) 'The case for industrial and general development of the smaller towns of West Africa.' In *La Croissance Urbaine en Afrique Noire et à Madagascar.* Paris: CNRS.

Hart, K. (1971) 'Migration and tribal identity among the Frafras of Ghana.' *Journal of Asian and African Studies*, 6 (1), 21–36.

Hart, K. (1973) 'Informal income opportunities and urban employment in Ghana.' *Journal of Modern African Studies*, 11, 61–89.

Hart, K. (1974) 'Migration and the opportunity structure: a Ghanaian case study.' In Amin, S. (ed.), *Modern Migrations in Western Africa*. London: Oxford University Press.

Harvey, D. (1973) *Social Justice and the City*. London: E. Arnold.

Harvey, M. E. (1966) 'Town size; town sites; urban land use.' In Clarke, J. I. (ed.), *Sierra Leone in Maps*. London: University of London Press.

Hauser, P. M. and Schnore, L. F. (ed.) (1965) *The Study of Urbanization*. New York: Wiley.

Hay, A. M. and Smith, R. H. T. (1970) *Inter-Regional Trade and Money Flows in Nigeria*. Ibadan: Oxford University Press.

*Heisler, H. (1974) *Urbanisation and the Government of Migration*. London: C. Hurst.

Henkel, R. (1979) *Central Places in Western Kenya*. Heidelberg: Geographisches Institut der Universität.

Hill, P. (1977) *Population, Prosperity and Poverty: rural Kano 1900 and 1970*. Cambridge: Cambridge University Press.

Hilling, D. (1966) 'Tema: the geography of a new port.' *Geography*, 51, 111–25.

Hinchcliffe, K. (1974) 'Labour aristocracy: a northern Nigerian case study.' *Journal of Modern African Studies*, 12, 57–67.

*Hinderink, J. and Sterkenburg, J. (1975) *Anatomy of an African Town: a socio-economic study of Cape Coast, Ghana*. Utrecht: Geographical Institute, University of Utrecht.

Hirst, M. A. (1970) 'Tribal migration in East Africa.' *Geografiska Annaler*, 52B, 153–63.

Hirst, M. A. (1973) 'A functional analysis of towns in Tanzania.' *Tijdschrift voor Economische en Sociale Geografie*, 64, 39–51.

Hirst, M. A. (1975) 'The distribution of migrants in Kampala.' In Parkin, D. J. (ed.), *Town and Country in Central and Eastern Africa*. London: Oxford University Press.

Hjort, A. (1979) *Savanna Town: rural ties and urban opportunities in northern Kenya*. Stockholm: University of Stockholm.

Hodder, B. W. and Ukwu, U. I. (1969) *Markets in West Africa*. Ibadan: Ibadan University Press.

Hopkins, N. S. (1972) *Popular Government in an African Town: Kita, Mali*. Chicago: University of Chicago Press.

Horvath, R. J. (1969) 'The wandering capitals of Ethiopia.' *Journal of African History*, 10, 205–19.

Hoselitz, B. F. (1957) 'Generative and parasitic cities.' *Economic Development and Cultural Change*, 3, 278–94.

Howard, A. (1975) 'Pre-colonial centres and regional systems in Africa.' *Pan-African Journal*, 8, 247–70.

Hoyle, B. S. (1967) *The Seaports of East Africa*. Nairobi: East African Publishing House.

Hoyle, B. S. (1972) 'The port function in the urban development of tropical Africa.' In *La Croissance Urbaine en Afrique Noire et à Madagascar*. Paris: CNRS.

Hoyle, B. S. (1979) 'African socialism and urban development: the relocation of the Tanzanian capital.' *Tijdschrift voor Economische en Sociale Geografie*, 70, 207–16.

Hoyle, B. S. and Hilling, D. (eds.) (1970) *Seaports and Development in Tropical Africa*. London: Macmillan.

Hull, R. W. (1976) *African Cities and Towns before the European Conquest*. New York: Norton.

Hutton, C. R. (1973) *Reluctant Farmers?* Nairobi: East African Publishing House.

Hyden, G. (1980) *Beyond Ujamaa in Tanzania*. London: Heinemann.

ILO (1972) *Employment, Incomes and Equality: a strategy for increasing productive employment in Kenya*. Geneva: International Labour Organization.

ILO (1976) *Growth, Employment and Equity: a comprehensive strategy for the Sudan*. Geneva: International Labour Organization.

Jefferson, M. (1939) 'The law of the primate city.' *Geographical Review*, 29, 226–32.

Jeffries, R. D. (1978) *Class, Power and Ideology in Ghana: the railwaymen of Sekondi*. Cambridge: Cambridge University Press.

Jenkins, G. (1967) 'An informal political economy.' In Butler, J. and Castagno, A. A. (eds.), *Transition in African Politics*, New York: Praeger.

Johnson, E. A. J. (1970) *The Organization of Space in Developing Countries*. Cambridge, Mass.: Harvard University Press.

Johnson, G. E. and Whitelaw, W. E. (1974) 'Urban–rural income transfers in Kenya.' *Economic Development and Cultural Change*, 22, 473–9.

Joshi, H., Lubell, H. and Mouly, J. (1976) *Abidjan: urban development and employment in the Ivory Coast*. Geneva: ILO.

Kabwegyere, T. B. (1979) 'Small urban centres and the growth of underdevelopment in rural Kenya.' *Africa*, 49, 308–15.

Kanyeihamba, G. W. and McAuslan, J. (eds.) (1978) *Urban Legal Problems in Eastern Africa*. Uppsala: Scandinavian Institute of African Studies.

Katz, S. S. and Katz, S. H. (1981) 'The evolving role of traditional medicine in Kenya.' *African Urban Studies*, 9, 1–12.

Kay, G. (1967a) *A Social Geography of Zambia*. London: University of London Press.

Kay, G. (1967b) 'The towns of Zambia.' In Steel, R. W. and Lawton, R. (eds.), *Liverpool Essays in Geography*. London: Longman.

*Kay, G. and Smout. M. A. H. (1977) *Salisbury*. London: Hodder and Stoughton.

Kayitenkore, E. (1967) 'La construction dans les zones de squatting de Kinshasa.' *Cahiers Economiques et Sociaux*, 5, 327–53.

Kennedy, P. T. (1980) *Ghanaian Businessmen*. Munich: Weltforum.

Kenya (1969) *Development Plan 1970–1974*. Nairobi.

Kenya (1978) *Human Settlements in Kenya: a strategy for urban and rural development*. Nairobi.

Kenya (1979) *Development Plan 1979–1983*. Nairobi.

Kileff, C. (1975) 'Black suburbanites: an African elite in Salisbury.' In Kileff, C. and Pendleton, W. C. (eds.) *Urban Man in Southern Africa*. Gwelo (Zimbabwe): Mambo Press.

Kilson, M. (1974) *African Urban Kinsmen: the Ga of central Accra*. London: C. Hurst.

Kimani, S. M. (1972) 'The structure of land ownership in Nairobi.' *Canadian Journal of African Studies*, 6, 379–402.

King, A. D. (1976) *Colonial Urban Development*. London: Routledge and Kegan Paul.

King, K. (1977) *The African Artisan: education and the informal sector in Kenya*. London: Heinemann.

King, K. (1979) 'Petty production in Nairobi.' In Bromley, R. and Gerry, C. (eds.), *Casual Work and Poverty in Third World Cities*. Chichester: Wiley.

*Krapf-Askari, E. (1969) *Yoruba Towns and Cities*. Oxford: Clarendon Press.

Kudiabor, C. D. K. (1977) 'Urbanization and growth pole strategy for regional development in Ghana.' In Mabogunje, A. L. and Faniran, A. (eds.), *Regional Planning and National Development in Tropical Africa*. Ibadan: Ibadan University Press.

Kuhn, M. W. (1970) *Markets and Trade in Omdurman, Sudan*. Ph.D. thesis, University of California, Los Angeles.

Kuper, H. (ed.) (1965) *Urbanization and Migration in West Africa*. Berkeley: University of California Press.

Kuper, L. and Smith, M. G. (eds.) (1969) *Pluralism in Africa*. Berkeley: University of California Press.

La Fontaine, J. S. (1970) *City Politics: a study of Leopoldville, 1962–63*. Cambridge: Cambridge University Press.

Langdon, S. W. (1981) *Multinational Corporations in the Political Economy of Kenya*. London: Macmillan.

Larimore, A. E. (1959) *The Alien Town: patterns of settlement in Busoga, Uganda*. Chicago: Department of Geography, University of Chicago.

Leblanc, M. and Malaisse, F. (1978) *Lubumbashi: un ecosystème urbain tropicale*. Lubumbashi: Université Nationale du Zaire.

Leeson, J. and Frankenberg, R. (1977) 'The patients of traditional doctors in Lusaka.' *African Social Research*, 23, 217–34.

Leslie, J. A. K. (1963) *A Survey of Dar es Salaam.* London: Oxford University Press.

Linsky, A. S. (1965) 'Some generalizations concerning primate cities.' *Annals of the Association of American Geographers*, 55, 506–13.

Lipton, M. (1977) *Why Poor People Stay Poor: a study of urban bias in world development.* London: Temple Smith.

Little, K. L. (1965) *West African Urbanization: a study of voluntary associations in social change.* Cambridge: Cambridge University Press.

Little, K. L. (1973) *African Women in Towns.* Cambridge: Cambridge University Press.

* Little, K. L. (1974) *Urbanization as a Social Process.* London: Routledge and Kegan Paul.

Little, K. (1978) 'Countervailing influences in African ethnicity.' In Du Toit, B. M. (ed.), *Ethnicity in Modern Africa.* Boulder, Colorado: Westview.

Lloyd, P. C. (1962) *Yoruba Land Law.* London: Oxford University Press.

Lloyd, P. C. (1967) *Africa in Social Change.* London: Penguin.

Lloyd, P. C. (1973) 'The Yoruba: an urban people?' In Southall, A. (ed.), *Urban Anthropology.* New York: Oxford University Press.

Lloyd, P. C. (1974) *Power and Independence: urban Africans' perception of social inequality.* London: Routledge and Kegan Paul.

Lloyd, P. C. (1979) *Slums of Hope? Shanty towns of the Third World.* London: Penguin.

Lloyd, P. C. (1981) *A Third World Proletariat?* London: George Allen and Unwin.

* Lloyd, P. C., Mabogunje, A. L. and Awe, B. (eds.) (1967) *The City of Ibadan.* Cambridge: Cambridge University Press.

Lock, M. *et al.* (1967) *Kaduna 1917, 1967, 2017.* London: Faber.

Mabogunje, A. L. (1962) *Yoruba Towns.* Ibadan: Ibadan University Press.

Mabogunje, A. L. (1964) 'The evolution and analysis of the retail structure of Lagos.' *Economic Geography*, 40, 304–23.

Mabogunje, A. L. (1965) 'Urbanization in Nigeria: a constraint on economic development.' *Economic Development and Cultural Change*, 13, 413–38.

Mabogunje, A. L. (1967a) 'The Ijebu.' In Lloyd, P. C. *et al.* (eds.), *The City of Ibadan.* Cambridge: Cambridge University Press.

Mabogunje, A. L. (1967b) 'The morphology of Ibadan.' In Lloyd, P. C. *et al.* (eds.), *The City of Ibadan.* Cambridge: Cambridge University Press.

* Mabogunje, A. L. (1968) *Urbanization in Nigeria.* London: University of London Press.

Mabogunje, A. L. (1970a) 'Migration policy and regional development in Nigeria.' *Nigerian Journal of Economic and Social Studies*, 12, 243–62.

Mabogunje, A. L. (1970b) 'Systems approach to the theory of rural–urban migration.' *Geographical Analysis*, 2, 1–18.

* Mabogunje, A. L. (1977) 'The urban situation in Nigeria.' In Goldstein, S. and Sly, D. F. (eds.), *Patterns of Urbanization*, Dolhain: Ordina 569–641.

Mabogunje, A. L. (1978) 'Growth poles and growth centres in the regional development of Nigeria.' In Kuklinski, A. (ed.), *Regional Policies in Nigeria, India and Brazil*. The Hague: Mouton.

Mabogunje, A. L. (1980) *The Development Process*. London: Hutchinson.

Mabogunje, A. L. and Faniran, A. (eds.) (1977) *Regional Planning and National Development in Tropical Africa*. Ibadan: Ibadan University Press.

McGee, T. G. (1967) *The Southeast Asian City*. London: Bell.

McGee, T. G. (1971) *The Urbanization Process in the Third World*. London: Bell.

McGee, T. G. (1973) 'Peasants in cities: a paradox, a most ingenious paradox.' *Human Organization*, 32, 135–42.

McGee, T. G. (1976) 'The persistence of the proto-proletariat.' *Progress in Geography*, 9, 3–38.

Maclean, U. (1971) *Magical Medicine: a Nigerian case study*. London: Penguin.

McMaster, D. N. (1968) 'The colonial district town in Uganda.' In Beckinsale, R. P. and Houston, J. M. (eds.), *Urbanization and its Problems*. Oxford: Blackwell.

McNulty, M. L. (1969) 'Urban structure and development: the urban system of Ghana.' *Journal of Developing Areas*, 3, 159–76.

McNulty, M. L. (1976) 'West African urbanization.' In Berry, B. J. L. (ed.), *Urbanization and Counterurbanization*. Beverly Hills: Sage.

McNulty, M. L. and Horton, F. E. (1976) 'West African urbanization: patterns of convergence or divergence?' *Pan-African Journal*, 9, 169–80.

Magubane, B. (1979) 'The city in Africa: some theoretical issues.' In Obudho, R. A. and El-Shakhs, S. (eds.), *Development of Urban Systems in Africa*, New York: Praeger.

* Manshard, W. (1977) *Die Städte des Tropischen Afrika*. Berlin: Gebrüder Borntraeger.

Marguerat, Y. (1975) *Analyse Numérique des Migrations vers les Villes du Cameroun*. Paris: ORSTOM.

Marris, P. (1961) *Family and Social Change in an African City: a study of rehousing in Lagos*. London: Routledge and Kegan Paul.

Martin, R. (1974) 'Housing in Lusaka.' In Hawkesworth, N. R. (ed.) *Local Government in Zambia*. Lusaka: City Council.

Martin, R. (1975) *Self-Help in Action: a study of site-and-service schemes in Zambia*. Lusaka: National Housing Authority.

Martin, R. (1982) 'The formulation of a self-help project in Lusaka.' In Ward, P. M. (ed.), *Self-Help Housing*. London: Mansell.

Mascarenhas, A. C. (1967) 'The impact of nationhood on Dar es Salaam.' *East African Geographical Review*, 5, 39–46.

Mascarenhas, A. C. (1973) 'Urban growth.' In Egero, B. and Henin, R. A. (eds.), *The Population of Tanzania*, Dar es Salaam: University of Dar es Salaam, BRALUP.

Mazrui, A. (1977) *Africa's International Relations*. London: Heinemann.

Mehta, S. K. (1964) 'Some demographic and economic correlates of primate cities.' *Demography*, 1, 136–47.

Meillassoux, C. (1968) *Urbanization of an African Community: voluntary associations in Bamako*. Seattle: University of Washington Press.

Meillassoux, C. (1971) *The Development of Indigenous Trade and Markets in West Africa*. London: Oxford University Press.

Memon, P. A. (1982) 'The growth of low-income settlements: planning response in the peri-urban zone of Nairobi.' *Third World Planning Review*, 4, 145–58.

Middleton, J. (1979) 'Home-town: a study of an urban centre in southern Ghana.' *Africa*, 49, 246–57.

Miner, H. (1953) *The Primitive City of Timbuctoo*. Princeton, N.J.: Princeton University Press.

Miner, H. (ed.) (1967) *The City in Modern Africa*. New York: Praeger.

Mitchell, J. C. (1956) *The Kalela Dance*. Manchester: Manchester University Press.

Mitchell, J. C. (1959) 'The causes of labour migration.' *Bulletin of the Inter-African Labour Institute*, 6(1), 12–47.

Mitchell, J. C. (ed.) (1969a) *Social Networks in Urban Situations: analysis of personal relationships in Central African towns*. Manchester: Manchester University Press.

Mitchell, J. C. (1969b) 'Structural plurality, urbanization and labour circulation in Southern Rhodesia.' In Jackson, J. A. (ed.), *Migration*. Cambridge: Cambridge University Press.

Mlay, W. F. I. (1974) *Recent Rural–Urban Migration in Tanzania*. Ph.D. thesis, University of London.

Mlia, J. N. (1975) 'Malawi's new capital city: a regional planning perspective.' *Pan-African Journal*, 7, 387–401.

Moller, V. (1978) *Urban Commitment and Involvememt among Black Rhodesians*. Durban: University of Natal.

Morgan, R. W. (1975) 'Fertility levels and fertility change.' In Caldwell, J. C. (ed.), *Population Growth and Socioeconomic Change in West Africa*. New York: Columbia University Press.

Morgan, R. W. (1979) 'Migration into Lagos.' In Udo, R. K. (ed.), *Population Education Sourcebook for Sub-Saharan Africa.* Nairobi: Heinemann.

Morgan, W. T. W. (1969) 'Urbanization in Kenya: origins and trends.' *Transactions, Institute of British Geographers,* 46, 167–77.

Mortimore, M. J. (1972) 'Some aspects of rural–urban relations in Kano, Nigeria.' In *La Croissance Urbaine en Afrique Noire et à Madagascar.* Paris: CNRS.

Mortimore, M. J. (1975) 'Peri-urban pressures.' In Moss, R. P. and Rathbone, R. (eds.), *The Population Factor in African Studies.* London: University of London Press.

Moser, C. (1978) 'Informal sector of petty commodity production: dualism or dependence in urban development?' *World Development,* 6, 1041–64.

Moughtin, J. C. (1964) 'The traditional settlements of the Hausa people.' *Town Planning Review,* 35, 21–34.

Muench, L. H. (1978) *The Private Burden of Urban Social Overhead: a study of the informal housing market of Kampala, Uganda.* Ph.D. thesis, University of Pennsylvania.

Murison, H. S. and Lea, J. P. (eds.) (1979) *Housing in Third World Countries.* London: Macmillan.

Muwonge, J. W. (1980) 'Urban policy and patterns of low-income settlement in Nairobi.' *Population and Development Review,* 6, 595–613.

Nabila, J. S. (1979) 'The processes of the decision to migrate in Ghana.' In Udo, R. K. (ed.), *Population Education Sourcebook for Sub-Saharan Africa,* Nairobi: Heinemann.

Nelson, J. M. (1979a) *Access to Power: politics and the urban poor in developing nations.* Princeton, N.J.: Princeton University Press.

Nelson, N. (1979b) 'How women and men get by: the sexual division of labour in the informal sector of a Nairobi squatter settlement.' In Bromley, R. and Gerry, C. (ed.), *Casual Work and Poverty in Third World Cities.* Chichester: Wiley.

Nigeria (1975) *Third National Development Plan 1975–80.* Lagos.

Norwood, H. C. (1972) 'Ndirande: a squatter colony in Malawi.' *Town Planning Review,* 43, 135–50.

Nwafor, J. C. (1981) 'The growth towards urban status of Kigali, capital of Rwanda.' *African Urban Studies,* 9, 39–56.

Nwaka, G. I. (1980) 'Owerri: development of a Nigerian State capital.' *Third World Planning Review,* 2, 233–42.

Obbo, C. (1975) 'Women's careers in low income areas as indicators of country and town dynamics.' In Parkin, D. J. (ed.), *Town and Country in Central and Eastern Africa.* London: Oxford University Press.

Obbo, C. (1980) *African Women: their struggle for economic independence.* London: Zed Press and Hutchinson.

*Obudho, R. A. and El-Shakhs, S. (eds.) (1979) *Development of Urban Systems in Africa*. New York: Praeger.

Obudho, R. A. and Waller, P. P. (1976) *Periodic Markets, Urbanization and Regional Planning: case study from western Kenya*. Westport: Greenwood.

O'Connor, A. M. (1968) 'The cities and towns of East Africa: distribution and functions.' In Berger, H. (ed.), *Ostafrikanische Studien*. Nürnberg: Friedrich-Alexander-Universität.

O'Connor, A. M. (1978) *The Geography of Tropical African Development*, second edition. Oxford: Pergamon.

O'Connor, A. M. (1981) *Urbanization in Tropical Africa: an annotated bibliography*. Boston: G. K. Hall.

Odongo, J. (1979) 'Housing deficit in cities of the Third World: fact or fiction?' In Murison, H. S. and Lea, J. P. (ed.), *Housing in Third World Countries*. London: Macmillan.

Odongo, J. and Lea, J. P. (1977) 'Home ownership and rural–urban links in Uganda.' *Journal of Modern African Studies*, 15, 59–73.

Ogendo, R. B. (1972) *Industrial Geography of Kenya*. Nairobi: East African Publishing House.

Ohadike, P. O. (1975) 'The evolving phenomena of migration and urbanization in Central Africa: a Zambian case.' In Parkin, D. J. (ed.), *Town and Country in Central and Eastern Africa*. London: Oxford University Press.

Ojo, G. J. A. (1966a) *Yoruba Culture: a geographical analysis*. London: University of London Press.

Ojo, G. J. A. (1966b) *Yoruba Palaces*. London: University of London Press.

Ojo, G. J. A. (1970) 'Some observations on journeys to agricultural work in Yorubaland.' *Economic Geography*, 46, 459–71.

Olatunbosun, D. (1975) *Nigeria's Neglected Rural Majority*. Ibadan: Ibadan University Press.

Ominde, S. H. (1968) *Land and Population Movements in Kenya*. London: Heinemann.

Onibokun, G. A. (1970) 'Nigerian cities: their rehabilitation and redevelopment.' *African Studies Review*, 13, 291–310.

Onokerhoraye, A. G. (1975) 'Urbanism as an organ of traditional African civilization: the example of Benin, Nigeria.' *Civilisations*, 25, 294–305.

Onokerhoraye, A. G. (1976) 'The influence of different cultures on the patterns of change in traditional African cities.' *Cultures et Développement*, 8, 623–45.

Onokerhoraye, A. G. (1977) 'The spatial pattern of residential districts in Benin, Nigeria.' *Urban Studies*, 14, 292–302.

Onyemelukwe, J. O. C. (1970) 'Aspects of staple foods trade in Onitsha market.' *Nigerian Geographical Journal*, 13, 121–39.

Onyemelukwe, J. O. C. (1972) 'Foodstuff price variation in the service area of Onitsha market.' *Nigerian Geographical Journal*, 15, 13–23.

Onyemelukwe, J. O. C. (1981) 'Urban slums in Nigeria.' *Journal of Environmental Management*, 13, 111–25.

ORSTOM (1969) 'Les petites villes de Côte d'Ivoire.' *Cahiers Orstom, Série Sciences Humaines*, 6 (1), 61–111; 6 (2), 3–92.

Oyebande, L. (1978) 'Urban water supply planning and management in Nigeria.' *Geojournal*, 2, 403–12.

Oyelese, J. O. (1971) 'The growth of Ibadan city and its impact on land use patterns, 1961 to 1965.' *Journal of Tropical Geography*, 32, 49–55.

Paden, J. N. (1971) 'Communal competition, conflict and violence in Kano.' In Melson, R. and Wolpe, H. (eds.), *Nigeria: modernization and the politics of communalism*. East Lansing, Michigan: Michigan State University Press.

Paden, J. N. (ed.) (1980) *Values, Identities and National Integration*. Evanston, Illinois: Northwestern University Press.

Pain, M. (1979) *Kinshasa: écologie et organisation urbaines*. Toulouse: Université Toulouse le Mirail.

Palen, J. J. (1976) 'Urbanization and migration in an indigenous city: the case of Addis Ababa.' In Richmond, A. H. and Kubat, D. (eds.), *Internal Migration*. Beverly Hills: Sage.

Pankhurst, R. (1961) 'Menelik and the foundation of Addis Ababa.' *Journal of African History*, 2, 103–117.

Parkin, D. J. (1966) 'Types of urban African marriage in Kampala.' *Africa*, 36, 269–85.

Parkin, D. J. (1969a) *Neighbours and Nationals in an African City Ward*. London: Routledge and Kegan Paul.

Parkin, D. J. (1969b) 'Tribe as fact and fiction in an East African city.' In Gulliver, P. H. (ed.), *Tradition and Transition in East Africa*. London: Routledge and Kegan Paul.

Parkin, D. J. (1974a) 'Congregational and interpersonal ideologies in political ethnicity.' In Cohen, A. (ed.), *Urban Ethnicity*. London: Tavistock.

Parkin, D. J. (1974b) 'Nairobi' (four papers). In Whiteley, W. H. (ed.), *Language in Kenya*. Nairobi: Oxford University Press.

Parkin, D. J. (1975a) 'Migration, settlement and the politics of unemployment: a Nairobi case study.' In Parkin, D. J. (ed.), *Town and Country in Central and Eastern Africa*. London: Oxford University Press.

*Parkin, D. J. (ed.) (1975b) *Town and Country in Central and Eastern Africa*. London: Oxford University Press.

Parkin, D. J. (1978) *The Cultural Definition of Political Response*. London: Academic Press.

Pasteur, D. (1979) *The Management of Squatter Upgrading.* Farnborough: Saxon House.

Payne, G. K. (1977) *Urban Housing in the Third World.* London: Leonard Hill.

Peace, A. J. (1975) 'The Lagos proletariat: labour aristocrats or populist militants?' In Sandbrook, R. and Cohen, R. (eds.), *The Development of an African Working Class.* London: Longman.

Peace, A. J. (1979) *Choice, Class and Conflict: a study of southern Nigerian factory workers.* Brighton: Harvester Press.

Peel, J. D. Y. (1980) 'Urbanization and urban history in West Africa.' *Journal of African History,* 21, 269–77.

Peil, M. (1970) 'The apprenticeship system in Accra.' *Africa,* 40, 137–50.

Peil, M. (1971) 'The expulsion of West African aliens.' *Journal of Modern African Studies,* 9, 205–29.

* Peil, M. (1972) *The Ghanaian Factory Worker.* Cambridge: Cambridge University Press.

Peil, M. (1975a) 'Female roles in West African towns.' In Goody, J. (ed.), *Changing Social Structure in Ghana.* London: International African Institute.

Peil, M. (1975b) 'Interethnic contacts in Nigerian cities.' *Africa,* 45, 107–21.

Peil, M. (1976) 'African squatter settlements.' *Urban Studies,* 13, 155–66.

Peil, M. (1977) *Consensus and Conflict in African Societies.* London: Longman.

Peil, M. (1979) 'Host reactions: aliens in Ghana.' In Shack, W. A. and Skinner, E. P. (eds.), *Strangers in African Societies.* Berkeley: University of California Press.

* Peil, M. (1981) *Cities and Suburbs: urban life in West Africa.* New York: Africana Publishing House.

Pellow, D. (1977) *Women in Accra.* Algonac: Reference Publications.

Pitte, J.-R. (1977) *Nouakchott: capitale de la Mauritanie.* Paris: Département de Géographie de l'Université de Paris–Sorbonne.

Plotnicov, L. (1967) *Strangers to the City: urban man in Jos.* Pittsburgh: University of Pittsburgh Press.

Plotnicov, L. (1970) 'Rural–urban communications in contemporary Nigeria.' *Journal of Asian and African Studies,* 5, 66–82.

Plotnicov, L. (1972) 'Who owns Jos? Ethnic ideology in Nigerian urban politics.' *Urban Anthropology,* 1, 1–13.

Pons, V. G. (1969) *Stanleyville: an urban African community under Belgian administration.* London: Oxford University Press.

Pred, A. (1977) *City-Systems in Advanced Economies.* London: Hutchinson.

Prothero, R. M. (1968) 'Migration in tropical Africa.' In Caldwell, J. C.

and Okonjo, C. (eds.), *The Population of Tropical Africa*. London: Longman.

Prothero, R. M. (1976) 'Population mobility.' In Knight, C. G. and Newman, J. L. (eds.), *Contemporary Africa*. Englewood Cliffs, N.J.: Prentice-Hall.

Rayfield, J. R. (1974) 'Theories of urbanization and the colonial city in West Africa.' *Africa*, 44, 163–85.

Redfield, R. and Singer, M. B. (1954) 'The cultural role of cities.' *Economic Development and Cultural Change*, 3, 53–73.

Richardson, H. W. (1980) 'An urban development strategy for Kenya.' *Journal of Developing Areas*, 15, 97–118.

Riddell, J. B. (1970) *Spatial Dynamics of Modernization in Sierra Leone*. Evanston, Illinois: Northwestern University Press.

Riddell, J. B. (1978) 'The migration to the cities of West Africa: some policy considerations.' *Journal of Modern African Studies*, 16, 241–60.

Riddell, J. B. (1981) 'Beyond the description of spatial pattern: the process of proletarianization as a factor in population migration in West Africa.' *Progress in Human Geography*, 5, 370–92.

Riddell, J. B. and Harvey, M. E. (1972) 'The urban system in the migration process: an evaluation of stepwise migration in Sierra Leone.' *Economic Geography*, 48, 270–83.

Roberts, B. (1978) *Cities of Peasants*. London: E. Arnold.

Ross, M. H. (1973) *The Political Integration of Urban Squatters*. Evanston, Illinois: Northwestern University Press.

* Ross, M. H. (1975) *Grass Roots in an African City: political behaviour in Nairobi*. Cambridge, Mass.: MIT Press.

Ross, M. H. and Weisner, T. S. (1977) 'The rural–urban migrant network in Kenya.' *American Ethnologist*, 4, 359–75.

Rouch, J. (1956) 'Migrations au Ghana.' *Journal de la Société des Africanistes*, 26, 1956, 33–196.

* Sabot, R. H. (1979) *Economic Development and Urban Migration: Tanzania 1900–1971*. London: Oxford University Press.

Sada, P. O. (1972) 'Residential land use in Lagos: the relevance of traditional models.' *African Urban Notes*, 7 (1), 3–25.

Sada, P. O. (1977) 'Environmental sanitation in urban areas of Nigeria.' *Nigerian Geographical Journal*, 20, 13–25.

Sada, P. O. and Adefolalu, A. A. (1975) 'Urbanisation and problems of urban development.' In Aderibigbe, A. B. (ed.), *Lagos: the development of an African city*. Lagos: Longman.

Safier, M. (ed.) (1967) *The Role of Urban and Regional Planning in National Development for East Africa*. Kampala: Milton Obote Foundation.

Saint-Vil, J. (1981) 'Migrations scolaires et urbanisation en Côte d'Ivoire.' *Cahiers d'Outre-Mer*, 34, 23–41.

Salau, A. T. (1977) 'A new capital for Nigeria.' *Africa Today*, 24 (4), 11–22.

Salau, A. T. (1979) 'Urbanization, planning, and public policies in Nigeria.' In Obudho, R. A. and El-Shakhs, S. (eds.), *Development of Urban Systems in Africa*. New York: Praeger.

* Sandbrook, R. (1982) *The Politics of Basic Needs: urban aspects of assaulting poverty in Africa*. London: Heinemann.

Santos, M. (1979) *The Shared Space: the two circuits of the urban economy in underdeveloped countries*. London: Methuen.

Schatz, S. P. (1977) *Nigerian Capitalism*. Berkeley: University of California Press.

Schatzberg, M. G. (1979) *Bibliography of Small Urban Centers in Rural Development in Africa*. Madison: University of Wisconsin.

Schildkrout, E. (1978) *People of the Zongo: the transformation of ethnic identities in Ghana*. Cambridge: Cambridge University Press.

Schlyter, A. and Schlyter, T. (1980) *George: the development of a squatter settlement in Lusaka*. Stockholm: Swedish Council for Building Research.

Schwab, W. B. (1965) 'Oshogbo: an urban community?' In Kuper, H. (ed.), *Urbanization and Migration in West Africa*. Berkeley: University of California Press.

Schwerdtfeger, F. W. (1982) *Traditional Housing in African Cities*. Chichester: Wiley.

Seck, A. (1970) *Dakar: métropole ouest-africaine*. Dakar: IFAN.

Seers, D. (1979) 'The congruence of Marxism and other neoclassical doctrines.' In *Rothko Chapel Colloquium: Toward a New Strategy for Development*. New York: Pergamon.

Segal, E. S. (1979) 'Urban development planning in Dar es Salaam.' In Obudho, R. A. and El-Shakhs, S. (eds.), *Development of Urban Systems in Africa*. New York: Praeger.

Seidman, A. (1974) *Planning for Development in sub-Saharan Africa*. New York: Praeger.

Sethuraman, S. V. (1976) 'The urban informal sector.' *International Labour Review*, 114, 69–81.

Sethuraman, S. V. (1977) 'The urban informal sector in Africa.' *International Labour Review*, 116, 343–52.

Sethuraman, S. V. (1981) *The Urban Informal Sector in Developing Countries*. Geneva: ILO.

Seymour, T. (1975) 'Squatter settlement and class relations in Zambia.' *Review of African Political Economy*, 3, 71–7.

Shack, W. A. (1973) 'Urban ethnicity and the cultural process of urbanization in Ethiopia.' In Southall, A. (ed.), *Urban Anthropology*. New York: Oxford University Press.

* Shack, W. A. and Skinner, E. P. (eds.) (1979) *Strangers in African Societies*. Berkeley: University of California Press.

Simms, R. P. (1965) *Urbanization in West Africa: a review of the current literature*. Evanston, Illinois: Northwestern University Press.

Sjoberg, G. (1960) *The Pre-Industrial City*. New York: Free Press.

Skinner, E. P. (1965) 'Labor migration among the Mossi of the Upper Volta.' In Kuper, H. (ed.), *Urbanization and Migration in West Africa*. Berkeley: University of California Press.

* Skinner, E. P. (1974) *African Urban Life: the transformation of Ouagadougou*. Princeton, N.J.: Princeton University Press.

Smock, D. R. (1971) 'Urban–rural contrasts in political values in Eastern Nigeria.' *Journal of Asian and African Studies*, 6, 81–90.

Smock, D. R. and Bentsi-Enchill, K. (eds.) (1975) *The Search for National Integration in Africa*. New York: Free Press.

Smout, M. A. H. (1977) 'Urbanization and development problems in Rhodesia.' *Journal of Tropical Geography*, 45, 43–51.

Soja, E. W. (1968) *The Geography of Modernization in Kenya*. Syracuse: Syracuse University Press.

Soja, E. W. and Weaver, C. E. (1976) 'Urbanization and underdevelopment in East Africa.' In Berry, B. J. L. (ed.), *Urbanization and Counterurbanization*. Beverly Hills: Sage.

Southall, A. (ed.) (1961) *Social Change in Modern Africa*. London: Oxford University Press.

Southall, A. (1971) 'The impact of imperialism upon urban development in Africa.' In Turner, V. (ed.), *Colonialism in Africa: vol. 3, Profiles of change*. Cambridge: Cambridge University Press.

Southall, A. (ed.) (1973) *Urban Anthropology*. New York: Oxford University Press.

Southall, A. (1975) 'From segmentary lineage to ethnic association: Luo, Luhya, Ibo and others.' In Owusu, M. (ed.), *Colonialism and Change*, The Hague: Mouton.

Southall, A. (1976) 'Forms of ethnic linkage between town and country.' In Arens, W. (ed.), *A Century of Change in Eastern Africa*. The Hague: Mouton.

Southall, A. (ed.) (1979) *Small Urban Centres in Rural Development in Africa*. University of Wisconsin, Madison. (Part forms a special issue of *Africa*, 49, 213–328.)

Southall, A. and Gutkind, P. C. W. (1957) *Townsmen in the Making: Kampala and its suburbs*. Kampala: East African Institute of Social Research.

Steel, R. W. (1961) 'The towns of tropical Africa.' In Barbour, K. M. and Prothero, R. M. (eds.), *Essays on African Population*. London: Routledge and Kegan Paul.

Steel, W. F. (1977) *Small-Scale Employment and Production in Developing Countries: the evidence from Ghana*. New York: Praeger.

Streeten, P. (1979) 'Development ideas in historical perspective.' In *Rothko Chapel Colloquium: Toward a New Strategy for Development*. New York: Pergamon.

Stren, R. E. (1972) 'Evolution of housing policy in Kenya.' In Hutton, J. (ed.), *Urban Challenge in East Africa*. Nairobi: East African Publishing House.

Stren, R. E. (1975) *Urban Inequality and Housing Policy in Tanzania: the problem of squatting*. Berkeley: University of California, Institute of International Studies.

*Stren, R. E. (1978) *Housing the Urban Poor in Africa: policy, politics and bureaucracy in Mombasa*. Berkeley: University of California, Institute of International Studies.

Stren, R. E. (1979) 'Urban policy.' In Barkan, J. D. and Okumu, J. (eds.), *Politics and Public Policy in Kenya and Tanzania*. New York: Praeger.

Stren, R. E. (1982) 'Underdevelopment, urban squatting, and the state bureaucracy: a case study of Tanzania.' *Canadian Journal of African Studies*, 16, 67–91.

Sule, O. R. A. (1979) 'Problems of solid wastes disposal in the metropolitan Lagos.' *Geojournal*, 3, 571–7.

Swainson, N. (1980) *The Development of Corporate Capitalism in Kenya 1918–1978*. London: Heinemann.

Swantz, L. W. (1970) 'The Zaramo of Dar es Salaam.' In Sutton, J. E. G. (ed.), *Dar es Salaam: City, Port and Region. Tanzania Notes and Records*, No 71. Dar es Salaam: Tanzanian Society.

Swindell, K. (1979) 'Labour migration in underdeveloped countries: the case of sub-Saharan Africa.' *Progress in Human Geography*, 3, 239–59.

Taylor, D. R. F. (1974) 'The role of the smaller urban place in development: the case of Kenya.' In El-Shakhs, S., and Obudho, R. A. (eds.), *Urbanization , National Development and Regional Planning in Africa*. New York: Praeger.

Temple, F. T. and Temple, N. W. (1980) 'The politics of public housing in Nairobi.' In Grindle, M. S. (ed.), *Politics and Policy Implementation in the Third World*. Princeton, N.J.: Princeton University Press.

Temple, P. H. (1969) 'The urban markets of greater Kampala.' *Tijdschrift voor Economische en Sociale Geografie*, 60, 346–59.

Thompson, R. W. (1978) 'Fertility aspirations and modernization in urban Uganda.' *Urban Anthropology*, 7, 155–70.

Thomson, J. M. (1978) *Great Cities and their Traffic*. London: Penguin.

Tiwari, R. C. (1979) 'Comparative analysis of CBDs in East Africa.' In Obudho, R. A. and Taylor, D. R. F. (eds.), *The Spatial Structure of Development: a study of Kenya*. Boulder, Colorado: Westview.

Todaro, M. P. (1969) 'A model of labor migration and urban unemployment in less developed countries.' *American Economic Review*, 59, 138–48.

Todaro, M. P. (1971) 'Income expectations, rural–urban migration and employment in Africa.' *International Labour Review*, 104, 387–413.

Trevallion, B. (1966) *Metropolitan Kano: report on the 20-year development plan 1963–1983*. London: Newman Neame.

Turner, J. F. C. (1969) 'Uncontrolled urban settlement: problems and policies.' In Breese, G. (ed.), *The City in Newly Developing Countries*. Englewood Cliffs, N.J.: Prentice-Hall.

Turner, J. F. C. (1976) *Housing by People*. London: Marion Boyars.

Twaddle, M. (ed.) (1975) *Expulsion of a Minority: essays on Ugandan Asians*. London: Athlone Press.

Udo, R. K. (ed.) (1979) *Population Education Sourcebook for Sub-Saharan Africa*. Nairobi: Heinemann.

UN (1976) *Economic Housing in Africa*. Addis Ababa: UNECA.

UN (1980) *Patterns of Urban and Rural Population Growth*. New York: United Nations.

UNCHS (habitat) (1981) *The Residential Circumstances of the Urban Poor in Developing Countries*. New York: Praeger.

Urquhart, A. W. (1977) *Planned Urban Landscapes of Northern Nigeria*. Zaria: Ahmadu Bello University Press.

Usman, Y. B. (ed.) (1977) *Cities of the Savanna*. Lagos: Nigeria Magazine.

Van Binsbergen, W. M. J. and Meilink, H. A. (eds.) (1978) *Migration and the Transformation of Modern African Society. African Perspectives 1978/1*. Leiden: Africa-Studiecentrum.

Van Den Berghe, P. L. (ed.) (1975) *Race and Ethnicity in Africa*. Nairobi: East African Publishing House.

Van Der Laan, H. L. (1975) *The Lebanese Traders in Sierra Leone*. The Hague: Mouton.

Van Velsen, J. (1960) 'Labour migration as a positive factor in the continuity of Tonga tribal society.' *Economic Development and Cultural Change*, 8, 265–78.

Van Velsen, J. (1975) 'Urban squatters: problem or solution.' In Parkin, D. J. (ed.), *Town and Country in Central and Eastern Africa*. London: Oxford University Press.

*Vennetier, P. (1976) *Les Villes de l'Afrique Noire*. Paris: Masson.

Vernière, M. (1977) *Dakar et son Double: Dagoudane-Pikine*. Paris: Bibliothèque Nationale.

Villien-Rossi, M.-L. (1966) 'Bamako, capitale du Mali.' *Bulletin de l'IFAN*, 28B, 249–380.

Vincent, J. (1971) *African Elite: the big men of a small town.* New York: Columbia University Press.

Ward, P. M. (1978) 'Self-help housing in Mexico City.' *Town Planning Review*, 49, 38–50.

Ward, P. M. (ed.) (1982) *Self-Help Housing: a critique.* London: Mansell.

Weisner, T. S. (1976) 'Kariobangi: the case history of a squatter resettlement scheme in Kenya.' In Arens, W. (ed.), *A Century of Change in Eastern Africa.* The Hague: Mouton.

Werlin, H. H. (1974) *Governing an African City: a study of Nairobi.* New York: Africana Publishing Company.

Wheatley, P. (1969) *City as Symbol.* London: University College.

Wheatley, P. (1970) 'The significance of traditional Yoruba urbanism.' *Comparative Studies in Society and History*, 12, 393–423.

White, G. F., Bradley, D. J. and White, A. U. (1972) *Drawers of Water: domestic water use in East Africa.* Chiago: University of Chicago Press.

Williams, G. (ed.) (1976) *Nigeria: economy and society.* London: Rex Collings.

Wioland, F. (1968) 'Les langues parlées.' In Sankalé, M. *et al.* (eds.), *Dakar en Devenir.* Paris: Présence Africaine.

Wirth, L. (1938) 'Urbanism as a way of life.' *American Journal of Sociology*, 44, 1–24.

Wolpe, H. E. (1974) *Urban Politics in Nigeria: a study of Port Harcourt.* Berkeley: University of California Press.

Works, J. A. (1976) *Pilgrims in a Strange Land: Hausa communities in Chad.* New York: Columbia University Press.

Zachariah, K. C. and Condé, J. (1981) *Migration in West Africa: demographic aspects.* New York: Oxford University Press.

Zambia (1979) *Third National Development Plan 1979–83.* Lusaka.

Zipf, G. K. (1941) *National Unity and Disunity.* Bloomington: Principia.

Index